# MEDIEVAL FRANCE

# MEDIEVAL FRANCE

## A COMPANION TO FRENCH STUDIES

EDITED BY

ARTHUR TILLEY, M.A.

FELLOW AND LECTURER OF KING'S COLLEGE, CAMBRIDGE



HAFNER PUBLISHING COMPANY
New York and London
1964

First Published in 1922

Reprinted by Permission
of the
Cambridge University Press

*Printed and Published by*
Hafner Publishing Company, Inc.
31 East 10th Street
New York, N.Y. 10003

Library of Congress Catalog Card Number: 63-16481

Lithographed in the U.S.A.
by Noble Offset Printers, Inc.
New York, N. Y. 10003

# PREFACE

THE aim of this volume is to present to the reader within a moderate compass a survey of the history (political, military, naval, economic), language, literature, and art of Medieval France. An initial chapter on geography serves as a setting both for this and for the companion volume on Modern France. The volume is the work of ten writers, of whom, as was inevitable, a considerable majority are Frenchmen. To the ready and generous cooperation of these latter special thanks are due, particularly to M. Langlois, to whom the heaviest task has fallen. In his chapter on the political history of France the reader may trace the gradual development of the monarchy from Hugh Capet, who had practically no power outside his own province of the Ile-de-France and the neighbouring districts, to Charles VIII, of whom, while still a boy, Philippe de Commines declared that he was "more feared and better obeyed and served by his subjects than any other prince on the earth." He said this with reference to the meeting of the States-General at Tours in 1484, which, representing, as it did, every province except Brittany, gave a signal proof of that unity which has ever since been France's greatest strength.

Another feature, besides the growth of monarchy and national unity, which cannot fail to impress itself on the reader of M. Langlois's chapter is the marvellous recuperative power shown by France after the Hundred Years' War. In an arresting passage M. Langlois compares the condition of the whole country during that war with that of the devastated area at the present day, and he points out that in spite of the greater effectiveness of modern artillery "war was formerly even more murderous, because of the epidemics and famine which modern civilisation can arrest or mitigate," and that "brigandage, though less pedantically methodical than that which the present generation has experienced, was hardly less thorough." But France recovered then, as she recovered later after the Wars of Religion and after the Franco-German War, and as she will recover again.

The Hundred Years' War interrupted the growing commercial prosperity of the country, especially its trade by sea, but even before the war philosophy, literature, and art (except for the illumination of books) had begun to decline. The great age of scholastic philosophy was the twelfth and thirteenth centuries; after that Duns Scotus introduced that reign of dialectic which was to render philosophy sterile and to exercise a baneful influence even on literature. Joinville, who completed his *Life of St Louis* in 1309 at the age of 85, marks the final close of that creative period of French medieval literature which began about the middle of the twelfth century with Chrétien de Troyes's *Érec*.

The great period of French Gothic architecture may be said to begin in 1163 with Notre-Dame de Paris and to end before the close of the thirteenth century with the choir of Beauvais. For sculpture, glass, and painting the thirteenth century was the golden age, but painting continued to flourish till much later. The name of Jean Pucelle fills the years from 1320 to 1350, and the *Très Riches Heures* of Jean Duke of Berry, the finest extant example of the illuminator's art, was still unfinished at the Duke's death in 1446. After that there was Jean Fouquet. But the whole story of French medieval art is one of singular interest and importance, and it has been told in these pages, from close personal observation, by two Englishmen with a knowledge and sympathy which cannot fail to stir the reader's imagination and deepen his admiration for the country that has produced such noble masterpieces.

Another story, that of scholastic philosophy, is told here by an English scholar. If its appeal is less wide and less moving than that of French medieval art, it is more international. Paris in the Middle Ages was the capital of intellectual Europe. If Abélard was a Frenchman, Bonaventura and Thomas Aquinas were

Italians, Albert the Great was a German, Alexander of Hales and William of Ockham were Englishmen, and Duns Scotus came probably from Scotland or Northern England.

The other chapters are the work of Frenchmen who are experts in their several provinces. Apart from the knowledge these chapters impart, they are particularly valuable as lessons in method and lucidity. That on French medieval literature should dispel the charge of uniformity and impersonality which Brunetière brought against it. It is true that in the Middle Ages the individual was of little account in comparison with the corporate body, whether religious or lay, and that authority and tradition discouraged any departure from the old ways, but in literature, as in art, personality from time to time emerged triumphant. The authors of the *Chanson de Roland* and *Aucassin et Nicolette*, Chrétien de Troyes, Jean de Meun, Joinville, Froissart, must have all been men of marked personality; the long cycle of poems of which Renart is the hero was originated by an individual writer, and there is much to be said for the recent theory of M. Ferdinand Lot that the prose *Lancelot* was the work of a single man; Villon and Commines, whom some critics have claimed as definitely modern writers, are but the latest medieval instances of that strong individuality which underlies every work of creative genius.

Considerations of space have made short and select bibliographies imperative, but, as these comprise, whenever possible, works which contain full bibliographies, and also the more important recent authorities, it is hoped that the reader who wishes also to be a student will find his way to the chief sources of knowledge.

The map of France is due to M. Gallois and the map showing the main routes of commerce to M. Halphen; Sir Thomas Jackson has provided the illustrations for his chapter on Architecture. One of these (Plate VII) is reproduced, by permission, from *The Sculptures of Chartres Cathedral*, by M. and E. Marriage (Cambridge, 1909). The proofs of the translated chapters have all been submitted to the writers of the original texts, and the editor has had the advantage of their corrections and suggestions. His thanks are also due to Dr Guillemard of Gonville and Caius College and to Dr Clapham of King's College for reading the proofs of Chapters I and V respectively, to Miss W. M. L. Hutchinson for suggesting some improvements in the translations and to Mr H. S. Bennett of Emmanuel College, for making the index. Finally he must express his gratitude to Mr A. R. Waller, the Secretary of the Syndics of the University Press, for much sympathetic advice and kindly cooperation.

A. T.

*December*, 1921

# CONTENTS

## CHAPTER I

## GEOGRAPHY

By L. GALLOIS, Professor in the University of Paris

### § I. *General Observations*



### § II. *General Description*

## CHAPTER II
## HISTORY

By CH. V. LANGLOIS, Director of the *Archives Nationales*

### § I. *Political and social conditions in 987*



### § II. *First attempts at Government. First advance of the King's authority*



### § III. *Rivalry of Capets and Plantagenets*



### § IV. *Evolution in the direction of Monarchy*

§ V. *External policy,* 1000–1328



§ VI. *Political conditions in* 1337



§ VII. *The Hundred Years' War*

§ VIII. *Political and social conditions from 1337 to 1494*



## CHAPTER III
## THE ARMY

By PIERRE CARON of the *Archives Nationales*



## CHAPTER IV
## THE NAVY

By CH. DE LA RONCIÈRE of the *Bibliothèque Nationale*

## CHAPTER V

## INDUSTRY AND COMMERCE

By L. Halphen, Professor in the University of Bordeaux

### § I. *Industry and Commerce before the 11th Century*



### § II. *Economic Revival of the Feudal Age*



### § III. *Corporate Organisation*



### § IV. *The abuses of the Corporation System*



### § V. *The great Mediterranean Trade down to the beginning of the 14th Century*



### § VI. *Ocean Trade down to the Hundred Years' War*



### § VII. *Land Trade and the Fairs of Champagne*



### § VIII. *Decay of French Commerce in the 14th and 15th Centuries*

## CHAPTER VI

## SCHOLASTIC PHILOSOPHY AND UNIVERSITIES

By A. G. LITTLE, M.A., of Balliol College, Oxford



## CHAPTER VII

## LANGUAGE AND DIALECTS

By A. JEANROY, Professor in the University of Paris

## CHAPTER VIII

## LITERATURE

### By Lucien Foulet



### § 1. *From* 1066 *to* 1337

## CHAPTER IX
## ARCHITECTURE

By Sir Thomas Graham Jackson, Bart., R.A., Hon.D.C.L. Oxford, Hon.LL.D. Cambridge, Associé de l'Académie Royale de Belgique

§ I. *French Romanesque*

## CHAPTER X

## SCULPTURE, GLASS, PAINTING

By M. R. James, Litt.D., F.B.A., Provost of Eton College



### § I. *Sculpture*



### § II. *Glass*

§ III. *Painting*



*In the bibliographies the place of publication is omitted for French books published at Paris and for English books published in London.*

CORRIGENDA

p. 57 *for* Manichaeism *read* Manicheism.
p. 177 *for* Plessis-les-Tours *read* Plessis-lès-Tours.
p. 410 *for* Agnes *read* Agnès.

# LIST OF PLATES



# MAPS

# CHAPTER I

## GEOGRAPHY

### § I. GENERAL OBSERVATIONS

**Extent and Position.** France, having had restored to her by the Treaty of Versailles the Rhine frontier which she had attained by the middle of the 17th century, is to-day the largest of the Central and Western States of Europe[1]. A mere inspection of the map will show that she is symmetrical and coherent in all parts, with similar proportions from north to south and from east to west. Brittany indeed juts out into the Atlantic almost as far as Cornwall, but this large peninsula is solidly attached to the mainland, and its long coast-line, favourable to navigation, is a source of activity and life. Bounded to the west by the Channel and the Atlantic, to the south by the Mediterranean, separated from Spain by the lofty mountain-chain of the Pyrenees, and from Italy by that of the Alps, France, except in part of the Jura and on the Rhine, has towards the north and east only artificial frontiers, and the difficulties she has always experienced in assuring her defence on that side have weighed heavily on her fortunes.

France occupies a unique position in Europe, for there the European continent, which becomes steadily narrower towards the west, attains its smallest width. It is only 472 miles from the Mediterranean to the mouth of the Seine: it is not 275 from the Mediterranean to the mouth of the Gironde. And nowhere are communications easier between the two seas. The high mountain barrier of the Alps, which, farther to the east, separates Italy from the Germanic countries, ends on French soil. Moreover, only a strait less than 20 miles wide separates France from Great Britain. The first remark made by a geographer (Strabo) on the country which has since become France refers

[1] Superficies of France including the island of Corsica, 212,658 sq. miles; Germany, which before the war had a superficies of 208,780 sq. miles, now does not nearly reach 200,000. Italy has about 115,000 sq. miles; the United Kingdom with the islands has 121,613 sq. miles.

specially to the convenience of the thoroughfares which she offers between the Mediterranean and the Atlantic.

**Formation of the French nation.** This ease of communication and this cohesion between the various provinces have had a great influence on the formation of the French nation. It is hardly necessary to say that there is no French race. France has undergone too many invasions, both warlike and peaceful, to allow a single physical type to persist. One finds in France long heads and round heads, fair people and dark people, light eyes and dark eyes. Anthropological research has enabled some predominant types to be localised here and there, but these same types are also found amongst the neighbouring peoples; none of them belong exclusively to the French nation. The language indeed is the same, but the linguistic frontier of French does not coincide with the political frontier; it overflows into Switzerland and Belgium. And French is almost a learned language, a language of civilisation, which has added itself to the local dialects, without superseding them. Although almost entirely derived from Latin, these dialects differed so much in the north and south that two literary languages have sprung from them. There was a Provençal literature. If it has not survived, it is because the north soon imposed its political supremacy on the south. It was not done without violence. But union was attained very quickly. It is noteworthy that, whatever means the monarchy may have used to bring about French unity, a focus of resistance was nowhere maintained, and every one, without mental reservation, adhered to the contract, as though some secret affinity drew one French province to another.

And yet there is great diversity between these provinces. One of the men who has known and described France best (Vidal de la Blache) has said that her chief characteristic is her variety. There is not, perhaps, in the world any country which, with equal surface, presents such various aspects of elevation, soil, climate, and, consequently, of vegetation and of cultivation.

**Relief.** The relief is specially the result of those movements of the earth which occurred at the end of the Primary period and towards the middle of the Tertiary period in that part of the terrestrial crust which has become France.

The trace of Primary folding is still very visible in Brittany, in the Ardennes, in the Vosges, in the Central Plateau, and on the Mediterranean sea-coast, in the small ranges of the Maures and of the Esterel. These foldings raised lofty chains which were continued to the west in the southern part of the British Isles, and to the east in Middle Germany. But even at the beginning of the Secondary period, they had been completely levelled by the slow process of erosion. In many places, seas encroached and took their place. At the beginning of the Tertiary period the Central Plateau was covered with lagoons.

The second period of folding, which occurred in the course of the Tertiary period, caused the elevation in the spaces between the old high-lands, first of the Pyrenees, then of the Alps. But these movements could not take place without disturbing in their neighbourhood the remains of the old massifs. Although Brittany and the Ardennes were not affected, or only very slightly, by the shock of the folding movement, the Vosges were lifted to the south and the Central Plateau to the east. In this latter district especially, the strength of the folding movement also showed itself by faults, between which depressions appeared. Such is the origin of the inland basins of Le Forez and La Limagne. And through these fractures escaped the eruptive matter which gave birth to the numerous volcanoes of Auvergne and of Vivarais[1].

It is thus definitely from the last Alpine fold-movements that the relief of the French soil dates. But the old mountains, more rigid in spite of the heightening they have undergone, have preserved their squat and table-like shapes. These are the lower mountains. The highest point of the Central Plateau is not more than 6187 feet, that of the Vosges 4678 feet. Much more majestic are the beautiful chains of the Pyrenees and the Alps, with their jagged peaks and their eternal snows. The Pyrenees rise to 11,135 feet in Maladetta, which is a little beyond the French frontier, and though Mont Blanc, with its 15,781 feet, is half in France, half in Italy, there are many other Alpine crests in French territory which reach or exceed 12,000 feet.

[1] Large fractures have also been produced in the Vosges mountains, which formerly was a part of the Black Forest. The Rhine plain, between Basle and Mayence, is a plain which has sunk. And there also, but outside French soil (in Breisgau and Hesse), volcanic eruptions occurred.

Outside these mountainous regions there are a few small isolated heights in the south of Normandy, which hardly deserve the too ambitious name of "Mont" which has been given to them. They are not more than 1368 feet. The "Monts d'Arrée" in Brittany are not more than 1283 feet. The conformation of the land in all the low parts of France is chiefly the result of erosion, which has carved out valleys and made the hard rocks prominent.

Between the old and the recent mountains, plains and plateaux fall naturally into three groups: in the north the Paris basin, bounded by Brittany, the Central Plateau, the Vosges and the Ardennes; in the south, the Aquitaine basin between the Central Plateau and the Pyrenees; and in the east, the plain of the Saône and the valley of the Rhône, between the Central Plateau, the Alps, and the Jura. This latter chain is a continuation of the Alpine folds to the north.

There is another consequence of all the movements which the French soil has undergone, namely, that the same rocks never crop out over any great stretch of country. The result is that the landscape changes in rapid succession. Among the various districts, there are some so characteristic that they have received popular names, handed down through the ages, regardless of administrative divisions. Such are the names of "pays," as they are called: Beauce, Brie, Sologne, Woëvre, valuable indications of natural divisions of France. They are nowhere more numerous than in the Paris basin.

**Climate.** The differences which arise from the elevation and from the nature of the soil are, however, lessened by the effect of the climate.

Situated almost midway between the Equator and the North Pole, France is a temperate country, which is not exposed to great and persistent cold, except in the high mountainous districts. But on this common ground the prevailing winds produce variations, and certain, more or less distant, influences thus affect the climate of France, i.e. the Atlantic, the Continent, and the Mediterranean.

First of all the Atlantic. The sea-winds of the west raise the temperature in winter and lower it in summer. Rain is chiefly brought by them. The sea-coast of Brittany has in January a mean temperature similar to that of Marseilles, but the fruit of the vine does not ripen there. These ocean influences weaken as one goes eastward. In Lorraine, and still more in Alsace, they have to struggle with the continental influences. If in winter it is colder there than in the centre of the Paris basin, the summers and autumns are just as warm; in Alsace the vine covers all the foot-hills of the Vosges. Severe winter cold can moreover occasionally spread all over the Paris basin. If regions of high pressure establish themselves in the north and east of Europe, especially in times of snow, the east winds, sweeping away the clouds, bring cold and frost even to the shores of the Atlantic.

Farther south, and sheltered by the Central Plateau, the Aquitaine basin is perceptibly warmer. The mean temperature for January is 40°·1 (Fahrenheit) in Toulouse while in Paris it is 36°·2 and 31°·8 in Strasbourg.

In the valley of the Rhône, winds of different directions meet in conflict, but in consequence of the trend of the valley these are north and south winds. Lyons has high summer temperatures, but somewhat severe winters, and hence belongs rather to Northern than to Southern France.

The true south (*le Midi*) is the Mediterranean country, Lower Languedoc, and Lower Provence. Here are no longer ocean influences, but uniformly dry winters and summers, under a sky of deep blue, with that clearness of atmosphere which throws into such bright relief the Mediterranean landscapes. Although the rainfall at Marseilles does not differ greatly from that in the rest of France, it occurs by way of abundant but rare thunder-showers, principally in autumn and spring, at the time of the equinoxes. Warm in winter, sun-scorched in summer, Provence nevertheless also experiences cold snaps, when its formidable "mistral" blows tempestuously, that violent wind which sweeps down from the high uplands of the Cevennes as soon as a strong barometrical depression establishes itself out in the Mediterranean. Only that part of the coast which is sheltered by the proximity of the Alpine barrier, the "Côte d'Azur," from Cannes to Nice and Mentone, is not exposed to these violent changes of temperature. The vegetation, whether spontaneously or introduced by man, is well-adapted to that dry climate. The most general tree is the olive, faithful companion to the Mediterranean, with its retinue of parasol pines and cypresses, often planted in lines so as to break the violence of the mistral.

Outside these Mediterranean districts, with the abundance and regularity of the rains, the forest appears, the forest of great trees with deciduous leaves: principally oaks, beeches, hornbeams, and birches. It still covers vast spaces in the east, especially on the chalky plateaux of Lorraine and Burgundy, and it is preserved in the beautiful woods which are the ornament of the region of Paris. If it has yielded elsewhere to centuries of clearing, in the west at least the tree remains, emerging from the hedges which uniformly surround the fields and pastures in this land of "Bocage."

Such are the most salient features of the physical geography of France. One would like to be able to follow through the centuries the endeavour of men to adapt this country to their uses, to watch their institutions and industries come into being, grow, and change, to learn also what these men were and what previously acquired habits and customs they brought with them, and how they fitted themselves for the kind of life which Nature imposed on them. These are questions which, in many respects, will always remain unanswered, even for the periods which belong to history, a province in any case reserved for special sciences—anthropology, ethnography, toponomy, history under its various aspects—in which much research is still necessary to arrive at results, often hypothetical. The task of the geographer is more modest. But in describing the present, if he wishes to understand it, he also must connect it with the past, for in our old European countries there remain too many traces of bygone life to permit geography to dissociate itself from history.

In this spirit we shall try to describe the principal regions of France.

## § II. GENERAL DESCRIPTION

To the north and east France exceeds the physical limits of the Paris basin.

**The Northern Region.** A wide zone of easy communication opens to the west of the lower slopes of the Ardennes. Through this the Scheldt makes its way slowly towards the mouth of the Rhine, and the Sambre flows to join the Meuse. No part of France has more often been trampled under foot by armies. It offers the shortest and easiest way to Paris through the valley of the Oise. There Picardy and Flanders meet.

Flanders owes its early civilisation to its position in Europe. Situated opposite the estuary of the Thames, at the point from which diverge the roads leading to the Rhine and the Seine, easily accessible by rivers which were early adapted to navigation, she was soon covered with towns which rapidly became centres of industry and commerce. The principal industry was that of wool, which was at first imported from England, and weaving has always remained solidly established in this district. In order to feed the men who crowded to these prosperous towns, agriculture very soon contrived to make the best of a soil which was not rich by nature. The maritime region, a region of reclaimed land, was snatched from the sea, as in Holland. The discovery in the 18th century that the Belgian coalfields were continued on French soil, and their successful working in the course of the 19th century, gave a new impetus to local activity. Great metallurgical industries have been established all along this basin, from Anzin, close to Valenciennes, to the outskirts of Béthune. But the population is chiefly gathered in the towns, Lille, Roubaix, and Tourcoing form to-day almost a single town, which, with the localities in its immediate neighbourhood, includes 655,000 souls. In addition to wool, cotton and linen are woven there. To serve these industries, a continuous line of canals has been constructed, joining up the French and the Belgian systems, from the Scheldt to the sea, which is reached at Calais and at Dunkirk. On this sea-front, the two ports of Calais and Boulogne have been fitted up to ensure a rapid crossing to England. Dunkirk, with its numerous docks, has become the chief commercial port of all this Northern region, which before the war was one of the most industrious parts of France, one of the best cultivated, and one of the richest. Its spirit of initiative may be counted on to repair the destruction it has suffered.

**The Ardennes.** By a long depression at the foot of the Ardennes the Northern region is in communication with Lorraine. The adjoining towns of Mézières-Charleville and Sedan are the stages on this road. The wooded uplands of the Ardennes belong only in a small part to France. The frontier does not form a salient in it except in the valley of the Meuse, a deep indentation, where the river describes narrow windings, leaving but little room for human dwellings. There, nevertheless, as round Mézières, there is a succession of metallurgical factories, utilising the cast-iron and steel of Lorraine, and receiving Belgian coal by the Meuse, an interesting survival of the small forges of bygone days, which worked the iron ores of the district by means of the fuel derived from the neighbouring forest. Another ancient industry, the cloth-trade, employs numerous workmen in Sedan and the neighbourhood.

**Alsace.** The boundary of Alsace on the east is clearly marked by the course of the Rhine. Before the river was confined by artificial banks, it was a real obstacle. Divided into numerous streams, it constantly threatened its banks, on which no town could be built. To the west rises the wooded range of the Vosges, but the Vosges end to the south with the Ballon d'Alsace, and the Alsatian plains communicate freely with those of the Saône by the wide gap of Belfort. To the north, beyond Donon, the wooded region of the Lower Vosges is only the end of the Lorraine plateau, sinking suddenly towards the plain of Alsace. And there also the routes are easy. The Roman road from Reims to Metz and to Strasbourg passed through what is incorrectly called the "col" of Saverne, and nowadays by the same route pass the main railway-line from Paris to Strasbourg and the canal from the Marne to the Rhine. Thus is explained the fact that Alsace has always kept up relations with France and that the influence of French ideas has predominated since the 17th century, in spite of the Germanic dialect spoken by its inhabitants. The efforts made by Germany to germanise them since 1871 is enough to prove that they were not German at heart. Never was Alsace so French in feeling as during the bitter period of German occupation.

It is a fertile and beautiful country. At the foot of the Vosges there is an uninterrupted succession of vines, orchards, and cultivated land, and this thickly-populated zone is continued in the valleys which penetrate the mountains. The chief towns are in the plains, along the valley of the Ill: Mulhouse, where some enterprising men in the 18th century introduced cotton weaving, which has spread thence to the valleys of the Vosges, even on the Lorraine side; Colmar; and, near the confluence, at the end of the Saverne road, at the point where the canals of the Marne and the Saône end in the Rhine and where the important navigation of the river now begins, Strasbourg, an old commercial town, which is preparing to become the great port of Eastern France.

**Lorraine.** Lorraine, which is another outpost of French civilisation, has more varied aspects, owing to the changes in the soil. To this she also owes her double rampart of limestone escarpments, the *Côtes* of the Moselle and the Meuse, crowned with forests, and decked with orchards and vineyards on their lower slopes. In the neighbourhood sprang up her three most ancient towns, the three sees of Metz, Toul, and Verdun. For these ramparts have gaps, through which roads have always passed. Verdun and Metz are on the old Roman road from Reims to Strasbourg; Toul and Nancy (which developed later in another gap on the Moselle *Côtes*) are on the more modern road which is followed by the railway from Paris to Strasbourg and the canal from the Marne to the Rhine. Through the uplands where the Meuse takes its source, there is easy communication to the south with the region of the Saône; here too, a canal flows along beside the roads and the railways. Communication with the north is not so easy. Beyond Trèves the Moselle winds between deep banks across the plateau of Hunsrück, as the Meuse does among the Ardennes, and the river has not been adapted to navigation. Fertile only at the cost of assiduous toil, Lorraine, as a whole, remains an agricultural country. The discovery of the most abundant bed of iron-ore in Europe under the uplands which dominate the left bank of the Moselle, is in course of transforming all the region which extends from Nancy to Metz and Luxemburg into a land of factories. The assignment to France of the Sarre coal-mines will hasten this transformation. The Meuse valley and the uplands which extend thence towards the west are not affected by this activity, and the transition from Lorraine to the chalky plains of Champagne is made by a wide forest-zone, which extends not only to the small group of hills in the Argonne, but also to the flat and marshy land which borders it on the south.

**Champagne.** This poor district had for centuries little life except in the valleys: but these afforded routes which led from the Rhône and the Saône to Paris and the north. On these roads were established those markets, the fairs of Champagne, so prosperous in the Middle Ages, where the Italian merchants came to buy the Flanders cloth. And there also they began to weave the wool obtained from the sheep of the country; the two chief towns of Champagne, Troyes and Reims, the old religious metropolis, still depend on the weaving industry. The vineyards, which clothe the lower slopes of the escarpment of the Ile-de-France, have been another source of wealth to Reims. The great cellars of the wine of Champagne are here and at Epernay, on the Marne.

**Picardy.** The chalky soil of Champagne is continued to the north-west in Picardy, without, however, reaching the sea, which is bordered up to the Somme estuary by low country and dunes. But in Picardy the chalk is covered with a thick layer of loam, one of the most fertile of soils, easy to till, which for centuries has assured the agricultural prosperity of this district. Here begins the cultivation of wheat on a great scale, highly specialised on this soil; and doubtless this has helped to make bread the favourite food of the French. One is not, however, surprised to find that Picardy has felt the influence of the northern industrial region. Amiens and Beauvais were and are weaving towns. Saint-Quentin was one of the most active centres of the French textile industry, and will be again, when her factories have been raised from their ruins. Moreover, their beautiful cathedrals show the proximity of the Ile-de-France.

**The country round Paris. Greater Paris.** The plateaux with calcareous sub-soil which surround Paris are also corn-lands, wherever they are not covered with forest: Soissonnais, Valois, Vexin, and that little ancient district of "France," between the Seine and the Oise, whence bread was brought to the markets of the capital. Thence the name Ile-de-France[1] spread to the whole province, of which Paris was the centre. To the east, between the Marne and the Seine, La Brie is wetter;

[1] In the Middle Ages a district between two rivers was often called an island. The "island" of France was at first only the little district situated in the angle formed by the Seine and Oise near their confluence.

but the dryness reappears on the monotonous and calcareous table-land of La Beauce, a land without trees, which extends to the neighbourhood of the Loire.

With the exception of La Beauce, these plateaux are not continuous. The Seine, Marne, Oise, and Aisne, to mention only the chief rivers, have carved wide valleys in them, which are the glory and beauty of the Paris district. Nowhere has erosion worked with so much effect as in the immediate neighbourhood of Paris. In Paris itself, the hill of Montmartre is nothing but the remains of the plateau of which larger fragments are found in the wooded hills which limit the northern horizon of Paris. The varieties of soil and of elevation permit a great variety of cultivation, which is helped by the mild climate. Building materials are on the spot: clay for bricks, gypsum for plaster, and, above all, that fine limestone, firm but easy to work, of which the Parisian monuments are built. To this is due the elegance of construction in the Ile-de-France, which is sometimes shown even in the churches of the smallest villages. If to all these advantages we add the facility of communication, either by the easily navigable rivers which flow together to this Parisian region, or by the table-lands which surround it in all directions, it must be owned that here was all that was necessary to attract men. From the day when the French kings fixed on Paris as the capital, its growth has kept pace with that of the French State.

Paris, the seat of the Government of France, whose public Services have not ceased multiplying and extending, Paris, the home of great schools, of great banks, the converging point of great railway lines, a base of commerce and industry—for there are numerous factories, especially in the northern suburbs—the literary, artistic, and scientific capital of the country, the favourite resort of foreigners, who are attracted to her by the beauty of her monuments and her position, and by the amenities of life—Paris has increased from 600,000 inhabitants at the beginning of the 19th century to over a million in 1846, and in the last census of 1921 reached 2,863,000. But this total only included the Parisians living inside the fortifications. We must add the number of those living in the suburbs, which are increasingly populated by people who have emigrated from the city, who are employed there, or who depend on it for their living, and we shall certainly arrive at a figure which was not far off four million inhabitants in 1911, and which has now been largely exceeded owing to the influx of population caused by the war.

**Normandy.** The Seine forms the link between Paris and Normandy. The name of this province is derived from its Norse invaders, whose physical type is still to be met with in some places, notably in the extreme north of the peninsula of the Cotentin, where they firmly established themselves. Normandy is an aggregation of districts showing noticeable differences due to the diversity of soil. First to the north of the Seine, separated from Picardy by the Fossé of Bray, a land of pastures and cattle-breeding, stretch the chalky plains of the Vexin of Normandy, covered, as in Picardy, with loam; then comes the damper district of Caux, where the sea comes dashing against the high chalk cliffs. In their hollows some little ports have lodged themselves, especially Dieppe, whose venturous mariners were distinguished in the days of the great discoveries. To the south of the Seine, and up to the borders of La Beauce, there are again corn-lands, more humid as they approach the coast. All these districts taken together form Upper Normandy, which is bounded to the west by the marly escarpment of the district of Auge. Its centre is the Seine valley. At the highest point to which the tide enables sea-vessels to ascend, and opposite the last bridge by which the river can easily be crossed, rose a town, Rouen, the solid wealth of which is still attested by the beauty of her buildings. She owed this wealth not only to her commerce, but to the weaving industry, which here again was that of wool. This is still carried on at Louviers and at Elbœuf, but at Rouen a transformation has occurred, and cotton-weaving has taken its place. Nowadays Normandy and Alsace are the two great centres of the cotton industry in France. But in course of time, especially since the tonnage of ships has increased, the port of Havre, which was created in the 16th century at the mouth of the Seine to replace some small sanded ports, has threatened the prosperity of Rouen. The two towns, formerly rivals, now share the traffic: Havre takes the passengers and the costly merchandise; Rouen the heavy goods: coal, wine from Algiers, wood from the north, American petroleum. The war has introduced other industries, metallurgy and chemical products. Placed at the point of contact between sea and river navigation, and commanding an excellent means of communication with the interior, thanks to the adaptation and canalisation of the Seine, Rouen is to-day a very progressive town and the outer port of Paris.

Lower Normandy extends to the west of the district of Auge over the calcareous plain of Caen, but it also projects on to the Primary rocks of Armorica, while including all the Cotentin peninsula. Here too there is a large town: Caen, a port on the Orne, not less remarkable than Rouen for her wealth of architecture. Lower Normandy was for long purely agricultural, but is now, as if reluctantly, becoming industrial. Like Lorraine, it appears to be much richer in iron ores than had been supposed from former workings, and a great industry is establishing itself at the gates of Caen, which is the port of exportation of these ores.

**The Uplands of Burgundy.** The south-east and the south of the Paris basin bring us back to calcareous uplands, which are a continuation of those in Lorraine.

Between Lorraine and the small granite massif of Morvan, which is a projecting spur of the Central Plateau, stretches a district of very old thoroughfares; the roads leading from the Saône to the Paris basin necessarily pass through it. The oldest of all, the Roman road, leaving the Saône at Chalon, reached the Yonne valley through the borders of the Morvan. Close by was Autun, capital of the Aedui, which was celebrated for its schools during the Gallo-Roman period. Later, near this same road was built Vézelai, to-day a simple market-town, but enriched with one of the most beautiful specimens of romanesque religious art. Close by also was Alesia, which witnessed the last conflict between Caesar and Vercingetorix, chief of the Gauls. Another road farther north utilised the rising Marne valley. The old city of Langres from its high promontory watched this long narrow pass, which is to-day followed by the railway from Paris to Belfort and Basle. The modern road lies between the two; it reaches Dijon, the fine capital of the Dukes of Burgundy, by the valleys of the Yonne and the Armançon. There the great international line from Paris to Lyons, Marseilles, and Italy has been constructed. From Dijon also runs the railway, across the Jura, which reaches Italy through Switzerland and the Simplon, and the line which forms the communication between Lyons and the Saône basin and Lorraine. Modern towns which command such a railway system have a great advantage and Dijon has greatly profited by it.

**Nivernais. Berry.** Interrupted by the hills of Morvan and its covering of marly plains, the band of limestone reappears on both sides of the Loire, another great waterway, which after Nevers is marked by a succession of little towns. It becomes wider on the dry uplands of Berry, a land of cereals, where sheep-breeding has since very early times maintained the wool industry. But the proximity of the Central Plateau is here shown by the sand and clay, produced by the disintegration of the crystalline rocks, which running waters have carried down to Sologne and the Brenne, a district of ponds which for long remained the most unhealthy in France, and which has only been rendered healthy in our day by a systematic drainage. Beyond the Brenne, to the west, the limestone uplands regain their full breadth in Poitou, the door of entrance to Aquitaine, which opens widely between the Central Plateau and the southern part of the Armorican uplands.

**Perche and Maine.** A wide belt of forest separates the valley of the Loire from the corn-lands of La Beauce to the north; but to the west of La Beauce a change takes place very rapidly. We come to the district of Perche, which has specialised in horse-breeding, thanks to its meadows. And at once the houses, which in the regions hitherto described were generally grouped into villages, become dispersed and isolated. For everywhere in this impervious ground there is water. This was also a great forest-land, and the isolation of the dwellings seems to have been caused as much by clearing as by the water which can be easily obtained. Here begins the region of the Bocage, characteristic of the west of France, where all the fields are surrounded by hedges. With a few exceptions, it includes Perche, Maine, and farther to the west, the ancient lands of Brittany and La Vendée. The scattered dwellings and the consequent independence of life are the principal reasons which have retarded progress in these districts of poor soil. They have remained more firmly attached to the past, and to its religious and social traditions. They still possess a resident nobility which has preserved its influence along with its landed property. A more detailed study would reveal many slight differences. The towns, more especially the large towns, escape this influence, but, as a whole, the west differs markedly from the regions which surround it, and at more than one point on its border the popular language marks the difference between the "Bocage" and the "Plain."

**The Valley of the Loire.** The Loire valley is not included in this last district. Spreading widely, even before Orléans, in its "vales" and its "warrens," it is distinguished from the poorer regions which surround it by the wealth of its cultivation, its orchards, and its plantations. And it is also, up to the suburbs of Nantes, the country of the vine. Tours and Saumur possess renowned vineyards. By the mildness of its climate, as much as by the richness of its soil, it deserves throughout its whole length the name which has been given to Touraine of "the garden of France." Architecture, assisted by good building materials, has always been in request. The old feudal fortresses clothed themselves with beauty, and there are collected the most finished types of the French châteaux of the Renaissance. Blois, Azay-le-Rideau, Chenonceaux, and Chambord are in the valley or its vicinity. And this valley was also a great route and a great waterway, in the days when navigation was content with small craft. Tours sprang up at the point where the road to Aquitaine branches off, Angers near the meeting of the valleys, which by the Maine shed their waters into the Loire. Issuing from the impervious soil of the Central Plateau, the river is unfortunately too unequal in its flow to lend itself to the necessities of modern navigation, and this is one reason why no industry has up till now established itself in this part of the valley. Perhaps a change is at hand, since an important deposit of iron ore has been found in Anjou, and since the deepening of the bed of the river now enables ships to ascend as far as the Maine. Only the maritime towns, Nantes and its outer port, Saint-Nazaire, present the appearance of real industrial activity. Nantes is on the high road to regaining the rank amongst French ports which it held at the time of the great colonial enterprises.

**Brittany.** In this western region the Armorican peninsula too has its special characteristics. Separated from Normandy and Maine by a belt of forest, which was for long a deserted border, Brittany for many years lived apart from French life. Repeopled in the 6th century by emigrants from the island of Britain, it has retained its Celtic language, along with certain traits of character. This language is still spoken locally in the western part. In spite of her slight elevation, Brittany possesses great variety of scenery owing to the diversity of her rocks, which have been carved by erosion. We must consider separately the deeply-indented coast, where each tide comes so far up the rivers that inland ports have been established on their banks, such as Morlaix and Quimper, and Vannes on the almost closed gulf of Morbihan, which is like a small sea. The whole coast is rich in cultivation, thanks to the seaweed manure, especially in the north, where the fertility of the soil, under a climate of extreme mildness, assures the early ripening of vegetables, which are the object of an important trade. Enriched moreover by its fisheries, the coast of Brittany is remarkable for its very dense population. Little by little, especially in the east, these maritime influences diminish as one penetrates inland. The principal town, Rennes, owes nothing to the sea. To the west, a whole district is almost deserted: the old spongy surface of the Landes, where a few rocks emerging from the ground recall the former fold-structure. But except on these barren moors, almost always wrapped in fog, the inland is improving daily, thanks to the fertilisers, which are brought to this poor soil by means of the railway. Brittany, which is a prolific country, sends numerous workers to the Parisian district. Her great military ports: Brest, Lorient, and one may add Cherbourg, at the end of the Cotentin, keep up the tradition of the navy. In no part of France, among soldiers as well as sailors, has the spirit of sacrifice and devotion to the country been carried so far as in rugged Brittany.

**Poitou and Charente.** Between La Vendée, another land of Bocage, which is a continuation of the Armorican range beyond the Loire, and the lower slopes of the Central Plateau, the calcareous uplands of Poitou offer a wide approach, as we have seen, to the Aquitaine basin. They are continued by the uplands of

Aunis and Saintonge, or, as is said, by the district of "the Charentes," which takes its name from the two departments of Charente and Lower Charente, which are crossed by this river. The two ancient towns of Poitiers and Angoulême are landmarks on the way from Tours to Bordeaux and to Spain, a historic road on which in the 8th century the Arab invasion coming from the Iberian peninsula was arrested, and which was followed in the Middle Ages by numerous pilgrims going to the shrine of St James of Compostella. The region of limestone only reaches the sea in two places, opposite the two long islands of Ré and Oléron. In the space between, vast bays, choked by the encroachment of the land on the sea, have gradually dried up and been occupied by men. In these flat marshes, always threatened with inundation, end the courses of the Sèvre, the Charente, and the Seudre. Such a coast offers little encouragement to navigation. Between the Loire and the Gironde only one port has been able to find room, namely La Rochelle, supplemented by La Pallice, a dock which has been made a little farther north. It was one of the chief ports of embarkation in the days when French colonisation was directed to America, and there were many natives of Saintonge among those who went to find a fortune overseas. But the hinterland has not enough resources to supply a great traffic. Employed in agriculture and the cultivation of the vine (brandy from the wine of Cognac) it also feels the attraction of Nantes and Bordeaux.

**The Aquitaine basin.** Less extended than the Paris basin, the Aquitaine basin has not the same varied resources. It also lacks a good navigable waterway, for, owing to its Pyrenean origin, the Garonne rises with dangerous suddenness, and its principal tributaries, amongst which the Dordogne may be included, coming from the Central Plateau, do not help to equalise its stream. The Garonne and Dordogne are not easily navigable beyond the point reached by the tide. The soil, which is chiefly formed of light particles proceeding from the erosion of the surrounding mountains, is easy to till and, thanks to a warm and rainy climate, necessities and superfluities are obtained from the land without much trouble. It has long been a land of moderate wealth, of properties of moderate size, where the birth-rate is unfortunately limited.

**Périgord and Quercy.** To the north, the limestone surroundings of the Central Plateau persist in Périgord and Quercy, a region of uplands, deeply indented by valleys, whose steep and often rugged banks yielded shelter to prehistoric man. The celebrated caves with rock-paintings at Eyzies are on the banks of the Vézère. In Périgord some sands, where forests have been preserved, overlie the limestone in several places. To the east, the drier table-lands of Quercy bear the same name of "Causses" as the great stone surfaces of the calcareous portions on the Central Plateau. But these Causses in Quercy are less desolate because of their lower altitude and a warmer climate. Quercy and Périgord, thanks to their unyielding soil, were districts of easy communication. A Roman road ending at Saintes on the Charente connected the towns of Cahors and Périgueux, which throughout the ages have remained the two chief urban centres.

**Gascony and Béarn.** To the south a wide flattened cone, formed of Tertiary rocks, leads to the Central Pyrenees, and its feeble rivers, diverging fan-wise, leave between them long monotonous uplands. This is the country which is often called the Armagnac, a land of varied cultivation and of vineyards, which the Garonne bounds to the north-east and east. It is joined in the west to other uplands, which are more extensively encroached on by two abundant streams, the Gave and the Adour, which descend from the Pyrenees. Here, on roads leading to the Pyrenean valleys, towns have been built: Tarbes, Pau, whose mild climate has made it a winter resort, Bayonne, the port of all this southern region, at the end of the road and the railway coming from Spain. In this neighbourhood the Basque language has been preserved, and it is also spoken on the other slope of the Pyrenees; its sphere was formerly more extended and it probably corresponds with the ancient Iberian language. Nowadays it is nothing more than a popular dialect, serving for local intercourses. The Basque, even if he adheres to his language, has become a whole-hearted member of the great French family.

**The Landes.** From the top of the uplands of Béarn, which command the Adour, the view extends endlessly over a sea of forests. Here begins the region of the Landes, covering the vast triangle contained between the Adour, the Garonne, and the perfectly straight coast which goes from the Gironde to Bayonne. Covered with fine sand, bordered towards the sea by a high barrier of dunes, behind which stretch pools, it was less than a century ago one of the most desolate parts of France. Sandstone formed by the cohesion of these sands retained the waters on the surface, and the shepherds of the Landes perched on high stilts and watching their flocks of sheep, which gave the only touch of life to these unhealthy solitudes, are no fable. Drainage and pine-plantations have made this region quite healthy. They have even enriched it as well, for the pines in this favourable climate yield an abundant supply of resin of which turpentine is made, and their wood is exported by Bayonne and Bordeaux.

**The Valley of the Garonne.** The valley of the Garonne serves as a link between the various districts of Aquitaine. Opening wide at both ends, near Toulouse and Bordeaux, it narrows in the middle near Agen, where banks of limestone interpose between lighter formations. It is prolonged to the east near the rising ground of Naurouze, the door of communication between Aquitaine and Languedoc, by a long valley, whose waters, formerly more abundant, have been turned aside to the Aude. The little stream which occupies it bears the significant name of Lhers mort. But here passes the shortest route from the Mediterranean to the Atlantic, the railway and canal still following the line of the old Roman road. Carcassonne is at the point where that road leaves the valley of the Aude, Toulouse where it reaches the Garonne. Built of brick, which does not exclude architectural beauty, Toulouse, in spite of some industries, still remains a great agricultural market, and its growth has not proceeded at the same rate as that of other great French towns. Montauban, another town built of brick, occupies a more modest place in the low valley of the Tarn. As one goes west, the Garonne valley has a more varied cultivation; maize, tobacco, early vegetables, fruit trees; and then we come to the great vineyards, which continue to make the fortune of Bordeaux. The gravels of the terraces which dominate the river, the limestone slopes of the "Entre-deux-mers," the alluvial soils of the low plain, all yield vintages which rival each other in delicacy. Bordeaux shows its well-established wealth by its fine stone buildings, for marine limestone here encroaches on the Aquitaine basin. This wealth is due to her commerce, which, thanks to regular lines of navigation, is to-day extending to the countries overseas. Nothing is needed but more numerous and better inland communications to make Bordeaux one of the great European ports.

**The French Pyrenees.** The jagged peaks of the Pyrenees form a magnificent background in the south to this Aquitaine basin. Their numerous, but short, valleys have for long lived a life apart, like so many little separate States, sharing the high mountain pastures with the folk from the other slope. This exclusiveness has not resisted the penetration of roads and railways. Their natural beauty and their celebrated hot springs have attracted many visitors. The mineral resources have caused factories to be built. Another source of wealth is now being exploited: the water-power of the streams and torrents. The power-stations on the French side already produce 350,000 horse-power, and they will produce much more. The Pyrenees already supply light, heat, and power in abundance to the plain: and by this means the two regions are becoming more and more intimately associated.

**The Central Plateau.** It has been said of the Central Plateau that it was the repulsive pole of France, in contrast to the Paris basin, which was the attractive pole. Although this statement is exaggerated, it is none the less true that by its divergent valleys it did not lend itself to the union of the various regions composing it, which must be studied separately.

**Limousin and Marche.** To the west, nothing in the relief marks the limits of the Plateau. We pass insensibly from the marly or calcareous soil of the circumference to crystalline rocks, most frequently granite, much decomposed on the surface. On this impervious soil, meadow-land has a great place: chestnut trees adorn the slopes; only the high and almost deserted summits have kept their appearance of landes. Here there is not enough to occupy a numerous population, and Limousin and Marche supply a strong contingent for temporary emigration. Almost all the masons who come to work in Paris are natives of these two provinces. Limousin, however, possesses one industry, that of porcelain-making, utilising the white china-clay of the district, and this industry has brought prosperity to its ancient capital, Limoges. Here pass the main road and now the railway from Paris to Toulouse, forming an additional route to that through Poitou.

**The Southern part of the Central Plateau. The Causses.** The same crystalline rocks are present in the south, quite close to the Aquitaine basin, in the Rouergue, the Lacaune Mountains and the Black Mountain, which overlook the depression of Naurouze and the valley of the Aude. For all this part of the Plateau has felt the repercussion of the Pyrenean movements and is much higher than the west.

These southern mountains are separated from the volcanic region by the calcareous high-lands of the Causses, deeply furrowed by the Tarn and its tributaries. Honeycombed with cavities which communicate with a whole labyrinth of subterranean passages where water collects, these high desolate surfaces with a severe climate do not lend themselves to anything but the breeding of sheep, whose milk is used to make Roquefort cheese. Nowhere in France is the population scantier.

**Auvergne.** We know the origin of the numerous extinct volcanoes of Auvergne: Cantal, Mont Dore and that strange chain of the Puys, near Clermont, whose eruptions have been witnessed by man. The same volcanic track is continued towards the south-east up to the Rhône, by the basaltic flows and the numerous peaks near the source of the Loire. The curious town of Le Puy is built at the base of two of these needles of eruptive rock. The decomposition of basalt produces a soil, the fertility of which is in great contrast to the poor neighbouring granitic land, and Auvergne rears fine breeds of cattle. But here also the land does not give occupation to enough people, and from Auvergne another stream of temporary emigrants flows to Paris; formerly water-carriers, they are now small coal-merchants or drivers of carriages or cars on hire. All this part of the Central Plateau, as a matter of fact, feels the attraction of the Paris basin, because of its inner plains, which all open to the north. Of these, the richest is that of La Limagne, fertilised by volcanic débris. The capital of Auvergne has always been on one of the lower slopes, which command this basin: formerly Gergovia, now Clermont-Ferrand, where the facility for finding work has brought into being a very active industrial centre.

**The Eastern Border of the Central Plateau.** This is the most elevated, because of the proximity of the Alps, and it is also the most varied, for some fragments of limestone have remained in places upon crystalline rocks, especially in the neighbourhood of Lyons, and farther south, opposite Valence. But what most distinguishes this eastern border is the presence of several coal-fields, the most important of the Central Plateau: the basin of Montceau-les-Mines, to the north, near which are placed the great metallurgical factories of le Creusot; the basin of Saint-Étienne in the centre, which is continued beyond the Rhône; to the south the basin of Alais. The largest production belongs to the basin of Saint-Étienne. Round this centre, which has become one of the great French towns, has been formed a powerful group of metallurgical industries, the most active after that of the north. And the influence of the Lyons weaving industry has also extended there. Saint-Étienne has specialised in the manufacture of silk ribbons. Lyons has in turn profited increasingly from the proximity of this coal-field.

**The Lyons district.** In the long valley of the Saône and the Rhône, Lyons is the vital point. Lyons, which was the religious and political centre of Gaul during the Roman epoch, very soon became also a commercial centre, thanks to the roads which radiated thence: to Italy over the Alpine passes; to the Swiss plain by the Upper Rhône; and in the west, to Le Forez and to the Loire. But the principal route was the waterway of the Rhône and the Saône from the Mediterranean to the north. Commerce brought industries, and Lyons has become the capital of the silk-trade. If there are not as many looms as formerly to-day in her precincts, it is because they have spread through the whole district, grouped in factories: in Dauphiné, in the Southern Jura, and even in Auvergne. In this way the great town has extended her influence, her activity, her intelligence, and her capital. Recently, she has become even more wealthy by the introduction of other industries: the chemical industry, brought there by the requirements of dyeing, and mechanical construction. Her importance cannot fail to increase, when the operations intended to tame the Alpine torrent of the Rhône and make it navigable for large ships have been completed.

**The Saône basin. The Jura.** To the north, the Saône basin is an exclusively agricultural district. Macon, Chalon, Bourg, even Dijon, are markets for land produce. Macon and Dijon are also markets for the rich local vineyards, for Burgundy is not inferior to Bordeaux in the warmth and delicacy of its wines. In a line at the foot of the "Côte d'Or" there is a whole series of little towns whose names—Gevrey-Chambertin, Nuits, Beaune—have been popularised by its most celebrated vintages.

In this fertile basin of the Saône end the valley of the Doubs, the road, and the railway which come from the pass of Belfort. The fortified town of Besançon, shut in a bend of the river, protects this crossing. At the boundary of the Jura and of the plain it served as the link between the two districts. It was one of the centres of exchange and it was always the capital of the successive political groups: the Gallic tribe of Sequani, and later the County of Burgundy or Franche-Comté. France offers more than one example of these unions between distinct but complementary regions round some town situated close to them. Only the northern part of the Jura, that of the grassy and forested uplands, felt the attraction of Besançon. To the south lies the Jura region of the great folded chains, which opens naturally towards the Rhône. Bugey, by its industries, belongs to the district of Lyons.

**The Rhône Valley.** Across these southern chains of the Jura, the course of the river, after leaving Lake Leman, is at first only a succession of gorges. It is above all a region favourable to the installation of power-stations. There will soon be constructed an enormous dam to form a waterfall, which will supply 200,000 horse-power, part of which will be conveyed to Paris. On leaving the Jura, and up to its junction with the Saône at Lyons, the river is the boundary of Lower Dauphiné. A land of plains and of uplands, where glaciers have left their traces, this district gradually becomes narrower towards the south up to the confluence of the Isère. The Rhône valley, well-situated between the old river terraces, there forms a narrow passage, effectively sheltered by the Central Plateau, where vines and fruit-trees yield famous fruit. Vienne, whence came the Roman colony which established itself at Lyons, and which still retains some remains of this distant past, has become an industrial town specialising in the weaving of common cloth. Beyond the Isère the valley contracts; the Alps draw nearer. Then, after leaving Valence, the edge of the Central Plateau deviates to the west. Here begins the region of the Cevennes, a mountainous off-shoot from the Central Plateau, deeply furrowed by the streams which join the Rhône. Nowhere is the contrast more marked than between these valleys, which are quite southern in type, and the highlands, where the snow still covers the ground late in spring. It is here, in these valleys of the Cevennes, that is best kept up the breeding of silk-worms, which was formerly carried on more widely in the whole of the Rhône valley, and the rapid streams work the "silk-throwing machines," which prepare the silk for the factories of Lyons. Below Montélimar, near the old episcopal town of Viviers, the river is compressed in a narrow gully, the door of entrance to the south, where the olive proclaims the proximity of the Mediterranean. The Rhône, without slackening its speed, widens more and more. In its neighbourhood and on its banks towns which recall past civilisations and history succeed each other: Orange, the Roman town, Avignon, the Papal town, and the two sister towns of Tarascon and Beaucaire, so prosperous in the days of the fairs, which attracted all the merchants of Europe; finally Arles, whose vast amphitheatre shows its importance in the days when the Roman galleys were anchored in serried ranks on the steep banks. Here begins the Rhône delta, including within its arms the Camargue, formerly poisoned by its pools, but now almost entirely drained, and added to the vineyards of Languedoc. On the left bank there is another desert, the Crau, where are welded together into a solid mass the pebbles once carried down by the Rhône and the Durance. And the river, obstructed by its own deposits which prevent the passage of any large ship, ends in lonely shores, far from the great port which is the real outlet of its valley. But this isolation is about to end. Great works are in progress with the object of connecting the Rhône directly with Marseilles. A tunnel has been cut through the chain of Estaque, giving access to the deep salt water basin known as the Étang de Berre, connected with Arles by a canal which is to be rendered navigable to the largest ships of the Rhône.

**The French Alps.** Through the valleys of the Isère and the Durance the Rhône gully communicates easily with the great region of the Alps, and real inner plains penetrate the mountain. Other valleys come to join them there, and this network ends in passes, the highest of which are not all on the frontier. There is, therefore, no impassable barrier and the high peaks glistening with snow can be turned more or less easily. Some political organisations were even formed on both slopes before there had been given to the line of the watershed an importance which it does not always in reality possess. The House of Savoy, native to Maurienne (valley of the Arc), owes its fortune to the fact that it held several Alpine passes, and the little State of Briançon extended on both sides of the pass of Mont-Genèvre. Thus is explained the fact that the French language is still spoken in the valley of Aosta, and as far as Susa in the river-valley of the Dora Riparia. Among these inner valleys there is none so rich as that of the Isère above Grenoble. It opens laterally to the outer world by wide passes, in which are placed the lakes of Annecy and of Bourget. It is continued to the south of Grenoble by another series of valleys, forming a pass to the Durance. Nowadays railways follow these old routes, connecting towns which were formerly the chief stages: Annecy, Chambéry, Gap, Briançon, and above all Grenoble, which has become the metropolis of the Savoy and Dauphiné Alps. For long devoted to agricultural and pastoral life, the French Alps now possess industries, thanks to the abundant water-power supplied by their streams. All along the most accessible valleys, in Maurienne and in Oisans, power-stations succeed each other almost uninterruptedly, producing chiefly aluminium, the ores of which are found in Provence. But this power, which, when effectually used, will represent the value of a large coal-field to France, is not all consumed in the mountains; it is conveyed by cables far away to Lyons, and even to Saint-Étienne, for the use of the metallurgical industry.

**Lower Provence.** Intersected by chains of bare limestone, in a line from west to east, Lower Provence is composed of a series of hollows, connected by valleys. It is a collection of little basins, where towns and villages are grouped among cultivated land. Amongst these depressions there is a longer and more continuous one, which bounds to the north the dark hills of the Maures, covered with pines and cork-trees. To avoid the very steep headlands on the coast, the Roman and later the modern roads have followed this inland valley. But the Roman road went directly to Aix, which has always been the capital of Provence, while the modern routes have felt the attraction of Marseilles. The coast in this eastern part has therefore remained isolated, and even to-day its life is distinct from that of the inland plains. There is a succession of small ports on the curving shores of the mirror-like sea, from Nice to the old Lacydon, which for centuries sufficed for the commerce of Marseilles. Hill-towns have sprung up on the headlands and many of their names recall their Hellenic origin. All this coast has been transformed: it has been enriched by the cultivation of flowers and early vegetables. Nice is a great winter resort, Toulon is a military port, and Marseilles, exceeding on all sides the limits of its old port, has widely multiplied its docks, without finding enough space for all its industries. We have seen above, that by piercing the Estaque chain, Marseilles is preparing to gain greater scope, thus assuring to herself the place which belongs to her among the great Mediterranean ports, opposite that other France which has been created on African soil.

**Lower Languedoc.** Lower Languedoc, which begins on the other side of the Rhône, does not possess the advantages of the Marseilles sea-front. Bordered by lagoons which are separated from the sea by sand reefs, it has only been able to acquire one artificial port, namely Cette. Here activity is inland, along the roads which connect Nîmes, the richest of French towns in Roman monuments and remains, Montpellier and Béziers, cities of the Middle Ages, and Narbonne, another Roman town, which, at the end of its lagoon, was long the great port of all this coast, at the point where it is joined by the Aude valley and the Aquitaine road. The plains of Lower Languedoc are to-day too exclusively given up to the vine, which even extends into the valley of the Aude, beyond Carcassonne, a curious relic of the past, dominating with its walls and towers the modern town, which has been built at its feet.

**Roussillon.** The low coast, edged with lagoons, extends to the end of the Pyrenees. Made narrower by the vicinity of the Corbières, it again widens in the warm plain of Roussillon, which recalls the Spanish "huertas." Then the rocky salient of the Pyrenees offers shelter to ships in its creeks. The deepest and safest of these, Port-Vendres, was in early times frequented by the Carthaginians. Between the plain of Roussillon and that of Ampurdan, on the other side of the frontier, the mountains become lower and are reduced to a simple chain. The pass of Perthus is not more than 951 feet. Inland, the valley of the Têt leads without obstruction to the high plateau of the Cerdagne, whence the waters of the Sègre flow to the south. Here, as at the other end of the Pyrenees, communication has always been easy, and the Catalan language has invaded the French slope. It is used as the local dialect in Roussillon and the Cerdagne, and, like Basque, does not imply any separatist sentiments. The citadel of Perpignan, which commanded these passes, is in a district thoroughly French.

In conclusion, a few reflections and figures.

One of the expressions which has most often recurred in the course of this too rapid description is that of agricultural country. In spite of the increasing importance of her industries, France actually draws her chief revenue from the land[1]. This is the result of her comparative poverty in coal (41,000,000 tons produced in 1913—265,000,000 tons in Great Britain—256,000,000 tons in Germany). 58 per cent. of the French nation are a rural population (23 per cent. in Great Britain) and almost half the population lives by work on the land. These cultivators are mainly landowners on a small or a moderate scale, who till their land themselves with the help of their families or a small

[1] 48 per cent. of the soil of France is arable land, 19 per cent. forests, 12 per cent. meadows and pastures, 4 per cent. vineyards, 17 per cent. is unproductive (especially mountainous regions). These figures are pre-war ones and do not include Alsace-Lorraine. France held the third place among the great wheat-producing countries with 89,000,000 metric quintals (figures of 1901–1910), after the United States (181,000,000) and Russia (173,000,000).

number of servants. A quarter of the agricultural land of France consists in properties of less than six acres. There are no agricultural operations on a large scale except on the rich soil of the Paris basin. The large proportion of small holdings has certainly retarded the progress of agriculture, but the continually increasing number of landowners on a small or moderate scale is one of the sources of strength of this profoundly democratic country, less exposed than others to revolutionary experiments.

This attachment of the French to the land and the slower progress of industries than elsewhere have also retarded the formation of very large urban centres in France. In the last census, in 1921, there were only 16 towns of over 100,000 inhabitants (instead of 43 in the United Kingdom and 47 in Germany). Amongst these towns, only five exceeded 200,000: Paris, Marseilles, Lyons, Bordeaux, and Lille; three only had over 500,000: Paris, Marseilles and Lyons. Paris was a long way ahead with her 2,863,000 inhabitants, really, as we have seen, with more than 4,000,000, if the suburbs are included[1].

The preponderance of Paris is the result of its position as capital. As the French monarchy evolved towards absolutism, Paris became the centre whence all orders were issued, whence all impulses were transmitted. The absolute government of Napoleon I made this dependence even more complete. Thus Paris has tended more and more to absorb all the living forces of the nation. But in attracting to herself writers, scientists, and artists, the great city has shone with incomparable splendour far beyond the limits of France. We need only recall the great part played by the University of Paris in the Middle Ages, and the influence which has been exercised all over the world by French thinkers. We may regret this excessive centralisation: it has at least had the merit of contributing in great measure to the moral and intellectual unity of France. To-day there is a tendency to reaction, to give more autonomy to the

[1] Greater Paris comprises more than a tenth of the French population. In 1911, this population was 39,601,000 inhabitants, while that of Alsace-Lorraine was 1,874,000, making a total of 41,475,000. At the census of March, 1921 the total was 39,194,550, including 1,695,156 for Alsace-Lorraine. The losses caused by the war (from deaths and decrease of births for the years 1914–1920) may be estimated at about 2,400,000.

great districts which have grouped themselves round the chief towns. The country cannot fail to gain in activity and initiative thereby. There is no fear that it will lose what has been its strength in the hour of great peril, the close union of all its children.

## BIBLIOGRAPHICAL NOTE

P. Vidal de la Blache, *Tableau de la Géographie de la France* (forming the Introduction to E. Lavisse, *Histoire de France*, I.). This book cannot be too highly recommended to those who wish to have a thorough knowledge of France. Michelet's *Tableau de la France* (*Histoire de France*, II. 1–110) still preserves its value as a work of art, but it cannot pretend to the same exactness. Mention also should be made of the very penetrating pages devoted to France by H. J. Fleure in his *Human Geography in Western Europe. The Making of the Future.* 1918.

# CHAPTER II

## HISTORY

### § I. POLITICAL AND SOCIAL CONDITIONS IN 987

BEFORE beginning a survey of the period of five hundred years in the political and social history of France, of which a broad outline is here to be given, we must briefly indicate the state of affairs prevailing at the accession of the Capetian dynasty and during the first and second generations which followed.

There was at this time a Kingdom of France, or rather "of the French," which was a fragment somewhat curiously carved out of the ancient "Romania." The frontiers of this kingdom were natural only on the west (the sea) and the south-west (the Pyrenees); on the north, east, and south-east, the purely arbitrary boundaries are only to be explained by the persistence of the lines drawn on the map of the Carolingian Empire, when in the 9th century it was divided between the sons of the Emperor Louis the Pious. Lothair, the eldest son, received as his share the two capitals of the Empire, Aix-la-Chapelle and Rome, with a wide road leading from one to the other, from the North Sea to the Mediterranean, between "France" and Germany. It was not long before "Lotharingia," the absurd buffer State thus constituted, was subdivided into Lorraine (Upper and Lower) and Burgundy; but the chance of immediately uniting these detached provinces to the western kingdom was lost; instead of this, they yielded to the attraction of the Germanic Empire. For this reason "France" in 987, instead of being bounded on the north and east by the Rhine and the Alps, as had been the case with Gaul, was bounded, to speak generally, by the Meuse, the Saône, and the Cevennes; beyond the Pyrenees, it included the Marches of Catalonia. It has taken centuries and cost torrents of blood up to our day to repair the very grave consequences of these partitions in the 9th century, which thus appear to be a perfect type of those accidental events whose disproportionate consequences are perpetuated almost indefinitely throughout the ages. But in 987 doubtless no one thought, as we think nowadays, that by reason of previous history, and ethnical, linguistic, and geographical considerations, it would have been better had the "Kingdom of the French" been originally somewhat differently designed; for we are wise after the event.

The unity of the kingdom consisted in the fact that there was only one king, who was recognised from Bruges to Barcelona. This king was in reality only nominally recognised and had hardly anywhere any power; but his dignity, of illustrious origin and magnificent traditions, both Roman and Carolingian, was even in abasement rich in inherent powers, which might develop, or disappear, according to circumstances. The Roman and Carolingian principles of authority were in danger of extinction in actual fact, but they survived as a memory and an ideal. At the end of the 10th century this ideal existed in a more or less latent manner and it was personified by the king.

In 987 there was a change of dynasty. This event, which for long was regarded as profoundly significant, has been much discussed by modern historians. It was at first thought that the Carolingians and the Capetians respectively represented antagonistic races. According to some, the accession of Hugh Capet to the throne was the reaction of the Latin race (Gallo-Roman) against the German invasion (as the Carolingians were certainly the chiefs of Frank tribes established in Gaul): "With the Capetian dynasty, and under its auspices, France shook off the influence from the other side of the Rhine." According to others, the Carolingians of the 10th century, successors of Charlemagne and romanised as he was, appear on the contrary as champions of the Roman ideas of unity, order, and centralisation; their fall was a protest against these doctrines, "and was the triumph of the feudal system brought to Gaul by the Germans." Augustin Thierry, protagonist of the theory of nationalities, considered that the accession of the Capetians, the first "national" kings of France, was a notable defeat of Germanism in Europe, while Jacques Flach[1] wrote in 1904:

[1] J. Flach, *Les origines de l'ancienne France*, III. 199.

"By the accession of the Capetians Germany triumphed." All these opinions are valueless; and the wisest thing to do is to hold the very simple view that the victory of Hugh Capet over the last of the Carolingians was the victory, which had been long preparing, not of a race, nor of a nation, nor of any principle whatever, but of a family still in the ascendant over another which was decadent. The date of 987 is not that of a "revolution"; it is only a convenient chronological mark.

At the close of the 10th century monarchy in France was therefore no more than *magni nominis umbra*, except in the province where the new royal family had previously been powerful under other titles. We know that this province was the Ile-de-France and the neighbouring districts, with Paris as their centre. The ancestors of Hugh Capet had formerly been masters also of Blois, Tours, Angers, etc.; but their possessions had diminished in proportion as they approached the hereditary throne, at the same time as the territorial support of the Carolingian dynasty entirely disappeared for reasons and under conditions which we need not consider.

The principality of the Robertinians, ancestors of the Capetians, was still in 987 a living reality, although it already seemed on the decline. But there were in the kingdom many other ruling families at different stages of their greatness. These must be considered so that we may be able to form an idea of the organised forces which were then active, for the existence of great feudal States, side by side and in rivalry, is what first strikes us in the France of the 11th century, where the monarchy was scarcely more than a lofty traditional abstract idea, and in some places hardly as much as that.

In the first place there were on the marches of the north and west certain duchies or counties which were more or less natural unities, already possessing marked and permanent characteristics: Flanders, Normandy, Brittany, and Aquitaine.

**Flanders** was a mixed State, which included Walloons (i.e. people of Roman speech) and people of German speech; it was situated between the kingdom of France and the German Empire, and was so wealthy and strong from the very beginning that it tended to increase at the cost of those who surrounded it. Count Baldwin V (d. 1067), who waged a victorious war with the Empire and was uncle and guardian of King Philip I of France and father-in-law of that Duke of Normandy who became King of England, deliberately established the centre of gravity of his "kingdom" at Lille, in Walloon territory; he was the leading personage of his time.

**Normandy** was a conquered land to which its Scandinavian conquerors had given a peculiar character by colonising part of it and organising it in an original manner. The extraordinary vitality of this State showed itself in the 11th century by its enterprises abroad, amongst which the conquest of England by Duke William was only an episode. We shall refer to it later.

**Brittany,** situated at the point of the mainland, seemed to be also a "kingdom" apart from that of France, isolated by the fact that its population was for the most part of a different race, language, and traditions (Celtic). This "kingdom" was not united at the end of the 10th century. There was rivalry for supremacy between the houses of Nantes and Rennes, who in their quarrels alternately called for the intervention of their neighbours, the Normans and the people of the Loire provinces; hence comparative weakness.

**Aquitaine** was the wide region without unity which stretched from the Loire to the Garonne and from the Atlantic as far as, and including, Auvergne, enclosing very varied districts, with populations for the most part of Provençal speech and a few who spoke "French." At the beginning of the 11th century, the Poitevins had overcome the people of Auvergne and the supremacy in this region was in the hands of the house of Poitiers. Their ostentatious ruler, Guillaume V (990–1020), had real power and kept semi-royal state.

Had the Duke of Aquitaine extended his power to Gascony (between the Gironde and the Pyrenees) and the region of Languedoc (between the Garonne and the eastern boundary of France in the south), he would have become the ruler of a southern state which, possessing its own civilisation, would certainly have imperilled "French" unity, which was then artificial. There is no doubt that the dynasty of Poitou persistently claimed this supremacy, or rather aspired to it, for this was in the nature of things. Now Gascony, a barbaric and archaic country like Brittany, whose centre of gravity had in the 10th century been evidently placed nearer to Navarre and Aragon than to Aquitaine, did in fact become united to the duchy of Aquitaine after the extinction of the principal line of local rulers, under the great Dukes of Aquitaine in the following century. But Languedoc did not fall into their power.

**Languedoc**, with Toulouse and Narbonne as its marts, was the real home of southern civilisation, which differed from that of the north, and was very capable of self-government. But in the 11th century the house of the counts of Toulouse, which was divided into several branches, was strong enough to hold its own against the Aquitanian power, but far from strong enough to absorb it. Its influence was moreover counter-balanced in all the south-eastern extremity of the kingdom by the rulers of the **Marches of Catalonia**, of which Barcelona was the capital; these rulers were rivals of the house of Toulouse, but their strength also was checked by successive divisions in each generation. Either the princely house of Toulouse, or that of Barcelona, might aspire to the leadership of the south; but neither of them was in a position to attain to it.

Now as to the eastern marches in the direction of Burgundy and Champagne.

The former unity of the territory colonised by the Burgondi was severed at the line of the Saône by the treaty of Verdun; the kingdom of France consequently only included part of this country—the **Duchy of Burgundy**, whose characteristics date from the time of Duke Richard the Lawgiver, who governed it for a number of years in the second half of the 9th and for the first half of the 10th centuries. The successors of Richard extended their power beyond the Saône, as he had done, and aimed at an increase of territory at the expense of the kingdom of Burgundy of the Jura. If the plan of reunion between the two Burgundies, which was certainly contemplated, had been realised, it would have created on this frontier, on an even larger scale, a state separating France and the "Empire," which might have become of great importance. But the ducal dynasties which succeeded each other in Burgundy after that of Richard were weak and achieved nothing great.

In the 10th century the supremacy of the Dukes of Burgundy became extended to the province of **Champagne.** But in the 11th century, as the result of a series of complicated events which are now fairly well known, this region fell into the hands of the family of a former *vicomte* of the Dukes of France, Thibaut the Trickster, who founded a great dominion in the country outlined by the towns of Chartres, Blois, and Tours. The master of Chartres, Blois, and Tours thus became also the master of Troyes, Meaux, Provins, etc.; and from 1027 onwards his possessions, which were more than twice the size of the land properly belonging to the Capetian kings, surrounded it on every side.

There remains **Anjou** (Angers-Saumur), in which there had arisen another dynasty, descended like that of Thibaut the Trickster from the former *vicomtes* of the original Duchy of France. The Angevin dynasty, having subjugated Maine, was in possession of power which might become formidable to its neighbours, especially to Normandy and Aquitaine. A brilliant future was in store for it.

Thus there were in the kingdom "feudal" States with shifting frontiers, some of which had become established, and all of which had become generally stronger during the half-century which preceded and that which followed the accession of the Capets. We must now form a clear idea of the political and social conditions in each of these States. There were certainly, in this respect, considerable differences between one province and another. But the resemblances were still more numerous, for the system which is generally described by the epithet "feudal" obtained everywhere at that time. As this system was not however peculiar to France, and as it extended, the same causes having produced the same effects, throughout nearly the whole of Western Christianity, it will be enough here to describe it briefly.

In the beginning, there was the Roman state of things, a system by which the citizen possessed land and slaves as his absolute property, subject to restrictions and charges imposed by the State in the public interest. At the time of the great Carolingians, this state of things, greatly altered by centuries of invasion and of Barbarian domination, still existed in some of its main features, at least apparently. But new phenomena had been produced, or had presented themselves—the decadence of the State, i.e. of public power, with the division or the seizure by violence or by more or less disorderly usurpation of its prerogatives; and the change in relations between the masters of properties and the men who lived on them. These immense changes in the course of the 10th century, the complicated machinery of which was by no means uniform according to districts, and which will always remain very obscure for lack of documents, are outside our subject. They were moreover by no means at an end at the period which serves us as a point of departure; they were not even quite ended by the time of St Louis. We may however try to sketch the really characteristic features of the system which became thus established in the course of three or four hundred years, considering rather the general tendencies and results than the actual processes of the evolution, the details of which were infinitely varied.

At this time, the land was cultivated by a population, relatively of great density, men of various conditions, amongst whom small proprietors and farmers, or *métayers* of the modern type, were nearly everywhere in a very small minority. For the most part established on the property of a master, some were serfs, others free. But the serfs, who were moreover continually decreasing in number as a result of emancipation conceded at a monetary price, were not slaves; the master granted them plots of land, which were handed from father to son, in return for dues and forced labour, which were certainly burdensome, but which gradually ceased to be *à discrétion*, i.e. not limited by local custom. The greatest difference between the serfs and other tenants was that their condition was still theoretically affected by traces of the old personal slavery—the master's right unconditionally to resume possession of the land he had granted, should the deceased serf not have left, in the direct line, a suitable descendant to continue his work; the master's right to object if his serfs renounced their tenures and their consequent duties towards him in order to move elsewhere, or if their daughters married outside his property (which is only a special application of the same principle). In practice, these rights were often redeemable and could be cancelled singly, just as exemption from all duties could be bought by emancipation properly so called. Now, the free tenants, like the servile tenants, were in possession of hereditary plots of land, in return for dues in money or in kind, for various loans (especially of labour on the land reserved for the master), and for taxes on removal. Actually the real difference between servile tenants and free tenants was therefore not very great and it always had a tendency to diminish. On both servile and free tenants alike there weighed charges to the advantage of the master, without analogy either in the ancient or the modern world, which were caused by the disintegration of public power and private appropriation of its prerogatives. Besides his other rights, fixed by custom, the master had, for instance, the right of exploiting the dwellers on his land to his own advantage, by establishing thereon administrative rules (*bans*) with lucrative results, such as monopolies (*banalités*), dues on traffic and on the sale of commodities, etc. Finally, almost everywhere, property was accompanied by "justice," and one of the chief sources of revenue for the master was produced by fines inflicted by his court of justice for all infractions, or for certain defined infractions ("high, low, and middle justice"), with the accessory profits of records and chicanery.

Who then was the "master" (*dominus*, lord) who enjoyed all these rights? He was sometimes, but not always, a great landowner, a layman or a cleric, whose possessions extended afar, over hill and valley. The world of masters, i.e. people whose common characteristic was to live without working, was as varied as that of the country people. But it was also hierarchic by nature.

In ancient times great estates were the rule; many communes nowadays in France have almost the same superficies as the Gallo-Roman properties whose limits, and even names, they have preserved throughout the ages. There were great lords who possessed several, or even many, of these ancient properties (or properties more or less recently constituted on the model of the older ones by the introduction on new ground of "colonists" to clear the land), each with his residence and his seignorial grounds. But there were also lords who had only one estate.

And, when we at last reach a time when documents enable us to judge the social state with some precision, it is obvious that there were a number of even smaller properties, some of very modest size, whose owner, if he had a family, must have found it hard to live "nobly." If a writer of the Middle Ages in France had, like Gogol and many other Russian novelists of the 19th century, thought of describing a round of visits to the neighbouring gentry, great and small, rich and poor, he would no doubt have drawn pictures analogous to those of the author of *Dead Souls*. Moreover we know from direct sources that in France there was soon a small, nay a very small, nobility, whose members lived by the exploitation of the few "souls" on their land, and whose younger sons were obliged to enter some princely court as servants in order to finish their education, and afterwards to adopt the profession of a mercenary soldier and seek adventures abroad so as to earn a living.

The practice among rich and great lords of surrounding themselves with young men who were serving their apprenticeship for the life of a gentleman, is naturally of great antiquity. And custom supplied it with special features in the Roman world as modified by the invasions. Between these great lords of Carolingian times and their armed servants, who were both servants and comrades, soon to be called *vassi* (vassals), relations of a character unknown in other states of civilisation became established: on the side of the overlord, protection and kindly familiarity; on the side of the vassals, devotion without subservience. At certain times, unascertained and no doubt differing in various districts, it was the custom that vassals of this kind should be recompensed and their livelihood ensured by the concession of land, i.e. by the grant of properties of greater or lesser extent, carved out of the larger estate of their lord. Such is the probable origin of a very great number of small estates of the 10th, 11th, and 12th centuries. The estate, secondary and derived, so to speak, granted in this manner, was properly the *fief*. Enfeoffment was therefore an act which created, or rather sanctioned, not only reciprocal obligations, but also a difference of rank, between him who granted and him who received the grant. And all the feudal hierarchy sprung from this elementary practice, as it was of a nature which could be repeated almost indefinitely, each vassal possessing a fief being in a position to enfeoff under-vassals, and so on. This fashion having spread, free men, small proprietors, in order to gain the protection of some powerful neighbour, soon formed the idea of delivering their land to him, on condition that he would return it to them by way of "fief." The land was thus divided up into seignories, one overlapping the other.

The feudal grant of land, or rather of the use of land, no doubt started with very simple conditions of sworn fidelity, indefinite and unlimited, and as a life-interest. But this did not last. At the beginning of the 11th century in France, fiefs had generally become hereditary like the tenures of the peasants, i.e. the son (and even, with local exceptions, the daughter) succeeded the father on condition of fulfilling in person or by proxy the same duties as the father to the holders of the lessor's rights. In the course of generations these duties became specified and consequently restricted, just as the serfs almost everywhere gradually obtained the substitution of fixed charges for exploitation *ad libitum*, or *à merci*. The feelings of whole-hearted fidelity which the grateful vassal had originally cherished towards the master who had "settled" him could hardly survive in his descendants towards the distant posterity of this forgotten benefactor. It therefore very soon became necessary to fix by a series of bargains the minimum of actual or symbolical service which the heir of a vassal was obliged to fulfil to the advantage of the suzerain as a sign of his traditional dependence, as a survival and in remembrance of the former total "fidelity." When this evolution was complete, the reciprocal duties of suzerains and vassals were the objects of as precise definitions as those of the lords and their villeins, and varied almost as much according to locality. *Liege* homage was distinguished from *simple* homage. The ceremonial of investitures was determined. The feudal use of land was burdened with military service (during so many days a year; in such and such a radius round the principal castle of the suzerain; under obligation for the vassal to lend his defensive material on requisition and without payment); money payments ("aids" in certain cases, and dues on removal and alienation); some forced labour (the obligation for the vassal to appear on certain dates at the court of the suzerain). The suzerain was moreover considered as the natural guardian of the younger children of a vassal who died. Feudal possession of land was no less burdened in all these ways than possession in villenage; and in the 14th century the wealthy townsmen of the *bourgeoisie* considered it even more harassing and less peaceful.

Moreover it must not be forgotten that the feudal system was, so to speak, constructed without a plan, by a kind of natural and secular growth; it was always very irregular, except in places where the system was artificially introduced in its entirety by ably led conquerors to countries where it was previously unknown. Enfeoffment originally signified absolute fidelity and a hierarchy; just as absolute fidelity was soon replaced by a sort of contract, so the primitive hierarchy was rapidly overthrown by the fact that very powerful nobles, having inherited, acquired, or seized new estates, became in this way the "vassals" of suzerains who were not their equals in power or social importance. The feudal hierarchy of properties lasted for long; that of persons lost a great part of its substantial reality when a number of nobles and even princes were found to be both suzerains and vassals. From the 12th century downwards the confusion of suzerainties and vassalages in France was inextricable.

That which in the feudal period most clearly characterised the condition of those who were not noble was, as we have seen, that their overlords had the power of exercising profitable rights over them, rights of an administrative and judicial order, which in our day belong only to public authority. What most characterised the condition of the nobles in their relations with each other was also, generally speaking, that they were exempt from the action of any authority of this kind. These people of no occupation were armed by their right of exacting definite military service to their own advantage from a larger or smaller number of their equals, who were their vassals; those who were wealthy had also the means of obtaining as many mercenaries as they wished among the poorer members of their own class. And *there was no organised police* to hinder them in the name of public interests from giving free play to their turbulence, their ambitions, or their feuds. They waged effective war on each other and when not actually so engaged they practised mock-warfare ceaselessly (jousts and tourneys). In this respect there is a striking difference between the French nobles in the Middle Ages and the Russian landowners in the days of the serfs, as depicted by Gogol and Turgenev. The latter were essentially peaceful because of the ubiquity of a very strict State police, but were all the more idle and corrupt; the former suffered, and above all made those around them suffer, from some of the inconveniences of anarchy, but they still retained some of the virtues kept alive by an active life. There may still be found to-day on French soil many seignorial dwellings of that age, in ruins, generally placed on high ground; these were fortresses, of which some were formidable, such as the donjons of Beaugency, Langeais, Étampes, Provins, and many others. The material and sentimental life led therein during the first centuries of the second part of the Middle Ages (after the year 1000) is now well known from descriptive contemporary literature, which is abundant and not sufficiently idealised to prevent us from obtaining an impression of reality.

In the feudal system each seignory was theoretically a complete and self-sufficient State, wherein there was no law, no tax, no police, in fact no organised force but that of the master. As to cohesion between seignories, which was originally maintained in great measure by the tie of vassalage, it ought to have decreased in proportion as this link became weaker. Yet we nowhere find total independence of parts or a multitude of tiny estates. We began this account by an enumeration of the vast groups of seignories, called "feudal States," into which the territory of the kingdom was divided in the 11th century. The fact is that our Western races are not anarchical. The confused remembrance of the former united state of things under the Roman plan still influenced them, and besides their instincts are such that it has never been necessary to exercise very heavy pressure to keep Frenchmen grouped and subordinated. The very great nobles, sometimes helped thereto by the fact that they were descendants of the former high administrative officials of the Carolingian Empire (dukes and counts, or governors of provinces), had little trouble in imposing the recognition of their authority throughout very extended regions. They naturally did so by the superiority of their forces, both financially (being incomparably the wealthiest) and military (having a very large number of personal vassals and the means of hiring many men). It was thus that they created the framework of estates which may be compared with real States; States in which the central power was indeed ill-supplied with means of action, and was more or less vacillating and precarious, but yet with enough influence to spread abroad to its advantage not only fear, but feelings of loyalty and a wish to collaborate in common enterprises. The founders of these feudal States were thus, on the very morrow of the disorder which accompanied the Carolingian decadence, the earliest agents of the great phenomena of recovery of which the French monarchy was the last word at the close of the Middle Ages.

Amongst all the "feudal States" mentioned above Normandy is unquestionably the most interesting to study, both because of the exceptionally high state of organisation which it seems to have attained at a very early date and because of the recent works devoted to this organisation. The central power seems to have been stronger there at an earlier date than elsewhere, strong enough to establish exactly what had almost disappeared in the other "feudal" districts—an official police. Even before William the Conqueror, the dukes imposed clearly-defined military service on their vassals, even enforcing their right to make general levies in case of common danger (public safety). They ensured the observance of their "peace," i.e. order, by a series of prohibitions, which their power enabled them to enforce; it was, for instance, forbidden to build new strongholds without permission; the right of private warfare was restricted in various ways; certain cases were, in all places, reserved for the jurisdiction of the duke. At the end of the 11th century, if not earlier, he had his own coinage, which was *the* coinage of the country, regular revenues, a fiscal administration, officials (called *vicomtes*), set over each district, who were not only agents of the province, but also representatives of his authority from every point of view, and finally, above them, at his court, the framework of higher jurisdictions for the control and direction of the local staff. Similar facts, which existing documents do not enable us to describe, may have existed at about the same period in other feudal States, but certainly nowhere with such precocity and intensity. As we know, the Norman rulers carried these traditional habits of theirs to their great conquests in England, Southern Italy, and the East.

The Church was always an element of capital importance in the social life of the Middle Ages. She was everywhere represented, with her hierarchy (the master-work of the remarkable genius of ancient Rome in the sphere of government), her doctrines, and her uniform ideals—her doctrine of obedience and her ideal of peace. Moreover the feudal system was bound up with certain modes of military service and the clergy were forbidden to bear arms. In the shipwreck of political unity and public order which explains the coming of the feudal system, it seems that the Church must have been by her professions a point of resistance to the general movement, and a force at the service of future reaction. For this, however, it was necessary that she herself should not be too greatly contaminated by the prevailing tendencies, which could not fail to affect her in some measure. To what extent then was she affected at the beginning of the 11th century in France?

Apparently modern historians are not quite agreed on this point, as we read in rightly esteemed recent works these contradictory statements: "Even at the periods of greatest confusion, at the time when the spirit of the century had most deeply affected the clergy, never did the Church adopt in her organisation a feudal principle; never did an inferior do homage to a superior, nor accept his office as a fief." On the other hand: "The bishops, having become great proprietors and great lords, allowed themselves to be tainted by the spirit of the new system; the habits and customs of the nobles exerted on them an influence very contrary to the nature of their office...." Striking facts are quoted in support of the latter argument: lords who turned the bishoprics of their domains into appanages for their children; bishops who succeeded each other from father to son; barons who had several episcopal sees in their personal possession and who handed them on to their heirs, etc. Other facts of an even graver character, because they were less exceptional than the foregoing ones, could be alleged. Bishops who were great landowners were led to distribute part of their estates as fiefs to vassals, and the position was such that the Councils of the Church forbade any further possessions of the Church to be granted to laymen as benefices, evidently because this practice was still common.

Not only lands, but also ecclesiastical offices and revenues, even parochial tithes, were enfeoffed; Orderic Vital mentions the gift made to Saint-Evroul, by a certain Fulk, of the archdeaconry "quem in feudo ab antecessoribus suis de archiepiscopo Rothomagensi tenebat"; Bishop Robert of Coutances (d. 1048) gave the prebends of his cathedral to his parents, who rendered him homage for them. Finally, whether the bishop were, or were not, of noble stock, he was a baron, as he had vassals; but did he not himself owe homage to the king, at least in some places? Was he not bound by the Carolingian custom to send, or lead, the men on his estates to the army of the prince? In short did he not hold his own ecclesiastical dignity in fief? Matters seem to have gone far in this direction, especially in the northern countries, but even further in continental Europe of the north and north-east than in France properly so called.

And yet, although a great number of varied and picturesque facts can be quoted to give the impression that the clergy and ecclesiastical dignitaries had become secularised and feudalised to a serious extent, these facts mainly refer to the more primitive parts of the kingdom (Brittany and Gascony). On the other hand, in comparatively civilised parts, such as Normandy, where we have seen from examples already given that the feudalisation of the Church had also made some progress, it is clear that this movement did not run counter to the normal tendencies of the ecclesiastical institution towards Unity, Order, and Peace. The first Norman dukes were, of all the founders of feudal States in France, those who exercised the most effective authority on the clergy of their dominions; the higher Norman clergy, which was often recruited from the ducal family and closely controlled by the ducal administration, at a very early date lent its power to help that of the duke. It is true that everywhere the higher clergy generally led somewhat profane, and occasionally scandalous, lives; reform was urgently needed; but the spiritual life and the mission of the Church in the world were not irretrievably compromised, in spite of everything. She was still, for instance, sufficiently animated by the spirit of her mission voluntarily to take a lead in undertakings such as movements for the "Peace" and the "Truce" of God. We know what was meant by those celebrated terms. The nations, weary of armed conflict, thirsted for peace; their most urgent need was for a police. When, as in Normandy, there was a chief of the State capable of assuring order by his own powers, nothing could be better; but, if not, the Church began at the end of the 10th century in some places to take the initiative in forming voluntary associations sworn to give their armed protection to defenceless folk, amongst whom the clergy held the first place (Peace of God); and secondly to forbid hostilities during feasts and at certain liturgical seasons under pain of the anathemas which they could pronounce (Truce of God). These attempts were at first considered utopian, were only partially carried out, and failed in the end; for public or national "peace" (the *Landfrieden* of the Germans) was not really obtained until later, and then only by the diffusion of methods like those of the Normans; but they possess at least the interest of proving the unfailing vigour of the episcopal institution during the darkest Iron Age which it has experienced.

The Church, then, was not thoroughly feudalised. There were moreover two Churches; the secular Church (bishops, etc.), more exposed, as is implied by its name, to the influence of the spirit of the age, and the regular Church, that of the abbeys and the monks, more retired from the world, better disciplined, and which represented a different conception of the religious life, and a zeal which called itself, and often was, intenser and purer. However, although it was held to be more detached from temporal things, the regular clergy had none the less been loaded with gifts by people who were pious, or at the point of death, and they were very rich. But at the feudal period even more than at any other "he who has land has war." The old Benedictine abbeys were also consequently obliged to conform to the necessities of the age and to supply themselves with regular defenders against the attacks of their neighbours, by granting to lay lords (who were called their *avoués*) dues which were levied hereditarily on the tenants of their estates. But they always endeavoured not to be made vassals themselves, neither by the barons, nor even by the bishops in whose dioceses they were placed. The essential claim of the monasteries of this time was for autonomy[1], for independence from all neighbouring domination, whether lay or episcopal; they made up for this by a profession of whole-hearted devotion to superior and distant authorities, such as the King and the Pope; especially the Pope. The most important of these monasteries, Vézelai and Cluny, had grown up during the 10th century in Burgundy, a district particularly given up to feudal disorder. Cluny was the perfect type, and became the metropolis, of these great republics organised like troops under an autocratic government; thanks to an uninterrupted succession of superiors of remarkable character, cleverness, and longevity, Bernon, Odon, Maieul, and Odilon—four abbots only between 910 and 1049—the monks of Cluny in a hundred and fifty years founded a vast monastic Empire, stretching across Europe like an archipelago of islets, with Cluny as centre; theoretically they acknowledged no head but the Apostolic See. If the great Roman traditions of the Church had been lost elsewhere, they would have been preserved here. The magnificent development of the Cluniac institution was, moreover, one of the first spontaneous symptoms of the general movement for ecclesiastical reform, which showed itself, under the guidance of Rome, during the second half of the 11th century, and which Cluny served with distinction when the way was clear.

Of the towns of this period we know hardly anything. In Roman Gaul there had been "cities" (*civitates*) and fortified places (*castra*), both possessing municipal institutions. After the invasions everything was changed. There were no municipal institutions anywhere. Many former "cities" were simple territorial possessions of their bishop; others belonged to a neighbouring baron; most were shared by several nobles; it was not, for instance, usual for the "city," properly so called, and the "bourg" (suburb), which had grown round it, to belong to the same master. Many *castra* had disappeared and in

[1] "Non fastibus regiæ magnitudinis nec cujuslibet terrenæ potestatis jugo subjiciantur." (Charter of the foundation of Cluny by Duke William in 910.)

other places, where there had formerly been only rural resorts (*villae*), people had flocked round the fortified residence of the landowner, or round the monastery which took its place, in such a way as to form what is now called in French a *ville*. It is calculated that only one out of every five of the urban groups of modern France is built on the site of a former "city"; four at least are former *villae* where, for many different reasons, which it is as easy to imagine as it is useless to enumerate, the population, formerly sparse, has become dense.

These towns, whatever their origin, were not, it seems, large enough to make town life very different from country life. There was little commerce, little industry. We may suppose that their inhabitants, necessarily having common interests and living inside narrow fortified enclosures, at closer quarters than the peasants in the open country, soon formed themselves into unions or confraternities, according to religion, or profession, for police, for mutual defence, etc., secret or open; this may be conjectured, but for want of documents nothing is known. It is only certain that, at the beginning of the 11th century the towns played an unimportant part in the social economy.

The principal defect in the very summary account we have just given is that the analytical touches of which it is composed are powerless to give an impression of the reality. In conclusion, we must at least add that the rudimentary and chaotic society of this age in France was overflowing with forces ready to emerge. On the eve of one of its finest periods of growth and expansion, the nation was full of youthful vigour.

### § II. FIRST ATTEMPTS AT GOVERNMENT. FIRST ADVANCE OF THE KING'S AUTHORITY

In each of the feudal States referred to above the same evolution produced itself with greater or less impetus and success in the course of the 11th and the first half of the 12th centuries—from anarchy to order; from the existence of almost independent seignories existing side by side to hierarchy, if not fusion; from the total absence of public spirit to the consciousness of a certain moral unity. The France of that period was not without analogy to the Europe of times much nearer the present day. Each of the States into which she was divided under the hegemony (for long very weak) of the royal authority had started on the path of internal improvement; had, or thought it had, its own interests, at least dynastic, the feeling for which tended to produce a kind of patriotism; and possessed ambitions beyond its frontiers and consequently a sort of foreign policy.

Each of these States has its history, internal and external, in the 11th and 12th centuries. We cannot enter into the details of each, which are indeed little known, but the general design is almost everywhere similar.

It is in Brittany that the movement of unification is most obscure. The dynasty founded by Duke Houël was obliged to exert all its energy to maintain itself against local rivals; furthermore, it fell into dependence on, and almost under the suzerainty of, the dukes of Normandy. Nor is there anything noteworthy in Burgundy, where the ducal dynasty was unopposed, but weak, having always been represented by incompetent men. The house of Blois-Champagne, originally divided into two branches, was, after the union of all its domains in the hands of Thibaut IV of Blois (1125) absorbed in a bitter rivalry with its neighbours in France properly so called—Capetian France. This rivalry prevented it from striking out an original line of conduct in administrative matters; it could only have acted systematically in this direction had it been victorious, which was not the case. In Flanders, on the contrary, there were soon firmly established princes who energetically punished the excesses of their nobles, great or small, princes such as Baldwin of the Axe and Charles the Good; the latter was assassinated on March 2, 1127, by men hostile to his "monarchical" work, which had injured them personally; but this quasi-regicide was only an accident. Yet it is not the Flemish State which chiefly deserves attention; for it was not there that the most characteristic phenomena were produced.

Nor was it in the south, which was divided between the great rival powers of Toulouse (Languedoc) and Aquitaine. The house of Toulouse had too great a struggle against its neighbours, who were stronger than itself (William IX, Duke of Aquitaine, several times temporarily occupied Toulouse for long years); it also took too great a part in the distant adventure of the Crusades, in the persons of its best rulers, Raimond de Saint-Gilles and Alfonse-Jourdain, to attend seriously to internal affairs. As to the dynasty of Aquitaine, after a troubled start, it had a brilliant period under William IX (d. 1127), the man who undoubtedly came nearest to realising the dream of a united Southern France, strong enough to resist the north; but it was a task too great for a young power, still poorly equipped, and William IX fell away from the hard-working simplicity of his ancestors. He enjoyed their heritage brilliantly, without establishing anything of consequence, or considering any one, not even the Church, whose support was then indispensable in all enterprises of government on a great scale. And his successor lost everything; we shall see how.

Thus the three States which are of capital importance to our point of view are Normandy, Anjou, and the Capetian State.

The Norman State was, as we have seen, far ahead of all the others. It was the first in France to make a display of regular government; and because of this, it was able to succeed in the conquest of England under Duke William in 1066. But the Norman dynasty almost lost this advantage after the death of the Conqueror (1087) by the unworthiness of his successor. William the Conqueror, knowing what his eldest son, Robert Courthose, was worth, left England, with the royal crown, to his second son, William Rufus; Normandy to the eldest. Robert, who was the kind of person who runs through the most splendid inheritance, a typical spendthrift, was duke for nineteen years. His indolence, which naturally caused disorder (for the time was not yet come when the governmental machine almost runs of itself, whatever be the incapacity of the men whom chance charges with its guidance), horrified the people, who had known a better rule. It was therefore comparatively easy for Henry Beauclerk, the youngest son of the Conqueror, who had succeeded William Rufus in 1100, to get rid of him; in the battle of Tinchebrai (September 28, 1106), Henry took Robert prisoner, and Normandy was again united to England. This was an event of great importance; especially because Normandy thereby resumed the thread of her excellent administrative traditions. Thus, about fifty years after the Conquest the island-colony of Normandy returned to her mother-country the benefits she had received.

In Anjou analogous events had occurred a little earlier. The patient work of the founders of the house of Anjou, which had increased by inserting itself like a wedge between the dominions of Blois, Normandy, Brittany, and Aquitaine, was on the point of being endangered after 1060 by an inefficient heir, chosen because he was the eldest—Geoffrey the Bearded. The part of Henry Beauclerk was here played by Geoffrey's younger brother, Fulk the Churl. But Fulk himself was not worth much. The greatness of the house dates from his two successors, more especially his grandson, Geoffrey the Fair (d. 1151).

It seems that the territories of this house were, in the middle of the 12th century, the freest from feudal troubles and the most securely held by the hand of the master. These territories were at this time considerable in extent, for to the original possessions (Anjou and Touraine) first Maine had been added; then in 1127 Count Geoffrey the Fair had married the ex-empress Matilda, daughter of Henry Beauclerk and heiress to Normandy and England. To secure this magnificent inheritance was somewhat difficult; but in the end Geoffrey was crowned Duke of Normandy at Rouen in January 1144. This marriage of 1127 virtually created, in favour of its issue, a house of Anjou-Normandy-England, with Brittany within its sphere of influence. Great future problems were thereby raised, especially the following: who, in the kingdom of France, would be strong enough to resist this new colossus, if it lived and prospered? The King?

The Capetian family, to whom in 987 the French crown had fallen, was even at that time no longer very powerful. Its chiefs, after Hugh Capet, did their best to turn to account the remains of the old landed property of the dukes of France in the 10th century, all that was left to them (Paris, Orléans, Melun, etc.—not more than three or four departments of modern France), by the same methods as their contemporaries, the feudal dynasties of Flanders, Champagne and Blois, Anjou, etc. They were sometimes allied to the one, sometimes to the other; in almost permanent difficulties with their nearest neighbours (Champagne and Blois); sometimes saved by the Normans, as at the accession of Henry I, sometimes at war with them (Henry I and Philip I against Duke William). The worst of them, Philip I (d. 1108), son of Henry I and a Russian princess, never ceased, at least during the first part of his reign, to strive with varying fortunes against the insolent and rapacious petty nobles of the dominions to which he was reduced, and to try by laborious and modest acquisitions to regain positive means of action and, as it were, a substance for his power. These princes were moreover too incompetent and also too weak to create and bring to perfection a regular administrative system similar to that of the Normans. Had it not been for the rights (unlimited, indefinite, and of little practical value) derived from the royal dignity, the house of Capet would not have been in the first rank of the feudal houses of the kingdom until the fourth successor of Hugh Capet. But at the moment when the event of 1127, full of threatening possibilities, occurred, the situation had already begun to change.

With Louis VI, son of Philip I, began the rise of Capetian power, which thereafter continued to increase throughout centuries, until it stood alone, thus realising national unity.

He was a large, active, and bold man. He remains in tradition as the man who cleared the feudal haunts, both to the north and to the south of the Seine, and thus undertook to accomplish a work similar to that of the early dukes of Normandy, of Baldwin of the Axe in Flanders, and of Geoffrey the Fair in Anjou. All through his life, in fact, he led punitive expeditions against the masters of the feudal fortresses in Ile-de-France, Beauce, and Picardy, who were disturbers of the peace—le Puiset, Couci, Monchi, Quierzi-sur-Oise, Néauphle, etc. He was obliged to destroy their donjons, which were then formidable stumbling-blocks, and the remains of which can still be seen in those peaceful villages of the outer suburbs of modern Paris, whither Parisians resort for their Sunday outings—Montlhéry, Château-fort, Chevreuse, Rochefort-en-Yveline and Gometz. In this respect he extended his operations to the country of the Loire—Meung, Château-Renard, Germigny, etc., as far as Berri and Bourbonnais. But this was far from being all that he did. Louis VI was the first of the descendants of Hugh Capet to act successfully out of his own domains. He repaired to Auvergne to defend the Bishop of Clermont against the count. He went to Flanders to punish the murderers of Charles the Good and to besiege in Lille Thierri of Alsace, one of the claimants to the succession. Finally, he did not hesitate also to attack the Anglo-Norman Empire of Henry Beauclerk, who had taken sides with Count Thibaut of Blois against him; for years he lent whole-hearted support to the son of Robert Courthose, who was claiming Normandy. Although not invariably successful (for he was beaten more than once, notably by Henry I), a series of lucky accidents saved him from failing in so many great enterprises and enabled him to come out of them with credit. Fortune even offered him a suitable compensation for the Angevin marriage of 1127, which seemed to threaten such fatal results to the greatness of the Capets. The eventual union of Anjou and Normandy, with Brittany and England in the background, seemed to be greatly counterbalanced when, ten years later, in 1137, Louis, the heir of the Capets, established and strengthened by thirty years of armed activity, married Eleanor, daughter and heiress of William X, the last Duke of Aquitaine, ruler of the whole of central and south-western France.

Hereafter only two families were rivals in the kingdom—the Plantagenets, the dynasty of Anjou-Normandy, with a foreign crown, and the Capets with the crown of France. It was inevitable that there should be a duel between them to decide which was to predominate.

## § III. RIVALRY OF THE CAPETS AND THE PLANTAGENETS. DECISIVE PROGRESS OF THE KING

The men of the second half of the 12th century, engrossed in the course of events and therefore not in a position to direct them, may frequently have thought that in the competition between the two houses success must attend the Plantagenets. The chief reasons why this appeared probable were as follows.

Louis VII, successor of Louis VI and husband of Eleanor, started in a deplorable manner by a series of misfortunes. First of all he undertook a Crusade in the East, whence he returned vanquished, humiliated, and, in addition, on bad terms with his wife. The minister bequeathed to him by his father,

Suger, Abbot of Saint-Denis, had kept all affairs in good order during his absence; Suger died in 1151. In 1152 Louis divorced Eleanor, who had given him no children, and two years later, Eleanor married again. And her second husband was—young Henry Plantagenet, already Count of Anjou and Duke of Normandy, and soon to become King of England by the death of King Stephen. Therefore not only was the vast Aquitanian dowry lost to the Capets, but it passed to the Plantagenets.

Henry II, head of this rival house, was moreover greatly superior to the Capetian king in energy and breadth of view. He was equally French in tongue and education, and, though he did not neglect Great Britain, where his work, of which we need not speak here, was of capital importance, his continental possessions were nearer to his heart than his kingdom overseas, and he even aspired to imperialistic dreams of almost European extent.

During the decade which ended in 1160 success attended him everywhere. Pope Adrian IV was an Englishman. Brittany seemed definitely to enter within his sphere of influence. In agreement with the Aragonese he revived the ancient designs of the dukes of Aquitaine against the counts of Toulouse. When Thierri of Alsace, Count of Flanders, started for the Holy Land, the care of his family and his possessions was entrusted to Henry. He had faithful servants, such as Simon de Montfort-l'Amaury, in the very heart of France properly so called. He even insisted on marrying his eldest son to the very young daughter of Louis VII by a second marriage, with the dowry of Vexin and the fortress of Gisors, the outpost of "France" against Normandy. The position of the Capetian king appeared at that time miserable by comparison.

Ten years later Henry II had still further extended his sphere of action. At Montferrand, in January 1173, Count Raymond V of Toulouse made liege homage for his fief to the Angevin representative of the line of Aquitanian dukes and the Count of Savoy bestowed his heiress on one of the sons of the Plantagenet king, one of whose daughters was at the same time betrothed to the King of Sicily, while another married in Castile. It is true that in the same year his sons, having arrived at the age of manhood, began to torment him with conspiracies for the division—during his life-time—of his "Empire," the Angevin Empire, whose cohesion was still recent and unstable. But he overcame them. And in 1177 he also acquired the county of La Marche. He had, besides claims to Berri and Auvergne, the dowry of another French princess, also promised to his house. What would have happened if Louis had not had a belated son by his third wife, Adèle de Champagne? In 1179, when this son was crowned and succeeded his father, who was in failing health, he was only fourteen years of age. If he had died prematurely, it would certainly not have been the Capet dynasty which brought about French unity.

But this son, Philip Augustus, was a second Louis VI. It was he who played the second game of the match against the Plantagenets, and he won it very quickly.

There were many dangers round him at his accession. Not only was Henry II master of the south and south-west of France, but the north belonged to the Count of Flanders, whose possessions had by marriage been extended to Valois and the Marne, and the family of Blois-Champagne, grouped round the Queen-mother Adèle and represented by intelligent leaders, appeared in the east as a living force which threatened to support or to oppose the young king in either case to the point of annihilation. In 1180 there was a breach between Philip and his mother, who took refuge in Normandy. In 1181, the Flemish, the men of Champagne, and the Burgundians formed a league against the sixteen-year old king, and a war of four years followed. At this distance, it is hard to understand how Philip managed to pass safely through this very critical period. No doubt each of the allies had his personal embarrassments, which prevented him from throwing all his weight into the struggle; moreover let us remember that this conflict, like all those of the same kind between feudal princes, did not possess the bitterness of a life and death struggle.

Under these circumstances, however, the Capetian family must have been already very firmly rooted to resist such a storm. For it is a fact that in six years, Philip Augustus, still quite a youth, shook off the guardianship of Champagne, drove back the Flemish, and brought the Burgundians into submission. Henry II was occupied at other points of his large and difficult field of action and did not move, while the German Emperor, Frederick Barbarossa, refused to intervene. He was ill-advised to refrain, as was shown by the immediate consequences.

About 1187, Philip Augustus resolved to attack Henry II, who was growing old, by exciting against him the enmities he had incurred during his long life, and more particularly the parricidal and fratricidal jealousies and hates of his brilliant and worthless family. Henry had quarrelled with his son Richard; the rebellious son was therefore welcomed at the French court as the personal friend of the King, and the legitimate owner, subject to homage, of the continental possessions of the Angevin Empire. In 1189 a short campaign by Philip and Richard led to the defeat of Henry and his death in that tragic despair which has been so pregnantly described by the anonymous biographer of William the Marshal.

All was not thereby ended, for the events of 1189 had only set at the head of the whole Angevin Empire a young and warlike ruler, Richard Coeur de Lion, instead of an old and weary politician. And it was in the nature of things that the friendship between King Philip and Richard the claimant should not endure between King Philip and Richard crowned. The Crusade in which Philip and Richard both took part did not, in fact, avert the inevitable rupture. A war of five years from 1194 onwards dates from the return of Richard. This war was more violent than usual, as on both sides it was waged by regular troops of mercenaries, and in it Richard certainly played the finer part and held the advantage. Philip was not crushed, but he was beaten and in evil case, when Richard was killed quite accidentally on March 26, 1199, in a skirmish with the men of the Viscount of Limoges.

Richard was succeeded by his brother John, a man as inferior to Philip Augustus as Louis VII had been to Henry II, and who had a possible rival, at least for certain foreign possessions of the Angevin family, in the person of a very young nephew, Arthur of Brittany. French policy immediately seized this powerful lever of Arthur's asserted rights to shatter the unity of the hostile power. It was under this pretext that the great final struggle between the Plantagenets and the Capetians began in 1202. The campaign of 1203 was disastrous to John, who was definitely forsaken by the barons of Anjou and Poitou, whom their leader, Guillaume des Roches, rallied to the cause of the Capetians. Then followed the violent death of Arthur in prison, which excited public feeling against his uncle. The whole of Normandy was conquered in a few weeks in the spring of 1204. Next came the turn of Aquitaine, where the last resistance was overcome in 1207–1208. Thus was achieved in a comparatively simple manner the great conquest of the west, which for the last hundred years had been the condition necessary to protect the Capetian monarchy henceforward from all serious danger in France.

The duel between the Plantagenets and the Capetians had already passed through so many phases that it was in no wise evident to contemporaries that this last decision was final. King John naturally adhered to his claims and remained in possession of the English crown, which would enable him to advance them when occasion arose. In pursuance of this, when in 1212 the counts of Boulogne and Flanders sought for allies against Philip Augustus, John's aid was not lacking. They planned to crush the common enemy in the north by the weight of the Germanic forces (the Emperor Otho of Brunswick, with the men of Flanders, of Lorraine, and of the Netherlands), while in the south-west John hoped to regain foothold between the Gironde and the Loire, where he still had partisans. This plan was actually carried out two years later, but it failed. John was routed at La Roche-au-Moine near Angers; and the French won a brilliant victory over the northern allies at Bouvines. The victory of Bouvines (July 27, 1214) had a tremendous result in France; it marks both the end of the feudal period, in which the royal dynasty had to struggle for the hegemony of the kingdom, and the entrance of the French monarchy into the front rank of important European policy.

The Capetian dynasty had a favouring wind at the beginning of the 13th century. The Plantagenets having been humbled, there remained little to be done in the north. Flanders was mastered; Artois, Picardy, Normandy, Maine, Anjou, Touraine, and Poitou were annexed; Brittany, vacant by the death of Arthur, was given to a member of a younger branch of the

Capets, Pierre de Dreux; Champagne had retired from all rivalry and, during the long minority of Thibaut IV, the King was almost as much master there as in his own dominions; Burgundy also, always the most docile of the great fiefs, was governed in the name of a minor. There remained only the south—Gascony and Languedoc. The danger of a confederation of the great southern nobles into a France of the south, independent of northern France, had no doubt become less since northern France had developed a preponderance of strength. But there was still a possibility of jealous independence, which might be embarrassing to the future of French unity. However this last danger was averted like the others at the decisive period of which we are treating, immediately after the battle of Bouvines.

The southern provinces possessed a language of their own, which differed from that of the north. Nor was that all. Exotic heresies of Eastern origin, not involving theological subtleties but essential points of dogma and discipline (Manichaeism), flourished there; insufficiently, indeed, to affect the whole population, but enough to make the Church anxious because of the support given to them by great nobles, such as the viscounts of Béziers, the counts of Foix, Comminges, Béarn, etc. Now these latter conditions were such as to provoke, and actually did provoke, a cataclysm, of which there would have been little danger without them. During the last thirty years of the 12th century they had already been brought to the notice of the northern rulers whose superior authority extended, on various grounds, to those regions—Louis VII and Henry II. Twenty-five years later they had not altered. But Pope Innocent III resolved to put an end to them. He did so by means of a crusade, which was preached throughout northern France from 1208 onwards, by permission of Philip Augustus. The King evidently authorised this crusade, but took no part in it, for he had other work to do and it seems he did not wish personally to embark on such an enterprise.

It was an atrocious war, full of fanaticism and pillage—a veritable invasion, which in a few years destroyed the characteristic civilisation of Languedoc, and whose fury far surpassed what the Holy See had foreseen or wished. The history of this great struggle can be sketched very briefly. At first Simon de Montfort, the chosen leader of the crusade, carried all before him; Peter II, King of Aragon, who tried to defend his vassals and his friends north of the Pyrenees, was killed at Muret (1213); the heretical nobles were dispossessed in favour of the conquerors. The hereditary chief of the southern nobles, Raymond V, Count of Toulouse, was, in spite of his submission, deprived of all his fiefs to the west of the Rhône by order of the Pope; the conquered territory was administered by men of the north after the manner of the north. Then a second period began, in which there was a reaction of the conquered people against the alien colonists; Simon de Montfort was killed at the siege of Toulouse (1218); the crusaders asked for official reinforcements from their native provinces, for Raymond VI, son of Raymond V, had undertaken a plan of revenge, which offered some hopes of success. The moment had therefore come for the king to make his appearance and to gather what he had allowed to be sown, when by the imposition of his "peace" he perpetuated the anarchic condition of affairs. Philip Augustus had already twice sent his son to the scene of battle with the royal standard, to find out what was going on. And no doubt he was on the point of acting at the time of his death (July 1223).

What he had intended to do was done by his son Louis VIII in 1226. A simple military expedition was enough; there was no resistance. The former estates of the house of Toulouse, recently possessed by Simon de Montfort, were divided into *sénéchaussées*, i.e. into districts, directly administered by officers of the king who had come from the north.

The work of Philip Augustus and Louis VIII was put to the severest possible test by the premature death of the latter, and by its inevitable result—the appointment of a foreigner (Blanche of Castile) as regent and as guardian of a child (Louis IX). The fact that it stood the test successfully proved that the dynasty had already passed the stage when such contingencies would almost certainly have led to disaster.

The attempts to destroy the work of Philip Augustus, which marked the first part of Louis IX's reign, are the natural epilogue of this very summary sketch. All the vanquished forces of the previous age—the Plantagenets, the high feudal nobility the people of the south—exerted themselves to profit by a chance which seemed so favourable, but without any success whatever.

And first, as to the high feudal nobility of the north. Their activities from 1226 to 1231 were no more serious than those which, four hundred years later, troubled the regency of Marie de' Medici or Anne of Austria. The most dangerous intriguer of this mediaeval Fronde was likewise a prince of the blood, that Pierre de Dreux, nick-named Mauclerc, to whom the head of the house had recently given Brittany. Count Thibaut of Champagne, with his sudden changes and his gallantries, and Philip Hurepel, Comte de Boulogne, an illegitimate son of Philip Augustus, are also very exact prototypes of people familiar to us in the 17th century. Is there any better proof, that the French monarchy under Louis IX, the child king, was not so very different from the French monarchy in the time of Louis XIV, the child king?

In the south, the treaty of Meaux, concluded in 1229 with Raymond of Toulouse, solemnly confirmed his ruin. The last Count of Toulouse only retained half of his estates for his life-time, under the most humiliating conditions, notably by promising to marry his daughter, the heiress of all his property, to a brother of the French king.

As to the Plantagenets, they, with their memories and their rights, were now represented by Henry III, son of King John. Pierre Mauclerc tried to arouse his ambition and obtain his help, but in vain.

However, sixteen years after the death of Louis VIII, and six years after the end of Blanche of Castile's regency, there was a sort of final convulsion. It began in Poitou, which was then an appanage of Alfonso, third brother of Louis IX, whose nobles had always been of a turbulent disposition. It was not, moreover, merely local, for Henry III, Raymond of Toulouse, Alfonso's father-in-law, and the few remaining southern nobles had been approached and had consented to join. But this was the end. Louis IX had but to make his appearance and order was re-established everywhere. Henceforth the house of Toulouse completely disappeared. As to Henry III, who was struggling with inextricable difficulties in England, the King of

France could certainly have taken advantage of his imprudent ambitions in 1242 to deprive him of his last continental possessions—Bordeaux and Gascony. Philip Augustus would certainly have done so. But his grandson acted in quite a different manner. In May 1258, after long parleys, he thought it his duty to celebrate the definite end of his struggles with Henry by restoring to him, as an act of pure grace, several provinces formerly confiscated from the Plantagenets—Périgord, Limousin, etc. He restored these provinces (which protested vigorously), in order that there might be a lasting peace, on the sole condition that the descendant of the Plantagenets should renounce the rest of the continental empire of his ancestors, i.e. Normandy, Anjou, Maine, etc., and should pay special homage to the French crown for all that had been left to him. Never having had to struggle seriously for life, he could afford himself the luxury of generosity and of scruples, which is always easier to a man of family than to a self-made man.

## § IV. GENERAL EVOLUTION IN THE DIRECTION OF MONARCHY

Thus the struggle for kingship, the decisive phase of which had lasted more than a century, resulted in favour of the family which had in theory held the sovereign power since the days of Hugh Capet. And it may be said that any other result would have needed the convergence of a long series of unfavourable chances, which was not, *a priori*, probable. It was not likely that the natural unity of France should be attained to the detriment of the dynasty which was specifically French, under the auspices of a rival line, to whom the possession of a foreign crown was rather a handicap than an advantage.

We must now consider the evolution which was taking place obscurely under the surface, while the changes—accidental in detail, but impressed as a whole with an almost inevitable logic—which have been sketched in the preceding paragraphs, occurred on the surface.

**The Church.** The reaction of the Church, true to her principles and her distant past, against the feudalism which threatened to invade her had begun in the 10th century (Cluny), and continued during the first part of the 11th. But at the end of the latter century, it suddenly assumed extraordinary acuteness, under the guidance of Rome, and particularly under the successors of Leo IX, Victor II and Gregory VII. There was a question of general reform: amendment of the clergy; correction of morals; an attempt to remove the ecclesiastical hierarchy from the influence of the "age" and of the powers of this world. The final goal of this movement, if carried to its logical conclusion, was the proclamation of the independence of the Church with regard to civil (or lay) powers, then—an easy transition—of its superiority to these powers—in a word, theocracy.

This movement, which appeared simultaneously throughout the whole of Christendom, was led in France in the time of Gregory VII by Papal legates of exceptional energy—Hugues de Die in the north, and Amat d'Oloron in the south. It proceeded with redoubled intensity during the pontificate of Urban II (1088–1099), a French pope, formerly prior of Cluny, who had none of the Italian pliancy and was much more uncompromising than Gregory VII himself. The movement finally subsided into a more moderate form under Pascal II and Calixtus II, which enabled it to arrive at partial results, allowance being made for actual conditions and for great reductions in the maximum programme.

It is needless to say that its thorough-going supporters only obtained partial satisfaction in the matter of moral reform; to achieve more it would have been necessary to change human nature. They succeeded, however, in reducing the worst abuses. Thanks to them, the secular Church, bishops and chapters, improved greatly in conduct and decorum; from this *revival* date the Canons Regular of St Victor and Prémontré. The regular Church was also rejuvenated—for the vitality of Cluny was spending itself away—by a large number of new Orders: Carmelites, Carthusians, White monks of Clairvaux and Citeaux, etc.

The supporters of the movement had proposed to free the Church from the authority of princes. In this respect, they obtained successes in form and appearance: princes ceased to present the spiritual investiture to prelates and to receive their feudal homage. But, in reality, in the new order of things, the princes had kept the essentials: control over the appointment of prelates and over ecclesiastical estates. And they kept, sometimes acquired it at the time of Reform, with the agreement of the greater part of the clergy, who in France saw in established authority, and especially in the royal authority, which was itself invested with sacred character, the greatest safeguard of "ecclesiastical liberties." Extremists may have wished to free the Church from the "State," but the majority wished for union, for association, and collaboration between the one and the other, which could not fail to result, as it actually did, in the subordination of the weaker partner.

The "Gregorian" movement did not "free" the local churches. At the most, it delivered them from the more humiliating traces of feudalism. But it left them in subjection to princes and in particular to the King. Its chief result was to impose on them, in addition, the monarchical authority of the Holy See, thus preparing, far ahead, the conflict between the two powers which marked the age following. But at this period of Reform nothing foreshadowed this conflict. In the continual struggles with the German Empire Louis VI was the ally of Popes Pascal and Calixtus, who found a refuge with him. In 1163 Louis VII received from Alexander III, who had similarly been offered hospitality in France, a well-deserved "Golden Rose." Philip Augustus had some fairly lively differences with Innocent III with reference to a matrimonial question (the repudiation of Ingeborg of Denmark) and to his policy in Germany, but not on the subject of his relations with the clergy of the kingdom. National monarchy and pontifical monarchy were then increasing on parallel lines and in agreement.

It was in the course of the 12th century that the French Church gradually assumed the character that she kept in the future: protected, but docile. The "Most Christian" kings of France defended and enriched her, but they soon made use for their political ends of her resources in men and money almost as they did their own—without attaching any importance to her objections, which were moreover always very discreet (there was no Thomas Becket in France), and now and then, if necessary, they did not hesitate to make slight use of the curb. The attitude of Louis IX, the saintly king, was typical on this point. He was fond of recalling the words of his ancestor: "In remembrance of the benefits which God has given to me, I would rather lose my rights than dispute with the servants of Holy Church"; but none the less he smilingly refused to listen to the angry bishops who accused him of having despoiled them.

The chief apple of discord between the Church and the princes was then, in France as elsewhere, and during the whole of the 13th century, the question of ecclesiastical tribunals and their jurisdiction. This question did not arise until long after the Gregorian reform, even after the death of St Bernard, and was started by a new influence, that of the revival of legal studies in the clerical world. It is important to define clearly its nature and extent.

In the social organisation of feudal times the bishop was invested with judicial powers in a two-fold capacity, as feudal lord and as bishop. He had a temporal court and a spiritual court. We may ignore the former, in which the bishop was represented by a layman (*vidame*, or advocate) and which had no special features. But in the spiritual court, the bishop—at first personally in synod, later by the intermediary of a judge *ad hoc*, the "official"—put forward a claim, after the revival of legal studies, to exercise exclusive judicial rights over:

1. the clergy, both in criminal and in civil cases, by reason of their profession;

2. certain categories of laymen, akin to clerics, such as crusaders, scholars, *miserabiles personae*;

3. all persons amenable to trial in certain cases: the innumerable cases relating to faith and the sacraments, the property of the Church and the clergy, vows and obligations under oath, sacrilege, witchcraft, heresy.

This list is not complete and differed in various regions. But it may easily be seen that it could be extended by analogy. Thus by this theory, not only was a substantial part of the population, with its property, removed from the power of the lay judge, but even within the ground which was left to him the competency of this judge was at every step limited by inexorable "taboos." We must add that although by this theory clerics were forbidden, under the most severe penalties, to submit willingly to a secular, in preference to a clerical, court of justice to settle their differences, the opposite was permitted, nay even recommended; the Church claimed the right of laymen to summon other laymen before the ecclesiastical tribunal *in actionibus personalibus*, thereby reserving to herself the possibility of a vast voluntary jurisdiction, with the resultant material and moral advantages. These extraordinary claims were formulated in the second half of the 12th century; and were to a great extent admitted. This seems at first sight surprising; for princes and kings should instinctively have aimed at the creation in their dominions of a juridical state of things, the necessary instrument of which was a regular and public court of justice, derived from their authority. How then did they allow the establishment and the progress of a rival court of justice which competed with theirs? This is explained by their original weakness, even more than by the superiority, however incontrovertible, of canonical procedure, which has been said to have justified the extension of the ecclesiastical tribunal by its benefits. In any case, it was inevitable that "privileges" of jurisdiction, so contrary to the Roman principle of unity in the State, so harmful to the private interests of princes, so irksome, and even annoying, to their agents, should be contested and quarrelled over as soon as the administrative officials of the growing monarchy began to realise their power and their duties. Now France was at that stage in the 13th century. This century was full of controversies and quarrels caused by the ceaseless antagonism of civil and ecclesiastical jurisdictions. But it is noteworthy that the influence of the royal government—of the central court—was at this period always exercised to restrain the zeal of its officials, never to excite it. Even in 1329, at the celebrated tournament of eloquence held at Vincennes, where this great problem was once again solemnly discussed, the King declared in conclusion that he had no intention of depriving the Church of any advantages conferred on her by custom; and matters remained as they were.

**Population of the towns and the country.** We will first consider the urban centres, which were of comparatively small importance in the preceding period and which, during the 11th century, underwent upheavals, after which their condition seems to have changed.

There is no doubt as to the cause of these upheavals; it was the general growth of material prosperity from the year 1000 onward. The population of the towns increased; the towns became enriched by industry and commerce. The state of things which previously existed, in the days of poverty, isolation, stagnation, and insecurity, now seemed unbearable. The memories of Roman antiquity and of Germanic antiquity were for long quoted by modern historians to explain the movement of emancipation which was brewing in the 11th, broke out in the 12th, and ended in the 13th centuries; we now realise that they had nothing to do with it.

The movement first appeared in the regions of very early prosperity—the Mediterranean provinces. It spread to the less favoured provinces of the north, along the great commercial tracks, in proportion as wealth developed.

The essential object of this movement, as regards the inhabitants of towns, was to shake off the arbitrary seignorial rule, which originally weighed on them, as we have seen, as heavily as on the country people. This common object was not everywhere attained in the same way. Several methods must be noticed.

The dramatic method of armed insurrection was not, as a whole, the commonest, contrary to what was asserted in the 19th century by Romantic writers. But it was the oldest, at least in northern France. It was resorted to at Saint-Quentin, Beauvais, and Arras, before 1100; at Noyon, Valenciennes, Amiens, Laon, Corbie, Soissons, Bruges, Lille, Saint-Omer, Ghent, Liège, etc., before 1150; especially against the ecclesiastical lords, bishops and abbots, who, for many reasons, were the most hostile to attempts at independence and who, at the same time, were not the most formidable of the great lords; more daring measures were therefore taken against them.

Elsewhere, the *bourgeoisie* of the towns had no need to resort to violence. The financial resources and armed forces at their command were such that by offering these adroitly for the service of their lords, or alternately to one or other of their various lords (in the towns shared by several), or even to the rivals or adversaries of their lords, they could impose their conditions without striking a blow. By using diplomacy, they had often only to obtain pay for their co-operation. Sometimes, the charter of enfranchisement was plainly bought for money from a prodigal or embarrassed noble.

At last there came a time when more than one noble saw clearly that it was in his own interest to forestall in some way the inevitable claims, whose success was, in the long run, assured, and spontaneously to grant carefully drawn-up statutes to the towns in his domains. The most celebrated case of this kind is that of the "Établissements," which Henry II, Duke of Normandy and Aquitaine, granted between 1169 and 1179, first to Rouen (whence the name of "Établissements de Rouen") then to a number of other towns in Normandy, Poitou, Saintonge, etc.

Thus some charters of emancipation were obtained by force; others were negotiated; others were granted. Under these circumstances, it is easily to be understood that they are not all similar. The common object, which was not everywhere attained in the same manner, was not, moreover, everywhere attained with the same degree of completeness and intensity. There were very varied systems, and many imperceptible transitions from one to the other. It is hard to classify them and the men of the Middle Ages never attempted to do so, but nowadays we have formed the habit of detaching two leading types and comparing the "commune" properly so called to the "*bourgeois* town."

The "commune," properly so called, was the last efflorescence of the feudal system. It consisted of a *bourgeois* group, which had introduced itself forcibly, or been introduced willingly, into the world of nobles, before the latter was closed *ne varietur*. It was a *bourgeois* group, which had proved itself fit to hold in fief the town in which it was settled and even other estates, to carry out the ordinary duties of a vassal and to hold vassals itself in turn. The commune properly so called, like the lord whose place it took, had its court of justice, its officials, its seal (often bearing some warlike emblem, like that of the barons), its donjon (the belfry), its militia and the right to use it for its private quarrels. It stands to reason, also, that the communal charters obtained by violence generally contain more extended rights of feudal sovereignty than those freely granted. The

"Établissements" of Rouen, for instance, only concede a minimum of independence—the degree of independence compatible with the maintenance of seignorial rights in everything which is important from the political point of view. This great charter, granted by the Plantagenets, spread by them all through the west of France, particularly leaves to the officers of the overlord the exclusive exercise of the higher justice, an effective control on the nomination and administration of communal magistrates, etc. So that the numerous towns in which these "Établissements" became "law" in the 12th century in fact only possessed the name and external prerogatives of the great *Communes jurées* of the north, which were really autonomous under a more or less lax suzerainty.

One step further, and we find communities which had neither extorted nor received the reality nor the external signs of feudal sovereignty, which are not consequently *communes* at all, but which none the less succeeded in obtaining from their overlord the establishment of regular rule, or, at the very least, guarantees against arbitrary rule, and various favours. These communities have received the name of "*bourgeois* towns" (an expression not known in the Middle Ages) from modern historians. They also have charters and "laws." About 1182 William of the White Hands, Archbishop of Reims, granted a charter of this kind to the little town of Beaumont in the Argonne; its spirit is very akin to that which is present in the wording of the "Établissements" of Rouen; it is true that there is no feudal personality; but the community of Beaumont is considered as a moral person, represented by elected magistrates, under the control of the seignorial officials; these magistrates are associated with the local administration to the common advantage of the lord and of those administered. The charter granted by Louis VII to Lorris in the Gâtinais, on the contrary, ignores the collective group of the inhabitants of the little town, but recognises their privileges limiting the rights of the overlord and other usual advantages. These typical "laws" of Beaumont and Lorris had a great success; the former spread rapidly in the north-east; the latter in the valley of the Loire, in Berri, and, outside the personal estates of the Capets, in Burgundy. Systems similar to these, with differences of detail, were established in the rest of

France, in all places where from the 11th to the 14th centuries "new towns" were created.

New town, "sauveté" (*salvitas*), "bastide"—these names were applied to new centres of population, created by the nobles, and most frequently by two nobles in conjunction, one lay and the other ecclesiastic, with the object of increasing the value of their domains. Between four crosses, set up at the four cardinal points to serve as the limits of the boundary, the plan of the future town was traced on the ground; the church, the town-hall, and the markets, public square, streets intersecting each other at right angles, and an outer wall. These towns created all at once—in the American fashion, so to speak—finally received a name and a charter. The name was sometimes chosen, especially in the south, from the list of famous cities in the world as then known, as was also the custom nearer our own day for the "mushroom townships" of the United States, which are called Paris, Rome, London, Syracuse, etc. Some small towns of the present day, which are former "bastides" of the 13th century, still bear the names of Pampelonne (Pampeluna), Fleurance (Florence), Cordes (Cordoba), Bénévent (Benevento), etc. The charter assured a safe place of refuge and permanent privileges to the colonists who settled there, and it generally included a short code of civil, penal, and administrative laws with tariffs (fines and taxes). It is very interesting to study the collection of these charters of new towns in the 12th and 13th centuries; it is possible by reading them to realise what under the voluntarily defined and limited authority of the overlord, or the associated lords (one of whom was often the King), was the *normal* aspect of town life.

*Normal.* There is in fact no doubt that the general course of events soon turned conclusively towards the type common to Beaumont, Lorris, and the new towns of the north and south, rather than to that of the feudal commune. The commune properly so called aged very quickly; it was born in the autumn of the feudal system, and when the latter became decadent, which was very soon, the commune passed directly from youth to a state of anachronistic survival. The Romantic historians have regretted this phenomenon, but owing to a mistaken idea.

They regretted it because the insurrections, which gave rise to most of the great communes during the first part of the 12th century, seemed to deserve their democratic sympathies. But the communalistic movement to which they refer was very slightly democratic in its sources and even less so in its consequences. In the beginning the insurrections almost everywhere took place on the initiative and under the direction, not of the lower classes of the population, but of the richest inhabitants, merchants and masters, united in friendly confraternities, religious or professional. The poor and the workmen, absorbed in anxiety about their daily bread, naturally served only as instruments; and, after freedom had been won, they were generally excluded from the circle of the communalistic association which enjoyed it. Most of the great communes were governed originally, and even more so later, by a narrow and exclusive aristocracy of property-holders, which kept for themselves the magistracies and consequently the effective power. This aristocracy was moreover divided and its leading families each had its own faction, whence arose frequent disturbances. At last in the 13th century it had already degenerated; it had lost all anxiety for public welfare; the communal funds, managed in the interest of the oligarchs, were generally in a bad state; and the lower classes of the townspeople, subjected to a yoke even heavier than that of the old seignorial masters, began to organise themselves in order to shake it off. In every commune a second revolution was threatening against those who had monopolised the benefits of the first. And it would certainly have occurred if a superior power, the very power which ensured order, peace, and bearable conditions of life for all, in hundreds of towns and villages which lacked in the dignity of *communes*, had not put an end to the fray.

We are thus led to explain the part played by the royal government in the history of the emancipation of the *communes* and urban populations in general. To believe in a primitive, systematic, and deliberate protection on its part, as was done until recently, would be foolish. The Capetian kings, contemporaries of the first risings which resulted in the formation of feudal communes, combated them with the greatest energy and with success in their own dominions, as is proved by the fact that no feudal commune (except Dreux and Senlis) succeeded in establishing itself in the personal domains of their house. There was never, in the Middle Ages, any *commune* in Paris. Under Louis VII, Orleans made an attempt in this direction, but it was crushed and never renewed. Although Louis VI confirmed the charters of some communes which had been snatched from great lords, he also helped other great lords to overcome other rebellions on their lands, according to the varying interests of his dynastic policy. Louis VII and Philip Augustus acted in the same way, although changed circumstances led them in their fight for the monarchy more often to support the forces antagonistic to the old feudal powers and, amongst them, the *bourgeois* aristocracies. Moreover to the monarchy the communes were much less dangerous than the barons. In the first place, in their struggles against their immediate adversaries in the feudal world, they had a tendency to place themselves under the protection of the Crown, the enemy of their enemies. Secondly and above all, in northern France there was never anything resembling the great federal leagues between city-republics, such as those constituted in Lombardy (the Lombard League against Frederick Barbarossa), on the Rhine, or even in the kingdom of Arles; vague attempts in this direction, made in Artois and Flanders during the 12th century, were unsuccessful. In France, instead of uniting with a view to political action, the free communes entered into competition with each other, thus remaining isolated and powerless; and, at the time of their decadence in the 13th century, their financial difficulties and the disorderly riots which took place supplied the King's officers with the opportunity for which they thirsted to meddle in their affairs and to confiscate what remained of their autonomy in favour of the central power. In the 13th century the King's officers succeeded in reducing the ancient communes established in the dominions of the great vassals to a condition very similar to that of the *bourgeois* towns, by interfering in their internal quarrels (sometimes for, sometimes against, the local aristocracy), by insisting on the liquidation of debts under their control, and by continual interventions—often justified because they were benevolent—in the matter of elections, of jurisdiction, etc. In short, when the evolution was complete, it was obvious that the increasing power of the urban population, like that of the

Church, was always exercised as a whole in favour of the royal authority and for the destruction of the feudal state of things.

**The Officers of the Crown. Administrative organisation.** From the moment when the irresistible ascendency of the monarchical authority showed itself, the subsequent course of events depended in great measure on the efficiency of the administrative means at its disposal. In this respect the Capetian rulers were for long in no way superior to other chiefs of feudal States in the kingdom; indeed, in the 11th century, the government of the dukes of Normandy was, as we have seen, greatly in advance of theirs. But this also changed in proportion to their progress and certainly was both a cause and an effect of this progress.

Nothing exact is known about the original methods of government of the early Capets. The Capetian King of the 11th century moved incessantly from one residence to another, accompanied by his family and a small court of knights and priests, servants, counsellors, and executive agents. This court was swelled by the crowd of barons and prelates who had business with the King and (especially at the great feasts) by the vassals and the faithful of various ranks, who appeared there under the same excuse, and for whom it was a duty, even more than a right, to appear. The King governed and carried on all the prerogatives of his office with the ill-defined help of this court, whose composition was always changing. On the other hand, he was represented at home, on his own lands, by "provosts," who were entrusted both with the seignorial receipts, and with police and legal matters, whose office was originally held in fief, but was subsequently let out on lease.

The court (*curia regis*) became improved little by little, by a process of internal differentiation, whose phases can be studied in detail after the 13th century. It would be long and difficult here to explain all the details in chronological order; but the general scheme of development was simple. It was always necessary that current affairs should be prepared, and even treated, by almost permanent members of the *curia*. And it stands to reason that, as business increased in volume and complication, a tendency to specialisation became accentuated in the members of these necessary assistants, the *curiales* properly so called. Now the King had to make decisions of various kinds "*in curia*"; he had to make decisions in political matters; he had to administer justice; finally he had to supervise the management of his agents, especially in financial affairs on which his own resources depended. Certain *curiales* therefore, clerks or laymen, must necessarily soon have specialised in the exercise of the judicial functions of the Crown, others in the control of local, and especially financial, administration; for these duties must soon, if not always, have required a fairly high degree of education and of technical knowledge. Never at any period has fitness been regarded as urgently necessary for decisions of general policy; but those who undertake these, sometimes too lightly, must at least be surrounded by people who are well-informed as to precedents, traditions, and routine-work; it is certain, *a priori*, that among the *curiales* there must always have been some who were particularly well-acquainted with the routine of internal and external policy. And yet, centuries passed before—at the expense of the former *Curia Regis*—there were formed "sovereign" Assemblies, really autonomous and distinct: *Parlement* for justice; "Chamber of Accounts" for administrative control; "King's Council" properly so called. And for a long time, even after these great bodies had already taken shape, the members remained interchangeable up to a certain point; and other traces of their original unity still persisted.

For local administration, there were still provosts, but the feudal character of their office had completely disappeared and their excessively independent position became modified when they were subordinated to new officials, called bailiffs or seneschals. The bailiffs and seneschals of the 13th century were officials similar to those of the present day, i.e. nominated, paid, superintended, transferable, and removable *ad nutum* by the central authority, and entirely under its control. At the beginning of the reign of Philip Augustus, they seem originally to have been members of the central *curia*, detached for temporary circuits; in 1190 they do not yet appear to have been settled in fixed posts within strictly defined boundaries. But a little later they were resident like the "prefects" of our day, and their jurisdiction extended over a radius which included a fixed number of provostships (and often several of the present departments). There they represented the King in all matters and with full powers. As royal judges of district courts, they held regular judicial assizes; they also served as intermediaries between persons amenable to justice and the supreme court which sat near the King, whose summons and arrests they put into execution. As financial agents, they transmitted the receipts from their districts, for which they were personally responsible, so many times a year. As administrators, they promulgated the commands of the King and saw that they were obeyed; they also themselves drew up regulations of local interest and published them in their own name. They were charged with the delivery of military summons, with the punishment of the refractory, and with the chief command of the permanent armed force serving as garrison in the *bailliage* or *sénéchaussée*. Finally, it was their general duty to defend the King's rights, of whatever kind, towards and against all men, not only in the district which they directly administered, but also in that of the neighbouring lords; the power of each bailiff in this respect therefore extended indirectly to a certain number of fiefs which were independent of his immediate authority. Precautions were, however, taken to prevent possible abuses or dangers. Bailiffs and seneschals were often transferred from one district to another, from one end of the kingdom to the other, so that they could not take root anywhere. The central court kept them strictly under control and in working order, by the necessity they were under of appearing several times a year at the judicial sessions or *parlements*, and at those of the "Commissions of Accounts." As well as this, and especially from the middle of the 13th century, the court sent *enquêteurs-reformateurs* frequently, or even regularly to all districts; these were travelling redressers of wrongs, charged in each place to receive the complaints of those under administration against officials of all ranks, from the top to the bottom of the hierarchy. For there were soon a large number of inferior officials under the bailiffs and the seneschals, not to mention the provosts and *bailes* (who were in the south what the provosts were in the north); judges, receivers, castellans, surveyors, foresters, money-changers, custom-house officers, notaries, sergeants, etc. The weakness for officialdom is of very old standing in France.

However, French officialdom in the service of the central power showed from its appearance in the 13th century that it possessed the same essential characteristics which it has preserved under all forms of government: somewhat conceited and meddlesome, no doubt, but honest and conscientious. It is surprising how trivial were the breaches of trust committed by bailiffs and their agents and minutely investigated by the "Inquirers" under the last Capetians of the direct line. Black sheep were rare among these officials, who were hard-working and energetic busybodies. They were proud of the fragment of power entrusted to them and watchful not to let it be violated, both on account of their personal susceptibilities and because of their feeling for the public interest. They had a passion for extending the rights of the authority which they represented, for on this depended the increase of their own importance. It was men of this type, originally recruited among the clergy and petty nobility of Ile-de-France, who at this time silently laid the very solid foundations of the Capetian monarchy.

The study of the activities of the administrative staff under the Capetians from the time of Philip Augustus has been systematically begun in our day; district by district; branch by branch of the *Curia Regis*; one method of procedure after the other. The extraordinary harshness of the local agents in dealing with anything which offered an obstacle to the free exercise of royal authority is the most striking feature. It was such that the central court was often obliged to exercise a moderating influence, which was not invariably merely apparent and formal.

It is of great interest, especially, to see how and by what use of violence or cunning the local agents constantly defeated rival jurisdictions and rival police; and what was the policy of the central court both in this matter and in the matter of taxes.

As regards jurisdictions, it is certain that the royal jurisdiction made great progress in the 13th century: (1) by the extension of the right of appeal from seignorial courts of justice to that of the King; (2) by the extension of the *jus praeventionis*, which gave to the royal courts of justice the right to summon before them any person in any cause whatever (except that the parties concerned could, if they wished, eventually demand to be tried by the judges to whom they were normally amenable); (3) by that of the royal safeguard, which conferred on the royal judges the exclusive cognisance of offences brought against it; (4) by the monopoly claimed by the royal courts of justice in the cases called "royal" (i.e. dealing with public peace or *ad regiam dignitatem*).

We must, however, be careful not to suppose that the central court had on this subject a deliberate and methodical policy of encroachment based on the Roman theories. The bailiffs themselves no doubt acted instinctively, without preconceived ideas, in accordance with contemporary habits of thought; and the central court never intervened in their spontaneous quarrels, either with the seignorial or ecclesiastical courts, except to moderate their zeal and condemn its excesses. There was in this respect a great difference between the attitude of the Anglo-Norman monarchy, which was deliberately hostile to the seignorial courts and soon systematically took every possible advantage of the theory of royal cases, and that of the Capetian monarchy, which left things alone, trusted to its lucky star, and simply profited by the natural play of the forces which tended to exalt it.

But the future of the monarchy depended above all on its power of obtaining money, and consequently hired troops, by means of taxation of a general character. It is obvious that no great results were possible as long as the King could only dispose of the revenues of his estates, like other chiefs of feudal States: the customary *cens* and *tailles*, feudal dues for alienation and occasional subsidies (*aides*), etc. On the other hand, the transition from this state of things to the modern system of public taxes was very difficult. The study of this transition, of which the King's officers were the more or less conscious instruments, is one of the most important in the history of France in the Middle Ages.

In the first place it is certain that the revenue from the King's domains was continually increasing, not only because of the territorial growth of the royal possessions, but from the fact that the King's power to collect in practice the positive dues to which he had a theoretical right as uncontested feudal suzerain, gradually became extended to a larger number of fiefs. Philip Augustus received from the most powerful barons relief duties which his predecessors would not have been in a position to demand. Louis IX and his successors were able to raise without much difficulty certain contingent subsidies, or aids, in cases foreseen by feudal custom (crusades, marriage of the eldest daughter, knighthood of the eldest son, etc.) throughout the whole kingdom, from their vassals, and also, in conformity with their feudal rights, from the vassals of their vassals, with the consent of the latter; their predecessors, even Philip Augustus himself, would not have been so successful in this, had they attempted it. Thus for a long time the royal revenues preserved their character of dues from landed property; no new principle was invoked; but these dues were increased and, above all, generally extended; which did not fail to create a state of things, leading up to a new claim. They were also sometimes altered so as to be collected more conveniently; it was in this way that many loans or dues in forced labour were replaced by taxes in cash. For instance, many towns soon compounded, more or less exceptionally, for the ransom of the military services which they owed under certain circumstances, by binding themselves to pay a definite sum each time. This sum, which represented the fine which could legally have been exacted in case of non-appearance, was the *aide de l'ost.* Thus was started a practice with far-reaching results.

Suppose for instance that this practice were extended to all those who owed the feudal service of arms and horses; and that, both to nobles and to the *bourgeois* communities, a choice were offered between effective service and the payment of a tax. In both cases the King would gain an advantage from this permission for the same reasons; it would be better for him to receive money, which would enable him to secure the willing services of professional soldiers, than the help of indifferent soldiers, troublesome, inexperienced, and without eagerness. Furthermore, suppose that the King were obliged by the needs of his external policy to make frequent use of his right as supreme suzerain to summon his feudal forces, or that national army which he had also the right to assemble in case of necessity, i.e. of public danger. Would not the great frequency of requisitions naturally lead to an ever-increasing tendency, among gentlemen as among commoners, to prefer the sort of tax instituted for dispensing with military service to effective military service? Finally, a time might come when freedom of choice was abolished and when the tax, replacing the feudal armed service compulsory for all, was demanded every time that the royal government thought it advisable to proclaim "a case of necessity," viz. when it pleased.

The evolution which took place did not in reality possess the simplicity and severity which it might have done. Besides, nothing in the Middle Ages developed simply, severely, or logically, because the evolutions always came about spontaneously, without foreknowledge or guidance, and because the variety of local conditions offered insurmountable difficulties to the rapid progress, uniformity, and synchronism of movements.

At the time of which we are speaking the price of ransom from military service was not uniform; the military taxes still bore an ambiguous character (it is not certain whether they were voluntary or compulsory). The King's legal officers had not only to demand them; they had to negotiate them. They had, each time, to negotiate the amount, the mode of assessment and of collection, with the commission to be paid to the intermediary, if not the "concession." In the second half of the 13th century, negotiations of this kind had gradually become one of the chief duties of the King's legal officers. They took place either in the central court, when the representatives of those liable to contribution repaired thither personally as suppliants for that purpose; or locally, by the consideration of the resident local officials, bailiffs or seneschals, or of one of the special delegates of the "court," when on tour in the provinces.

It would be very interesting to study, as has not yet been done, what can to-day be learned of the procedure of these negotiations. Sources of information are not lacking. We should then see that political life was far from being non-existent at that time in most of the French provinces. The King's officers had actual dealings not only with the magistrates of such and such a town, with the attorneys of such and such a great lord, but sometimes with the delegates of some, or all, of the towns of a district; with local assemblies of nobles, or with the representatives of all the nobles of the district; or even with local assemblies in which both nobles and "commons" were represented. It is thereby proved that in the 13th century the nobles and the "common" people were everywhere in France accustomed to deliberate in the same manner as the clergy in their diocesan synods, whither repaired other delegates from the court to discuss at the same period and under the same conditions the financial contributions to be paid by the Church for the royal needs in the pressing necessities of the Crown. Of course no record of all these meetings has been preserved, and authentic minutes are rare; but there is no doubt that, amidst more or less vehement protests, conditions were often attached before the contributors would agree to the measures proposed on behalf of the King; lists of complaints were drawn up, i.e. an enumeration of grievances for which redress was demanded. The ingenuity of the King's legal officers was displayed in obtaining in every case as much material advantage as possible without yielding anything more than unimportant promises in return. Generally, after much talk, the King's representative promised to reward the goodwill of the assembly by issuing royal letters in which the substance of the complaints presented was incorporated after revision, with formulas of notification, admonition, or prohibition. Most of the charters granted after the end of the 13th century to Churches, to the nobles, and to the common people of various French provinces were thus drawn up. They are valuable as showing both the modest desires of the earliest deliberative assemblies held in France of which traces have not entirely disappeared, and also the sort of cunning used towards them by the representatives of the government.—There were present, in every stage of development, elements the tendency of which could not fail to become accentuated in the near future. This was the origin of the "States-Provincial" and "States-General" of a later age.

## § V. EXPANSION OF FRANCE AND EXTERNAL POLICY FROM THE 11TH CENTURY TO THE ACCESSION OF THE HOUSE OF VALOIS

At the beginning of the 11th century—the point at which this sketch started—France was still only the nebula of a nation, in which vast centrifugal forces were at play. During the subsequent three hundred years she began to emerge clearly and to become consolidated. She even began to measure herself with her neighbours and, at the period which has been considered up till now, the question of hegemony among the Western nations had already arisen.

But it was in the 11th century, when the nucleus of the nebula was still barely formed, that the most wonderful external events took place. At no time did the men of France go forth with such generous enthusiasm to greater enterprises. The spontaneous feats of their vigorous youth must be rapidly recalled.

It is at first sight paradoxical that feudal life should encourage, or even permit, long voyages and distant expeditions, for most of the peasants were bound to the soil, and the nobles were normally shut up, each in his own castle. But the very monotony of their existence inspired them with a wish to see the world and the very ancient custom of long pilgrimages, by satisfying this desire, helped to encourage it. About 830 there was discovered in Galicia an old tomb of white marble, which was at once for some unknown reason assumed to be that of the Apostle St James, son of Zebedee. It became established as a pilgrim resort and was already popular in the 10th century; it was soon so much frequented by French pilgrims that the old Roman road from the Pyrenees to Compostella was called *camino francès*. In the same way, the principal road to Rome by the Alps was called, at least from the beginning of the 12th century, and probably earlier, *via francesca*, the road of the French. Besides these there were also the pilgrim resorts of Southern Italy, Monte Cassino, and the church of St Michael at Monte Gargano; and the East, with the Holy Places, to which, under the rule of the Moors of Egypt, access was not difficult. Along these great main roads, whose track was dotted with minor sanctuaries, there flowed a continuous stream, fed from several sources: penitents, on whom the pilgrimage was enjoined for the expiation of their sins, or as a temporary banishment; pious folk in search of salvation; people suffering from boredom, who felt the call of distant lands; younger sons who sought for action and employment. It has recently been shown that it was for this vast and varied public, amongst which there were many of the best of each generation, that the first heroic poems, localised at the stages of the pilgrim roads, were composed. Analogous phenomena may still be observed nowadays in Brahminic India, where the great roads are continually trodden by men of all conditions in pilgrim garb; but there is this great difference that the pilgrims of our Middle Ages were men of action rather than contemplatives.

The pilgrimage of St James of Compostella soon brought about armed expeditions of French nobles into Spain, to help the native Christians in their struggle with the Moors of the Peninsula. Such were those of Roger de Toeni, lord of Conches in Normandy (1018); of Gui-Geoffroi, Duke of Aquitaine (1063); of Ebles, Comte de Rouci in Champagne (1073), this last under the auspices of the Holy See; of Eudes I, Duke of Burgundy and his barons, which were constantly renewed during the twenty years subsequent to 1075. The Cluniac Order, whose mother-house was in Burgundy, then undertook a kind of ecclesiastical colonisation of Spain reconquered from Islam, which had the result of developing the military immigration of Burgundians into those regions; it was a Burgundian prince who was the first Count of Portugal.

In 1016 Normans from Normandy, on the way home from a pilgrimage in Syria, lent a helping hand to the inhabitants of Salerno in Southern Italy, whom the Saracens were harrying. Finding the work easy and the profits considerable, they soon returned in greater numbers under the leadership of Raoul de Toeni and the sons of Tancred de Hauteville. A regular stream of immigration set in; and in those wild parts of Apulia and Calabria there were battles and intrigues for forty years, as a result of which one of Tancred's sons, Robert Guiscard, became vassal, and protector, of the Holy See, master of Southern Italy, and soon of Sicily, which was reconquered from Islam in ten years (1062–1072). Robert Guiscard, who in 1076 became the son-in-law of the heir to the Greek Empire, planned to obtain the mastery of the Adriatic and of the whole Mediterranean; he established himself at Durazzo and dreamed of the imperial crown of the East. But he died at the age of seventy (1085). Moreover, the strange romance of the Normans in Italy did not end with him, for in 1130 the Two Sicilies were made into a kingdom in favour of a branch of his family, and in the 12th century this kingdom was one of the two best organised States in Europe, as well as being the home of a colonial civilisation, quite original and comparatively "modern" in character.

This is not the place to dwell on the conquest of England by other Normans of Normandy under the leadership of Duke William in 1066; the readers of this work know all about its cause, progress, and results. It must however be said that the two best organised States of Christendom in the 12th century were the Two Sicilies and England—both Norman colonies.

Finally the available surplus of the French population also overflowed at the same period into the East in great numbers. The first Crusade, i.e. the first great international expedition for the deliverance of the Holy Places and the struggle with Islam in Asia, was determined on by a French Pope, Urban II, in a Council held in the heart of France, at Clermont, in 1095. And there was a preponderance of French combatants in the later Crusades. It was not actually for this reason that the Orientals, by a custom which has persisted until the present day, applied the name of "Frank" to all Westerners—for this Eastern custom goes back o the time of Charlemagne, when the "Frank" Empire was regarded as identical with Western Christianity—but the fact is unquestioned.

The four States founded in Asia by Western crusaders after the first Crusade had as their rulers great French-speaking lords, who came from provinces of the Empire which bordered on the kingdom of France (Godefroy de Bouillon, King of Jerusalem; his brother Baldwin, Count of Edessa); an Italo-Norman prince (Boemond of Taranto, at Antioch); one of the great feudatory princes of southern France (Raymond of Toulouse, at Tripoli). Most of the feudatories of these rulers, who divided the newly conquered territory between them, came from the French kingdom, like Jocelin de Courtenai, who, in 1101 penetrated as far as the region between Mesopotamia and Syria. It was a native of Champagne, Hugues de Payns, and a Flemish knight, Godefroi de Saint-Omer, who, probably in 1119, founded the military order of the Temple to come to the help of pilgrims by policing the roads which led to the Holy Sepulchre. About the same time some French gentlemen transformed the charitable work of some merchants of Amalfi into the Order of the Hospitallers of St John, which, although sprung from a different idea, soon associated itself with the Templars to form a sort of joint police-force for Christian Palestine. The civilisation of the "Frank" States in the East was originally entirely French—the imposing remains of the fortresses which were built in the 12th century on the desert marches of those countries are enough to prove it.

Later, during a century and a half, France continued to send reinforcements in this direction. When the Turks succeeded in overcoming the State of Edessa (1144) there was at Vézelai in Burgundy, under the inspiration of St Bernard, a meeting similar to that presided over by Urban II fifty years earlier; King Louis VII went in person. When Jerusalem succumbed to the blows of Saladin in 1187, Philip Augustus joined in the movement which drew all the kings to the East, including those of Germany and England; he took little interest in it and did not play a brilliant part; but his countrymen had again an important influence on the new Christian States of Cyprus and Little Armenia. Meanwhile Jerusalem remained in the hands of the Turks; and at the beginning of the 13th century, another effort was made to regain it. In 1199 a great expedition for this purpose was formed in north-eastern France, chiefly in the dominions of the Counts of Champagne and of Blois, and those of the barons of that neighbourhood. This expedition, which is called in France the "Fourth Crusade," ended after curious vacillations of policy in the conquest of Constantinople and the destruction of the Byzantine Empire (1204). On the ruins of this Empire there soon blossomed a cluster of Latin feudal seignories. Baldwin, Count of Flanders, became Emperor; Louis of Blois took over Nicea and Bithynia; Hugues de Saint-Pol was made lord of Demotica, etc. The Burgundian family, La

Roche, held the duchy of Athens; and the principality of Achaia, or Morea, was conquered by Geoffroi de Villehardouin and Guillaume de Champlitte; a considerable part of ancient Greece thus became French and this was the most lasting result of the crusade of 1204. Under the government of the La Roche family the duchy of Athens survived until the battle of the Cephisus (1311), by which it was transferred to the Catalans. The principality of Achaia, which was quite independent under the three Villehardouin rulers, Geoffroi I, Geoffroi II, and William (1209–1278), was in the 13th century one of the most prosperous of the Mediterranean States; French influence was all-powerful at the court of Andravida, as described in the very interesting *Chronique de Morée*; and the ruins of the great castles built at that time by the French masters of the country may still be seen all over the Peloponnesus, at Acro-Corinthus, Mistra, Kalamata and Maïna.

The three last great expeditions of Western Christianity against Islam in the 13th century (in 1239, 1248, and 1270) were carried out by the French single-handed, or almost single-handed. The method of direct attack on Syria was abandoned. The Christians settled in the East were not anxious for an influx of new pilgrims and considered that it would be better to strike at the heart of the Mussulman power which held the command of the Eastern Mediterranean—Egypt; and they succeeded in convincing the Western powers. They thought that if "Babylon" (Cairo) fell, the dependencies of the Sultan of Egypt in Asia, above all Palestine, would more easily be conquered and Egypt itself would be a magnificent prize where new Western colonies might be established; there seemed no reason against it. The fact that this plan, when first attempted by bands of German and Frisian crusaders in 1221, was checked, did not discourage them. The diplomatic triumphs of the Emperor Frederick II, who, by means of an agreement with the Sultan of Cairo, succeeded in reviving the Christian kingdom of Jerusalem for a time in his own favour (1229), seemed to indicate that the solution of this problem really lay on the Nile. When Thibaut de Champagne, King of Navarre, was heavily defeated near Gaza in November 1239 and most of his comrades were taken to Cairo as prisoners, this opinion was confirmed. So in 1248, when Louis IX of France with a great French army had established his base of operations at Cyprus, he decided to adopt the plan followed by the Germans in 1221. The history of the second Egyptian campaign, which, like the first, opened with the capture of Damietta, is familiar to us from the *Mémoires* of Jean de Joinville, who took part in it. Circumstances were favourable and, had greater prudence been exercised, the result might have been different. As it was, it ended in disaster. The King was taken prisoner and held himself bound in honour to pay to the Sultan's assassins the enormous ransom he had promised them. And when he was released, he went to Syria, where he spent three years waiting for reinforcements which never came. The time was not yet ripe for European domination in Egypt.

If Louis IX had been a different man, it is probable that the French, disillusioned by such unhappy experiences, would have desisted from further Eastern ventures, especially as in France people were beginning to think vaguely that the King of the country had more important things to do at home than to waste his resources overseas. But Louis IX was a saint. In spite of publico pinion, he did not relinquish his plan, for he was sincere in his idealism. Moreover, like the *bona fide* crusaders of 1204, who were sent to Constantinople when their aim was Jerusalem, his sincerity was without his being aware of it exploited as a blind force to be used in the game of political combinations. He wished to deliver Jerusalem and in 1270 he landed at the ruins of Carthage near Tunis, because the local sultan owed money to his brother Charles of Anjou, King of Naples and Sicily, who succeeded in using Louis as a pawn in his political game. There he died. "But that is another story," which we are about to tell. How had a Capetian prince, closely connected with the reigning house of France and himself rich in French possessions, Charles of Anjou, become master of the old Norman colonies of Southern Italy; how did he claim the hegemony of the Mediterranean in the same manner as Robert Guiscard? We must go back a little to explain this. For this is no longer a question of the spontaneous expansion of a young people, but of the beginning of a foreign policy of the modern type by a nation already formed.

As long as the real power of the Capetian dynasty was almost nominal in France, each of the feudal States established within the boundaries of the kingdom had a sort of foreign policy; the kingdom as a whole did not possess one, or rather, its almost fictitious rulers, the first Capetian kings, had no aims beyond the instinctive desire to defend their immature State against the pretentions of the German Empire, with the resolution not to abandon the claims of their own predecessors to the regions between France and Germany (formerly Lotharingia); "To prevent the Germans from encroaching on the boundaries of Gaul," as wrote Hugh Capet to Basil II of Constantinople. But they were too weak. Robert, son of Hugues Capet, could not prevent the last King of Burgundy from solemnly transferring his crown to the German Emperor (1027). The support which Henry I lent to Duke Geoffrey of Lorraine against the Emperor Henry III did not avert the defeat of the duke. Under Philip I the position was complicated by the conquest of England by the Normans; the State of France thus found itself face to face, not only with the Imperial State, but also with a very alert foreign kingdom, which had a foothold in France itself and might possibly ally itself with the Empire when occasion arose. This possibility became a startling reality in 1124, when Henry Beauclerk, King of England and Duke of Normandy, formed an alliance with the German Emperor Henry V against Louis the Fat. For the first time since the 10th century the Germans invaded the French kingdom through Lorraine in the direction of Reims. But in the time of Louis the Fat the monarchical tide, which had been slack for a century, had already resumed its flow. The national peril of 1124 was the first occasion when northern France, realising a common danger, rose as one man to defend itself under the Capetian standard.

In 1124 the danger was more apparent than real, and a simple demonstration was enough to avert it. But it recurred later in very different proportions.

It threatened to recur under Louis VII in the time of Frederick Barbarossa, the first German emperor to form a deliberate plan of uniting to the Empire by close bonds the regions of Romance language situated between France and Germany, especially the kingdom of Arles, over which the holders of the Holy Roman

Empire exercised only a somewhat vague supremacy. If Frederick Barbarossa had acted in concert with Henry II of England, as the two princes had agreed in 1157, the attempt of 1124 would have been renewed under conditions much less favourable to the Capetian king. Louis was saved by the difficulties caused to the Emperor by the schism which followed the death of Pope Adrian IV (1159) and by the ambitious schemes of Henry II, which extended to Savoy and Italy and were thus of a nature to disturb the imperial party.

The decisive game, thus postponed under Louis VII, was, like so many others, played by Philip Augustus and lasted for several hands. First of all, Henry VI, Barbarossa's son, took up the hostile attitude assumed by his father forty years earlier, in 1157. But he allowed himself to become thoroughly involved in Italy and died prematurely. The King of France was then induced to take sides in the struggle for the succession of Henry VI, the candidates for which were the dead emperor's infant son (the future Frederick II), his brother Philip of Swabia, and Otho of Brunswick, nephew of the Angevin kings, who was supported by northern Germany and the Pope. After the death of Philip of Swabia (1208) Otho of Brunswick was elected; but Philip Augustus, this time in agreement with the Pope who had quarrelled with his *protégé*, put forward a new rival to his relentless adversary, who was increasingly pledged to the Angevin kings; this new candidate was Frederick, heir to the Hohenstauffens. Thus the King of France had become important enough to take an active part in the making and unmaking of the Emperor. There ensued the great coalition of 1213–1214 between all the enemies of the Capetian dynasty, of which we have already spoken. The alliance of the German Empire with the Norman and Angevin Kings of England, which had hung over France as a deadly menace for nearly a hundred years, thus became realised and put to trial by combat. The battle of Bouvines shattered it, and from this victory dates a new era in the fortunes of France.

The existence and the supremacy of France were assured at one blow on July 27, 1214 at Bouvines. The second successor of Philip Augustus might have misused this supremacy by undertaking over-ambitious enterprises. Or he might simply have made use of it to complete his grandfather's work methodically in two directions: (1) first by depriving the Angevin King of England, Henry III, son of John, of the precarious remains of his continental possessions; (2) by gaining over the princes of the Empire who ruled the territories bordering the French kingdom, especially those of the Romance countries beyond the Rhône, the Saône, and the Meuse, so as at least to make the linguistic frontiers coincide with the frontiers of France, or of French supremacy. But St Louis did neither the one nor the other and never thought of doing it. On the contrary, we have seen that because of scruples of conscience and to establish a spontaneous and really Christian peace founded on the recognition of just claims he allowed Henry III to retain Aquitaine. Nor was this all—he proposed to settle all old difficulties existing between the kingdom and its neighbours in the same conciliatory and disinterested spirit. Thus by the treaty of Corbeil in May 1258 he arranged the questions caused by the rival claims of Aragon and France. The King of Aragon was also Count of Barcelona and as such might be claimed as a vassal of France, since in Carolingian times the County of Barcelona had been an annex of France (in the heading of Catalan diplomas, up to the end of Louis VII's reign, the year of the kings of France was given); on the other hand, he could put forward some claims with regard to Languedoc. But the rights of France in Catalonia and those of Aragon in Languedoc, although of a nature to serve as pretexts for endless quarrels, were both equally illusory, for ever since the accession of the Capetian kings Catalonia and Languedoc had inclined towards opposite poles. At Corbeil compensation was wisely awarded to both sides. And in this matter also Louis IX believed that he had assured a lasting peace.

So unusual an attitude, the sincerity of which was beyond all doubt, gained for the King of France in the third quarter of the 13th century a moral force which was magnificently complementary to his material power, and a position as arbiter surrounded by universal respect. The dynasty was indeed fortunate to have been successively represented at important junctures by a man who could seize fortune by violence and by another who could sanctify the proceeding.

And yet Louis IX, with his firm determination to maintain the balance of power and a harmonious peace based on the *statu quo* in order to help the honest crusade of simple souls for the deliverance of the Holy Sepulchre, the great aim of his life, could not help sanctioning the indirect expansion of his house, so irresistible was at that time the growing power of France. Finally he was himself unwittingly involved thereby in the whirlpool of Mediterranean intrigue, as we shall now see.

"In 1265 a military expedition left France for the purpose of establishing a Capetian prince, Charles, Count of Anjou and Provence, the youngest brother of St Louis, on the Sicilian throne. Its purpose was to realise at length, and in such a way as to settle the matter beyond all doubt, one of the objects which had for three centuries been paramount in the policy of the Holy See[1]."

For three centuries one of the chief objects of the Holy See had been to prevent the German emperors from annexing Italy as an integral part of the Empire. They had hitherto succeeded in this by relying on the help of the Normans in the Two Sicilies. But when the Emperor Frederick Barbarossa of Hohenstauffen realised his great scheme of marrying his heir to Constance, heiress of the Norman kings of Southern Italy, the danger became acute. Hence the desperate struggle which broke out between Frederick II, Emperor and King of Sicily, on one side and Gregory IX and Innocent IV on the other. Frederick died in 1250 and his son Conrad four years later, after which the policy of the Holy See consisted in maintaining anarchy in the Empire. In Southern Italy there was a choice between two alternatives: either to annex to the Papal States the heritage of Constance, a fief of the Holy See, whose confiscation had been pronounced by Innocent IV at the Council of Lyons in 1245 (which was soon seen to be impracticable), or else to enfeoff it to some new dynasty. In 1252 Innocent IV ordered his notary, Master Albert of Parma, who throughout three Pontificates was the mainspring of the international negotiations relating to the *Negotium Siciliae*, to offer Sicily to Richard of Cornwall, brother of Henry III of England,

[1] E. Jordan, *Les origines de la domination angevine en Italie*. Paris, 1909.

and, in case of refusal, to Charles of Anjou, brother of the French king. This idea of summoning a foreign prince to Italy for the defence of the Holy See as a counter-stroke to the possible return of the Germans and Ghibellines had infinite consequences throughout centuries.

Innocent IV had hesitated between England and France, but he gave the first choice to the English prince. His second successor, Urban IV, who was French by birth, decided on Charles of Anjou, when it became evident that it was time to proceed from intention to action. It is impossible to exaggerate the importance of the chance which, after the death of Pope Alexander IV on May 25, 1261, made the Sacred College choose as his successor Jacques Pantaléon, a former *curé* of Laon, born in Champagne, for many years employed by Innocent IV as a diplomatic agent in Germany, and rewarded first by the bishopric of Verdun, then by the patriarchate of Jerusalem. He took the name of Urban IV. In the conclave which elected him the partisans of the agreement with England were in a majority; Jacques Pantaléon was nominated from sheer fatigue after vain attempts to gain the necessary two-thirds majority of the votes for some one else. The King of France had no hand in it. And yet Urban IV, one of whose earliest acts was to appoint three of his compatriots to the Sacred College, all three trusty counsellors of the French king and members of his court, was the first of the intermittent series of Francophil Popes, which in fifty years, after equally intermittent reactions and a sharp conflict between Philip the Fair and Boniface VIII, ended in the Avignon Popes and the "Babylonian Captivity."

Although the Holy See in 1261–1262 abandoned its plan of conferring Sicily on Prince Edmund, son of Henry III (at the same time that the Empire and the senatorship of Rome were conferred on his uncle Richard of Cornwall), this was naturally for reasons quite unconnected with the previous history of relations between the Holy See and the French and English crowns (of which it is therefore unnecessary here to recall the fluctuations). It was caused by prevalent circumstances and under the general influence of the accession of a French Pope. At the beginning of 1262 at latest Master Albert of Parma was at the court of Louis IX, charged to sound him on the subject of the enfeoffment of the kingdom of Sicily either to himself or to one of his sons.

There was something very tempting to Louis IX in the offer of a kingdom such as Sicily, situated in the middle of the Mediterranean, which might be of great assistance in the work of Crusades and of Eastern Christianity; and he attached no importance to the claims of the Hohenstauffens, inasmuch as they were represented by Manfred, a natural son of Frederick II and actual king of the contested kingdom. For, at a period when Henry III of England had declared himself ready to undertake the *Negotium Siciliae* in the service of the Holy See, Louis had bound himself by the treaty of Paris in 1259 to supply the pay for two years of five hundred knights in aid of that holy enterprise, the expulsion of Manfred. But if his conscience was quite clear on this point, it was not so easy on the subject of the eventual rights of Conradin, Frederick's grandson, and still less so as regarded the rights which the English princes might have derived from the concessions granted to them by Urban's predecessors. He therefore refused for himself and his sons. All that the Papal diplomatists could obtain, by representing that the rights of the English princes had lapsed owing to their lack of means, was permission to offer what he had refused to his brother Charles of Anjou (May 1263). But this was the main point. For acceptance was now certain; there remained only to arrange conditions; and the King was necessarily led to discuss these conditions in detail, as after all, his brother's successful intervention depended on him: it was obvious that Charles of Anjou was powerless to carry out any serious enterprise if Louis did not give his approval, authorise his subjects to take part in it, and allow the Papal agents to make levies on the Church in France in his name so as to finance it.

The expedition to Southern Italy for the deprivation of Manfred was considered as a crusade and received the Pope's encouragement by the grant of privileges generally reserved for journeys to the Holy Land. This was not the first occasion on which the Holy See had caused a crusade thus to be preached against Christians. In 1179 the third Lateran Council had likened those who enrolled themselves to fight against the

Albigenses of Southern France to the crusaders who defended the Holy Sepulchre; and we know that the lands of the Albigensian nobles were "offered as prizes" to the faithful who seized them with the permission of the Church. A further step was taken when in 1199 Innocent III granted to any one who undertook to fight against Markward of Anweiler, Manfred's supporter, in Sicily the same spiritual favours as the crusaders "against the perfidy of the Saracens," because "Markward, being in alliance with the Saracens in Sicily, was preventing Christians from succouring the Holy Land." After this, political crusades followed each other closely; against Frederick II, against Viterbo, against the Tuscans, against the Pallavicini, etc. In the second half of the 13th century it had become regarded as natural that a battle with the political opponents of the Pope should be considered as pious a work as a crusade itself; and this idea obtained everywhere, especially in France when a man like Louis IX accepted it implicitly in 1261, after some hesitation. This confusion of ideas was ingeniously supported by the accusation, always brought against the political adversaries of the Pope, that they were either heretics, or else allies of the Saracens and hinderers of the crusades. More than one French knight who had taken part in Louis IX's Egyptian expedition now enlisted in that of Charles of Anjou against Manfred, without having any clear idea of any difference between the two.

In 1265 Urban IV was replaced by a former counsellor of Louis IX, Gui Foulcois, even more subservient to the house of France than his predecessor, who was thoroughly imbued with the great doctrine of theocracy and had at least tried to impose somewhat severe conditions on Charles of Anjou, before actually entrusting him with the command of the crusade against Manfred. Events now moved more rapidly; the campaign, which had taken several years to prepare, was decided in one month. On February 26, 1266, the Sicilian army was heavily defeated by the French at Benevento; and this victory, endorsed at Tagliacozzo in 1268 and confirmed by the death of Conradin, delivered the whole kingdom into the hands of the Capetian prince.

The triumphant establishment of the French in Italy under

the direction of Charles of Anjou in 1266 was an event of the first importance in European history. The consequence to which we have already referred, i.e. the diversion to Tunis of the last crusade of St Louis, which was caused by the intrigues of the first Angevin king of Sicily, was only in the nature of an episode. We must pause to consider some others.

Charles, Count of Anjou in his own right, was also Count of Provence in imperial territory by his marriage with the heiress of the last count. He had always been adventurous, so much so that in 1253 he enlisted in the service of the Countess of Flanders against William of Holland, King of the Romans, in a quarrel which, had it been successful, would have brought him the county of Hainault (another imperial state). By means of Provence and as Provençal sovereign he had begun to be active in Northern Italy long before there had been any question of his accession to the throne of the Hohenstauffens. Looking across the Alps he had planned to descend in 1258 into the plains of Northern Piedmont. It was therefore natural that, when he was offered Sicily, Urban was anxious to bind him by definite promises; for the Pope did not wish German ambition in Italy to be replaced by French ambition, and German imperialism by another foreign supremacy. But under Clement IV the necessity of speedy action against Manfred swept away all the previously arranged precautions. And the victor of Benevento, as well as being master of a centralised kingdom which had been very well governed ever since its foundation by the Normans, soon became the common protector throughout Italy of the party which, in the internecine struggle of each city, prided itself on being the party of the Holy See—the Guelf party, the Angevin party, the French party, the anti-Ghibelline party, the anti-German party. It was thereby decided that Italy, which had escaped from the domination of the Hohenstauffens, should not become, as Innocent had hoped, a federation of free states under the freely recognised authority of the Holy See, but should remain the battle-ground of foreign influences, amongst which French influence henceforward held the first place.

The following are some of the very important results of the summoning of Charles of Anjou, which was risked by

Urban IV, but on which an Italian Pope might perhaps not have ventured:

(1) The influx into Southern Italy of a new contingent of French colonists, chiefly from Anjou and the neighbouring provinces.

(2) The attraction of one of the two great Italian parties towards France, and in consequence, a perpetual temptation for the French princes to interfere in Italian affairs.

(3) Finally, "the establishment of the Angevins in Sicily seemed like an outflanking of Germany by France. The extermination of the Hohenstauffens in Italy marked the close of the most brilliant period of German history in the Middle Ages. Germany, given over to anarchy and driven from Italy, beheld its influence diminishing in the world as the result of a French victory, at the very moment when France, in full possession of all her powers, became the arbiter of the West[1]." In the 19th century Germany had not yet forgiven 13th century France for the death of Conradin.

Nor was this all. The only important point on which Charles of Anjou had been obliged to give definite promises to the Holy See was that as King of Sicily he bound himself not to compete for the Empire (the Holy Roman Germanic Empire), so that he should not emulate the proceedings of Frederick II. But he had not forsworn the Empire of the East, nor any other crown, and at the highest point of his power he actually attempted to gain an Empire. Heir (by the treaty of Viterbo in 1267) to the rights of Baldwin II, Latin Emperor of Constantinople *in partibus*; suzerain of the Franco-Grecian principality of Achaia, by the marriage of his son to the heiress of the Villehardouins; established in Corfu and proclaimed King of Albania at Durazzo; in alliance with all the enemies (Serbs, Bulgarians, and Wallachians) of the Greek Empire which had recently been restored; he conceived the idea of uniting under his sceptre all the "Frank" territory of the Eastern Mediterranean, up to and including the kingdom of Jerusalem. The subjection of Tunis was also in his mind, as was proved by the events of 1270, when so many Frenchmen with their king found death there. Perhaps he even aimed at Egypt? Formidable indeed for a moment was this

[1] E. Jordan, *op. cit.*, p. 613.

power which wished to gather into one hand all that remained of all the previous Western ventures in the East.

So much for Italy and the East; but Louis IX was the son of a Castilian princess, and Spanish affairs, up till then quite beyond the ken of the French kings, interested him on that account. He strengthened the ties of his house with the princes of the Peninsula by three marriages.

The first negotiation between the crowns of France and of Castile of which there is any record in the archives took place in 1265. It dealt with a plan which had no less an aim than to unite the two kingdoms under one sceptre by a marriage between the heir to France and the heiress to Castile. The French heir having died and the Castilian heiress having lost her title by the birth of a son to Alfonso X, a new scheme was evolved: to marry the Infante Ferdinand de la Cerda, heir to Castile, to a daughter of Louis IX. Further, Philip, Louis's second son, who had become heir to France by the death of his elder brother, was married to a princess of Aragon. Finally, the kingdom of Navarre, which in 1234 had fallen to Thibaut, Count of Champagne, nephew of the last native king, and which, since then had only escaped by the help of France from being conquered by the Castilians or the Aragonese, now entered naturally into this scheme of marriages; and Thibaut II, King of Navarre (1253–1270), followed Louis IX, his father-in-law, to the Tunisian crusade.

As a result of all the events just described, the immediate successors of Louis IX found themselves under the necessity of devoting part of their attention and of their activities to Mediterranean policy, in which all the Eastern, Italian, and Spanish problems soon inevitably became involved in such a manner as to create enormous difficulties. At the end of the 13th century there was a somewhat painful settlement of all these problems, which had the effect of bringing back the French monarchy to questions nearer home.

Only one point was arranged satisfactorily: that of Navarre. When the last king of Navarre of the house of Champagne died in 1274, he left only a daughter, Jeanne, under the guardianship of her mother, Blanche d'Artois. There was then a violent reaction in the country against French influence; it was abetted by the neighbouring countries, Castile and Aragon. But a royal army was sent from France and crushed it, and the Infanta Jeanne, having been restored, married the heir to the Capetian throne, Philip the Fair (1284). From 1285 to 1328, as a result of this marriage, France and Navarre had the same sovereigns and Navarre was governed as a French seneschalship.

Another isolated question was settled, but in a less brilliant manner—Castile. When Ferdinand de la Cerda died prematurely, there was a fear that his very young children by Blanche of France might be robbed of their rights to the throne. In 1276 their uncle Philip III of France took their part; this was the first armed intervention of this kind undertaken by a Capetian king in the affairs of a foreign kingdom. There was an active beginning which failed miserably. Then Philip III had no more leisure to interfere in Castilian anarchy and ceased to retain part of the nobles of the country in his pay. The Infantes de la Cerda were definitely deprived of the succession of Alfonso X, and French influence in this region waned.

Finally the undertakings of Charles of Anjou, with which the French monarchy had become increasingly associated after the death of Louis IX, ended in disaster, and France was involved.

The wonderful fortunes of Charles of Anjou were bound up with the presence in the See of St Peter of Popes who were inclined to continue the work of the French Popes during the years from 1260–1270, especially of Clement IV; they depended also on the support of France. Now, at the court of Rome Charles had enemies, who were justly alarmed by his ambitions and they nearly balanced his friends in the papal elections; after a long interval, Clement IV was replaced by a peace-loving and neutral Pope, Gregory X; and some of Gregory's successors, like Nicholas III (Orsini), were frankly hostile. After the death of Louis IX, Charles of Anjou had thought out a singularly bold plan for ending the great Interregnum in Germany—that the imperial crown should be conferred on his nephew, Philip, the new King of France. Gregory X put an end to this idea by furthering the election of the first of the Habsburgs (1273) as King of the Romans. Nicholas III forced the King of Sicily to relinquish the office of senator of Rome and to evacuate Tuscany. In France also Charles had enemies, amongst whom was the Queen-mother, Margaret of Provence, his sister-in-law, who had claims on the succession to Provence, which he had seized. However all these difficulties were overcome when, in 1281, the Angevin party in the Sacred College succeeded in conferring the Papal dignity on the Cardinal of Santa Cecilia (Martin IV), not merely French like Urban IV and Clement IV, whom he had served, but even more whole-heartedly devoted to the Capetian princes, both in Naples and in Paris. Then Charles of Anjou, having been reinstated in the senatorship of Rome and having come to an agreement with the Venetians, prepared his great enterprise against Byzantium to re-establish the Latin Empire of the East. At this time the French court was likewise well-disposed towards him. He was apparently at the zenith of his career.

His reverses began with the general rebellion in Sicily, known as the Sicilian Vespers (March 31, 1282). If this event had merely resulted in the ruin of Charles of Anjou's lofty plans in the East, and in the separation of Sicily from the kingdom of Naples, it would hardly deserve mention in this sketch of the history of France. But it unloosed other forces. Pedro III, King of Aragon, had married Constance, daughter of Manfred, the natural son of Frederick II. He was summoned by the Sicilians when they revolted against Angevin domination and he accepted from them the Sicilian crown. Charles of Anjou tried to obtain revenge by inciting Martin IV to revive the procedure formerly employed by Urban and Clement against Manfred. The *Negotium Siciliae* was renewed on new grounds, against a new adversary, as *Negotium Aragoniae*; it was thought expedient to have recourse to the same weapons: the outlawing of the enemy, the proclamation of a Holy War against him, the offer of his States as a fief of the Holy See to some prince capable of holding them. Formerly it was Charles of Anjou who victoriously wielded the Papal sword in the "crusade" against Manfred. But against Pedro of Aragon, Charles of Anjou, now vanquished and imperilled, planned that it should be offered to the King of France himself.

Thus the peaceful and disinterested policy of St Louis led, logically enough, to the invasion of the kingdoms of Aragon and Valencia in 1285 by his son, Philip III. The King did not actually accept these kingdoms from the Holy See for himself; but he was authorised by a great and almost national assembly of prelates and barons to let his second son Charles of Valois be invested with them. As to the "crusading" army which crossed the frontier of Roussillon, and then the Pyrenees, to support the claims of this other Charles, it was similar to the army which twenty years earlier had conquered at Benevento and Tagliacozzo; but this time it was the army of France, led by the King in person under the royal standard, as at Bouvines.

This expedition to Aragon in 1285 was the first war of foreign conquest personally undertaken by a Capetian king. Its results were most unfortunate. Philip III died on his return and in the same year there also died Pedro III, Charles of Anjou and Martin IV.

**Philip the Fair and his Sons.** At this time the States of Western Christianity were organised and arrayed in opposition to each other. A diplomatic history would be possible, but would be very complicated. Old quarrels lapsed; new ones came into being. The position of France must be clearly defined.

(*a*) As regarded the Spanish peninsula, there was peace. Navarre had been acquired. There was no occasion, nor any desire, for further intervention in Castile. Philip the Fair, whose mother was a princess of Aragon, settled the unhappy affair of 1285 as quickly as possible by persuading his brother to renounce his pretensions to the crown of Aragon (1295). No further attention was paid to the States beyond the Pyrenees.

(*b*) The same cannot be said of the Italian peninsula. There, although Sicily had been lost, the Angevin monarchy survived in the south, with its agents and plans, its intrigues in Rome and in the kingdom of Arles, its hatred of Germany, its patronage of the Guelf party, and its partisans at the French court. Italy continued to attract the French and to depend on them. In 1301 Charles of Valois, the former Papal candidate for the throne of Aragon, made a descent beyond the Alps with five hundred men-at-arms, by invitation of the Pope, Boniface VIII, who conferred on him full powers for the pacification of Italy (in favour of the Guelfs), and he undertook the re-conquest of Sicily on behalf of Charles II, King of Naples, but without decisive result. In the same year he married Catherine de Courtenai, daughter of the heir to the last Latin emperors of Constantinople and of a daughter of Charles of Anjou, and he carried out many negotiations, during his stay in Italy and subsequently, to prepare the way for an Eastern expedition to gain possession of his wife's crown. In 1308 there was even an expedition on his behalf under the command of a captain of Picardy, Thibaut de Chepoix. After which the everlasting Pretender transferred his rights to his son-in-law, Philip of Taranto son of Charles II. Charles of Valois was in all respects like a poor copy, caricatured and faulty, of the founder of the Angevin dynasty.

But the real reason why the King of France kept his eyes fixed on Italy was Rome. The competition for the Papacy is one of the chief facts in the political and religious history of the period. In the second half of the 13th century there had been three French Popes. Would there be another? This question of capital importance was solved by the stormy pontificate of Boniface and its results.

Under Boniface VIII it became obvious that in summoning the French to guarantee the independence and assert the authority of the Papacy against the Germans there had been no change for the better. What actually did the famous *différend* between Philip and Boniface amount to? Boniface, a Roman of the old stock, who was elected in December 1294, was far from being originally inclined to an anti-French policy; even in 1301 we have seen that he warmly welcomed the armed intervention of Charles of Valois. But he was proud, violent, uncompromising, imperious, and grandiloquent. This was enough to cause sudden quarrels on burning or trifling matters (of one of which we speak later) between him and the court of France, where men of the same mental type were then in power; and it was shown on this occasion that in a bitter war, when all scruples, all precautions, and all traditional courtesies were disregarded, a Sovereign Pontiff, however fine his language, was very weak; while a King of France, master in his own dominions, whatever might be his temporary embarrassments elsewhere, was very strong. In 1302 Boniface VIII "fulminated" Bulls, in which the theocratic views of his predecessors as to the relations between Spiritual and Temporal matters were vigorously expressed. Nevertheless he was contumeliously treated in France and personally insulted, "seized" even in his own town of Anagni by a jurist of the French court (Guillaume de Nogaret), who had put himself at the head of the Pope's private enemies from the Roman Campagna (1303). Thus there had been Popes subservient to France, and now an independent Pope, in disagreement with France, had suffered unheard-of humiliations. The last straw was that the outrage at Anagni remained unpunished. On the day when Boniface died, Charles II, King of Sicily, entered Rome to "protect the Conclave." Moreover the Pope elected by this conclave, Benedict XI, although faithful to the memory of Boniface, was powerless to avenge him. And his successor, elected at Perugia in 1305 by an assembly almost exclusively composed of Italian cardinals, mostly partisans of Boniface, was Bertrand de Got, Archbishop of Bordeaux, French by birth, who never set foot in Italy, and was the first Avignon Pope. The history of the conclave at Perugia is very obscure. But the result was clear: from Clement V onwards the extraordinary fact came to pass that the court of Rome left Rome, settled itself to the north of the Alps, close to the Capetian king, and that the Church of France, generally so submissive to the national dynasty, now took in hand the guidance of the Universal Church.

(*c*) After Italy Germany, and after the Papacy the Empire. In this other sphere the French monarchy also showed its power after the close of the great Interregnum. It may even be thought that in the interest of the future it should long before have systematically made this the scene of its chief activities, had more wisdom been displayed. The French monarchy at the end of the 13th and in the early years of the 14th centuries, still in full and increasing vigour, would inevitably take advantage of its undoubted preponderance and of the permanent disorder of the decadent Empire, to bring into closer relations with itself the regions of Romance language which in Carolingian times fluctuated between France and Germany. Steps were actually taken in this important direction. Would it have been possible to go further? The undertaking was perhaps not as easy as it pleases us to imagine nowadays.

In any case important progress was made.

And first, as to the kingdom of Arles. About 1285 the agents of the French king already treated the bishop of Viviers (which was not entirely subjugated until 1307) and the Count of Valentinois as their master's subjects. In 1292 the bourgeois of Lyons placed themselves under the protection of the King of France, who more than ever behaved (as he had begun to do) as though he were at home in this great imperial town; *civitas de regno nostro existens* it was called after this, twenty years before the treaty of April 10, 1312 definitely recognised his possession of it. In 1294 Philip the Fair purchased the liege homage and the military support of the Dauphin of Vienne; and in October 1310 he entered into a formal alliance with him. By the convention of Vincennes (March 1295) Otho IV, Count Palatine of Burgundy, abdicated and betrothed his heiress to one of the sons of Philip the Fair, and the King of France was straightway appointed administrator of his States to represent the future bridegroom, in spite of the local nobility, who were brought to reason and then conciliated; after this, Franche-Comté was lost to the Empire. Even the Count of Savoy, who had hitherto been hostile, seemed to be reconciled when in 1302–1304 he took part in Philip the Fair's campaigns in Flanders. But the importance of these and other analogous facts must not be exaggerated; the kingdom of Arles was so far only encroached on, not acquired. There were such bitter feuds between the barons who shared it that it was easy for France to find partisans among them; but the enemies of her partisans became hostile to her; and they all changed sides as soon as there was a shifting of alliances. Dauphiné itself, generally favourably disposed (which caused a contrary attitude in Savoy), oscillated in this way until the middle of the 14th century; the definite cession of Dauphiné to France, balancing that of Franche-Comté by Otho IV in 1295, only took place in 1349. Under the last Capetians of the direct line, the situation in the kingdom of Arles was moreover complicated by the rival influences of the two powers which acted in concert in questions of general policy, the Capetians of France, and the Capetians of Naples who were masters of Provence. The very transference of the Papacy to Avignon complicated matters yet further. Finally there was still hesitation between the two possible ways of acquiring the kingdom of Arles—whether to acquire it gradually by the detachment and absorption of small parts, or to acquire it as a whole by the concession of the crown of Arles to the King of France himself, or to a prince of his house. Philip the Fair coveted this crown for himself, or for his son who was already Count of Burgundy. Under Charles IV there was a plan to re-establish the kingdom of Arles in favour of Charles of Valois. Philip VI of Valois even tried to obtain the whole Rhône valley for himself or for one of his family in this manner.

Similar events occurred all along the rest of the frontier between France and the Empire. In 1284, to help the Aragon "crusade," Martin IV had granted to Philip III the right to levy a tithe on Church property, not only in the kingdom of France and the kingdom of Arles (the provinces of Besançon, Lyons, Vienne, Tarentaise, and Embrun), but in all the ecclesiastical provinces of the Empire which bordered French territory (Liège, Metz, Toul, and Verdun). Many of the princes of these regions between the Rhine and the North Sea had come within the sphere of French influence, especially after the marriage of Philip III and Marie of Brabant. Under the last Capetians of the direct line France encroached a little in this direction as in the kingdom of Arles: in Hainault and in Barrois as in Franche-Comté; some ecclesiastical seignories, such as Toul, Verdun, and Metz, towns which to-day are eminently French, came for the first time under her protection, like Viviers and Lyons. The King of France had there a number of partisans and dependants (Montbéliard, Luxemburg, Lorraine, Holland, etc.) as he had in the Rhône valley, but equally unstable and liable to change sides. And finally, just as in the kingdom of Arles the instinctive and prudent policy of gradual dismemberment and partial acquisition, when occasion offered, was pushed forward, without being formally adopted in preference to that of eventual candidatures for the crown, which, if successful, would result in immediate possession of the whole state, so the last Capetians of the direct line, while they increased their power to the north-east by modest degrees, did not lose sight of their designs on the imperial crown, which Charles of Anjou had suggested as an inducement to the head of his family immediately after the time of St Louis. After the death of Albert of Austria, Charles of Valois offered himself as a candidate for the Empire; he was rejected. But Charles IV, the last Capetian of the direct line, came to an agreement with Leopold of Austria in July 1324 and put forward his own claim, with the warm approbation of the Avignon Pope, John XXII.

It is not surprising that, at the beginning of the 14th century, the heads of some people in France were turned by all these events. France, united and compact, was in the first rank of Western nations and was advancing towards the Rhine and the Alps; her allies, the Capetians of Naples, enclosed Italy between their dominions of Provence and Piedmont in the north and their kingdom in the south. The Latin kingdom of the east was entirely French. The Holy See had been transferred from Rome to Avignon and the Pope was, and must inevitably in future be, a Frenchman. The imperial dignity itself, which would have crowned all these successes, did not seem unattainable. In contemplating all this, irresponsible advisers were bound to arrive at a kind of optimistic intoxication and at visions of a universal monarchy held by France for the benefit of mankind. The writings of one of these men, Pierre Dubois, an obscure official, have been preserved. Less than a century after Bouvines, his imagination wandered through a world of gorgeous visions: the Pope was willingly, or by compulsion, to yield his temporal power in Italy to the King of France, as also the suzerainty of the Holy See over the three kingdoms which recognised it, England, Sicily, and Aragon; help was to be given to the Infantes de la Cerda, and thereby Castile too was to be forced to acknowledge itself a vassal; finally, "Let the King take to himself the throne of the Caesars; he will fix the centre of European policy for ever in France; he will pacify Germany and Italy; having united the East under his sceptre, he will then lead it to the conquest of Asia." This state of mind was not peculiar to Pierre Dubois; a French missionary in India, Brother Jordan Catala, wrote to Avignon about 1329: "Credo quod rex Franciae posset totum mundum sibi subjicere et fidei christianae, sine aliquo alio eum juvante."

Nevertheless there were some contemporary facts of a nature to recall clear-sighted people to a sense of proportion. After all, in international politics everything is decided by force of arms. Now Philip III had not been successful in his Aragonese war. Philip IV, in his turn, made war on Flanders and England; and these adversaries, people of minor importance in the vast dreams of Pierre Dubois, in reality caused him much trouble; all his available strength was hardly enough to get the better of Flanders, although on this occasion he strained it to an extent which imperilled the maintenance of his own authority over his people. So far there had only been skirmishes with England; but it immediately became obvious that in this direction lay the chief obstacle between the Capetians and the excessive ambitions cherished by some of their supporters. The great defeat of the French knights by the Flemish at Courtrai (July 1303), although it was retrieved, nevertheless remained the forecast and omen of the French military disasters during the Hundred Years' War.

## § VI. POLITICAL PHENOMENA AT THE OPENING OF THE HUNDRED YEARS' WAR

As a pendant to a sketch of the manner in which the material power of France became consolidated, there should be another on the origin of her spiritual individuality. But all that can here be said on the subject is that the characteristic temperament of the French people showed itself in the 12th century—that is, as soon as an abundant and living literature enables us to judge of it—with the essential qualities and defects which clear-sighted foreigners have since recognised. It is for this reason that France stands out as one of the oldest nations of Europe.

Yet the France of Philip Augustus and of St Louis differed greatly in appearance from the France of the last Capetians of the direct line. After the lapse of a hundred years, from the beginning of the 13th to the beginning of the 14th centuries, the colour of events was, so to speak, no longer the same. Circumstances had changed. The same fundamental temperament reacted differently because of the new conditions of external life.

During these hundred years France had passed from the defensive for her existence to the offensive for supremacy. The enterprises for this object, especially during and after the last quarter of the 13th century, cost vast sums and stupendous efforts. Now great expenditure of national energy generally causes grave results in the political and social order, the point of departure of which is—in critical times—the necessary increase in taxation. Wars, expenditure, taxes, and other means of raising the necessary funds for the governing authority; consequences resulting from the proceedings of the government and the re-distribution of wealth; reaction of the people against this upsetting of customs and of previous economics; all these follow each other inevitably. The crisis of this kind which declared itself in the time of Philip the Fair was the first, and is one of the best known, in the history of France.

The wars which caused this crisis were those of Philip III with Aragon and those of Philip IV with England and Flanders. The war with Aragon had been disastrous. Those with England and Flanders were difficult but inconclusive. There is no need to mention their causes, which are well known. Gui de Dampierre, Count of Flanders, and Edward I of England were both great vassals of France, one for Flanders, the other for Aquitaine, and as such they were equally exposed to the interferences of the law officers of the French crown. And there were also many other reasons why they should unite, as they did in 1296–1297, to try to re-open questions which had been settled at Bouvines. It is enough to recall the chief vicissitudes of the struggle. There were formidable forces on both sides; on the one side England and the thickly populated and very rich country of Flanders, aided also by most of the princes of the Low Countries (Brabant, Holland, and Guelderland); on the other, France and her allies, who were enemies of her opponents (Cambrai, Hainault, Luxemburg, Scotland, and Norway). They were so formidable that both sides hesitated to engage seriously; and there was difficulty in assembling and mobilising the forces, much more numerous than in the past, which were considered necessary. Hence innumerable summons and warlike preparations, both by sea and by land, followed by little or no result, but terribly costly, even without allowing for subsidies to allies. There was no pitched battle between the French and the

English, and the treaty of 1303 merely re-established the respective positions of Edward and Philip on the same footing as ten years earlier. In Flanders the French started with some successes and established the royal authority in the great towns of the country; then there was an insurrection in Bruges, similar to the Sicilian Vespers, which gave the signal for revolt; and the French knights were defeated at Courtrai (1303). The campaign of 1304 was marked by two successes, the naval victory at Zieriksee in Zealand, and the advantage gained at Mons-en-Pevele, which enabled the French to conclude a satisfactory treaty with the count the following year, to the detriment of the large Flemish towns and on payment of a war indemnity (treaty of Athis-sur-Orge, 1305). But the conventions of 1305 were only ratified by the towns in 1309 after many difficulties. They were modified later, because they had not been carried out (it was at this time that part of the Walloon provinces of the County, above all Douai and Lille, were "transported" to the King). As the execution of the treaty was still delayed, military demonstrations on the frontier of Artois again appeared necessary. There was thus an *ost de Flandre* in 1313, another in 1314. After the death of Philip the Fair, there was yet another in 1315, which, like the previous ones, fell back somewhat ignominiously without doing anything. It merely marked time and money flowed in streams. Philip V tried to end the affair by making concessions, but the bad faith of the Flemish was such that he too was obliged to prepare an expedition, which only ended in further negotiations without any fighting. Under Charles IV the events of the early days of Philip the Fair seemed to be recurring, as if nothing had happened. Charles of Valois, who had taken Gascony from the English in 1295, took it from them again in 1324; the following year the King called an *ost* at Saint-Omer against the Flemish; but Gascony was soon given back and the *ost* of Saint-Omer did nothing.

Such were, broadly speaking, the inglorious events which, combined with the normal increase in other expenses of all kinds, were enough to create in France (and in England too) such grave financial difficulties that the previous equilibrium of these countries was profoundly disturbed.

So as to keep pace with the expenses of the preparations for war, continued for so long from year to year, the royal government of France, to speak only of that, was obliged to increase taxation, to contract loans, etc. These operations are always difficult on a large scale, and more so at a period when all experiments in such matters still had to be made.

And first as to taxes. Every one—clergy, nobles, and "common" people—was overtaxed.

The French clergy had for some time paid taxes on their revenues, or "tithes," granted to the kings by the Popes to meet the expenses of the crusades, or of expeditions similar to crusades. The kings had thus formed a habit of depending on the ecclesiastical tax to defray their war-expenditure. Having used the clerical subsidy in the war with Aragon in 1284, the royal government wished to employ it again in their war with England ten years later. Then Boniface VIII, prompted by complaints, issued in an irate mood (February 25, 1296) his Decretal *Clericis laicos*, which in general terms forbade all secular rulers, under pain of excommunication, to demand or receive exceptional subsidies from the clergy, and forbade the clergy to pay such without the permission of the Holy See. This decretal, which opened hostilities between Philip and Boniface, gave rise in France to a campaign of pamphlets in which the principle of the royal levy on the property of the clergy "for the defence of the kingdom" "in case of necessity," of which the King was to judge, was vigorously upheld. "What! the priests had grown fat on the liberality of princes and they refuse their help in case of need!" The Pope yielded this time quickly enough and the French Church obediently voted two double tithes in 1297, a biennial tithe in 1299, a tithe in 1303, while she paid in 1304 a double tithe, or a fifth, asked for, if not literally ordered, by the King.

Nor were the nobles exempt. The holders of noble fiefs were in principle exempt, because they were bound to give personal military service. But those who were prevented from giving it, or who wished to absent themselves, were allowed or obliged to compound by giving financial assistance. Thus in 1302 those nobles in possession of at least forty *livres* revenue, who had not attended the *ost*, were obliged to contribute at least a fiftieth per cent. of their property. In May 1303 those in possession of fifty *livres* revenue were taxed to the half of their income, or a quarter if they were burdened with debts or children. In October of the same year they were compelled to help the King by providing him with one mounted and equipped man-at-arms for every five hundred *livres* of revenue. In 1304 a new tax of a fifth was levied on the revenue of the nobles.

Those not of noble birth were taxed as severely. In 1295 there was a levy of a hundredth part on capital or property of ten *livres* or over, of a two-hundredth part on property of five to ten *livres*, and a tax equal to the price of a day's work on the very poor. In 1296 a fiftieth was levied on the same conditions. In 1297 a twenty-fifth was demanded from those who possessed more than a thousand *livres*, a fiftieth from those who had less. In 1300 a fiftieth. In 1302 a fiftieth from those who had at least two hundred *livres* of personal property, instead of the military service which they owed. In 1303 taxes were imposed of a fifth on revenues above a hundred *livres* in land, of a twentieth on personal property above five hundred *livres*; on another occasion, a tenth on revenues between twenty and a hundred *livres*; a fiftieth on personal property between fifty and five hundred *livres*. In 1304 a hundred non-noble families were bound to supply six fully equipped sergeants, two of them to be cross-bowmen; the communities which did not wish to equip sergeants had to give a sum proportionate to the number of men whom they were bound to supply.

Moreover these repeated and very heavy levies on income and capital were far from being all that the tax-payers had to pay during the period of years between 1294 and 1304, which we have here taken as an example. In 1291 the royal government established a tax of two *deniers* in the *livre* on all transactions which took place within a period of six years, paid half by the vendor, half by the buyer, which affected all classes of the community. In 1295 it ordered a *maltôte*, i.e. a proportionate tax on all essential commodities (wine, wheat, salt), whether owned or sold; there was a second *maltôte* in 1296, which was also levied on cattle. After 1297 and after 1304 the Church paid annates, or the first year's income from a vacant living, in addition to tithes. There were also "loans and gifts," more or less forced loans, more or less voluntary gifts, which the King's legal officers went about soliciting or negotiating everywhere, especially in 1296 and in 1302.

It is hard to form an idea of the immense unrest caused by such measures, which were mostly new and, as regards their frequent recurrence, unheard of. Even in our day the establishment of the income-tax has caused great difficulties in France, and a levy on capital has not yet been resorted to. It must be remembered that in preparing the lists for assessment the oath of the contributor was not always accepted as sufficient; the collectors were sometimes asked to verify statements. And there were accessory difficulties in the Middle Ages; thus the great lords, no longer powerful enough to prevent the King from collecting these national war-taxes from their vassals as well as from his own, were still strong enough to grant their consent to this measure as a concession to be paid for by the assignment of a certain percentage of the receipts to themselves personally. Thus the great feudal lords, such as the Count of Flanders, the Duke of Burgundy, the Duke of Brittany, etc. only allowed the levy on their lands of the first fiftieth in 1296 on condition that they should keep half the receipts for themselves; the other barons kept a third or a quarter.

Further, in addition to the greater frequency of calls to arms, so burdensome because of the expense of self-equipment, and to the enormous increase in taxation of all kinds, there occurred monetary crises of extraordinary violence. The debasement of the royal coinage, which was also a kind of tax to the advantage of the Crown, became constantly aggravated between 1295 and 1306, with the result that the standard of coins was depreciated, incomes shrank, the normal agreement of the legal and commercial proportion between gold and silver was dislocated, change was scarce, prices were inflated, and exchange transactions caused by the competition of coins of various standards were multiplied. Owing to the continued remonstrances of the prelates and barons who made a "return to the good coinage of the time of St Louis" an essential condition in their grant of subsidies, the government of Philip the Fair in June 1306 proclaimed its determination of returning to the old standard.

But the transition was very difficult as it was inevitably accompanied by the depreciation of a large part of the money then in circulation. Minute calculations of value were requisite. A number of provisions and regulations on the mode of paying farm-rents, leases, debts, and arrears, followed each other without supplying a solution for all the problems raised by the counter-reform and without putting an end to the list of litigious cases. Moreover the experience thus gained of the inconveniences both of debased coinage and of a sudden return to the system of good coinage did not prevent the royal financiers from resorting to fresh debasements, the profit from which was immediate and very considerable, alternating with fresh returns to the "coinage of St Louis." The chronicler Geofroi of Paris states that in 1313 many people were ruined and "left the country," and that the variations of exchange interfered with every kind of liberality as well as with business. Geofroi's feelings were shared by many others, and royal commissioners were sent to explain in the towns, châteaux, etc., what were the causes which had "moved the King to act as he had done." These commissaries were charged to persuade the people by clever speeches to conform to the regulations, or if necessary force them to do so.

It may be supposed that, although most people lost by the great variety of coinage and the constant fluctuations in exchange, others must have gained, especially the professional financiers. But even the money-dealers were treated with extreme severity by the government of Philip the Fair. Jews were, like Christians, subject to taxation, and in 1297 they paid in addition a fourteenth as a war-subsidy. On one and the same day in 1306 all the Jews in the kingdom were arrested and their property and account-books seized from one end of France to the other; they were expelled in a body and there was a rigorous recovery of their debts to the advantage of the King. The merchants and "Changers" of Lombardy and Tuscany, who were called "Lombards" in the 13th and 14th centuries, were mostly established in powerful companies which at that time exploited France and the other Western kingdoms in the same manner as the Western capitalists of the 19th century exploited the new or backward countries of the East and the Far East. They were bankers, tax-collectors, money-changers, etc. It was to them that the King applied when he required an immediate advance. One of them, the Florentine who was called "Monseigneur Mouche" (Musciato Guidi), was the principal financial agent of the royal government during the first part of Philip the Fair's reign; the great levies of 1295 and 1296 were collected by means of his "purveyors" or employees. But after the death of "Monseigneur Mouche," his property was sequestrated by the King, as had previously been that of the great Florentine banker of Provins, Renier Accorre, the King's pantler, receiver of the royal estates in Champagne, and as was later that of Mache de Maches, money-changer to Charles IV. In 1311 all the Lombards settled in the kingdom suffered a fate similar to that of the Jews in 1306—arrest, confiscation, and wholesale expulsion. Finally the pre-eminently Christian bank which belonged to the Templars was attacked in spite of its religious and international character. It is well known that kings, princes, and even private individuals, had in the previous century come to regard the monasteries of this Order as places to which they could with perfect safety consign money in current account. The Templars also undertook money transfers by means of deeds between their houses in different countries. Their house, or Temple, in Paris served as Crown Treasury throughout nearly the whole of the 13th century. Philip the Fair himself made use of this establishment until 1295, and again in 1303 after a lapse of eight years. It is not yet exactly clear why, nor at what date, there arose in the court of France the design of ruining the Order of the Temple, but the fact remains that all the Templars in the kingdom were simultaneously arrested in October 1307 on a preposterous charge of heresy, which, pressed with stubborn animosity by its promoters, ended five years later, at the Oecumenical Council of Vienne, owing to the weakness of Pope Clement V, in the suppression of the Order. It is impossible now to prove that the financial activity and wealth of the Order were the causes of its misfortunes; but it is hard to believe that considerations of this kind had nothing to do with it. In any case, Jews, Lombards and Templars were alike treated very harshly, and the mercilessness of Philip's government in this respect has contributed not a little to the dark view taken of that government by posterity.

It is moreover certain that the new generation which was at the head of affairs under the last Capetians of the direct line differed greatly from those who had surrounded Louis IX. They were characterised by an impudent and cunning audacity, to which nothing was sacred; by the use they made both of abominable calumnies and extreme violence against those they wished to ruin; by a sort of gloomy imagination, and a bitterness of hatred beyond belief. Any one who now studies the numerous "affairs" of that time—the campaign against Boniface when alive, the more atrocious campaign against his memory, the campaign against the Templars (which reminds us of the proceedings of the State Inquisition in Spain), the hitherto unheard-of court scandals, such as that of the three daughters-in-law of Philip the Fair—feels as though he were living in a nightmare. Contemporary nerves were tried, not only by the new and ever-increasing difficulties of life, but by repeated and unexpected events, wherein people saw everything which had hitherto been generally respected publicly loaded with abuse. Such circumstances were very likely to lead to a revolutionary situation. Under the influence of all these causes there were actually movements whose nature it is interesting to examine; all the more because, as has been recognised in our day, "it is rather in the 14th century than in the 13th that the true differentiation of French and English institutions began to be worked out[1]." Until then, "the English and French administrative and constitutional development were very closely akin." It was under the influence of circumstances somewhat similar to those which we have just described in France, that in England "the aristocratic control permanently restricted the scope of the English monarchy, without depriving it of its national and representative character." What in this respect happened in France?

The levies in the time of Philip the Fair caused some protests, such as those of the Cistercian Order in 1296, those of the Flemish and the insurgents of Montpellier and Langres in the same year against the first fiftieth. In the winter of 1306–1307, after the

[1] T. F. Tout, *Chapters in the administrative history of mediaeval England*, I. 8. Manchester, 1920.

re-establishment of good money, there were riots in Paris and Châlons when the season for paying rents arrived. But nothing serious happened before the end of the reign. Monarchico-feudal society was too firmly established for disorderly movements from beneath to create a serious danger of anarchy. The weakness of Churchmen was poorly disguised by their emphatic eloquence. And we must not forget that the fiscal agents of the Crown acted with comparative caution: the sums received from the vassals of the barons were shared, as we have seen, with the barons; friendly arrangements were generally arrived at with the magistrates of large towns; there was certainly no insistence on the payment of contributions which were too hard to recover; finally, the King's officers were well accustomed to deal with local assemblies. Danger to the monarchy could come from those assemblies only if they combined to demand guarantees and to impose positive conditions before granting the subsidies which for long had nominally been asked for, but actually exacted.

The government of Philip the Fair apparently toyed with this danger by multiplying not only local, but also general and formal, assemblies. All the ordinances by which it enforced the levy of new taxation were preceded by the formal declaration that they had been prepared with the help of the prelates and barons. On the other hand, it took pains several times to strengthen its policy by the solemn approbation of public opinion, expressed by authorised representatives of the Orders of the whole kingdom assembled in its presence. This had already been done under Philip III to obtain the consent of the prelates and barons of the kingdom to the crusade of Aragon. In 1302 on the occasion of the quarrel with Boniface the King published his intention of conferring on grave questions which touched the safety and welfare of the kingdom with the prelates, barons, "et aliis nostris ejusdem regni fidelibus et subjectis"; and a largely attended assembly was actually held on April 10 in the nave of Notre-Dame de Paris. In 1308 he again felt the need of associating the nation with himself in an unheard-of proceeding—the trial of the Templars—for he wished to use the *vox populi* to over come the doubts of Clement V on this point (Assembly of Tours). And in the preamble of the fiscal ordinance of Château-Thierry (October 1303) the King expressly excuses himself for having held "deliberation and counsel" with only a few prelates and barons "because we could not in this matter summon all our prelates and barons of the kingdom as soon as necessity required." Obviously the idea was beginning to dawn that assemblies called to decide on the question of subsidies should not consist solely of people whom the King had not only at hand but in his hand. And why should they not have had as much latitude as those which in 1295, 1302 and 1308 were summoned to express popular approval for the royal policy? Possibly Enguerrand de Marigni, the great financier of the second half of the reign, was thus led in August 1314 to summon to the Palais de la Cité in Paris an assembly of this kind to submit the question of financial support, which had to be forthcoming in circumstances more critical than ever before. Unfortunately we have little information about this assembly, which was apparently only asked to approve without debate, as had been done in 1302 and 1308. But it was natural that plenary assemblies summoned either to approve an important political step, or to assist the Crown in the matter of subsidies, should not always content themselves with meek acquiescence.

In 1314 general assemblies were still silent and docile. Public discontent and uneasiness showed themselves otherwise.

The levies on the capital, the income-taxes and the *maltôtes* ordered in 1313 and 1314 for the prosecution of the endless struggle with the Flemish put the finishing touches to the anger which had been accumulating for a long time. In November and December 1314 leagues to resist fresh exactions were formed in several provinces and these leagues became federated. We are in possession of the constitution of the League of Burgundy (nobles, clergy and "commons"), and that of the League of Forez; and of the "alliances" of these two leagues with each other and with those of Champagne, Vermandois, Beauvaisis, Pontieu, and the territory of Corbie and Artois. The constitution of the League of Burgundy established it on a permanent footing so as to oppose the "unreasonable things" which the King might do, or had already done; there were to be general meetings every year at Dijon on the Monday after Low Sunday, and, if necessary, during the intervals between the sessions at the summons of elected "governors"; etc. The deeds of confederation show that arrangements of a similar kind were adopted in each of the confederated districts. In the lands only which directly depended on the Crown, except Vermandois, there were none of these new organisations. It is moreover certain that everywhere the initiative and the guidance of the movement was undertaken by the petty nobility: the great feudal lords held aloof and were looked on with suspicion; the Duke of Burgundy's name does not appear in the Burgundian League; the Leagues of Artois and Anjou eventually opposed the Countess of Artois and the Count of Anjou with even greater zeal than they did the royal government.

As for the programme of the malcontents, it unanimously demanded that duties should no longer be levied and that there should be reforms. But they did not elaborate a petition of common grievances on the second point, even in the federated districts. During the winter of 1314–1315 assemblies of all kinds were held throughout the whole kingdom laboriously to draw up a list of abuses to be corrected. Their representatives then presented these lists successively and in great disorder to the court about March 1315, without co-ordination or agreement. As usual, the Chancellor's office hastened to issue under the royal seal "Charters" in which the substance, and sometimes the actual text, of their grievances were incorporated, with certain corrections and reservations, in the form of concessions and privileges granted by the King. Each province thus obtained its "Charter," or even several (when certain articles were omitted in the first hasty draft); Charters to the Normans, the *Languedociens*, the Burgundians, the people of Champagne, the people of Berri, the people of the *Basses Marches* (Poitou, Touraine, Anjou, Maine, Saintonge and Angoumois), etc. What opinion should be held of these documents, of which there are a considerable number? Failing a Great Charter of the kingdom, it would have been a great achievement if the movement of 1314 had really bestowed on each French province a charter of liberty, intelligently drawn up and provided with guarantees.

Unfortunately the Charters of 1315 give a very unfavourable impression of the public spirit, and even of the intelligence of the men who drafted them. Every question has been approached without method and without breadth, from unimportant aspects, in the interest of a caste and never in the general interest. As regards administrative and judicial matters they lay special stress on complaints about the King's officers having infringed superannuated rights, which were no longer justifiable in any respect. In matters regarding taxation they protest against a large number of petty abuses, without elevating the tone of the discussion or fixing the conditions under which the King should henceforth be allowed to require pecuniary sacrifices from the nation. They do not even know how to demand guarantees for the miserable reforms they claim; the chief remedy for all ills seems to them to be the regularising of an institution established by St Louis, that of the circuits of *enquêteurs-réformateurs* for the inspection and punishment of local officials of the Crown; several charters agree in asking that these should be carried out every third year. And as they were not able to evolve means of self-protection, their only resource was thus to appeal from the representatives of the royal authority to their hierarchical superiors. The only provincial charter of 1314 which contains some slight indication of a desire to obtain recognition of principles and guarantees, as well as somewhat precise regulations on the details of procedure, is the Charter of the Normans; this was also the only one which eventually survived in the honourable position of a local Great Charter. In fact the royal government got off very cheaply on this occasion after a crisis which might have been fatal. The malcontents were paid in words and were satisfied with the concessions, masked with restrictions and reservations, which were lavished on them; they had not even the excuse of believing these promises to be sincere, as the royal Chancellor had previously granted similar charters, always without effect. Consequently the most distinct impression to be derived from the study of events in 1314–1315 is that of the strength of the monarchy and the extreme weakness, both material and intellectual, of the forces opposed to it at the beginning of the 14th century. Moreover these leagues and alliances of 1314, apparently so alarming, quickly disappeared, almost without a struggle (except in Artois) and without leaving a trace.

During the reigns of Philip V and Charles IV the assemblies held *coram rege* to deliberate on internal and external policy, on subsidies and coinage, and also on the "reformation of the kingdom" (assembly of March 30, 1321), were frequent. But they have not yet been properly studied. It can only be said that at this time general assemblies of representatives of the whole kingdom, which were brought into fashion, if not started, by the government of Philip the Fair, were almost abandoned. A marked tendency towards sub-division showed itself; each order began to be consulted by itself, and the orders of each of the great provinces of the kingdom (Languedoïl, Languedoc) by themselves. Apparently it was not thought desirable that the representatives of the nobles and those of the towns, who had combined in the spontaneous "leagues" of 1314–1315 and in the "alliances" of those leagues, should have further occasions of meeting and of acting in concert. Moreover, if it then seemed preferable to summon the orders of each great province singly on their own territory, it may indeed have been to avoid eventual alliances, but there is no doubt that it was chiefly to reduce the expenses of the deputies. For it must not be forgotten that to hold a seat or elect a representative was not yet considered as a right to be cherished, but rather as a tiresome duty; firstly because the journeys to the meeting-places were irksome, and secondly because every one knew by past experience that if the King summoned his subjects, it was to demand what they were by no means anxious to grant, and they had not yet realised that they could refuse or even parley *in his presence*. Under Philip V the unwillingness of those summoned to appear at the place of meeting was evident. It became absolutely necessary to repeat regional summons, and actually sometimes, as in November 1318, to subdivide the regions, and even in this way it was not always possible to avert parliamentary strikes on the part of the order of nobles, always the most inclined to absent themselves. It is hardly necessary to dwell on the profound difference between contemporary France and England which such a state of mind reveals. However, certain precedents were established, which circumstances might develop.

## § VII. THE HUNDRED YEARS' WAR. GREATNESS AND DECAY OF THE HOUSE OF BURGUNDY

After the time of St Louis the growth and expansion of France were almost suspended for about a century and a half. This crisis is known as the "Hundred Years' War," because its most critical period (from 1337 onwards) actually lasted one hundred years. We shall here consider its general effect, and as we are now dealing with comparatively simple and familiar facts, which are moreover in part common to the histories of England and France, this sketch will be more than ever reduced to absolute essentials, and almost to an outline.

The permanent peace which Louis IX wished to establish between England and France was a vain dream, so long as the King of England remained the vassal of the French King for his continental possessions. So false a situation could not continue indefinitely. Either the work of Philip Augustus would be crowned by the total expulsion from France of the successors of William the Conqueror and the Plantagenets, or else the latter would take advantage of dynastic accidents and of a lucky turn of fortune to displace the Capetians (as had appeared possible at some periods, and probable in the 12th century), and seize the crown of France. Under Philip the Fair and his sons there were only inconclusive skirmishes, and the least that can be said is that the second hypothesis now appeared very improbable.

But a singular succession of dynastic accidents culminated in 1328. One of the conditions of the reconciliation between Philip the Fair and Edward I had been the marriage of Philip's daughter to the future Edward II. When this marriage was celebrated Philip the Fair had a flourishing family of three sons; and it was impossible to foresee that fourteen years after his death those three sons would all have died without male heirs, and that a question of the succession to the crown of France would arise, in which Edward III of England, the son of Edward II and Isabella, would be in a position to put forward claims as the representative of his mother. This however is what happened in 1328; by the death of the last of the three sons of Philip without a direct male descendant, Philip, son of Charles of Valois, and nephew of Philip the Fair, eldest male of the male line, was crowned King of France without opposition (May 19, 1328)[1]. But it was now possible to argue in favour of Edward III, the eldest male of the female line, that although in France women could not inherit the throne, they were none the less capable of transmitting to their sons the rights which they were not qualified to exercise personally. It is certain that without this extraordinary accident events would not have taken the course which they subsequently did. There would have been wars between England and France; but there would not have been a war in which the crown of France was at stake, in other words, a war of conquest. Thus among all the princely marriages of the Middle Ages which have decided the course of history, that of Edward and Isabella, which seemed so harmless when it was arranged, was perhaps the most fatal.

We need hardly mention the early years of the reign of Philip of Valois. He started well with a signal victory at Cassel against the Flemish towns, which were still hostile. He took an interest in Italian politics (in which, like his father, he had played a personal part before his accession in agreement with the Capetians of Naples); and in German politics, in concurrence with the Pope and the house of Luxemburg (King John of Bohemia, son of the Emperor Henry VII). He made very serious preparations for an expedition to the East which in 1336 seemed on the eve of upheaval. The disturbances of the early years of the 14th century, which might still almost be regarded as signs of growth, were allayed; the King of France seemed more than ever to be the foremost personage of his time, his kingdom the strongest, and his court at Vincennes the most magnificent in the West. This was the moment when the great war broke out.

Edward III's challenge to Philip, "the self-styled King of France," was in October 1337. The immediate causes of this insulting step were recent incidents showing the profound hostility between the two countries, which had occurred in Guienne, Flanders, and Scotland. As in the time of Philip the

[1] The kingdom of Navarre was now separated from the kingdom of France, because female succession was allowed there. It therefore fell in the direct line to the daughter of Louis X, who was married to Philip of Evreux.

Fair, the two opponents entered the lists each with a train of allies recruited among the princes of the Empire, England with the help of the Flemish communities, France supported by the Scots.

The first campaign in 1339, in which Edward III took the offensive, was inconclusive and recalled those of Philip the Fair and Louis X, both by the enormous amount of preparation and the negative result. Nor was that of 1340 any more definite, in spite of the naval victory of Sluys, carried off by the English and Flemish. But in 1341 there was a new theatre of war in Brittany, where the succession of Duke John III, who left no heir male, was disputed by two claimants; one of these, Charles of Blois, being seconded by the French-speaking Bretons and supported by France, and the other, Jean de Montfort, who had on his side the Celtic-speaking Bretons and England.

For years the two sides faced each other in all the theatres of war and waited for an opportunity to engage seriously. The first invasion of France by an English army which was crowned with success was in 1346. The culminating point of the invasion, which started in Normandy, was the battle of Crécy (August 26), the greatest military disaster experienced by France since Courtrai. The capture of Calais by the English on August 4, 1347, was the result of the ensuing campaign. Then the opponents paused for a while, exhausted. It was during this time of relative calm that Philip VI, whose incapacity had caused so many misfortunes to his country, died (August 1350).

His successor was no better and he was very badly advised. Moreover his accession witnessed the rise in France of one of those princes of the royal family, of whom there were so many subsequently, always ready to come to an understanding with the enemies of the kingdom, to help them, and to act traitorously for the furtherance of his personal ambitions. This part was played for the first time in the reign of King John by his cousin Charles the Bad, grandson of Louis X, King of Navarre in his own right, and also in possession of considerable territory in Normandy. He was himself a more or less serious candidate for the French throne and was ready to act in concert with Edward III failing anything better. This was an additional trump in the English hand.

The war was not seriously resumed until 1355 when the Prince of Wales made a successful advance into Languedoc. In 1356 the same prince formed a bold plan of starting at Bordeaux and marching across the land of France to meet an English army which had landed in Normandy; on the way he fought the decisive battle of Poitiers (September 19), in which the French King was taken prisoner. This was the first instance in the Middle Ages of the capture of a king and was most significant in the circumstances under which it occurred.

The equanimity of the French people, already shaken fifty years earlier after the battle of Courtrai by much smaller misfortunes, was shattered by the severe and repeated blows of Crécy and Poitiers. Defeated nations are inevitably subject to disturbances in which they become disintegrated, especially in capital cities. The governments which have led them to defeat then disappear, or are obliged to consent to more or less permanent changes. In the next paragraph we shall see what in this respect were the consequences of the extreme sufferings and humiliations in the France of King John's day.

These sufferings were terrible, infinitely worse than any which had been known hitherto. Permanent war was waged not only by great armies but even more by ubiquitous bands of foreign mercenaries (English, Welsh, Navarrese, Italians, Spaniards, Lorrainers, Germans), who, under the banner of one or other of the belligerents, lived on wide-spread pillage, extending to districts which had been at peace for centuries, and even to the outskirts of Paris.

In 1359 there was the possibility of a peace which would have given the western half of France, including Normandy, Maine, Anjou, and Touraine, to the King of England *in full and sovereign right,* as well as the suzerainty of Brittany. King John in his prison accepted this peace, but the government of the Regent, i.e. that of his son the Dauphin, would not consent to it. It seemed as though a final campaign would be enough to settle it all in Edward III's possession, and it was undertaken. There was no decisive result. Every one was exhausted and peace was therefore arranged at the conference of Brétigni in April 1360. France was divided; the King of England was to have Guienne, Poitou, Saintonge, Angoumois, Rouergue, and a great part of the present department of Pas-de-Calais, *in full and sovereign right,* as well as an enormous ransom. But even at this price peace was not restored to what remained of Capetian France. It was still infested by licensed mercenaries, who roamed about in bands; and the King of Navarre was threatening to take them into his pay so as to dispute with the King the inheritance of the last duke of the first house of Burgundy, who died on November 21, 1361.

The Hundred Years' War was like a clock whose pendulum twice made a double oscillation in opposite directions, forwards and backwards; going forward to the depth of misfortune for France, then by a sort of reaction back to a more favourable position. The death of King John marked the close of the first of the four oscillations; the second began at this moment, viz. at the accession of Charles V, and did not, so to speak, reach the end of its course until the beginning of the 15th century.

The tide seemed to have turned at the accession of the new king, who was greatly superior to his father and ripened by the trials of his regency. First a very good professional soldier of Breton origin, Du Guesclin, in the service of the French crown, dispelled the menace from Navarre by lucky operations in Normandy against the bands and garrisons of the Navarrese king (spring of 1364). But in the autumn of the same year this success was counterbalanced by the battle of Aurai, when Jean de Montfort, the English candidate for the duchy of Brittany, with the help of English troops annihilated the army of the French candidate, Charles of Blois, who was killed; on that day Du Guesclin was taken prisoner. The consequent peace, concluded in April 1365 at Guérande, left Brittany in the hands of the Anglophil dynasty, under the condition of homage to the Capetians; and Charles V had to pay a ransom for Du Guesclin. Subsequently Du Guesclin led the unemployed soldiers, who had to be removed from France, to Castile, where there were two claimants, as recently in Brittany, one supported by France, the other by England. As Du Guesclin went to the help of the one, the other almost immediately received assistance from the Prince of Wales, who was watching events from his court at Bordeaux. The French leader was again captured and his ransom had again to be paid. But the Francophil claimant, Enrique de Trastamare, was in the end successful, and the activities of the mercenaries were thus at least temporarily transferred beyond the Pyrenees.

However the peace concluded at Calais on October 24, 1360, in accordance with the conditions agreed to at Brétigni, had not been carried out in all respects. A fraction of the Gascon nobility, amongst whom Jean d'Armagnac was the most conspicuous figure, did not wish the sovereignty of their province to be transferred to a foreign crown. After protracted and crafty manoeuvres intended to gain time, this state of things led in May 1369 to a resumption of the Franco-English war, which reopened all questions. Du Guesclin was now appointed *connétable*, or Commander-in-Chief (October 1370), and the Black Prince, who was ill, returned to England and died there.

During the ten years which followed, the principal military vicissitudes were the conquest of Saintonge and Poitou by France; the capture of La Rochelle (1372); a lively intervention in Brittany, whose duke was obliged to take refuge in London (1373); the failure of a great English advance after the manner of the Black Prince, which, in pursuance of new tactics, was allowed to proceed without being given any opportunity for a new victory, and which melted away without any result; the final downfall of Charles the Bad in Navarre and the seizure of his Norman possessions. Du Guesclin died during an expedition into Languedoc in July 1380, on the occasion of another fruitless advance from Picardy into Brittany through the valley of the Loire, which was carried out by Buckingham. Then Charles V died in September of the same year, without having succeeded in persuading the successor of Edward III to conclude the treaty he desired so as not to bequeath the task of continuing the struggle to his young son. It is possible to deduce his view of the advance made in recovering the ground formerly lost by his father from the conditions to which he would have consented and which the English refused to sign: he would have allowed Edward III's successors to retain Quercy, Périgord, Rouergue, Saintonge as far as the Charente, and Angoumois, but *under his suzerainty*, and he wished to impose an indemnity for the rest of the territory which had previously been conceded and which he would now have regained (Pontieu, Limousin, Poitou, Aunis, etc.).

The advance made can also be measured in another way. At the lowest ebb, France had ceased to interest herself in European politics. But Charles V made it an object of his activities. The Emperor Charles IV paid him a visit in Paris to confer on his son the Dauphin for life the office of imperial viceroy of the kingdom of Arles, where the King of France had undertaken to continue the gradual progress of his ancestors. The former ambitions of the Capetians as regarded Italy were revived when Queen Jeanne of Naples, who had no heirs, adopted the eldest brother of the King of France, Louis of Anjou (June 29, 1380). Finally and above all Charles V was induced to take steps to maintain the Holy See in the same position towards France as it had held since the beginning of the 14th century. Urban V, who had rendered him great services, was nevertheless the first of the Avignon Popes to recognise the necessity of visiting Italy; he did so and returned in 1370. Gregory XI, who sprang from a family entirely devoted to the Valois, also went to Rome; but he died at Anagni in March 1378. The election of his successor, held at Rome under pressure from the Romans, led to a schism; for the Sacred College first elected an Italian, Urban VI, and then on reflection and when free from coercion, Robert of Geneva (Clement VII). Charles V and Jeanne of Naples declared themselves in favour of Clement VII, as did also the friendly princes of Spain, Scotland, and the provinces of the Meuse and Rhine; England and Flanders naturally supported Urban. This was the beginning of the Great Schism[1].

After the death of Charles V and until the accession in England of the second Henry of the Lancastrian dynasty, the great war was almost suspended by constantly renewed truces. During this time French activity again spent itself lavishly in Italian affairs, in German affairs, and above all in civil wars.

Louis of Anjou, the heir chosen by Jeanne of Naples and crowned by Clement VII, was the founder of the second house of Anjou, whose claim on Southern Italy reverted to the royal house of France a century later and then furnished the excuse for beginning the celebrated expeditions of Charles VIII in the

[1] See below, p. 144.

Italian peninsula. Louis died while struggling with the difficult task of conquering the Neapolitan kingdom (1384); but his son succeeded him and about 1389 a very far-reaching plan was devised in agreement between Clement VII, Charles VI, the young King of France, and his brother Louis, Duke of Touraine (Louis d'Orleans), who was married to the daughter of Giovanni Galeasso Visconti, lord of Milan, by which alliance he had become possessed of Asti. The King himself was to bring to Rome his Pope, Clement VII, who would then enfeoff Louis d'Orleans in perpetuity with the States of the Church in Central Italy, under the name of the Kingdom of Adria. To have one French prince in the south of the peninsula, another in the centre (with aspirations towards the north), such was the plan for the root and branch destruction of Urbanism. This plan was still in contemplation in 1393 and that year a singular incident seemed to offer an opportunity of beginning operations: the aristocratic party in the Republic of Genoa summoned the French to help them against the popular party, first appealing to Prince Louis, later to the King himself. For over eight years (1401–1409) Genoa was governed in the name of the lilies of France by Marshal Boucicault, who even established the rights of Genoa over Savona, Monaco, the island of Elba, etc. on behalf of France, making warlike expeditions as far as Cyprus. The romantic southern adventures of a past day seemed about to be resumed.

As regarded Germany it was another member of the Capetian family who played a similar part to that of Prince Louis in Italy. In 1363, King John had conferred the duchy of Burgundy, vacant by the death without heirs of the last duke of the former dynasty, on his favourite son, Philip the Bold. In 1369 Charles V arranged a marriage for this Philip, his brother, the results of which were of exceptional gravity; the bride was Margaret, daughter of the last Count of Flanders, and heiress to the counties of Flanders, Burgundy, Artois, Nevers, Rethel, etc. A power stretching from the Low Countries almost to the Rhône was thus established to the east of the French kingdom, as formidable as that of the Plantagenets had formerly been in the west. Duke Philip, whose States were thus sandwiched between France and the Empire, and depended on both, soon formed a German policy. He arranged marriages between his children and those of

Albert of Bavaria, who had inherited Hainault, Holland, and Zealand, and the mouths of the Meuse and the Rhine. The marriage of his nephew, Charles VI, to Isabel of Bavaria was arranged at the same time. In 1388 he involved Charles, who was still very young, in an expedition against the Duke of Guelderland, a former ally of Charles V, and forced the Duke thereby to change sides; this was done to please the Duchess of Brabant, whose heir Philip the Bold wished to be. This expedition into Guelderland, which failed, was one of the reasons which decided Charles VI to free himself that year from the control of his uncles, particularly his uncle of Burgundy.—A few years later, the Emperor Wenceslas of Germany was deposed; he was a great friend of Louis of Orleans, who had over-reached him for the sake of his Italian plans. Robert of Bavaria was elected king of the Romans in his place (1400); like all the Wittelsbachs, he was very well disposed towards Philip of Burgundy, who circumvented him in his plans for the Empire.—Lastly in 1395 Hungary, threatened by a Turkish invasion, asked that a crusade to help her should be organised in the West, and the Duke of Burgundy's eldest son led to Buda an expedition containing the flower of the French nobility, always ready to engage in chivalrous and distant adventures. This expedition was wiped out in the battle of Nicopolis (September 25, 1396).

Finally as to the civil wars. A distinction must be made between two kinds; those which sprang from the sufferings of the people and those caused by rivalry between two princely factions.

Even the time of Charles V was not exempt from disorder caused, like those in King John's time, by fiscal troubles and by overwhelming misfortunes. Nor was England free from similar disturbances after the death of Edward III, and it was actually the revolutionary movements in England under Richard II which at this time accounted for the prolonged pause in the struggle between the two nations. During the childhood of Charles VI, in 1382, there were riots in all the large towns. But local outbursts of popular anger were at that time easily quenched with blood. Even the great organised communes of Flanders, who had revolted against their count, were crushed by the knighthood of France, led by the King in person (at the instigation of Duke Philip, prospective heir of the Count of Flanders, his father-in-law), in the battle of Roosebecke (November 27, 1382), when Courtrai was avenged. The repressive measures taken everywhere after Roosebecke were atrocious. After this there were no more popular outbursts except when connected with the fluctuations of rivalry between factions, of which we have yet to speak.

At the beginning of the 15th century King Charles VI was hopelessly insane, and in the deplorable lack of a supreme authority, two factions made their appearance: that of Orleans and that of Burgundy. They opposed each other everywhere and in everything; in the matter of the schism, in the affairs of Italy and Germany, and even on the important subject of England. There was a question whether in order to put an end to the Schism France should withdraw her support from the Avignon Popes, Clement VII and his successor; the theorists of the University of Paris proposed this course; Burgundy approved; Orleans remained faithful to Benedict. In the Empire and in Italy, Orleans, who was an ally of the house of Luxemburg and hostile to the Wittelsbachs, and son-in-law of the Visconti, thwarted Burgundy, who had joined the party of the Wittelsbachs against Luxemburg and that of Florence against the Visconti, on all points. In the important affair with England, the Duke of Burgundy was in favour of the continuance of truces and of peace, because of his interests in Flanders; Orleans supported the opposite view, especially after the tragic death of Richard II, whom he claimed the right of avenging as the natural protector of Isabella of France, Richard's widow, and his own niece and future daughter-in-law.

Finally Orleans and Burgundy both put forward claims to govern in place of the King; popular sympathy was with Burgundy, that of the great nobles with Orleans. However the Duke of Orleans was assassinated in Paris on November 23, 1407, by order of John the Fearless, son of Philip the Bold, second Duke of Burgundy. Such was the origin of the civil war, which quickly developed from reciprocal invective to armed conflict. On the side of the new Duke of Orleans, who had married the daughter of Count Bernard d'Armagnac after the death of Isabella of France, were most of the great lords, Berri, Brittany,

Bourbon, Armagnac, Albret (the party was called "Armagnac" because of the contingents brought from Gascony by the two last-named nobles); on the other side were Burgundy, his family, and his allies on the imperial frontiers.

Here ended the second swing of the pendulum of fate. The third, which was in the same direction as the first, but even more alarming, began by the massacres of the Armagnacs in Northern France in 1410; and both parties had the audacity to approach the King of England to beg for his help in return for promises of the most disgraceful character. At that time there was in Paris (1412) a fresh attempt at the reformation of the government by the people, of which we shall speak later and which had a similar fate to the preceding attempts.

Henry V of Lancaster who succeeded his father as King of England on March 20, 1413, resolved to take advantage of circumstances to revive the policy of Edward III. Conditions had never been so favourable.

The invasion was prepared militarily and diplomatically with the greatest care. In August 1415 there was a crushing offensive; Harfleur was taken, thence the English marched on Calais across country as Edward III had done in 1346. We know what happened at Agincourt on October 25; there was a fresh slaughter of the nobles and the Duke of Orleans was taken prisoner, like King John at Poitiers.

In 1417 matters became even worse. The English army conquered Normandy systematically and captured Rouen after a famous siege. The army of the Duke of Burgundy took Paris from the Armagnacs, who had kept the unhappy King and his family in confinement since the beginning of hostilities. For two years invasion and civil war raged simultaneously.

In 1419 John the Fearless was assassinated at Montereau during a conference with the Dauphin Charles. And this incident decided the Burgundian party, which, though constantly maintaining a somewhat suspect attitude, had hitherto preserved appearances, to cast in their lot with the invaders. Rather the English than the Armagnacs! National feeling seemed to have vanished.

Matters ended in the Treaty of Troyes (May 20–21, 1420),

by which Charles VI, the mad king, renounced and banished his own son Charles, declaring him illegitimate; adopted Henry of England as his heir and gave him his daughter in marriage, meanwhile allowing him to keep Normandy and the rest of the conquered territory as appanages; and finally entrusted him with the government of the kingdom. And it was not necessary to impose this treaty on Paris, for Paris, Burgundian at heart, welcomed it. Elsewhere no doubt there was some resistance. But a final expedition by Henry V in 1421–1422 drove back across the Loire those partisans of the Dauphin who were still in the field. To achieve total conquest now seemed to be only a question of time.

The third swing of the pendulum had been singularly rapid and never has France been reduced to such straits.

The fourth on the contrary was very slow. The unexpected death of Henry V on August 31, 1422, may be regarded as its starting-point; Charles VI died three months later.

At the end of 1422 the Dauphin, now Charles VII, was still recognised in the direct dependencies of the Crown to the south of the Loire—Berri, Touraine, Poitou, most of the Central Plateau, Languedoc, Lyonnais and Dauphiné; and also in the great fiefs of this region whose chiefs were prisoners in England—Orleans, Bourbon and Angoulême. He had also a governmental staff, which having been expelled from Paris by the Burgundians, had followed him, and some very good professional soldiers as was the custom of the day. The position was therefore not desperate. If he had been a man of mettle, the struggle against the Anglo-Burgundians, however unequal, might have been immediately resumed, with some hope of success. But he was degenerate, indolent and pleasure-loving, a prey to parasites and favourites of the lowest kind, and subsequently to women as well; he was afraid of action and let everything go. He himself was the greatest danger to any cause which he defended.

Consequently Henry V's death did not at once arrest the progress of the English advance. Between 1422 and 1428 the Duke of Bedford, regent of the kingdoms of England and France in the name of his nephew Henry VI, also occupied Maine. In

August 1424 at Verneuil he carried off as signal a victory as Agincourt over the best opposing army.

Under these deplorable circumstances the first ray of hope came from France herself; the spirit of the race spoke.

It was natural that the English government, intelligent and exact, but necessarily severe, should not be beloved by the provinces which it ruled. The immense majority were neither Burgundians nor Armagnacs. Anything objectionable in the Treaty of Troyes could not fail in course of time to arouse national feeling, even in the states of the Duke of Burgundy and in Normandy, which were always particularly well-treated by the invaders. And any one who was suffering was led to feel himself hostile at heart. The Anglo-Burgundian sway to the north of the Loire was therefore much less stable than it seemed. Nevertheless a flash of lightning was necessary to illumine the situation and clear the atmosphere.

Now occurred the magnificent episode of Joan of Arc, a peasant of the Meuse, simple, natural, and eloquent, who during her short career expressed in deeds and words the inarticulate feelings of the people from whom she sprang. The army of France, to whom Charles VII consented to give her as a fetish, forced the English army to raise the siege of Orleans (May 8, 1429), and defeated it again at Patay (June 18). Then followed the journey to Reims for the coronation (July 17). But the King would no longer allow himself to be led by the heroine after the failure of an attack on Paris (September 8). Henceforward she was set aside. Then she decided to take action with a few faithful followers only, and was captured in a trifling skirmish (May 23, 1430). The royal government took no interest in her fate; the Chancellor Regnault de Chartres wrote to the people of Reims that she had been taken because she had insisted on following her own desires, and moreover that her place had already been taken by a shepherd of Gévaudan, who would do as well as she had done. She was burned at Rouen on May 30, 1431, after a trial the reports of which are an eternal monument to her strength of soul and her humanity.

This episode being closed, matters resumed their previous course. There were private wars between the nobles in the non-invaded parts of France, raids and insurrections in the invaded parts, and almost total inactivity of Charles VII. The confidants of this prince, who were often changed, always seem to have thought that it was impossible to deliver the kingdom by armed force, and relied chiefly on their negotiations with the Burgundian party, with a view to dissociating the latter from the invaders.

The negotiations between the government of Charles VII and that of the Duke of Burgundy, Philip the Good, ended at last in 1435 with the Treaty of Arras: Philip forgave the King for the murder of his father and denounced the Treaty of Troyes, which had resulted from it; in return, Charles VII ceded to the house of Burgundy, already so powerful, the county of Mâcon and the "towns of the Somme," i.e. all the possessions of the Crown beyond the Somme; moreover, Philip the Good was exempted for life from the suzerainty of the King for all his French possessions. The English were invited to conclude a permanent peace at the same time, but refused. They were offered Normandy and Guienne in fief; on their side they declared that, if the so-called King of France would abdicate, Henry VI would go so far as to grant him in fief those parts of France which he actually held. This was the position in 1435.

After the Treaty of Arras the Franco-English war was resumed under new conditions. Now England, abandoned by Burgundy, experienced some difficulties in her turn; the Duke of Bedford, who had carried on the work of Henry V, died and there was discord between the English princes; on April 13, 1436, the French triumphantly re-entered Paris, and a great avenging expedition, which was despatched from England in 1443, was a failure. In 1444 the government of Henry VI would have been content to retain Normandy and Guienne with full sovereign rights. But the French government saw that luck had turned and would only consent to truces which lasted until 1449. The exhaustion of both sides was terrible; but in France it was enormously aggravated by the incessant brigandage of mercenaries, for whom war, under whatever flag, had for nearly a hundred years been only an opportunity for pillage.

The years which followed the truces of 1444 were well employed in France, after the manner of Charles V, in the formation of regular troops, instead of the former undisciplined bands; they were very badly employed in England, where under a weak and peace-loving king who had inherited the mental feebleness of his grandfather, Charles VI, and who had married a dowerless French wife, daughter of René of Anjou, the civil war of the Two Roses had broken out, a pendant, *mutatis mutandis*, to the conflict between the Armagnacs and the Burgundians. At the expiration of the truces, the whole of Normandy was reconquered by the French in a year; Guienne, which had been English for so long and which was the only part of the kingdom really attached to its masters overseas, was reduced with much more trouble; but at last Bordeaux, the pre-eminently English continental town, fell on October 19, 1453. All England's continental possessions had been lost, except Calais.

The years from 1449 to 1453 were for England what the years from 1415 to 1420 had been for France. And to complete the parallel of the reversal of parts, before very long the English factions were in their turn soliciting foreign alliances; the Red Rose, Charles VII; the White Rose, Burgundy.

In 1453 the Hundred Years' War may be regarded as ended. But France was not yet free to follow her destiny; Burgundy still remained. We shall see how this last obstacle was overcome.

**Greatness and decay of the house of Burgundy in the 15th century.** The Hundred Years' War created conditions very unfavourable to the evolution which was in progress towards the monarchical acquisition of French territory by the disappearance or destruction of great fiefs. Thanks to these conditions, some old houses, such as Brittany, were enabled to survive. Others, which had not previously existed, came into being; these were founded by younger sons of the Capetian house. The chief dynasties of these princes with "appanages," who eventually became as dangerous to the royal power as the old houses, were in the 15th century Bourbon (Bourbonnais, Auvergne, Forez, etc.), Anjou (Anjou and Maine), Orleans (Orleans, Blois, Valois, etc.), and above all, Burgundy (Burgundy, Flanders, and Artois).

Two of these dynasties had great possessions outside France; the house of Anjou were in possession of Provence, of claims to the Two Sicilies, and, after 1430–1435, of the duchies of Bar and Lorraine in the Empire; the house of Burgundy, to whose rapid growth we have already referred, had Franche-Comté and the Low Countries. Duke Philip the Good, son of John the Fearless, almost doubled the extent of his possessions in the Low Countries, which he made the centre of his government, for, by various methods, he annexed the duchies of Luxemburg, Brabant, and Limburg, the county of Namur, Hainault, Holland, Zealand, and Frisia. By his alliance with England he advanced the frontiers of this new Lotharingia in France to the line of the Somme; and the confirmation of this encroachment was the price of his reconciliation with Charles VII. He was actually almost as powerful as the King. But there was not room for both. The house of Burgundy must either absorb the whole of France or be ruined.

The intermediate solution—an agreement between the very great lords under the auspices of the house of Burgundy to limit or annul the royal power and establish a sort of aristocratic rule—was definitely excluded by the national temperament, then as always. Subsequent to 1437 there were several coalitions among some of the nobles (the most celebrated of which, in 1440, called *La Praguerie,* was connived at by the Dauphin, who detested his father); but they were easily dispersed by the royal policy.

Philip the Good wished to be a king, but not originally to be King of France. Two-thirds of his states lay outside the French kingdom and by the Treaty of Arras he was dispensed from doing homage for the French one-third. He had enough territory to form a new kingdom under the nominal suzerainty of the Empire; a kingdom of Low Germany, on which all the seignories on the left bank of the Rhine, including Lorraine, would have depended. This plan failed. Charles VII's government succeeded in thwarting it by supporting all those in the region referred to and in Germany whose interests would have been affected by it. Charles VII pursued an anti-Burgundian policy in the imperial court of the Habsburgs, in Germany and on the left bank of the Rhine; it was as a whole successful and was the beginning of the cordial relations between the French Crown and the Swiss. Several times it seemed as though war were about to break out between France and Burgundy on some excuse or another (and they were innumerable), especially in 1444 and 1470. The Dauphin Louis, when he revolted against his father, took refuge in Burgundy; on the other hand, Charles the Bold, Count of Charolais and son of Philip the Good, when he quarrelled with his father, opened negotiations with France. However at this time matters were settled without an appeal to arms. The latent hostility did not break out until after the death of Charles (1461) and Philip (1467), between their sons, who, having respectively become king and duke, resumed their natural parts with all the intensity of their age and of their characters. The last important act of Duke Philip, enfeebled and under the sway of his favourites, the Croÿ, who had been bribed by Louis XI, was to consent in 1463 to the King's redemption of the Somme towns, a possibility foreseen by the Treaty of Arras, but which would never have been realised if the house of Burgundy had retained the almost preponderant position towards France which she had held in 1435. The restitution of the Somme towns was a sign of what was about to happen. However any development seemed still possible.

Everything depended mainly on the personal courage of the heads of both houses and on the matrimonial alliances which chance or diplomacy might bring about. If, instead of being very sagacious, Louis XI had resembled his ancestor Charles VI or his cousin Henry VI; if, instead of being moody, rash, impulsive, quarrelsome, and crazy with pride, the successor of Philip the Good had been a politician; if Louis XI had not had a son (he had only one, a very sickly one); if Charles the Bold had had a son; if he had married, as was suggested, Anne, the daughter of Louis XI, who became Anne de Beaujeu; if his only daughter and heiress, Marie of Burgundy, who was betrothed to, or courted by, so many princes, had married any one but Maximilian of Austria, the history of the territorial development of France would have been different. Even if, at the beginning of his reign, after the new *Praguerie* of 1465, called the War of Public Welfare, between the King and most of his great vassals, and after the battle of Montlhéry, Paris had abandoned Louis XI and the latter had fled to the Swiss or to the Duke of Milan, as he so often confessed to the historian Philippe de Commines that he had been on the verge of doing, what might not have happened? What actually did happen was as follows.

During the early years of his reign Louis XI suffered some cruel humiliations; after Montlhéry he was obliged to make concessions to the great lords leagued against him, and these concessions were not only humiliating, but dangerous, for it was on this occasion that he was obliged to give back to Charles the Bold (who had not yet succeeded his father) the Somme towns, which had been ransomed in 1463, and to add to them another part of Picardy. In 1468 the position was very critical and the King fell into the hands of Charles the Bold at Péronne; he only obtained his freedom on degrading conditions. At the same time, the "great Western Duke" revived the designs of Philip the Good on the Empire, with a view to the establishment of a new kingdom in Lotharingia; in various ways Liège, Guelderland, Upper Alsace, and the middle part of the Rhine fell into his hands; he thus succeeded in linking the two halves of his States—the Low Countries and Burgundy. In addition, the Duke of Lorraine was forced to grant him right of passage for his troops across Lorraine (1473). But the crown which would have consolidated all this into a kingdom was denied to him, as to his father, by the jealous and uneasy Emperor.

The war between Louis XI and Charles the Bold did not actually break out until 1470, and it was not a duel without seconds. The Duke had innumerable enemies in the east—(the Swiss, Lorraine, the large towns on the Rhine from Basle to Cologne, etc.). He had to defend at all points a dominion which, being new, was not particularly secure. As the brother-in-law of Edward IV of England he could indeed hope for English support; and in 1474 Edward IV actually contemplated reconquering "his kingdom of France" in agreement with Charles. We now know, but contemporaries naturally did not know, that the Hundred Years' War was over. Yet the day of great expeditions was past. There were still skirmishes, and negotiations, and threads crossing each other in all directions; in the middle of this web lurked Louis XI, who since the 15th century has been compared to a spider, with Duke Charles, a noisy and capricious drone, for his predestined prey. In August-September 1475 the English danger was averted and a long truce was arranged between France and Burgundy. The quarrelsome disposition of the duke now turned blindly against Lorraine and the Swiss. It led to his own overthrow by the Swiss at Grandson and Morat (1476) and to his death outside Nancy (1477). The great succession to Burgundy was thus unexpectedly vacant.

It was immediately divided. At this time Louis XI could no doubt still have arranged a marriage between Princess Marie, the sole heiress, and his son. He preferred to confiscate to the French crown those parts of the territory within the boundaries of the kingdom (Picardy, Artois, Flanders, and Burgundy), as well as Hainault and Franche-Comté, which were outside, while he left the rest to his allies the princes of the Empire. But these operations were not without difficulty. And as Marie died in March 1482, leaving two children by her marriage with Maximilian of Austria—Philip the Fair and Margaret—Louis XI now thought it prudent to moderate in some measure the demands he had made five years earlier and to return to the matrimonial method, so convenient and safe. The Dauphin was therefore betrothed to Margaret of Austria, who as dowry would bring him Franche-Comté and Artois; Burgundy still remained confiscated. It was thus that the Low Countries, left to Philip the Fair, became Austrian and were, for ever, lost to France.

All was not yet over. At the date we have reached, France had safely survived the English and the Burgundian dangers. She even began to turn her eyes again towards her southern frontiers, more especially to Spain, whose crown was coveted by Louis XI as great-grandson of John I of Aragon; on this pretext he made war against John II and was thereby enabled to annex Roussillon in 1475. But he could not prevent the marriage of Isabella, heiress of Castile, to Ferdinand, Prince of Aragon (1469), and a plan of betrothal between the daughter born of this marriage and the Dauphin Charles failed. Thus France had henceforth three enemies, all more or less bitter, who possessed claims against her: (1) England (the King of England, who retained Calais, was still King of France *in partibus*); (2) Austria, mistress of the Low Countries, who remembered that she had been robbed of part of Charles the Bold's heritage; (3) the new power Aragon-Castile, which regretted Roussillon and kept an eye on Navarre. When Louis XI died in August 1483 it seemed for a while as though these three adversaries were about to have an opportunity for a common revenge.

The only part of the kingdom which still enjoyed a kind of feudal independence was Brittany, which during previous centuries had over and over again entered into alliances with the enemies of the kingdom; Duke Francis II had only daughters to succeed him. Here again there were marriages which might turn out fortunate or fatal. They would have been very fatal if, as was decided by the Breton government in 1486, the ladies of Brittany had been married, one to Maximilian of Austria who had meanwhile become King of the Romans, the other to his son. The Kings of England (Henry VII) and of Aragon were very anxious that these arrangements should be effected, and the French army which invaded Brittany in 1488 to prevent it had to face not only the men of Francis II but also Anglo-German contingents, whom they encountered in the battle at Saint-Aubin du-Cormier (July 27). Anne, the elder and the heiress, did in fact marry the King of the Romans by proxy in December 1490; but a year later this contract was declared null and void and Anne took finally Charles VIII, son of Louis XI, as her husband, with the characteristic proviso that if Charles died without children she was to contract a second marriage only with his successor. Maximilian, Henry VII, and Ferdinand of Aragon were all too distracted with other anxieties to carry out their planned coalition; and the marriage between Charles and Anne, or rather between France and Brittany, in 1491 brought the unity of the kingdom to perfection.

Two new series of events began about this time. On the one hand it became evident in 1492 that great Italian wars were about to break out. Even in the darkest days of her struggle for life France, thanks to the persistent claims of the houses of Anjou and Orleans, had never lost interest in the affairs of the peninsula; Charles VII and Louis XI had even tried three times to re-annex the lordship of Genoa; Louis XI, who was married to a princess of Savoy, had claims to Savoy and he was the protector of Florence and Milan. In her new fullness of power the first use which France made of her regained security was to act in this direction. On the other hand an accident raised up against

France, victorious after a century-long struggle with the Anglo-Angevin colossus and the Burgundian colossus, a third and last power capable of aiming at her dismemberment. If Ferdinand of Aragon and Isabella of Castile had not had an only daughter as sole inheritor of their united possessions; and if this daughter had not married Philip the Fair, with his rights in Germany and in the Low Countries, France would probably have passed much earlier through the phase of European hegemony to which she seemed destined by her past history.

## § VIII. POLITICAL AND SOCIAL PHENOMENA FROM THE ACCESSION OF THE HOUSE OF VALOIS TO 1494

We must now study the effect of the Hundred Years' War on the spontaneous evolution of political and social conditions in France.

And first, did the misfortunes of those times act more efficaciously than those of the preceding age in causing great political changes? We saw how the movement of 1314 failed. What was the result of the later movements which the crushing defeats of Philip VI, King John, and Charles VI inevitably provoked?

Philip VI carried on negotiations with his subjects to obtain the money necessary for his wars in the same manner as the last Capetians of the direct line. But after Crécy he was made to listen to some plain speaking from the assemblies called for this purpose, especially in 1347. In these negotiations the idea—it had already been put forward under Philip V—was beginning to assert itself that the assemblies which voted taxes might insist on choosing the agents for their collection and even for their distribution. It was by no means evident yet that these tendencies would not develop quickly into free institutions.

But this became obvious during the celebrated crisis caused by new disasters, which began in 1355 and lasted three years. The general assembly of the deputies of Languedoïl, collected in Paris in December 1355 and March 1356, clearly established the following principles: indirect taxes under the form of taxes on business transactions and the *gabelle* on salt, or else direct taxes on income; no exemptions; levies to be made by "elected" officials; application of the money raised to be decided not by royal officials, but by commissaries of the States-General.

The assembly prorogued itself *proprio motu* so as to receive at a later date the accounts of its commissaries, and to advise according to circumstances. Thus the monarchy was put under guardianship and there was an attempt to substitute a new authority and administration for the royal authority and administration. This point had been reached before the battle of Poitiers (September 19, 1356); afterwards the young Dauphin, who took the place of the captive King, had to deal with the same men, but they were greatly excited by the course of events and even more firmly resolved to take in hand the control of affairs. Leaders appeared: the former advocate Robert Le Coq, Bishop of Laon; Étienne Marcel, Provost of the Merchants of Paris; and Charles Toussac, a fine orator. But these assemblies of 1356, which were very large (eight hundred men, although there were no southern deputies present, as the southern provinces had their own assemblies) and very mixed, devoid moreover of any parliamentary experience, and deliberating in the atmosphere of a large, divided, and nervous town, could not fail to make mistakes. And although the former royal government was momentarily overwhelmed by the weight of reverses brought on by its own mistakes, it still possessed the immense advantage of secular traditions and the blind confidence of the majority; a revulsion in its favour was certain as soon as the new men made any mistakes or committed any excesses. Yet mistakes and excesses were inevitable.

Under these circumstances the Dauphin Charles displayed great dexterity. He evaded the first and most formidable attack of the States-General after Poitiers in October and November 1356. In January 1357 there was strife on the subject of a change of coinage ordered by the King's officers; at the injunction of Étienne Marcel, who urged Paris to a general strike and a resort to arms, the Dauphin yielded and the operation was abandoned. However by February it became evident that the deputies of the States-General were to a great extent tired of attending; the nobles especially were absent; and Paris was assuming a dangerous preponderance in the assembly as regarded future reforms. These reforms were now really definite and were expressed in writing; the Dauphin sanctioned them without making any difficulties; this was the Great Ordinance of

March 1357, of which more anon. But a few weeks later the prince allowed it to be clearly understood that he intended to act as though this document were not in existence; and his party, which was always numerous, gave renewed causes of offence. This stormy situation ended in a riot (February 22, 1358), in which some of the Crown councillors were massacred; it was on that day that Étienne Marcel presented the Dauphin with a red and blue cap, the colours of the town. But subsequently the provost committed the mistake of allowing Charles to escape; and thereby everything was lost. Actually the ground of dispute seemed thenceforward to be changed; nothing more was heard of the struggle for the control of public money against the autocratic and arbitrary methods of its disposal hitherto; instead the view was put about in the name of the Dauphin that the insurrection of Paris had been made in alliance with the King of Navarre (a disgraceful candidate for the Crown, who was taking advantage of the troubled times) against legitimate authority. Everything was brought into play: an appeal was made to the hatred of the nobles for the *bourgeois*, to the jealousy of Paris felt by other towns; people went so far as to apply to the States-General and their agents the accusations of exaction and corruption which had been launched by them against the royal administration. Then the men of Paris, abandoned to their own devices, were driven in self-defence to deserve some of the reproaches addressed to them. They now actually sought for the help of Charles the Bad, who was strongly suspected of treachery to the national cause, and the Anglo-Navarrese troops. At the outbreak of the Jacquerie, an unruly rising of the peasants in the region to the north-east of Paris against the nobles, which manifested itself in the burning of châteaux, the Paris *bourgeoisie* allowed itself to be compromised, although it differed in every way from these poor insurgents, who were destined for the gibbet. In July 1358 the obstinate partisans of Étienne Marcel were in the minority, even in Paris, and the Provost of the Merchants was assassinated. His statue now stands in front of the Hôtel de Ville in democratic Paris, because he was the first man in French history to give premature expression to generous sentiments on behalf of the people.

The 1355–1358 movement failed like that of 1314–1317 and partly for the same reasons, with this difference that in 1314 it was the petty nobles who were in control, whereas forty years later it was the *bourgeoisie*. But in both cases there was no co-ordination of effort and no power to realise ideals. The chief difference was in the respective programmes of the two abortive revolutions. That of the men of 1314 had been worthless. That of the men of 1355–1358, such as it appears in the remonstrances of those years, and (with some exceptions) in the Great Ordinance of March 1357 (however badly it may have been drawn up) which sanctioned them, has a certain scope: improvement of the governmental staff by the supervision of some delegates of the States; administrative reform from top to bottom of the hierarchy; establishment of the principle of State intervention in the direction of public matters (truces with the enemy, decisions on coinage, imposition of special war-taxes and direct control of their yield); establishment of the principle of the rights of subjects to arm themselves and offer forcible resistance to "injustices," such as the improper requisitions of royal officials and the pillage of soldiery. Unfortunately the only provisions of the Ordinance which did not remain a dead letter were those which satisfied personal rancour; there was indeed some "improvement" of the staff, but all thorough reform of institutions or morals, all principles or deductions from principles were lost in 1358, when the monarchical reaction triumphed. Or rather, only reflections of them remained in the governmental practice of the time of Charles V.

There were still reflections, for if the monarchical administration of Charles V was greatly superior to that of his immediate predecessors, of which there is no doubt, this was certainly the result of the disturbance which the ideas and the attempts of 1355–1358 had caused in traditional arrangements. Charles V and the new generation of councillors satisfied without the States some of the desires which the men of the States had formulated in the decade between 1350 and 1360, particularly as regarded improvement of the coinage. And can we for instance believe that the Valois kings at the end of the 14th century would occasionally have applied the Aristotelian maxim that all magistracy is elective, by proceeding to the election of some of their chief officials (by ill-defined electoral bodies, indeed), if there had not been in the middle of the century this kind of outburst of parliamentary activity (in the modern French sense of the word "parliamentary")? Finally Charles V to a great extent adopted the administrative organisation which the States of 1355–1358 had improvised for the levying and the expenditure of special subsidies or taxes. He even maintained the use of the term *élu* for the officials entrusted with assessment and collection, who had been really "elected" by the contributors in the system instituted by the States, but whom he changed into royal officials nominated by the Crown. Thus, consciously or unconsciously, Charles's monarchy made use of all that suited his convenience in the innovations of the revolution which had failed.

However the Hundred Years' War went on and a fresh period of material and moral suffering inevitably led to fresh disorders. There were such in 1380–1381, almost at the same time as those with which the name of Wat Tyler is associated in England; in France as in England, the King, although young and badly advised, by means of massacres easily overcame these disorderly movements of the people in revolt against the social order. On the top of this came thirty years of foreign and civil war, catastrophes, ruin, and exhaustion. At the beginning of the 15th century, in the general disorganisation and bankruptcy, the royal government, under the influence of the Duke of Burgundy, had recourse to the dangerous expedient of summoning the States-General of Languedoïl, which had been successfully avoided for a long time. Only districts under the Burgundian sway were represented in the States which assembled in Paris in January 1413; its history closely repeated that of the assemblies, equally reduced by abstentions, of half a century before; and in the background, John the Fearless, Duke of Burgundy, now played the part which had formerly been that of Charles of Navarre. The people of Paris, who were carrying on revolutionary demonstrations daily in the streets to support and encourage the States and impress the Dauphin as in the time of Étienne Marcel, were this time called *Cabochiens*, from the name of one of their leaders, the knacker Simon Caboche. The Ordinance of May 26, 1413, which is called

"Cabochienne," is the exact counterpart of the Great Ordinance of March 1357. It does not mark any advance and is rather a repetition. The improvement of the great governmental bodies (which seemed to deteriorate in proportion as they were "improved") again appeared as the chief point, with a collection of regulations, formerly vainly enacted, for administrative reform. It was again repeated that officials should be elected by constituencies, not directly chosen by the supreme authority. But the political intelligence of those who drew it up was obviously inferior to that of their predecessors. They neither established nor attempted to establish any control of the monarchy by the nation; nothing about the future part to be played by the States-General; and their remedies were much more superficial than those of Étienne Marcel. Their ideal was a regular monarchy and not in any sense a limited monarchy. Moreover the Ordinance was never applied. It was formally annulled in September of the year in which it was promulgated, as having been extorted by violence.

Subsequently France fell too low for misfortune to rouse her in this way. Northern France passed under English government, which did not bring about the importation of English institutions. In the part left to Charles VII, to the south of the Loire, the practice of State Assemblies, general or partial, at first remained in force. But it soon degenerated. These assemblies became mere machines for voting the financial proposals of the Crown and their docility reminds us of the early assemblies of this kind, under Philip the Fair. The reasons for this are very obvious: as long as it was necessary to defend what was left of France and to reconquer what was lost, the crying need of the struggle for life prevented any thought of liberty; and when the King had driven out the foreigners, the prestige which he gained by this great achievement silenced all criticism. Finally the practice of summoning general assemblies of Languedoïl fell into disuse. After 1435 the *aides* (indirect taxes) which until then had been exceptional and provisional in principle, became permanent, i.e. they recurred automatically every year; and soon afterwards the same thing happened to the *taille* or direct taxation. This was done by clever jugglery which roused no serious protests. The war-taxes, *aides* and *taille*, were henceforth levied even in times of peace on the pretext that they were used for the maintenance of the army, which was at all times necessary (*Si vis pacem*, etc.). As for the local assemblies (Provincial States), which had also been summoned in the past to discuss the amount and assessment of taxation, and which were in the habit of adding here and there "increases" to the royal taxes (now called the additional centimes) to provide for local requirements, the yield being administered under their authority—even these were only very occasionally summoned after about 1450. Thus came into being two connected phenomena, permanent royal taxation, and a permanent royal army, without discussion, consultation, or conditions, whence sprang the absolute monarchy of modern times.

The government of Louis XI was a despotic government. The States-General of 1468 were summoned by him only to vote for his policy in the matter of appanages and they expressed only one wish—that the King should henceforth act alone, according to his own judgment in cases of difficulty, "because the States cannot be easily assembled."

Nevertheless although representative government was lethargic, it was not dead. Throughout centuries it retained enough vitality to be always regarded as a supreme resource in critical conditions—and every one knows that the destruction of the monarchy in 1790 was the result of one of these resurrections. The first took place at Tours in January 1484 during the regency which followed the death of Louis XI. It is of great interest to observe how the Beaujeu family, which was then exercising the office of regency in the name of Charles VIII, gently disposed in that year of an assembly where, in the apparent absence of personal power, it seemed possible that every question might be, and in fact was, re-opened. This meeting of the States-General is the first of which there exists a detailed account in the form of a journal: the diary of Jean Masselin, canon and deputy for the *bailliage* of Rouen. This is why historians have sometimes attributed exaggerated importance to it. The fact is that for the very clever advisers of the late king in the service of the regency it was a pastime to dissipate this menace, more apparent than real, by a suitable distribution of individual favours, concessions on points of secondary importance, promises lavished without any intention of fulfilment, and free and easy proceedings in the end. The States-General of Tours obtained from the Chancellor Guillaume de Rochefort in the name of the King a formal recognition of the principle that "a tax must be sanctioned," but as soon as they were dispersed, the principle was no longer observed; and as they were rather slow in dispersing, the said Guillaume de Rochefort dismissed them summarily. The diary of Jean Masselin shows above all things the timidity, awkwardness, and lack of public spirit of most of the deputies, and the dullness of the privileged orders in striking contrast to the cleverness of the royal party. In 1484 three centuries still separate the monarchy, then more flourishing than ever, from its fall under the blows of men similar to Jean Masselin.

**The Church.** The hundred and sixty years which followed the accession of the Valois form a very agitated period in the history of the Church in France.

We have seen that during the preceding period the Holy See was moved from Rome to Avignon; that Urban V visited Rome in 1367, but returned; that his successor also visited Rome ten years later, and died there. The Sacred College, influenced by the shouts and threats of the Romans who demanded a Roman, or at least an Italian Pope, elected Bartholomew Prignano, Archbishop of Bari (Urban VI). But as it was composed mainly of creatures of the last "Limousin" Popes, they reconsidered the matter a little later, and at Fondi, under the protection of bands of Gascon soldiery, they proclaimed Cardinal Robert of Geneva, who took the name of Clement VII (September 20, 1378). Hence the famous "Schism," for Christianity was divided between the two Popes.

Charles V did all in his power to support Clement VII. He imposed him easily enough on France, where he met with no resistance except in the ranks of the international University of Paris, and on his allies outside France. But, as was natural, his enemies made common ground with England in the camp of Urban.

If this Schism were prolonged, it would be for the Papal power a crisis analogous to that of the Hundred Years' War for the monarchies engaged in that struggle. It would reduce it to a state of weakness, since it might lead either of the competitors to make advances, to compromise, and to moderate his claims so as to gain or keep partisans. There was moreover a danger that Churchmen of all nations might become emancipated while considering means of putting an end to a disgraceful schism, even to the length of wishing to interpose as arbitrators in the quarrel. One step farther and they might claim to control and reform the government of the Church, in which omnipotence had developed its inevitable abuses, and might appeal to memories of a distant past when Councils enjoyed an authority superior to that of the Roman pontiffs. What causes of trouble in a world which up till then had been strictly disciplined!

Now the University of Paris had witnessed, without taking part in them, the political troubles of 1355–1358, wherein the bishop Robert le Coq had none the less played a prominent part; but this great clerical republic had felt the reaction. It was moreover a centre of free thought. The means of putting an end to the Schism were soon examined and discussed there; and one of the expedients contemplated was naturally that the Universal Church should be consulted by means of a Council. There was also the "way of concession," viz. the voluntary and simultaneous retirement of both competitors; and, if they refused, the "withdrawal of obedience." It was the latter method which was first tried. In May 1398 after fruitless attempts to persuade the Avignon Pope to "yield," an assembly of the clergy of France, who met in Paris, proclaimed the withdrawal of obedience and the provisional independence of the National Church as regarded all Papal authority. Thereby lapsed all the powers of the Papal agents in France, which, as a result of successive and secular encroachments by the Holy See on the liberties of local churches, were immense; to suspend them was to allow their oppressive characters to be measured from a new standpoint; and if the suspension were long and the freedom appreciated, would it be possible to make people submit unconditionally again to the yoke? Actually the variations of royal policy caused the restitution of obedience to Benedict XIII in 1403; but the disappointment of most of the clergy and especially of the University of Paris at this return to the old methods was great and agitation was thereby increased.

As a result of a campaign inaugurated in 1406 by the University of Paris, the assembled clergy of France again proclaimed the withdrawal of obedience. This time the withdrawal was partial, but was even more characteristic than a total one. For with the approval of the royal government, the assembly distinguished between the powers of the Avignon Pope; without totally rejecting his authority, it declared him to be deprived of the right of conferring livings in France and of the power of taxing the National Church for his own advantage. Were these measures provisional or final? It is obvious that the tendency to wish for their permanence was increasing. In May 1408 the two rival Popes were moreover both deposed and absolutely repudiated. The Holy See was declared vacant and the French Church organised itself for the duration of the vacancy.

It is well known that the Schism was only ended by the election at the Oecumenical Council of Constance of Cardinal Colonna, who took the name of Martin V. It had lasted over forty years and the Church of France had thereby formed, or rather enormously developed, the turn of mind afterwards described as "Gallican"; an increased horror of Papal taxation because for a while it had been free from it; and the habit of appealing from the present government of the Universal Church with its principles of absolutism to the tradition of ancient Christianity in questions of canonical elections, the authority of Councils; etc. This was a state of mind which was approved and adopted by the Crown councillors, not of course from love of liberty, but in the interests of the lay monarchy, their own monarchy, which abhorred all division of authority.

It must have been obvious to Martin V and his successors, who had to defend the rights of the Holy See in a new world, that the Schism had not lasted so long with impunity.

At the beginning of the 15th century the current of opinion was so strong in favour of defending the rights of Councils in matters of government and discipline that Martin V, the Pope elected by the Council of Constance, found himself obliged to assemble another General Council to deliberate on questions of ecclesiastical reform which had not been settled at Constance. It was on February 1, 1431 that he summoned the Council of Basle. In the history of the Church, this famous council occupies a place which is not unlike that of the States of 1356 in the history of France. It was actually a first attempt under critical circumstances at Parliamentary government, a struggle to replace autocracy by a representative and deliberate body, for the reform of abuses and of the Commonwealth "in its head and in its members." Such were the analogies; it is needless to dwell on the differences, of which one, in the case of the duel between the Council and the Pope, was the physical distance between the antagonists (one in Rome, the other in Basle), which in times when communications were not rapid led to extraordinary misunderstandings and to the prolongation of hostilities for many years. At Basle the clergy and universities of France exhibited the greatest energy on behalf of the party which was keenly anxious to reduce the Papal power radically and which finally, in June 1439, proclaimed the deposition of Eugenius IV who had succeeded Martin V, and set up an antipope. The Council of Basle is thus the first parliamentary assembly which (metaphorically or otherwise) cut off the head of an autocrat. It however ended by collapsing miserably into confusion, disorder, weakness, and anarchy.

The Holy See in the end triumphed over the General Councils and monarchy persisted in the Church as it had persisted in France in the middle of the 14th century; but nevertheless it did not emerge from this affair without leaving, so to speak, some of its wool on the bushes. While the tragi-comedy for the determination of the supreme authority of the Church was being picturesquely unfolded on the stage of the Basle Council, the National Churches in every country were, in agreement with civil authority, reconsidering their relations with Rome from a practical point of view, so as to find a *modus vivendi* which, without destroying anything, might limit the Roman claims. In France, for instance, the Councillors of Charles VII in 1438 sought to obtain the logical result of the principles established by the reformers of Basle concerning the system of relations between the Church of France and the head of the Universal Church. This produced the Pragmatic Sanction of the same year, which reduced to a minimum the rights of the Holy See as regarded appointments to ecclesiastical preferment; abolished "reserved cases," prospective graces, annates, and unnecessary summoning of cases to the court of Rome; these were the chief sources of ultramontane exactions, against which the French clergy of the Middle Ages had striven vainly, and they were all dried up by this act. As long as Charles VII was alive this "Gallican" Pragmatic Sanction was firmly maintained. Louis XI was subsequently faced with the question whether it would not be better to appease the Pope by abrogating it, subject to the threat of re-establishing it should not the Popes in return be sufficiently complaisant on other points in the diplomatic game. He thus made play, all through his reign, with the Pragmatic Sanction, which he abolished in 1461, and with the bugbear of a General Council to which he referred on occasion. The French Church, which was terrorised by him, moreover faithfully followed him in all his changes; whatever zeal she may have displayed in the 15th century against Rome, she certainly never showed then, nor at any other time either before or since, an independent spirit in her relations with the King.

The Hundred Years' War ruined a vast number of churches, monasteries, and hospitals in France. The story of their martyrdom down to 1380 has been told simply and artlessly in our days, from collected sources of differing value, by Father H. Denifle in his book *La Désolation des églises, monastères et hôpitaux en France.* It is certain that at the end of the 15th century the Church was much poorer than a hundred and fifty years before, not only absolutely but relatively. Her social importance had diminished. And everything coincides to show that this material decadence was accompanied by grave irregularities and fatal laxity. The 15th century is the only time in the history of France in the Middle Ages when no great monastic Order was founded; on the contrary the decadence of the old Orders, the reformed Benedictines of the 11th and 12th centuries and the mendicant Orders (Dominicans and Franciscans) of the 13th, was becoming intensified. It was at this time that there was a silent accumulation of the causes which in the following century provoked the Reformation.

**Other Social Classes.** The Hundred Years' War caused enormous destruction of wealth and of human life, and consequent economic and social upheavals. It is impossible to give an idea of this in so brief a sketch.

And first, it is impossible to convey an idea of the destruction. Words are powerless. "An endless and terribly monotonous succession of massacres, burnings, pillage, ransoms, rapes," says Father Denifle, who has devoted himself to the collection of episodes of this kind narrated in contemporary documents. "Few places remained inhabited," says the *Journal d'un Bourgeois de Paris*. "Few people are in the country," wrote the Premonstratensians of Mondaye in 1388, "and they have fled for the time of the wars." *Raritas populi* was the cry of all the provinces. Words are weak, and statistics, which would be eloquent, are lacking. There are none, for instance, about the Black Death of 1348–1349: it is only stated that a hundred thousand people died in Rouen; that for long in Paris the number of victims rose as high as eight hundred a day; that the town of St Denis counted sixteen thousand dead at the end of the epidemic; that at Narbonne a quarter of the population perished; etc. As a specimen may be quoted some figures accidentally preserved in an inquiry at the end of the 15th century on the depopulation of Quercy; the former three thousand households of Craissac were at the date of inquiry reduced to thirty; at Concorès there remained only twenty out of a hundred and fifty; Cahors had lost half, not of its solvent households, but of its inhabitants. And there is no doubt that such figures were in no way exceptional. Elsewhere there are references to lands which remained uncultivated for ten, fifteen, or twenty years; and these cases also were not uncommon. French people are better able to-day to imagine by analogy the likely result of a hundred years of insecurity, not indeed absolutely continuous, but constantly recurring, of invasions and of raids. No doubt modern artillery is more effective, but fires have always been destructive, and war was formerly even more murderous, because of the epidemics and famines which modern civilisation can arrest or mitigate. Moreover the ills brought about by the presence of armies were not then localised in the neighbourhood of a "front"; hostilities degenerated into acts of brigandage, less pedantically methodical than those which the present generation has experienced in Flanders, but hardly less thorough; and armies, friendly or hostile, or free lances, all equally organised for "loot," everywhere marched and counter-marched. In short when we read the contemporary writings of the time of Charles V, Charles VI, and the first part of Charles VII's reign, we receive the impression of an intolerable state of things. It was not literally intolerable, since it was tolerated, but assuredly it was accompanied by indescribable sufferings.

Like all great wars, this war, among other consequences, brought about a certain decomposition of those classes in society which had previously occupied an upper or middle position, and the rapid rise of the lower classes; new poor and new rich; depreciation of wealth and assured position, and a too high appreciation of labour and new enterprises. This process must be described with some detail.

The nobles of the second and third ranks, which in the 13th century formed the real middle class of the kingdom, were decimated and ruined to a greater degree than any other class. They were decimated by the hecatombs of their young men for many generations and ruined by the depreciation of the customary receipts in money on which they lived and by the enormous simultaneous increase in the price of commodities and service. Their lands passed into other hands and were bought by commoners who had become enriched by work, by speculation, or by the exercise of domestic, administrative, financial, or judicial offices in the service of princes. Of the families of this class there remained only those who had been singularly favoured by the course of circumstances, or, in name only, those who took the step of regilding their coat of arms by marrying the daughters of upstarts. And this process continued, becoming more and more marked, until the fall of the monarchy. The prejudices of the nobles did not disappear, but the day of the mediaeval nobility was over; its place was taken by another: all those in possession of fiefs were ennobled at one fell swoop by Louis XI in 1470 in return for monetary aid.

On the other hand the scarcity of labour and the general increase in the price of service improved the condition of the peasant class. Tenants took great advantage of this to lighten their obligations and to decrease the proportion due to the landlord in the division of produce between capital and labour;

and in those places where it was necessary to bring back into cultivation tracts of country which had reverted to solitude and weeds as a result of devastation, the property changed hands owing to the demands of the colonists who came to clear it. At the end of the 15th century the French peasant was consequently in a more independent and altogether better position than his like two centuries earlier, when France was richer.

The towns, protected by their walls, with few exceptions suffered less from the direct results of war than the country; but the insecurity of transport naturally caused the greatest injury to industry and commerce, on which the great centres of population lived. During the Hundred Years' War many industrial corporations disappeared; many workmen were obliged to leave their native towns to seek for work elsewhere; and the Italian merchants abandoned the markets of France, which they had formerly colonised commercially; it was at that time that the German Rhine assumed its great importance as the way of communication between Italy and the North, because France had become impossible to traverse. These changes however did not all occur without compensations. For when activity began to be resumed, even before the end of the war, the work of restoration was undertaken by the initiative of French business men and not by foreigners. The career of a great captain of industry and of national and international commerce, like Jacques Coeur, who was an exporter and importer in the Levant, a shipowner, a mineowner, who was interested in the silk and paper industries, etc., in France and abroad, had no precedent and would not have been possible under the Capetians of the direct line. As soon as order had been restored, business increased with extraordinary energy, and in the great towns of France it passed into the hands of a *bourgeoisie* to a great extent new, which had sprung either from the old *bourgeoisie*, or from the old urban proletariate, some of whose representatives, and, above all, whose descendants began to hold public offices, both lucrative and honorary, and to acquire land. Below these there was a new proletariate of whom little is known except that it was voluntarily nomadic, as a result of the habit contracted during the war of going to work in any place where work was to be found; and which was held with a very tight hand—for the new *bourgeois* aristocracy, which had arisen out of the disturbances of the Hundred Years' War, seems at once to have taken severe precautions to defend themselves against a continuance of the tendency to rise, which would have been prejudicial to them. This *bourgeoisie* showed itself a somewhat harsh oligarchy, domineering over workmen, who, conscious of their weakness in a world in which all the social powers would unite to crush them, did not resort to defensive coalitions against the exploitation of which they were the victims except as a last resource. As a whole the condition of the proletariate in the towns had not changed to the same extent as that of the same class in the country.

"When we consider the full extent of all the evils recorded in my work," writes Father Denifle in conclusion, "we cannot to-day imagine how it was possible to emerge from them. Although I admire in general the tenacity of the French people, I particularly admire the generation which lived at the end of the 14th century...." The generations which lived during the Hundred Years' War did in fact display a degree of recuperative power which is astounding. French art was never more original, more delicate, nor more fruitful than during these unhappy times. After a lapse of five hundred years there still remain in France a number of buildings, and, in collections, a quantity of furniture, manuscripts and other charming and sumptuous objects of that age, which testify to the extraordinary vitality of the highest forms of national civilisation during the course, or on the morrow, of the deepest political abasement. Never has the magnificence of the princely courts of the 14th and 15th centuries been surpassed; this would be of no importance, for we know from current experience that extreme luxury becomes developed in times of misery; but never was luxury freer from vulgarity, nor the framework of life in general more noble. It is incredible what a great people can bear without causing the creative power within it to falter.

## BIBLIOGRAPHY

A. Molinier, *Les sources de l'histoire de France des origines aux guerres d'Italie* (1494), 6 vols. 1902–1906.

*Histoire générale*, edd. E. Lavisse and A. Rambaud, vols. I–III, 1892–1894.—*Histoire de France*, ed. E. Lavisse, vols. II–IV.

The principal monographs, which are very numerous, are given in the bibliographies appended to the separate chapters of the two preceding works. Below are mentioned a few works, which have, for the most part, appeared since the publication of the *Histoire de France*, and which are specially distinguished for novelty and originality.

§ I. J. Flach, *Les origines de l'ancienne France*, 4 vols. 1886–1917. F. Lot, *Fidèles et vassaux*, 1904; and other works by the same author. P. Lacombe, *L'appropriation du sol*, 1912. Charles H. Haskins, *Norman institutions*. Cambridge, Mass., 1918.

§§ II, III and IV. The principal authority for the political history of the 12th and 13th centuries is the late Achille Luchaire, *Histoire des institutions monarchiques de la France sous les premiers Capétiens*, 2 vols. 1883; *Manuel des institutions françaises—Période des Capétiens directs*, 1892; *Les Communes françaises à l'époque des Capétiens directs*, 1890.

Our knowledge of the administrative history (see above, pp. 71 ff.) has been greatly advanced by the recent work of M. Borrelli de Serres, *Recherches sur divers services publics du xiii^e au xvii^e siècle*, 3 vols. 1895–1909. Cp. *Journal des Savants*, 1905 and 1910. As types of monographs, very limited in scope, but excellent in quality, may be cited: Michel, *L'administration royale dans la sénéchaussée de Beaucaire au temps de saint Louis*, 1910. H. Waquet, *Le bailliage de Vermandois aux xiii^e et xiv^e siècles*, 1919. E. Perrot, *Les cas royaux*, 1910.

§ V. On the relations of the *chansons de geste* to the pilgrimage routes, see the capital work of J. Bédier, *Les légendes épiques*, 4 vols. 1908–1913.

E. Jordan, *Les origines de la domination angevine en Italie*, 1909.

§ VI. The very important questions of which a sketch is given in this section and which relate to the history of the royal taxation will be shortly discussed by M. M. Jusselin in a considerable work, based on original documents, of which the provisional title is *Les impôts royaux en France sous les règnes de Philippe le Bel et de ses fils*.

The movement of 1314 has been exhaustively studied by A. Artonne, *Le mouvement de* 1314 *et les chartes provinciales de* 1315. 1912.

§§ VII and VIII. The history of the reign of Charles V has been recently re-written throughout with the greatest care by R. Delachenal. Three volumes, carrying the history down to 1368, have appeared (1909–1916).

Father H. Denifle proposed to write the history of *La Désolation des églises, monastères et hôpitaux en France* during the whole Hundred Years' War, but only the first part, down to 1380 (2 vols. 1897–1899), has appeared.

# CHAPTER III

## THE ARMY

By the sixth century the successive invasions of Gaul from the North were over, and the victorious Franks substituted their own military organisation for that of the Romans which they had destroyed. Their system lasted throughout the Middle Ages, subject, however, to profound transformations. But of its evolution through all these centuries it is only possible to give the essential characteristics, and no more than this will be attempted here.

In Gaul under the Merovingian kings, as at all times and in all countries, military organisation and social organisation were closely related.

It was, in principle, the duty of every free man owning land to serve in the army on reaching the age of fifteen. At first only the free men of Germanic or Frankish descent were called up, but it soon became customary to summon also those who were of Gallo-Roman origin. Permanent service was not required of them. As soon as the expedition for which they were levied was over they were disbanded, and they were rarely kept as long as six months. Generally speaking, the army broke up on the approach of winter.

The royal call to arms or *hériban* was sent to the dukes and counts. These made it known to the men of the territory which they governed, and assembled and led them to the appointed rendezvous. Defaulters were punishable by fines.

A soldier in Merovingian times received no pay and no allowances for clothes or weapons. His only hope of gain lay in spoil and plunder. And this hope produced volunteers in sufficient numbers to form the basis of the army, which was brought up to full strength by contingents requisitioned, as far as possible, from the regions bordering on the theatre of war: for the king wished and was expected to spare his subjects and not to abuse their willingness to serve or wear out their patience by too general and too constantly repeated levies.

On the whole the military organisation of the Merovingian kings closely resembled that of the ancient Germans and proceeded directly from it.

Under the Carolingians a notable change took place. Charlemagne knew how to make himself obeyed. Furthermore he found himself obliged to carry on wars longer and fiercer than those of the preceding age. He kept the instrument of war which his predecessors had left him, but he retempered and strengthened it.

Recruiting continued on the same principle. All free men possessing land were subject to military service. The age when service began was raised from fifteen to twenty.

On the Emperor's call to arms, which was transmitted by the count, the bishop, or the *missus dominicus* acting for him, a soldier had to report at the appointed time and place, with arms and equipment, a change of clothes, and some food. Absentees were punished.

The period of service lasted three months on an average. Even thus limited it was a heavy burden for small holders, insufficiently compensated by the scanty spoils won in the course of distant campaigns in Germany or Spain. Attempts, therefore, were made by the Emperor to lighten it, first by avoiding general levies and then by introducing exemptions even in partial levies. A capitulary of the year 803, for instance, shows that owners of a certain amount of land, four *manses* and upwards, owed personal service; owners of two *manses* must combine to furnish one fighting man for every four *manses* of ground. A later capitulary, dated 807, calls up owners of three *manses* and upwards. Those who possessed more than twelve *manses* must serve on horseback.

But an army composed of landowners only would not have sufficed. The emperor had recourse at the same time to the class of "beneficiaries."

In the rude society of the eighth and ninth centuries isolation had its dangers, and it was customary for an individual in humbler circumstances to "recommend" himself for protection to some powerful layman or ecclesiastic who was called his *senior* and whose *vassus* he became. The *vassus* owed military duties to the *senior,* and in many cases the *senior* granted him, as payment or reward, the usufruct, or, as it was then called, the "benefice" of a piece of land. Sometimes a freeholder by recommending himself to a *senior* for protection caused his freehold to become a "benefice."

The Merovingian kings had already followed this practice, as well as the dukes and counts. The Carolingian Emperor still further extended its use. It had the advantage of attaching to him by close personal bonds a devoted following. But he had, on the other hand, to allow a *senior* who brought his own *vassi* to the army to keep command over them. This state of things had the disadvantage of placing the *senior* between the sovereign and his subjects and so preparing the way for feudalism.

In the course of the tenth century social changes took place in France of which, for want of documents, we know little. By the eleventh century we find that important modifications have taken place in the military system.

To obtain troops, the Capets, who succeeded to the Carolingian dynasty, appealed both to their own vassals of the royal domain and to the feudatory lords of the crown and their vassals. But from both these sources they could only expect limited support. The fact was that the "benefice," which could be withdrawn and which implied an unconditional military obligation, had been replaced by the hereditary "fief," to which only an intermittent military obligation fixed at an average of forty days in the year was attached.

With men whose period of service is so short it is impossible to form a military force worthy of the name. This is why we see the armies of the period more and more composed of a new element—mercenary troops. From the twelfth century, whether among the king's knights, of more or less noble descent, or among his "sergeants" on foot or on horseback, or among the light-armed troops, cross-bowmen or archers, professional soldiers are numerous in the armies of the Capets.

Exaggerated importance has sometimes been attached to the part played in the king's army during this period, particularly under Philip Augustus, by the militia of the non-noble communes of the royal domain. These communes were required to rise in a mass and come to the king's help on proclamation of the levy of vassals and sub-vassals. But the king was not inclined to resort to this extreme measure, which might offer more drawbacks than advantages, and he declared himself satisfied on receiving from the communities contingents of men-at-arms recruited and equipped by them or, instead, the money required to raise and pay them.

It was by establishing little by little throughout the kingdom, as well as in the royal domain, the double principle, that military service was owing to the king and that exemption from it could be obtained for money, that the French kings succeeded in creating a standing army and a royal system of taxation at one and the same time.

One example of the application of this policy may be quoted. In 1302 a great need of troops arose from the rebellion in Flanders. And this is how Philip the Fair met it. He first called up for a period of four months all commoners possessing a stated minimum of wealth, either in goods or property. Next, at the close of 1303, in view of the next year's campaign, a fresh summons was issued, by which commoners of the domain and of the kingdom had to serve either in person or in the proportion of so many men per group of householders. This was appealed against, and the king moderated his demands, allowing, in particular, the townships and villages of the domain to pay for exemptions at the rate of two *sous* a day per man. These exemptions proved numerous and the money which they brought in was used for the enrolment, at half a *sou* a day per man, of infantry from Dauphiné and the South of France and of cross-bowmen from Italy. The army so constituted and numbering 60,000 infantry won the battle of Mons-en-Pévèle.

Speaking generally, recruiting in the thirteenth century and the first half of the fourteenth century continued on the same spasmodic lines as in the preceding period. Its evolution was slow and by sudden leaps. The system of pay and the command of troops underwent some changes. But to make it a reliable instrument of warfare the king's army still needed organisation by statute. This was to come, under the stress of necessity, in the Hundred Years' War.

In 1351 under John the Good, by an ordinance which determined the organisation of all troops, infantry were to be formed into *connétablies* of twenty-five to thirty men. Their equipment and pay were fixed. But much more important were the reforms brought about by Charles V.

They consisted first of all in permanently establishing in the king's army a preponderance of mercenary bands. The king scarcely made any further attempts to enroll men-at-arms individually. Rather, extending a practice which appeared as early as the thirteenth century, he relied on *routiers*, leaders of mercenary bands, for the hire of their troops to him. He had, indeed, no choice in the matter, for the state of war had become almost permanent since the middle of the fourteenth century and greatly increased the number of the mercenary companies, which were joined by all whom thoughts of battle and plunder attracted. This living force had to be looked for where it could be found. The system insured a permanent nucleus of troops, but it was not without drawbacks. For these adventurers grouped round their captains, and the captains themselves were with difficulty brought under discipline. Fraud, too, was common: there was always a danger that the captains, who were not over-scrupulous about such practices, were making false returns to the pay-masters, showing more troops than they possessed.

To combat this abuse, which would have been fatal to his finances, if allowed to spread, Charles V, like his predecessors, ordered returns (*montres*) to be as frequent and as exact as possible. But above all—and this was really his own and his counsellors' achievement—he did his best to get the army under better control and to make of it an organic whole with an order of battle, a fixed strength, cadres, and a graded staff.

Such was the object and such in great measure, after some preliminary failures, was the effect of the great ordinance of 1374. How then was the king's army organised at that period? The main strength of it rested on the mounted companies of men-at-arms and archers or cross-bowmen in the king's pay. Each company consisted of a hundred men. It was commanded by a captain who held an order from the king or his lieutenants and was responsible for keeping up the strength of his company. He had to show true returns and not to tolerate absence without leave.

Next came the infantry, which included contingents of militia furnished by the communes, whether of archers or cross-bowmen, and companies of *routiers*, professional soldiers, archers, cross-bowmen, or pikemen, who, in the main, were foreigners. In the fourteenth century Genoese cross-bowmen were held in high repute and much sought after.

The army might still include as accessory troops feudal contingents raised in the customary way. But these vestiges of past times were now rarely met with and are only mentioned to recall their existence.

Lastly, there were artillery serving the new guns already in use, as we shall see later; pioneers, sappers and miners for siege operations; and troops belonging to the base, particularly the pay-corps, which played so important a part in an army of mercenaries and which had been divided since 1366 into *trésorerie ordinaire des guerres* and *trésorerie extraordinaire des guerres* according to the permanent or temporary service of the troops which it paid.

The higher command was in the hands of the king's lieutenants, who were princes of the royal blood or great vassals, and of the Constable of France, under which title Du Guesclin held the supreme command. One step below these were the two marshals and the master of the cross-bowmen, and under them the captains with more or less wide powers.

This army strongly constituted by Charles V suffered seriously from the general disorganisation which marked the following reign. To restore it was one of Charles VII's chief tasks; a task which proved difficult and which could only be accomplished by stages in the intervals between campaigns.

In his first ordinance dated 1439 Charles VII tried to bring back into force the provisions of 1374, but in vain. In 1445, after the truce of 1444, a new ordinance followed and was better carried out.

The two characteristics of Charles VII's army were the companies known as *compagnies d'ordonnance* and the *francs-archers*.

The *compagnies d'ordonnance* were cavalry units of a nominal strength of a hundred "lances," each "lance" consisting of six men. There were twenty of these companies, forming a total of some ten thousand men. They were commanded by captains chosen by the king and subject to his dismissal. Garrison towns were assigned to them. Their pay was at the rate of 30 *livres tournois*[1] a month per "lance."

These companies were the pick of the army; they were sent into battle at the decisive moment. They were really the same as the companies of Charles V's organisation, reconstituted, re-inforced, and with more strongly marked characteristics of regularity and permanence.

The *francs-archers* were a more original institution, in a sense, but they were not as important as they were long thought to have been. They had come into existence spontaneously and in rudimentary form under Charles V. Companies of archers had been formed in the towns and in country districts. They met on Sundays for target practice. The nobles had looked askance on the movement and had succeeded in preventing it from spreading, at least in the country districts. Townships and villages kept their militia and continued in time of war to furnish the king with archers and cross-bowmen.

Charles VII set himself to make a fuller use of this spirit of competition and willing service. In 1448 he entrusted by ordinance the control of local forces to inspectors chosen on the spot. A fresh ordinance, dated 1451, replaced these inspectors by captains, each of whom was entrusted with a fixed territorial command, and laid down the conditions of pay and service for the free-archers (or cross-bowmen). One of these was to be supplied by every fifty households. He had to keep his arms and equipment in good order before him and hold himself in readiness to start at once when the call came. In the field he received pay from the king; in peace-time he was free (*franc*) from taxation, whence his name.

These free-archers were never more than an auxiliary force. There is only a distant and vague analogy between them and the national infantry of modern states. On the field of battle they played a scarcely more important part than that of the feudal contingents, which still continued to be raised at certain times

[1] Money struck at Tours was worth $\frac{1}{5}$ less than Paris money; thus a *livre parisis* was worth 25 *sous*, a *livre tournois* 20 *sous*.

in certain reigns. Charles VII's successor Louis XI added to their number and in 1469 reorganised them. The kingdom, as far as the free-archers were concerned, was divided into four main commands. Each command had to furnish 4000 infantry (pikemen, archers, cross-bowmen) and 500 pioneers. Orders were issued concerning the distribution and command of troops and their pay. But these reforms did not improve the quality of individual free-archers as soldiers, and they were only to a limited degree effective.

On the whole at the end of the fifteenth century the really strong elements in the king's army were the paid professional troops: the *compagnies d'ordonnance*, the foreign detachments of infantry, and the artillery. These constituted a powerful instrument of warfare soon to be put to the test in Italy.

After this rapid survey of the recruiting and organisation of the armies in general, a few remarks are necessary on arms and methods of warfare.

In the sixth century the Merovingian army was made up almost exclusively of infantry irregularly equipped. Some wore helmets and body-armour, but many others used the skins of animals for protection, as their Norse ancestors had done before them. They carried shields and fought hand to hand (missiles were as yet little used) with the sword or the *framée*, a kind of axe. In the seventh century the proportion of horsemen increased; missiles reappeared, and also the pike; the defensive armour of infantry improved.

The art of war had at that time fallen back into its infancy. Campaigns were mere plundering raids, in which bands of adventurers sometimes reached as far as Italy and the ancient Germanic realms. There were no lines of communication or supply. The raiders lived on the invaded country and left it only when they had exhausted its resources. They had few means of conducting a regular attack on a fortified place. An attempt would be made to storm it: if it failed, the attackers did not persist; they retired and went elsewhere. A battle was nothing but a series of single combats; the idea of manœuvre was for the time being abolished.

In the eighth and ninth centuries there are two salient points to notice. There was on the one hand an increase in the proportion of cavalry (it would be more correct to call it mounted infantry for it constantly fought on foot), a slow increase as yet under Charles Martel and Charlemagne, but a more rapid increase under their successors, particularly Charles the Bold, who in his capitulary, dated 864, perhaps out of a desire to possess a more mobile system of defence against the Norman raiders, aimed at a general use of mounted troops. On the other hand there was constant improvement in defensive armour: protection was afforded by means of leather and steel, steel helmets, coats of mail, and even, as early as Charlemagne's day, full armour.

In the course of the two succeeding centuries the familiar aspect of the feudal army, the army of the first crusade, became stereotyped. Cavalry had grown to be the main element, the infantry though still more numerous being subordinate to it. The unit of this army, and which was in a sense its portrait in miniature, was the feudal troop which issued forth from such and such a fief: at its head the lord, possessor of the fief, mounted and clad in armour from head to foot; beside him, similarly equipped and mounted, a few men-at-arms, and with them several foot-soldiers to help them in the fight and protect their horses against the enemy's infantry. In the open this feudal cavalry fought on horseback with sword and lance according to the now accepted practice; to take part in a siege they dismounted. Missiles, so long out of use, had returned to favour, with improvements: thus, when, in 1066, William the Conqueror's army embarked for England, it included a strong force of archers, a fair number of whom carried steel cross-bows.

In the twelfth century under Philip Augustus and his foe, Richard Coeur-de-Lion, a real efflorescence of military science took place. It was seen in fortification and siege warfare. "Poliorcetics," the engineer's art, had never quite fallen out of knowledge, even under the Merovingian kings, because the Roman system of fortifications had remained partially intact and had not ceased to be made use of. Progress was made once more in these arts in the course of the unceasing struggles between the feudal lords and of the frequent attack and defence of castles which these struggles involved. By the end of the twelfth century great skill both in constructing and in storming powerful fortifications had been acquired. It will be sufficient to recall among many instances the celebrated siege of Château-Gaillard. It was during the attack on this formidable castle of Richard Coeur-de-Lion, which overlooks the Seine on the heights above Les Andelys, that the engineers and sappers of the king's army so much distinguished themselves, particularly in their use of war material, which from that time onward became an important item, both in bulk and variety.

During the same period however a want of knowledge continued to be shown in the conduct of operations in the open. Let the famous battle of Bouvines be taken as an example. On July 27, 1214, Philip Augustus's army, which had been encamped south of Tournai, marched on Lille in three "battles"—advance-guard, main body, rear-guard—each composed of cavalry and infantry and advancing in column. It was beginning to cross the River Deule at Bouvines bridge, when the Emperor Otho's army appeared in its rear. The French army turned about and deployed and the engagement began. There was confusion, however, and no attempt at keeping together; successive mêlées of cavalry, a series of single combats, were all that took place. The infantry played a secondary part. The communal militia of Philip Augustus's army were broken by the German and English cavalry. These were, however, routed in turn by the French cavalry, which went on to destroy by repeated charges the Comte de Boulogne's infantry, who were drawn up in squares.

In point of weapons there was little difference between the armies of Philip Augustus and St Louis. In both the cavalry bore knightly arms and equipment: the large *hauberk* of mail with its hood, the conical head-piece known as a helm (*heaume*), the sword, lance, and oblong shield (*écu*). The infantry had a light *hauberk*, an iron or leather hat, a pike or a mace, or else used missiles. The use of the steel cross-bow, which shot a bolt (*carreau*) more formidable than an arrow, became more and more widely spread. In the army which landed at Damietta in 1248, out of a total of 50,000, 5000 were cross-bowmen. The army of the Comte d'Artois, which was defeated at Courtrai in 1302, and which also numbered some fifty thousand men, placed in the field 10,000 French or foreign cross-bowmen.

At the beginning of the fourteenth century the discovery was made which was to revolutionise the equipment and operations of troops, that of gunpowder. It was first used in 1324 in Lorraine, Spain, and Italy. France was slower to become convinced of the importance of the discovery, but she afterwards made up for lost time. From the outbreak of the Hundred Years' War, about 1335–1340, artillery using gunpowder was in current use in the French king's army.

At first the new artillery was not differentiated from the old, because the use of gunpowder was only at the experimental stage, whereas catapults were the familiar arm. This, however, did not retard the development of the new arm. Even before Charles V, under John the Good, the king's artillery included a large variety of bronze cannon. Progress continued throughout the following century. At the end of the Hundred Years' War the king's artillery possessed abundant war material, parks, magazines, and a well-trained *personnel*, and had become a force to be reckoned with. In the last battles fought against the English, at Formigny and at Castillon, its share in the success was large.

Besides the artillery proper, in order that the fullest results might be obtained from gunpowder a one-man portable fire-arm had still to be invented. And towards the end of the fifteenth century it was invented in the form of the arquebus (*hacquebute*, later *arquebuse*), which replaced the hand-culverin (*coulevrine*) requiring two men. The arquebus was eventually to turn into the musket. It was not until 1470 that soldiers bearing portable fire-arms left the artillery park to take up their stand in the ranks of the infantry.

At the close of the Middle Ages, the king's army showed many survivals of the past in its composition, its arms, and its tactics, along with germs of far-reaching changes in the future. The fifteenth century foot-soldier with his light helmet (*salade*), his coat of leather, cloth, and metal (*jacque* or *brigandine*), and his cross-bow and firing-rest, was very much like the infantryman of the fourteenth or even the thirteenth centuries. And still more like his forerunners was the horseman of the *compagnies d'ordonnance* with his heavy armour. As for the battle, it had scarcely changed in type during the whole course of the Hundred Years' War. But the use of gunpowder had already and once for all introduced that new element of fire-power which was to be the characteristic of modern warfare.

## BIBLIOGRAPHY

Boutaric, *Institutions militaires de la France avant les armées permanentes*, 1863. Fieffé, *Histoire des troupes étrangères au service de la France*, 2 vols., 1854. L. Dussieux, *L'armée en France, Histoire et organisation depuis les temps les plus reculés jusqu'à nos jours*, 3 vols., 1884. Prenzel, *Beiträge zur Geschichte der Kriegsverfassung unter den Karolingern*, 1887. G. Koehler, *Die Entwickelung des Kriegswesens und der Kriegsführung in der Ritterzeit*, 2 vols., 1886–1890. Lt.-Col. Belhomme, *Histoire de l'infanterie en France*, vol. I., 1893. Ch.-V. Langlois, *Le service militaire en vertu de l'obligation féodale*, and *Le service militaire soldé*, in *L'armée à travers les âges*, 1st series, 1899.

The chapters on the army in *Histoire de France*, ed. E. Lavisse, vols. II—IV.

# CHAPTER IV

## THE NAVY

In a country which is bounded by the sea on the north, west, and south-east the navy has come under numerous foreign influences, which have left their mark on the language. One may even ask oneself whether the French race did not accustom itself to sea-faring as a result of the Greek, Roman, Breton, and Scandinavian invasions, which successively burst on her shores. There is nothing so symbolical in this respect as the marriage of the daughter of a Ligurian chief to the captain of a Phocaean galley, to which fact Marseilles owes its origin, six centuries before our era. The Phocaeans, who came from Asia, introduced us to maritime commerce, and strove with other Asiatics, established at Carthage, for the conquest of the markets of the ancient world. If Euthymenes of Marseilles was less bold than the Carthaginian Hanno, and did not in Africa pass beyond the Senegalese river of crocodiles and hippopotami, his compatriot Pytheas outsailed Himilco in the exploration of the northern seas, and pushed on to the Shetland Isles and the Arctic Ocean, where navigation is checked by the icebergs or "lungs of the sea."

### § I. THE GALLO-ROMAN NAVY

The Punic Wars gave Marseilles an opportunity for satisfying her instinct of rivalry against Carthage. As soon as Rome had become a maritime power, and when the naval victories of Duilius in Sicily and of Cornelius Scipio at the mouth of the Ebro in 260 and 218 B.C. had destroyed the supremacy of the Punic fleets, Marseilles threw in her lot with the victors. She became then a base for naval operations and the point of departure for their infiltration into Gaul; *Aquae Sextiae* (Aix), the first Roman colony, dates from 123 B.C.

But when Caesar wished to subjugate the Phocaean city in 49 B.C., the fleet of Marseilles engaged battle with Decius Brutus, prefect of the Roman fleet; the naval battles of the Ile du Levant and of Tauroentum were defeats which cost Marseilles her ships, her treasures, her arms, and her engines of war; and she was subjected to the supervision of a naval station, which was created by Julius Caesar at *Forum Julii* (Fréjus). Seven years before, Brutus had crushed the fleet of the Veneti off the Breton coast, after a terrible struggle which had lasted a whole day. The Gallic fleet having been thus destroyed, Caesar embarked five legions, half of his cavalry, and 4000 Gallic horsemen on the Liane, at a point where the coasts of Gaul bend towards the north. One evening, when the wind had ceased blowing from the north, Caesar left PORTUS ITIUS. On the morrow, 54 B.C., he disembarked in Great Britain. In vain did the kings of Cantium (Kent) attack his *Castrum navale* in order to destroy the ships drawn up on the shore under the shelter of an entrenchment. They were repulsed and forced to pay tribute.

To secure the defence of the British channel, the Romans organised a naval station near Portus Itius. At the foot of the Gallic *oppidum Gesoriacum*, the name of which was changed to *Bononia Oceanensis* (Boulogne-sur-Mer), was stationed the *classis Britannica*, which was formed after the model of the Pretorian fleets of Misenum and Ravenna. Caligula, who honoured it with a visit in the year 40 A.D., ordered the construction of a lighthouse of vast proportions, the twelve stories of which were each smaller than the one below, and which held a light at the height of two hundred feet. The *Tour d'Ordre* (*Turris ardens*) or *Old Man* did not fall until 1644. Natives of all the provinces of the Empire, Africans, Asiatics, Dalmatians, Pannonians, the sailors of the triremes of Boulogne swarmed on both sides of the British channel, with their brickwork stamped CL. BR. and their *ex votos* to Aesculapius, Neptune, and Apollo. For the prefecture of Boulogne had posts on the other side of the strait, for instance at Dover, where there still exists a fragment of a Roman lighthouse. This fragment, the Bredenstone, serves as a seat for the Lord Warden of the Cinque Ports at the ceremony of his investiture. In the 5th century the Boulogne fleet disappeared. The invasion of the Franks was beginning.

## § II. THE VIKINGS

The great movement of monarchical centralisation which took place in the Scandinavian countries during the 9th century caused the exodus of many liberty-loving warriors. Bearing with them from the paternal house the pillars with the heads of Thor or Odin, which had adorned the household seat, they flaunted these sacred emblems of home in the sight of new countries; and, whithersoever fate carried them, they threw an axe ashore to mark their seizure of the land. This proceeding was unobjectionable in the half-deserted countries of Iceland, Greenland, and perhaps of American Vinland. But it was not so in Western Europe.

The people fled at the sight of their long-ships, with heightened prows, whence grinned the head of a dragon or a serpent (for which reason they were called *drakkar* or *snekkar*), 22·76 metres long, by 5 metres wide, and 1·75 in depth—these are the dimensions of a long-ship, dug up near Christiania, in which there still reposed the body of a viking, in the carved seat whence he directed the working of the ship. The dragons came safely up the rivers; in 841 they appeared before Rouen, in 843 before Nantes, in 887 before Paris. The capital barred the passage of the river to their seven hundred boats by two fortified bridges. She repulsed the scaling-ladders and fireships directed against the bridges; a siege of ten months heroically borne wearied the assailants, whose withdrawal was purchased by Charles the Fat. One of these vikings, Rollo the Dane, established himself so firmly at Rouen that Charles the Simple preferred to come to terms with him, and, by the treaty of Saint-Clair-sur-Epte, in 912, ceded Neustria, which became Normandy. The vikings took wives there.

Once again the law which governs conquests, the reaction of the conquered civilised race over the victorious army of barbarians, fulfilled itself. The children of the Northmen and the Neustrian women learned their mother's tongue, with only one exception: the terms unfamiliar to women, the Scandinavian sea-terms, persisted. They have remained up to our day, not many having fallen out of use. Thus the terminology of our ocean-going seamen is the last vestige of a vanished language, the language of the runes on the lions of the Piraeus, and towards the North, on the rocks of Greenland, the language of the Icelandic sagas, wherein we find the origin and the primitive meaning of our commonest sea-terms: *quille* or keel ("Kjöll," backbone), *tribord* or starboard ("styri-bord"), *haubans* or shrouds ("hofud-band," neck-band), *lof* or luff, *ralingue* or rope, *tillac* or deck, *girouette* or weather-cock ("vedr-viti," indication of weather), *étambrai* or framework, a round hole in the deck, through which the mast passes ("tappr," cork), etc., etc.

The Norman dukes kept up a strong liking for the navy. One of them was proud of the name of "duke of pirates"; and Duke William, having in 1066 put forward a claim to the throne of England, a crowd of great lords, bishops, and abbots of Normandy promised him ships, one twenty, another sixty, a third a hundred. On the 27th of September the flotilla appeared at the mouth of the Somme, as soon as the gilded weathercock placed at the top of the ducal mast had pointed its arrow towards the north. Some days later (October 14), the victory at Hastings made William the Conqueror King of England.

On the same date, the sons of a small noble of the Cotentin, Robert Guiscard and Roger, being summoned to fight the Arabs of Magna Graecia and Sicily, formed the vaguely-defined states of which there were so many in Southern Italy into the Kingdom of the Two Sicilies. The naval victory at Corfu in 1084 consolidated it. This was one of the first regular battles of the Middle Ages; Robert Guiscard had known how to avail himself of the tactical science of the Greco-Venetians, and his four squadrons of five ships each, supported by light vessels, were successful against the heavy Byzantine craft.

## § III. INFLUENCE OF BYZANTINE CIVILIZATION

Now, the Byzantine navy was the only regular war-navy which existed at that time. Western emperors and Carolingian kings were so little anxious about the defence of the seas that they applied to the neo-Greek navy for the protection of their coasts against the Saracen invasions: "Thy master has no ships," said Nicephorus Phocas to one of their ambassadors; "but as for me, I am powerful on the sea; let him say a word, and my fleet will force all his rebel ports to return to their obedience."

It was thus that in the 9th and 10th centuries dromonds, carabs, and flat boats (chargers, crabs, and tortoises), from Byzantium, lighted at sea by "catships," made their way to our Provençal coasts, where the nautical vocabulary—*estoire* (from στόλος, fleet), *eschar* (from σχάριον, stocks), *issartia* (from ἐξαρτήσις, rigging) etc. long betrayed the neo-Greek influence. But we retained the words without penetrating the spirit of Byzantine strategy; the swift dromonds, whence a battery of siphons poured forth Greek fire in flaming torrents, became in our hands heavy ships, robbed of the terrible weapon, of which we had not discovered the secret, and which Ives de Chartres thought to be made of resin and grease.

## § IV. THE TRANSPORTS OF MARSEILLES AT THE TIME OF THE CRUSADES

The ships were sometimes of quite high tonnage. As permits of travel between the Latin cities and the infidel country were limited by Papal bulls to one or two vessels, those interested gave the *absolved ships* such vast proportions that the statutes of Marseilles forbade more than fifteen hundred pilgrims being embarked in any one ship. What admirable maritime legislation we find in the statutes promulgated between 1253 and 1255 by the great Provençal city! All possible guarantees for security were assured to the pilgrims and the crusaders—but not comfort. And how could a passenger demand comfort, when, thanks to the competition between Marseilles and Genoa, the price of a voyage to the Holy Land had fallen to sixty sous for the first class, forty for the second, thirty-five for the third and twenty-five for the fourth! The first-class passengers enjoyed the airy deck-cabins, the second class those between decks, the third had the right to the stuffiness of the lowest deck, and the fourth to the stench of the stables. Each pilgrim received a numbered ticket, after previous inscription of his name and that of his backer in a register, which was kept in duplicate, one copy being preserved in the communal archives. Three *inspectors* were appointed for the Palestine convoys, and watched to see that the regulations were strictly enforced; experts, foot-rule in hand, calculated the number of places available on board, and took care that the scale of charges, marked by three tags painted white, should not be exceeded by any covetous captain. *Sea-consuls*, chosen by the municipalities of Marseilles, Aigues-Mortes, and Montpellier, were embarked as judges to arbitrate in disputes and to provide for emergencies which might arise. Finally, in the sea-ports of the Levant, the passenger found help and comfort with the resident *consul*, which each of the great Mediterranean ports employed there; the Levantine *fondachi* were private companies occupying a special quarter, in which the customs of the home city were maintained.

## § V. THE FIRST NAVAL WAR IN THE MEDITERRANEAN

The kingdom had still neither navy nor port—Marseilles belonged to the Counts of Provence—when the crusades of St Louis brought him face to face with this unpleasant fact. So he provided himself with a fortified port. In the solitude of unhealthy marshes, Aigues-Mortes, a declining city, doomed to a lingering death, sheltered the great ships which were bought as transports by the saintly king; his transport was the *Paradise* when he died on crusade.

His son, Philip the Bold, when throwing himself into the adventure of the war with Aragon, imperiously felt the urgent necessity of a war fleet. He collected a hundred galleys, from Pisa to Narbonne. But experience was to teach him that, even if vessels can be collected, strategy and admirals cannot be improvised. The twenty-five galleys of Guillaume de Lodève, surprised in the port of Rosas by eleven Catalan galleys, tried to surround their adversaries. But the unfortunate French soldiers under a rain of steel which swept their decks, fell stricken by the terrible arrows of the Catalan crossbowmen; artillery had triumphed over side-arms. Some weeks later, on the night of September 9, 1285, the French fleet received its death-blow. As it was proceeding in column of sail, with masked fires, between the two islets which have been named the Ants, "Las Hormigas," on account of their narrowness, the redoubtable Aragonese admiral, Roger di Loria, appeared out of the shadows, and falling on the fleet, sank the galleys by ramming them. A second squadron had turned the French flank. No resistance was possible. The great Neapolitan admiral, Henri de Mari, who was in command, turned tail and succeeded in escaping from the scene of slaughter by imitating Loria's signals. Deprived of food, the army was obliged to retreat and recrossed the Pyrenees behind the litter of a dying king.

## § VI. FROM THE CONQUEST OF NORMANDY TO THE CONTINENTAL BLOCKADE

Surrounded on three sides by powerful vassals, the Capet kings had no sure hold on the sea, except in Picardy. The Duke of Normandy was by conquest King of England and had by marriage acquired Guienne, Saintonge, and Poitou. To relieve the pressure, Philip Augustus allied himself with the Bretons, who also felt the weight of it. John Lackland had seized the English crown to the detriment of his nephew, Arthur of Brittany, whom he had stabbed to death. Attacked in front by the French troops, and from the rear by the Bretons, in three years, 1202–1204, he lost Normandy and Poitou. He was in danger too of losing England: seventeen hundred ships under the command of Philip Augustus were to cross the Channel, when on May 31, 1213, they were surrounded in the port of Dam and destroyed by fire; this surprise was executed by the English sailors, under the command of William of Salisbury and Renaud of Boulogne. "The French know little of naval methods," sadly concluded Philip Augustus.

Nevertheless his son Louis disembarked in the Thames. A sailor who had joined his party after having in the first place followed the fortunes of John, Eustace the Monk, whose exploits have been told in an epic, had robbed the English of the mastery of the seas. But the naval battle near Sandwich, where he met with his death on August 24, 1217, was the salvation of England. A fortnight later, Louis, being cut off from communication with France, signed peace, and abandoned all pretensions to conquest; he even renounced the Anglo-Norman Islands, which Eustace the Monk had occupied in the days when he was still in the service of John.

A latent cause for war existed between the two countries, because England still kept a foothold in Guienne. In the reign of Philip the Fair relations became so strained that he hastily provided himself with a fleet-of-war in the Western Ocean. Everything had to be found, in 1294, material and tactics, personnel and arsenals. All Europe was put under contribution: the Hanseatic towns and the Basques sent ships; Norway promised three hundred vessels; a squadron came from Provence, and from Genoa came ship-builders, who organised the arsenal at Rouen, the *clos des Galées* or enclosure of galleys. An army corps was ready in the camp at Boulogne, but the Dukes of Harcourt and Montmorency were novices at sea. Summoned from Genoa, the great leader of the Byzantine fleets, Benedetto Zaccaria, did not arrive until later. For want of an admiral the campaign failed.

Together with the plan of invasion, another plan was elaborated. Abandon force; bring cunning into prominence; for Napoleonic victories substitute victorious treaties; and you can compare Philip the Fair with Napoleon. To these two rulers, so different in genius, the same anxiety, the same deficiency in naval command, inspired the same policy—the *Continental Blockade*. The ports of Europe from Gibraltar to the polar sea, from the Sicilian coast to the end of the Baltic, were closed to England. But in 1296 the river arteries of the Rhine and the Gironde remained open to British trade, in spite of the cruises of Admiral Othon de Coucy, and thereby England was saved.

## § VII. THE HUNDRED YEARS' WAR

The continental blockade was the prelude of the hand-to-hand struggle which France and England were to wage with each other for a Hundred Years. The death of Philip the Fair without male heirs brought into conflict his grand-nephew and his cousin, Edward III of England and Philip of Valois, who both claimed the crown of France. Philip replied to the pretensions of the English king by mobilising the Norman fleet, by the *Journée des Normands*, thinking to repeat the exploit of William the Conqueror. But he had made the mistake of dismissing two squadrons of Levantine galleys, one of Genoese Ghibellines, the other of Guelfs from Monaco, who in 1338 had given him the mastery of the Channel. His fleet now only consisted of two hundred heavy ships, encircled by the royal barges, which a plan of action had arranged in three divisions, the vanguard being given to men from the Seine, the main body to the men of Dieppe, and the rear-guard to the men from Lower Normandy.

In a narrow bay, the point of which then extended as far as Bruges, but which the polders have filled up, twenty-five thousand men were about to start for England when Edward III himself shattered their attack. He drove them into a corner in the impasse of Dam and Écluse (now Sluys) where the admiral Quiéret had anchored, in spite of the sinister lesson formerly given to Philip Augustus, and in spite of the wise counsels of the Genoese Barbavera, who wished to fight at sea. Surrounded by the English fleet, taken in the rear by Flemish pillagers, crushed by the fire of twelve thousand archers to which only four hundred crossbowmen could reply, the French sailors were pressed against great dykes, such as Dante describes in his *Inferno*. In a hopeless attempt to make their way out, they made an onset on a large hull with its mast topped by a crown, whence floated a standard quartered with the arms of France and England. But a crowd of knights made a rampart of their bodies before Edward III; the action was definitely lost and had a decisive result. The loss of a hundred and ninety ships and twenty thousand men left the French disarmed, and the tide of invasion turned.

The remains of the fleet could only delay this result by a final sacrifice. If the siege of Calais has rendered famous the name of Eustace of Saint-Pierre, it is only fair that with his memory should be associated that of the sailors, who at the risk of their lives ran the blockade and revictualled the town for a year: such men as Enguerrand Ringois of Abbeville, who captured later and summoned to swear allegiance to Edward III, replied, "Never," and was thrown into the sea.

"The fleet should be proportionate to the necessities of the city." This principle, formulated in the *Politics* of Aristotle, which had just been translated by Nicholas Oresme, counsellor of Charles the Wise, ruled the conduct of that king. Fifty barges and galleys, which had been built in the *clos des Galées* at Rouen, gave the command of the Channel to the admiral, Jean de Vienne, and by repeated diversions in 1378, 1380, and 1385, caused anxiety on the other side of the Channel, paralysed the despatch of reinforcements and thereby greatly helped the operations of the High Constables Du Guesclin and Clisson on the Continent.

Charles VI wished to improve upon his father. But the *Great Army of the Sea,* assembled in 1386 at the very place where we had suffered the two disasters of Sluys, was never able to threaten England. The stormy season was enough to break it up. The King's madness allowed everything to drift.

The only ray of glory which shone on the French navy came to it from a marshal of France. Marshal Boucicaut, Governor of the town of Genoa, which had given itself to us, felt himself bound by the interests of the people under his administration. He brought help to Constantinople, where the Genoese had an important colony, raised the blockade of their settlement at Famagusta, sacked the Mussulman port of Beyrout, and on October 7, 1403, engaged the Venetians in the naval battle of Modon. In spite of the epidemic of influenza, which weakened his crews, he carried off the victory.

In the Channel, the kingdom no longer had a fleet: the *clos des Galées* was disused. France was ripe for invasion. The awakening was terrible. It came at Agincourt. In haste, the admiral, Guillaume de Narbonne, summoned several Genoese carracks from the Mediterranean, where a campaign had been carried on. With eight of these he attempted to bar the entrance of the Seine to three hundred ships full of troops on August 15, 1416. Half of his squadron perished: the last four carracks "got away with honour," a truly French sentiment; honour was saved, but the cause was lost, and Normandy again became English. And English it was to remain, until an outburst of patriotism, aided by Joan of Arc, freed the country. In 1453 there remained to the English only one place in France—Calais.

## § VIII. THE CANARIES AND "THE GREEN ISLAND"

The Hundred Years' War had not destroyed the initiative of our seamen. In the way of discoveries they had out-distanced most nations. If one can believe a 17th century traveller (Villaut de Bellefonds), they had placed settlements ("Petit-Dieppe and Petit-Paris") on the Ivory Coast and the Gold Coast about 1364. The authenticity of these expeditions from Dieppe has caused violent discussion, and so far no positive proof has been found; the *Briev estoire del navigaige Monsire*

*Jehan Prunaut au reaume de la Guinoye*, which was produced as a reference, is an imitation or a forgery.

On quite another footing, and a sure one, stands the narrative of expeditions to the Canary Islands, which the Middle Ages had endowed with the charming name of the Fortunate Isles. The Pope had conferred the investiture of them on the Admiral of France on November 15, 1344, when he bestowed on him the title of *Prince de la Fortune*. It was some years since the Genoese, Lanzarotto Maloisel, had undertaken their conquest, without leaving any other trace but his Christian name, which is still borne by one of the islands. Admiral Louis d'Espagne, Prince de La Fortune, did not become "King of the Canaries." On the way he abandoned his enterprise, which was again undertaken in 1402 by an unassuming chamberlain of the Duke of Orleans, Jean de Béthencourt. Supported by Gadifer de La Salle, seneschal of Bigorre, he occupied four islands of the archipelago, but failed in his attempts on the Guanchos of Grand Canary. He colonised the green plains of Ferro Island with peasants from the Caux district, while workmen and craftsmen collected, under the guidance of two priests and two sergeants of the people, round Santa Maria de Bethencuria at Fuerteventura, and near the cathedral of Rubicon on Lanzarote. At the bottom of a great ravine, in a circle of mountains, Santa Maria de Bethencuria is still standing. But since June 30, 1454, when Spain turned out the heirs of the Norman knight, the archipelago has been held by the Catholic King. The epic, which was chronicled by the chaplains of the expedition, was for ever closed. *Le Canarien*, who told it, has been forgotten.

A curious belief was the cause of our visits to another archipelago. In a record of the year 1483, we read that the captain of the royal ships was sent in haste "to the Green Island and Country of Barbary to cure any thing which closely concerned the welfare and health" of the king. Saint-Jacques, otherwise called Cape Verd Island, enjoyed a unique reputation; leprosy was cured there by bathing in the blood of great turtles; it was whispered that Louis XI actually believed himself to be suffering from leprosy. But no weight would attach to these rumours, reported only by one chronicler, Thomas Basin, were they not confirmed by the mysterious expedition to the Green

Island, whereby a light is thrown on the atrabiliary disposition of the lord of Plessis-les-Tours. For leprosy was a living death.

## § IX. PROTECTION BY FORCE OF ARMS UNDER LOUIS XI

Louis XI presents a curious figure. "One would say that he had been brought up in Italy," was said of him by foreigners, and Machiavelli would have found in him a model. The Hundred Years' War left us face to face with distressing economic problems; it had removed the commercial axis of Europe from the Rhône and the Seine towards the Rhine. In order to correct this and to bring back to the fairs of Beaucaire the trade of the Levant, which showed a tendency to become diverted to the States of the Duke of Savoy, the royal silversmith, Jacques Cœur, had, in 1442, obtained from the States of Languedoc bounties in aid of navigation, "the navigation of galleys being the principal source of the substance and nourishment of the country." And he received half-a-dozen galeasses to carry on trade with the Levant and the Barbary ports.

Louis XI, even bolder than the silversmith, contemplated becoming in the West the broker of the Levant. And his little fleet of warships had the task of preparing the way by expelling our competitors. In the rare leisure left to them by the wars of Louis XI against the English, the Bretons, and the Aragonese, Vice-Admiral Guillaume de Casenove, called Coulon, and Captain George Palaeologue de Bissipat, descendant of the emperors of Constantinople, practised protection by force of arms. They denied the Hanseatic traders access to the Straits of Dover, kept the Venetians out of the Straits of Gibraltar, and fought with the Flemings and even with the Genoese, whom they crushed on August 13, 1476, in the naval battle at Cape St Vincent.

But the King reckoned without the nation. First of all with the help of the Genoese, later with the assistance of his "good towns" only, he hoped to form a *Compagnie Générale de navigation dans le Levant*, with a capital of 100,000 livres; by giving it a monopoly he would have realised immense profits. But the delegates of the "good towns" of France, assembled at Tours in 1482, did not agree to the King's wishes. They refused to subscribe and made havoc of his plans. In answer to the royal prohibitions the nation upheld the contrary view, the reciprocity of treatment for "all foreign nations." On the morrow of the Hundred Years' War the first war between Protection and Free-trade took place. And Protection emerged from the struggle vanquished.

## BIBLIOGRAPHY

Ch. de La Roncière, *Histoire de la marine française*. 2nd edition. 5 vols. 1906–1920. Vol. I, *Les Origines*. Vol. II, *La Guerre de Cent ans; Révolution maritime*. A. Jal, *Archéologie navale*. 2 vols. 1839. V.-J. Vaillant, *Classis britannica...* Arras, 1888. J. Steenstrup, *Études préliminaires pour servir à l'histoire des Normands et de leurs invasions* in *Bulletin de la Société des Antiquaires de Normandie*, X (1882), p. 187. E. Duprat, *Les relations de la Provence et du Levant du Ve siècle aux Croisades* in *Congrès français de Syrie* (1919), fasc. II. Z. Pardessus, *Collection des lois maritimes antérieures au XVIIIe siècle*, 1828–1847, IV, 299. *Pacta nautarum* (1248), ed. A. Jal, in the *Collection des Doc. inéd. sur l'hist. de France, Doc. historiques*, I, 609. *Roman d'Eustache le Moine, pirate fameux du XIIIe siècle*, ed. Fr. Michel for the Société de l'histoire de France. 1834. N. Harris Nicolas, *A History of the Royal Navy*. 2 vols. 1847. Marquis Terrier de Loray, *Jean de Vienne, amiral de France* (1341–1396). 1877. Delaville le Roulx, *La France en Orient au XIVe siècle*. 1886. *Le Canarien: livre de la conquête et conversion des Canaries* (1402–1422), ed. G. Gravier, Rouen, 1874; ed. P. Margry, 1896.

# CHAPTER V

## INDUSTRY AND COMMERCE

FRANCE, properly so called, did not, in the Middle Ages, play so important a part in industry and especially in trade as did the great Italian Maritime Republics. Nevertheless, during several centuries, she occupied a place of the first rank in the business world (as it is nowadays called), of which she was only to be robbed by the misfortunes of the Hundred Years' War. This justifies the inclusion in this volume of a special chapter on the subject.

### § I. INDUSTRY AND COMMERCE BEFORE THE 11TH CENTURY

Even in the Ancient World Gaul took an active part in world-commerce. Thanks to an excellent system of roads, which linked up one part to another, thanks also to the Mediterranean ports, she attracted not only the Western traders, who came more especially to seek the agricultural products of her fertile soil, but also those from the Eastern parts of the Roman Empire, who brought thither the spices, medicinal plants, silks, and precious stones of Asia.

But the centre of the world's gravity was then in the Eastern Mediterranean, and the Barbarian invasions occurred before Gaul was able to consolidate the economic position to which she seemed entitled by her long and hospitable sea-front.

The invasions entailed, if not ruin, at least a general retrenchment of economic life; the difficulty and insecurity of communications, joined to the instability of social conditions, tended to limit productive effort to local requirements. Property became concentrated in the hands of a few large proprietors, and each large estate organised itself with a view to self-support. The owner planned the production on his land of all that was necessary for the normal feeding of those who lived there, and he collected round his house the various trades which were indispensable for the construction and preservation of buildings, of furniture, of tools, and of work for his clothing and that of his staff, etc. With the exception of the oriental products which were still being disembarked in the Mediterranean ports by the merchants of Syria or the real Byzantine countries, commerce ordinarily consisted in no more than simple transport of raw materials, and of those manufactured articles which were locally unobtainable.

The formation of the Carolingian Empire, through the whole extent of which Charlemagne succeeded in assuring the rule of the "Frankish Peace," enabled the inhabitants of Gaul during that time slightly to enlarge the limits of economic life and to play once more an active part in the commerce of the world —forming and reforming direct commercial links with distant lands. But the decay of Carolingian rule and the incursions of freebooters of all races, which were among the most unfortunate consequences of this decay, abruptly arrested this attempt. From the middle of the 9th century onwards, the seas were infested with pirates, Scandinavians in the north and west, Saracens in the Mediterranean; while the highways of France and the neighbouring countries were molested by bands of Hungarians, Slavs or Danes. From the economic point of view it was a period of retrogression, comparable only to the days of the great invasions.

## § II. THE ECONOMIC REVIVAL OF THE FEUDAL AGE

It was only in the course of the 11th and especially of the 12th century, that the industrial and commercial world re-established itself in France, after the havoc and plunder of all kinds committed in the first days of the feudal period. There came, as it were, an influx of new blood, an immense desire for improved conditions, and also, it seems, an increased birth-rate, which rendered available a large number of workers and also created new requirements. This was a period when much forest-land was cleared and many marshes were drained, resulting in the rapid improvement of the conditions of workers and of the tools at their disposal.

What has been stated about cultivation is equally true of industry. There was at that time in every direction of human activity a wish to increase production, to augment the yield of the workshops as well as of the fields, which is explained by the return of a period of relative peace, bringing with it a noticeable improvement in communication by sea, river, or land. Without running undue risks, a neighbouring country might supply from its surplus any deficiency caused by an insufficient production in certain materials. Consequently, specialisation, which is the primary condition of commerce on a large scale, could be boldly undertaken.

Considered as a whole, France, which is primarily a rural and specially an agricultural country, specialised in agricultural products. Certain districts, such as those bordering on the basin of the Seine, such as La Beauce, or La Brie, increased their yield of cereals, and could thus become exporters of grain, without, however, being able to rival countries such as Sicily, Apulia, or Campania, which had become perfect granaries in the times of the Hohenstauffens. A great part of the western, south-western, and southern districts, particularly Gascony, Saintonge, Poitou, Anjou, Languedoc, and, in the east, the region of Burgundy, devoted themselves to the culture of the vine, which tended to drive out some of the other kinds of agricultural industry, so much so that after the 14th century, in Gascony, the late arrival of a wheat supply almost reduced the countryside to famine.

Wines and grain thus became products available for trade in ever-increasing quantities, subject to various circumstances and to local conditions, such as those in the two instances quoted above.

However, some districts of France were able to turn to industrial specialisation, thanks to the new facilities for food-supply which were available. This was the case with nearly all the northern zone, which even now remains pre-eminently the French industrial district, along with its natural adjunct, Belgian Flanders, which was at that time part of the kingdom of France. This region was then, and to a great extent still is, the country of the manufacture of woollens. There was woven the wool of the sheep raised either in the Flemish regions, or on the dry and chalky soil of Artois and Champagne, or even of those imported from the wide English pastures. The latter were soon beyond competition, for England had more and more specialised in the breeding of sheep after the 13th century, thus sacrificing to the assured profits of the sale of their fleeces the uncertain profits and low returns of comparatively poor agricultural production. All the large French towns of the north and some of those of the north-east were what was then called "woollen" towns, e.g. Arras, Douai, Lille, Saint-Omer, Cambrai, Valenciennes, Abbeville, Amiens, Beauvais, Saint-Quentin, Reims, Châlons, and (in Belgium of the present day) Ghent, Bruges, Ypres, and Tournai. In all this district the weaving-looms were always increasing in number, and throwing on the markets an ever-growing stock of merchandise, the quality of which was soon appreciated throughout the world.

Moreover, this was not the only part of France where cloth-trade was carried on. Near the poor and dry land of the Crau, of Quercy, of Corbières, or of Les Causses, where sheep-breeding is still specialised, weaving-looms became more and more numerous; at Avignon, at Figeac, at Villefranche d'Aveyron, at Rodez, at Castres, at Carcassonne, at Limoux, and at Montpellier, famous for its beautiful crimson cloth, which was dyed by the use of the *kermès* or cochineal, found in the country round. Weaving was also carried on in Normandy, especially about Rouen, and in Berry, where also the country is suitable for rearing sheep.

## § III. CONDITIONS OF INDUSTRIAL WORK AND THE CORPORATE ORGANISATION UP TO THE MIDDLE OF THE 13TH CENTURY

While many districts thus struck out their own line independently of their neighbours as regards production, work became organised within new limits and according to new methods.

The important fact was the creation of a real industrial class, which stood in opposition both to the agricultural and to the noble class.

Before the 10th or 11th century, one cannot, as a matter of fact, discern an industrial class. Industrial work was done partly, as we have already seen, on the estate of the overlord, either by the labour of serfs, or by paid employees, who produced the essentials of life for him and his retinue in his own workshops; very few things being bought from neighbouring estates. Besides this, in some places the proprietor had granted the right of cultivation to some small tenant, who added some little domestic industry to his land-culture; one, for instance, growing flax on part of his land, or raising a few sheep, and working with his wife and daughters at spinning and weaving, sometimes in sufficient quantity to be able to sell a few ells of cloth or linen each year.

But as time went on, it was evident that these artisan-tenants were becoming multiplied and that the seigniorial workshops were losing their importance. This can easily be understood: it was, indeed, much simpler and also more economical for a lord of lesser importance to obtain woollen materials from some of his tenants, who would do the work for him by way of rent or would sell him what he required.

Thus in the 10th and 11th centuries a body of artisans began to separate itself more and more from ordinary tenants, especially near the great monasteries and important churches: they collected "under the monastery," as the old texts say, forming a new class of tenants, who worked with their hands, but who left off more and more completely their work in the fields for combined labour in the workshop, and whose holding henceforward was only the house (*mansio*) which they occupied, and sometimes a little garden and the court (*curtis*) which belonged to it. An urban population thus sprang up, forming large industrial *bourgs* or *faubourgs*.

In these *bourgs* and *faubourgs*, and often within the limits of old towns which revived, these artisan-tenants now grouped themselves in streets and quarters, the street of the weavers, the street of the smiths, the street of the potters, the street of the tanners, the street of the mercers, etc. The lords saw at first only advantages to be gained from this increase in the artisan population, for it was to them a double source of income: first by the number of tenants, whose rents would enrich them, and secondly, by the provisioning of the local market, which gave to the lords a revenue from the imposition of taxes and often of heavy fines.

This evolution once begun soon became accelerated. After the middle of the 11th century the artisan population became a power. Indispensable to the life of the country, they demanded rights. The lords granted these more or less willingly, more or less hurriedly, but finally the working class everywhere won its cause, and, strengthened by the struggle which it had often had to sustain in order to obtain a "place in the sun," it soon supplied itself with a complete organisation, within limits of which industrial life could henceforward develop itself.

The characteristic, if not universal, feature of this organization was the rule of the "corporation."

We know what was meant by this. It was originally the association, or, to use an expressive modern term, the syndicate of all the workmen employed in the same trade. Having been freed at the cost of long and violent effort from the domination of tyrannical lords, the workers succeeded from the 12th century onwards in obtaining recognition of the privileges and "customs" of their groups: these concessions gave them formidable power. There are some towns, particularly in the south, where even nowadays the workmen remain individualistic, and where many artisans do not belong to unions; but in the districts where industrial activity is greatest —above all in the north—the union is so strong and also so exclusive, that an artisan who refuses to join it is in danger of being crushed and is condemned to disappear.

The records which show us this struggle between the union and the free artisan, between the union and non-union men, are numerous and very interesting. The latter naturally attempted to interest in their cause the feudal lords, who were in general little inclined to favour the powerful unions of workmen. Thus, in 1224, in the northern suburbs of Paris, the Parisian weavers who were not affiliated to the weavers' corporation and who for this reason were being persecuted as disloyal competitors, were supported by the Abbot of Saint-Denis and the Royal Constable, Mathieu de Montmorency. But this was exceptional. King and lords alike were usually obliged to yield sooner or later to this inevitable result; at the end of the 12th century, Henry II of England, in his capacity of Duke of Normandy, granted to the corporation of Rouen tanners the exclusive right of practising this trade in the town and suburbs of Rouen; on the other hand, the clothworkers of Bruges had to wait until the beginning of the 14th century before they obtained a similar monopoly from Louis de Nevers, Count of Flanders. But in the end, sooner or later, the triumph of the corporation is a general fact.

In the beginning, this corporation was only an association of artisans, employers or for simple workmen, freely joined together with a view to loyal collaboration, and with the object of mutual defence and protection. The control of the association was assured by an administrative council—the council of the "wards" (*gardes* or *eswardeurs*), or the council of the "jurors" (*jurés*), or even the council of the "consuls" (to use the language of southern France)—of which all the members were elected, often by a direct universal vote. They chose their own president, who in the north was called "mayor" (*maieur*). The council of the "jurors" and its president supervised the increase in membership of the corporation, controlled its finances, and examined its productions, on which depended the good name of all those who belonged to the corporation. They had very wide powers, but their government was of short duration, generally for a year, and they had to render an account of it at the general meetings of the corporation.

Their revenues came from the annual contributions paid by the members, increased by the entrance fees paid by new recruits, by donations and by legacies, which they might be called on to receive. All these funds were employed for the common good. Part was applied to the purchase of real estate; another part was placed to the credit of the benevolent fund (if the union possessed one, as frequently was the case), and was thenceforward employed in sickness, in disablement, for funeral expenses, etc. Yet another part was reserved for the expenses of union feasts and holidays, for the celebration of religious services, for the feast of the patron saint under whose protection the corporation was placed, finally for legal expenses; for the unions could provide justice for themselves, and used and abused it.

The internal discipline of the corporation was regulated by statutes, which each new member swore to observe. We soon find therein established the division into three categories of manual workers: the "master," the "man" or *valet*, and the "apprentice."

The "masters" were those who owned their workshops, or to use the contemporary term, their *ouvroirs*. Originally, their numbers were not limited: any one might become a "master," provided he had sufficient capital to start with and offered professional guarantees. But at first there were no other restrictions on men becoming masters; or at least one does not find any recorded in the old statutes.

Professional skill was acquired by apprenticeship. The future workman was apprenticed at an age which the statutes fix at a minimum of ten years, and which was commonly about twelve years. The oldest statutes lay down in great detail the rules which were to govern the apprentice's treatment; they lay stress on the necessity that the master should be proficient in his business before taking in the child whom he is to instruct in the trade; on the duty, furthermore, of the corporation to assure itself that the master who wishes to take an apprentice is able to supply him with the suitable material and moral conditions of life. The chief anxiety, as we read in a Parisian record, is that the parents who apprentice their children should not "lose their money," and that the apprentices themselves "should not lose their time." Masters were also forbidden to take too many apprentices at the same time; some statutes even forbade them to take more than one. They demanded on his behalf good food, sufficient clothing, and they fixed the minimum of his pay. On the other hand, as the interests of the corporation demanded that the apprentice should really learn his business, they required from him a minimum time of apprenticeship, careful work, and forbade him to leave the workshop without the permission of the master, who had such entire authority over him that he might even inflict corporal punishment if needful.

When the young man was out of his apprenticeship, he could start in business, and open a workshop, that is to say, get himself recognised as "master." If, however, he lacked means to start, he might either, as in our day, go to some master as workman, or "man," or else still remain in this capacity with the master who trained him.

Hiring was done almost in the same way as nowadays. There were no employment bureaux, properly so called, but in the open air, in certain streets or public places consecrated by custom, in front of certain houses, or taverns, workmen in search of work usually gathered: thus in Paris, in the 13th century, we know that workmen seeking employment as fullers were to be found at the apse of the church of Saint-Gervais, in front of the house with the sign of the Eagle. Hiring was arranged freely between the parties, generally the only essential condition being that the workman could prove that he had been through his apprenticeship; sometimes it was added, that preference should be given to one's own townspeople to the exclusion of strangers or foreigners; finally, in principle, all undesirables were eliminated, thieves, rakes, and notoriously bad characters, whom the council of the union reserved the right of excluding from membership at any subsequent time.

As a rule, even the rate of pay might be freely discussed between employer and employee. There were however customary rates, which the corporation was careful to preserve: it attempted both to prevent prices being spoiled because certain masters offered too high rates, and also to prevent the workmen from demanding unreasonable rises. Here is already seen the anxiety to maintain the established state of things, the fear of dangerous novelties, which soon gave to the corporations a strongly marked character of narrowness of outlook and of exaggerated conservatism.

The corporation statutes naturally take a great place in the regulation of industrial work. Therein we find fixed the length of the working day, which varied according to the season from about eight hours of actual work to nearly twelve. Night-work was only allowed under exceptional circumstances, but when it was arranged for, it was compulsory for all corporation workers. It was moreover a characteristic feature of the organisation, that it was applied in the same manner to all members and was intended to subject them all to the same hours and to the same conditions of work. In all the workshops where the same trade was carried on, at the appointed hour work was begun at the sound of the bell rung from the municipal belfry; the hour of the midday meal was similarly announced, later the hour for the resumption of work, and finally, in the evening, the hour for rest.

The statutes also frequently contain the declaration of working days. Whether trade was bad or good, there were eighty or eighty-five days (including Sundays) on which work must cease, to which must be added Saturdays and the vigils of legal feasts, on which work stopped about 3 or 4 o'clock in the afternoon, in order, at least theoretically, to allow the workmen to be present at the vigil observances, and in some towns work on these days had even to cease at noon.

All these measures only aimed at avoiding the inequalities or the abuses, of which the "masters" or the "men" might be the victims. But in practice, it is only too evident that they were bound to degenerate into a corporate tyranny which destroyed all spirit of initiative.

This tendency showed itself even more in that part of the statutes which aimed at regulating manufacture itself. Bent on avoiding bad workmanship and faulty production, which would damage the good name of the work turned out by the workshops of their town, the councils of the corporations very soon conceived the idea that they must insist on uniformity of production from all their members. Even the choice of raw materials was rigidly limited, the head of a business, or "master" of a workshop, only being allowed to use certain kinds of wool, leather, wood, fats, or dyes, prescribed by the "wards," or "jurors" of the corporation. Regulations on this subject sometimes went so far, that in the middle of the 13th century, at Douai, the coffin-makers were forbidden to use other wood than deal. At the same period, the Paris coopers were only allowed by their own rules to use four wood-essences specified by name.

Raw materials could, moreover, only be used in certain ways, in accordance with certain rules, from which it was forbidden to depart. Thus at Châlons-sur-Marne, in 1244, it was ordained by the statutes of the clothworkers, that at least 6 lbs. of alum must be used in the dyeing of each piece of green or "brunette" cloth. A Douai statute of about the same date dealing with the "fulling" of cloth, ordered that five measures of "grumiel" (or lard) should be used for undyed cloth, three for cloth of the colour of peach-blossom, four for plain linsey-woolsey and two for a violet linsey-woolsey; these quantities might not be changed without incurring a penalty of 20 silver *sous*. Everything was the subject of regulations, the length of the pieces of cloth, their width, their weight, and the number of threads in the warp and the weft.

The clothworking industry was by no means an isolated instance. The shoemakers also had their rules, by which (to continue to take our instances from the town of Douai, about which we are exceptionally well supplied with documents) they could only make certain styles and use certain leathers: those who made fancy footwear were only allowed to use "Cordovan" leather, that is a kind of morocco; those who manufactured goods of average quality might only use cowhide; and those who made goods of a low class were only permitted to use sheepskin. A mixture of leathers was absolutely forbidden, and, moreover, the soles were to have a different look, according as the shoes were of the first, second, or third grade.

As regards the tailoring of garments, regulations were so circumstantial that there was no detail of cut, of stitching, of trimmings, and even of linings which was not mentioned. Thus it is laid down that a doublet must be made of three thicknesses, one of new cloth, one of pure thread, and one of a mixture of thread and cotton (which was called "fustian"). Two of these thicknesses formed a cover, within which was placed a stuffing which was to be composed exclusively of cotton.

All production was thus regulated, and offenders against the rules were liable to penalties, which extended to temporary exclusion from the trade (for a month, 40 days, a year or more), and even to banishment from the town for one or two years, occasionally for five or ten years, or even more.

## § IV. THE ABUSES OF THE CORPORATION SYSTEM (13TH AND 14TH CENTURIES)

Nevertheless corporation rule, at the time when most of the regulations which we have quoted were elaborated, was still essentially a democratic rule; the tyranny to which the members submitted was, at least theoretically, willingly accepted by each of them. In some of the statutes, the consent of all "masters" and all "men" is expressly stipulated. But in the second half of the 13th century a tendency to oligarchy showed itself, and became really acute in those districts where, by reason of its expansion, industry had become important, and no longer produced for the local markets, but for wholesale exportation. This occurred for instance in Flanders and Artois, where in the middle of the 13th century the cloth-trade had reached such a height that those of the masters who had large capital at their disposal had become the real controllers of the industry.

These great "drapers," or "cloth-merchants," as they were called at the end of the 13th century, were already leaders of industry. They bought wool in considerable quantities on the English markets, stocked it in their warehouses, carrying off likewise the dye-stuffs of the French markets; often also they cultivated on their lands, on a large scale, the plants from which the dyes were obtained. They did not yet possess factories, but each of these "merchants" employed a large number of workmen, or of "masters" in a small way, whom he supplied with materials and who depended for their livelihood on the work which he distributed regularly to them. Often too it was the "draper" who provided them with a workshop and tools, the rent or purchase-price being taken off the pay given on account of work done.

Masters on a small scale tended more and more to become paid employees, while only those who traded on a large scale were really employers. And as all these leaders of industry had common interests, and as they required agreements in order to regulate prices, they in their turn formed syndicates, outside the limits which had been planned by the corporations, forming "guilds" of great merchants, which very soon succeeded in monopolising the executive offices in the administrative councils of the corporations themselves.

The relations between the merchant-princes and the small employers hired by them became acute at the end of the 13th century. Bitter struggles began. From 1280 onwards, in Champagne, in Flanders and other places, strikes broke out, which were harshly suppressed by the heads of industry, who succeeded in securing control not only of the corporation councils, but of the municipal offices: they retaliated with measures such as the prohibition of meetings and of carrying arms; they imprisoned the leaders, and even condemned some to death. The struggle went on with varying fortunes. For a time in Flanders the workmen succeeded in seizing the power, thanks to political events, but finally the working-class had the worst of it. In the 14th and until the beginning of the 15th century we find in the northern districts these great cloth-merchants forming real dynasties in the face of a numerous working-class, succeeding each other from father to son in the same business, and, thanks to their capital, continuing to control the markets and govern the corporations.

In smaller and less-important industries, as for instance in the Parisian district, the position remained apparently more in accordance with the early ideals. But here, too, an oligarchical character gradually showed itself; the masters endeavoured to make "mastership" into a caste monopoly, which succeeded, like the merchant princes of the north, in dictating the laws of the corporation.

Everywhere, allowing for variations, the consequences were alike: the corporation councils came to be drawn from an ever-narrowing ring of employers, who were less and less studious of the general interests, and more and more of their own, and who perpetually twisted the regulations in favour of the employers and in a selfish and narrow protectionist sense. After the 14th century, obstacles were carefully piled up to prevent a simple workman becoming a master; high fees, which were constantly raised, were demanded from him; under the pretence of requiring a proof of capacity, the execution of a long, complicated, and costly "masterpiece" was exacted; often the obligation of a minimum period of work under the same master was insisted on; and, naturally, all these precautions and expenses were omitted or extraordinarily lightened, when the applicant was the son or the relation of a "master." At the end of the 14th century the guild of "masters," in more than one town, was perpetuated by heredity, and already in the 15th certain rules, as for instance those of the Poitiers locksmiths, declare officially that only the sons or sons-in-law of "masters" could attain "mastership."

The "masters," thus recruited in an ever-narrowing manner, not only actually seized the "offices," but moreover were often the only people eligible for the positions of "wards" or "jurors" and they even came to have the sole right to elect these. The corporation councils thenceforward only represented the "masters," in reality as in law.

In these conditions, the position in smaller and less important industries degenerated into violent opposition between the hereditary oligarchy of the employers and the working proletariat, as it had done in the great industries of the northern districts. In the 15th century, the struggle was nearly incessant. It was above all acute regarding the question of pay, which the masters tried to keep at an unalterable rate, in spite of the constant rise in the cost of living, while the workmen combined in support of their claims and in hope of success.

These "combines" were absolutely forbidden by the statutes, but the workmen collected secretly, and formed "trades-unions," brotherhoods, or *devoirs,* of which the most celebrated was that of the working masons, the "free-masons." The members of these secret societies recognized each other by mysterious signs, assisted each other, and placed themselves in a position to resist the official corporations, which had become the property of the masters.

This struggle was injurious to industrial production, not less than the narrow and destructive strictness which hindered all initiative, and which was the perverted work of the corporation rules. Decadence was precipitated thereby, even in the districts least touched by the Hundred Years' War, which caused so much ruin. On the other hand, this war was fatal to the cloth industries, which had made so magnificent a start in the northern districts of France, by dislocating the commercial relations between these districts and the English wool-market.

However, during the preceding centuries the French industries had gained so fine a reputation that France stood in the first rank of countries which exported manufactured goods. In what manner and by what routes was this exportation carried on? what were, generally speaking, the volume and method of the commercial movement of which France was the centre? This we shall now proceed to explain.

## § V. THE GREAT MEDITERRANEAN TRADE UP TO THE BEGINNING OF THE 14TH CENTURY

We must distinguish between trade by sea and trade by land.

Until the middle of the 13th century all the chief trade of Europe was almost exclusively carried on by means of the Mediterranean, or, at least, the Mediterranean traffic regulated all commercial activity in Europe. The reason for this must be looked for in the important part which Levantine products had assumed in Western life.

There was a demand first of all for spices from the East—those famous spices coming from lands to which the bold navigators of the 15th and 16th centuries sought to find the shortest routes with such determination and at the peril of their lives. The strong foods and aromatic drinks of the Middle Ages required an enormous amount of all kinds of condiments—cinnamon, ginger, pepper, cardamoms, cloves, nutmeg, galanga—without which everything would have seemed to them tasteless. They even put pepper into pastry! And to satisfy these imperative gastronomic requirements, Arabia, India, Ceylon, the Moluccas, and China had to be called on for contribution.

Their pharmacopeia likewise demanded a great number of plants and aromatic substances, which only Asia and Egypt could supply, as, for instance, camphor, tragacanth, mastic, cassia, rhubarb, scammony, and zedoary.

Sugar also came to them from the East; from the East, incense, balm and most scents; from the East too a great part of the dye-stuffs, which the manufacture of cloth, so highly developed in France, could not do without. Such were "brazil-wood" (from its colour of red embers) and gum-lake, which were imported from India, Indo-China, and Sumatra; indigo, which was brought from India, Persia, and Upper Egypt; finally alum, which was necessary for the preparation of the cloth before it was plunged into the dyeing-vats (now called steeping in alum), and which was also required for leather industries. We must also add silk from Syria, Persia, and China, cotton from India, Egypt, and Syria, ivory from Ethiopia, pearls from Ceylon and the Persian gulf, and all the precious stones, doubly precious in Western eyes for their exquisite beauty and the miraculous virtues which were attributed to them.

The great marts for all these Levantine products were in the Eastern Mediterranean, especially at Alexandria and in Syria; a great future was in the hands of those Western traders who could succeed in gaining the mastery of these markets, and in thus securing the vast profits which could be gained by the importation of the products there accumulated.

For a long time the Italian shipowners, who had a serious start of their French rivals, were able to exclude the latter, although Frenchmen were numerous in the crusading armies and in the Christian states which were founded in Syria at the end of the 11th and beginning of the 12th centuries; and the Genoese and Pisans, with the Venetians, kept an almost complete monopoly of the Eastern trade for a hundred years.

They did more than this: they schemed to prevent the French shipowners from taking part in anything more than coasting trade. Thus, in the course of the 12th century, Genoa was strong enough to impose successively, first on Narbonne, then on Montpellier, then on Arles and Saint-Gilles, treaties by which the sailors of these ports were forbidden to do more than to sail along the coast, and might not go farther than Genoa itself to the East, and the frontiers of Mahomedan Spain to the West. The mighty and tyrannical Genoese republic only allowed, for the transport of pilgrims, a strictly limited number of French ships to sail every year, e.g. one only from Narbonne.

The grasp of Italians on Mediterranean commerce had become such that they treated the French coasts like those of Greece, Asia Minor, Syria, and Africa, as districts to be exploited. The Genoese and Pisans had transformed the coasts of Languedoc and Provence into settlements for their countrymen, had assigned to themselves warehouses, rights and wide immunities, and had ended by seizing almost all export and import trade. Nothing so clearly shows the complete subordination to which the French maritime towns of the Mediterranean had been reduced than the treaty concluded in 1174 between the Genoese and Raimond de Saint-Gilles, Count of Toulouse and Provence, by which the latter abandoned to the former all rights of trading freely on all the coasts of Languedoc and Provence from La Turbie to Narbonne, and placed under their control all the traders of his states, absolutely forbidding the last-named "to navigate, or cause navigation by sea for the purpose of trade except under the authority of the consuls and commune of Genoa."

But in the last years of the 12th century and the beginning of the 13th the situation changed. Weakened by a continually reviving war, which had brought them to blows with each other for nearly a century, and which was to go on for nearly another century, Genoa and Pisa were no longer in a position to exercise their tyrannical supervision over the maritime towns of the French Mediterranean coasts. Gradually these towns became bolder and succeeded in wresting commercial initiative from the hands of their rivals; by degrees Narbonne, Montpellier, Saint-Gilles, Arles, Marseilles, and the small ports of the Provençal coast were able to take a place, and soon an important one, in the commercial navigation of the Mediterranean.

Naturally there could be no question of eclipsing their formidable Italian rivals. Moreover, the French ports, with the exception of Marseilles, were too precariously situated to be able to hope for equality; neither Montpellier, where access to the open sea was only attained by two "graus," or channels (the channel of Maguelonne and the channel of Melgueil), nor Saint-Gilles, nor Arles on the Rhône, were directly accessible to big ships; even Narbonne, because it was choked with mud, was inconvenient of access; Aigues-Mortes had a port in the 13th century, on the clearing of which the kings of France had spent great sums, but it was always being threatened by the sand. On all the Provençal coast trade with the interior was hampered by the fact that the political vicissitudes of the 9th century had brought all the country on the left bank of the Rhône into close relations with the Germanic Empire.

Nevertheless, in the 13th century, the shipowners of Provence and of the Languedoc ports rapidly regained the ground which their Italian rivals had stolen from them. Free at length to sail the high seas under their own flag, without having to seek permission from the Genoese or the Pisans, they, too, founded counting-houses in Syria. There appeared for instance at Saint-Jean d'Acre, at the beginning of the 13th century, a street called "rue des Provençaux" (*vicus* or *ruga Provincialium*), where naturally natives of Marseilles were in the majority. The merchants from Montpellier soon imitated them.

The Christian states in Syria and Cyprus gave wide facilities to the activities of the merchants of France; in return they obtained privileges connected with the customs, concessions of wharves and warehouses, and the right to have their own consular jurisdiction. Their field of action became extended and in a few years reached to the Byzantine countries, and later, in the western basin of the Mediterranean, it made an expansion which was full of promise; from the first half of the 13th century onward, they were in continuous commercial relations with the whole of North Africa, from Ceuta to Tunis. This is specially true of the Marseillais. In these districts too, they had their counting-houses and their consuls, and they obtained advantageous commercial treaties from the Mahomedan authorities. At the same time, Barcelona, the Balearic Islands, and even the western coasts of Italy were regularly visited by their ships; for after having been for long tributaries of the Italian shipowners, the French were quickly in a position to treat with them on a footing of equality, and all exemptions which were granted in French ports were generally now immediately reciprocated by similar exemptions in Italian ports. This is shewn by the fact that in the second half of the 13th century, Provençal vessels which came there to load and unload merchandise were becoming numerous, and the French maritime towns obtained there concessions of docks and exemptions, and appointed consuls to look after their interests.

At first their ships went to distant places in search of the same Levantine products which formerly only Italian ships brought, and they tried to take from the latter some part of the import trade. It was difficult to supplant them completely as regards northern France, because, as we shall see, the land routes helped the merchants of the Italian peninsula to reach the great markets of Champagne and Flanders in equal or even superior conditions of speed and security; but in southern France, at least, the importation of precious spices, of aromatic essences, of dyes, and of silks was thenceforward chiefly in the hands of the traders of Languedoc and Provence, who delivered them at the great local fairs, especially at the celebrated fairs of Beaucaire. The markets of North Africa enabled them to add the importation of leather and skins, particularly sheep-skins, a great part of which they forwarded to northern France, as also wool, which was used chiefly as material for the local weaving.

In exchange for these goods, they exported the products of French industries and agriculture; they sailed laden with good cloth from Montpellier or Avignon, from Reims or Châlons, or from the northern towns; they carried bales of linen from Champagne or Lorraine, cargoes of strong armour manufactured in the forges of Poitiers, furs, raw materials, such as iron, tin, or copper, precious metals, wine also (which in spite of the veto of the Koran, was bought from them in the African markets), fruits, especially almonds, nuts, chestnuts from the south, Provençal coral, etc. They also re-exported to the ports of Africa or Spain or in the Balearic Isles, part of the commodities brought from Syria or Egypt. In a word, they succeeded by dint of energy and perseverance in conquering by main force a commercial position of great importance in the Mediterranean and particularly in the western Mediterranean.

## § VI. OCEAN TRADE UP TO THE HUNDRED YEARS' WAR

In the beginning, the Atlantic and the northern seas played a smaller part than the Mediterranean in the commercial history of France, because the risks of distant voyages were not compensated for, as in the Mediterranean, by the considerable profits gained by those who devoted themselves to trading with the countries of Africa or the Levant; and one may even say, that ocean navigation was not to assume its full importance until the day when the idea of reaching by the West the countries whence spices were obtained, developed itself in the minds of the great merchants.

Nevertheless, long before that time the Atlantic and the northern seas were crossed by trading-vessels, which brought into contact the various maritime provinces of western France, and facilitated their exchanges with the northern French provinces, not less than with England, Ireland and Scotland. The vicissitudes of political history, which in the 12th century led to the union of almost all the west of France in the hands of the king of England, increased commercial activity, which tended to develop between the latter country and all the French ports on the Atlantic and the Channel. In Normandy itself, the port of Rouen, which had long been in continuous relation with the coasts of Great Britain, received important commercial rights from the English sovereigns, and until the province was conquered by Philip Augustus it remained the chief port for the export of the wines of Burgundy, which were brought down by the Seine river-boats. But it was above all the Atlantic ports, which benefited by the position; with the exception of Bayonne, which was also in commercial relations with Spain, the traders of these ports sent their cargoes to the countries of the northern seas—Great Britain and Ireland, Normandy and Flanders.

The intercourse thus established in the time when Henry II of England ruled from the Bresle to the Pyrenees survived the partial decay of this sovereignty (which in the 13th century was reduced to the region between Guienne and Gascony), and even increased with the improvement in conditions and navigation.

Bordeaux was the best-known port: it is the natural outlet to the western seas for the whole of Gascony, for the whole of Languedoc, for the central plateau and for the Aquitanian plain. Its export trade is pre-eminently that of the district of which it is the capital, that is to say the wine trade, and we quote some figures which give an idea of the volume of trade which was already carried on there at the end of the 13th and beginning of the 14th centuries. In 1293 and 1296, one single company of English merchants came to load hogsheads to the amount of 20,000 pounds sterling, at the time of the vintage; a few years later we find that the English court bought for its own use between 1000 and 1500 hogsheads annually. These were only a few purchases amongst many, for Bordeaux despatched its wines even to Scotland, or rather, for want of bold enough native shipowners, consigned them to this destination by English ships. Moreover the Bordeaux merchants had assured markets in all the northern ports of France, for instance, in Calais, Bruges, and Gravelines. In return, the English ships arrived in Bordeaux with cargoes of cloth, linens, corn, lead, copper, and other raw materials or manufactured goods which were lacking in the neighbourhood.

Farther north, Oléron, La Rochelle, Saint-Jean d'Angely, Niort, on the Sèvre, which was then navigable, and Nantes, exported wheat and salt from Aunis, wool and wines from

Saintonge, Poitou, or Anjou, and also did a large amount of business with the countries of England and Flanders.

If we put together all the information gathered from the records dating from the second half of the 13th century concerning the commercial activity which was thus established by ocean routes between the countries bordering the North Sea and the English Channel and the French Atlantic ports, the impression is gained of a volume of trade which swelled with extreme rapidity. At the beginning of the 14th century in the port of Calais alone, despite its secondary importance, we notice annual deliveries of wines from Gascony or Poitou which run into thousands of tuns: in 1314, nearly 2600; six years later more than 2700; and in 1315, nearly 14,000, of which it is true a great part (7873 tuns) represents an exceptional amount, destined for the royal fleet.

Naturally as the trade on the high seas developed, it became organised. Shipowners of the same district combined in defence of their common interests. At the beginning of the 13th century the shipowners and sailors of Bayonne had already formed a benevolent society for mutual insurance, which was called "Navigation Society" (*Societas Navium*), whose statutes have come down to us. They form instructive reading. We see the desire of the members to protect each other, and also a fierce spirit of exclusiveness against anyone who refused to join. Thus, with only a few lines' interval, an article (no. 17) provides that, if the ship of any member shall be in distress at the mouth of the Adour, it shall be immediately succoured by the other members of the society, to the cessation of all other business, and another article (no. 24) adds directly that it is forbidden, under penalty of a fine of ten pounds, to come to the aid of non-members.

It was above all during voyages that ships required to help each other. For, in addition to the dangers of storms and reefs, trading-vessels were at once exposed to all kinds of grave risks in the Atlantic, which did not exist to the same extent in the Mediterranean. One must remember, to appreciate the courage and spirit of enterprise of French traders of the Middle Ages, that after the 12th century there was an almost incessant state of warfare between France and England, which resulted in privateering being carried on almost continuously in the Atlantic and the North Sea off the French coasts, even before the Hundred Years' War. Let us merely consider the exploits of a privateer, such as the Picard Eustace the Monk, in the first quarter of the 13th century: he was an unfrocked Benedictine, who had become the seneschal of the Count of Boulogne, was dismissed by the latter for peculation, and thence passed into the service of King John of England; he then specialised in piracy, laying waste the Anglo-Norman islands, sailing up the estuary of the Seine, even penetrating the Eure as far as Pont-Audemer, thus repeating the deeds of the old Norse pirates to the injury of the king of France, until the day when, John having been excommunicated (1212), he preferred to pass over to the camp of Philip Augustus, moved thereto by a conscientious scruple, which is astounding in such a pirate. He now played his part of a highwayman on the open seas on the other side.

In the presence of such dangers, maritime trading became a trial of strength. Nevertheless, braving traitorous attacks, braving capture, even braving the blockades of the French or English coasts, the shipowners of the Atlantic or North Sea ports pursued their business in good or bad days; they attempted to avoid the enemy patrols—English, if they were under the French suzerainty, French, if they were under the English suzerainty, at the time when the English kings occupied part of the French territory in their capacity as dukes of Aquitaine or of Normandy—and in order to be able to hold their own, they armed their ships.

Most of the statutes of navigation count upon this arming, both in the Mediterranean, where (in default of privateering properly so called, which was there less general) pirates were on the watch, as well as in the Atlantic, where the privateer was the real danger. Each vessel was to be provided with arbalests, few or many, more or less powerful, according to the tonnage, and at least part of the crew was to be armed with defensive and offensive weapons, the number and calibre of which varied in accordance with the size of the boat they manned; finally, vessels were advised not to venture singly, but always to sail in convoys.

Thanks to all these precautions, French sea-trade was in full swing, both on the Atlantic and in the Mediterranean, at the time when the Hundred Years' War was about to break out. Between England and Flanders on one side, and the French Atlantic ports on the other, dealings had never been so brisk: the conditions of navigation had so greatly improved that the Levantine products destined for Great Britain, and inversely, the English goods consigned to Mediterranean destinations, instead of being sent by the land routes of western and northern France, began to take the Atlantic route, connected with Narbonne by Toulouse and Bordeaux, and the Genoese traders ventured to pass the straits of Gibraltar, and began to frequent the ports of western France.

## § VII. LAND TRADE AND THE FAIRS OF CHAMPAGNE

Notable as was the part played by the French sailors in great maritime commerce, it was nothing compared with the leading part taken by France in trade by land, for it can be said without exaggeration that for a long period France was the great international market of European trade.

There were very simple reasons for the great part she played. Up to the 14th century intercourse by sea between the Mediterranean countries and the ports on the North Sea was still rare, in spite of all we have said; only a very few ventured to risk their cargoes by passing the straits of Gibraltar, and to face the long and perilous voyage from the Provençal or Italian coasts to the coasts of the Atlantic, the English Channel or the North Sea. Now the Levantine commodities and the industrial products of southern countries accumulated in the ports of Italy, Provence, and Languedoc, while, on the other hand, in the north of France were gathered manufactured goods, produced in the workshops of Flanders, Artois, and Picardy. It was inevitable that some means of direct exchange should be established between these two zones, the Mediterranean zone and the zone of northern France.

From Italy, two great roads, old Roman roads, led to this northern zone: the Mont-Cenis road, which passed through Turin, Susa, the valley of the Maurienne, Chambery, Lyon, and thence to Mâcon, Chalon-sur-Saône, and Langres; and the Great St

Bernard road, which went by Aosta, Martigny, Lausanne, Pontarlier, Besançon, Dôle, Saint-Jean de Losne, Dijon, and eventually also to Langres (or directly from Besançon to Langres), whence by Troyes, Châlons-sur-Marne, Reims, Vervins, or Soissons-Bapaume it went to Tournai or Lille and Flanders. From Provence, the great road led by the valley of the Rhône to Lyon, whence once more it arrived at Langres, then to Troyes, and beyond to Châlons. At the same point, going by Sens, there converged also the most frequented great Roman roads of the west and the south-west, notably the two roads from Bordeaux, one by Périgueux, Limoges, Bourges, the other by Saint-Jean d'Angely, Poitiers, Tours, Orléans, and also the road from Nantes by Angers, Tours, Orléans. To the same point again led the river route of the Seine, which could be navigated as far up as Troyes, and similarly, to the north-east, the roads coming from Cologne, Mayence, or Strasbourg.

It is enough to trace on a 13th century map the great channels of communication which then existed to realise that a great road-centre of capital importance was situated in the district of Champagne. The merchant arriving from Genoa, Pisa, or Venice, from Marseilles, Arles, or Montpellier with his cargo of sugar, spice, or dye-stuffs, his bales of African furs and of leather from Cordova or Tuscany, his silks, his beautiful embroidered tissues; the armourer arriving from Paris or Poitiers; the drysalter from Nantes or Ancenis, there encountered the wool-merchant from England, the cloth-merchant from Bruges, Ghent, Lille, Douai, or Arras, the linen-merchant from Champagne or from the banks of the Rhine. It must naturally have occurred to them that it would be simpler to transact business with each other in the towns in which they must perforce meet on their way, than to continue their journeys.

Moreover fairs had long become established at similar great cross-roads, both in France and abroad, for instance the fairs of Fréjus, Saint-Gilles, and Saint-Raphael in Provence, which were much frequented by Italian traders; the fairs of Beaucaire, Nîmes; those of Bourges; those of Limoges at the point where the roads from Sens, Saintes, Perigueux, and Clermont-Ferrand crossed; those of Orleans, Tours, and Angers; the three great annual fairs at Caen, where the road from Rouen to

Cherbourg and the road from Tours and Le Mans crossed; the two fairs of Evreux, at the intersection of the Rouen-Chartres and the Paris-Caen roads; the fairs of the Paris district, especially the one of Lendit at Saint-Denis, one of the most ancient fairs in France; the great Flemish fairs, above all the four greatest, Thourout, Bruges, Ypres, and Lille.

But although these fairs were well-placed, Champagne was even better situated. Accordingly, the fairs which sprang up in this district, on the great transverse road from Flanders to Italy, became pre-eminently the fairs of Europe at the end of the 12th century and in the 13th. This movement was aided by the fact that Champagne was a rich and prosperous country, inhabited by a hard-working population, which had already known long years of internal tranquillity under the intelligent administration of a feudal dynasty of peace-loving counts. Champagne, crossed in every direction by an exceptionally close network of roads, kept in good repair, seemed destined to be a meeting-place for merchants. At nearly every cross-road, within a few miles of each other, great fairs established themselves and attracted customers: at Vitry-le-François, Chateau-Thierry, Reims, etc.

Among all these fairs of Champagne, six soon assumed special importance: the two annual fairs at Troyes, the fair at Bar-sur-Aube, the two fairs at Provins, and the fair at Lagny-sur-Marne, which was nearest to Paris. These fairs followed each other at short intervals, and their duration was so timed, that as soon as one ended, or soon after, another began. Each of these six fairs lasted forty-nine days, with the exception of one at Provins, which only lasted forty-six. The whole series therefore occupied a total of two hundred and ninety-one days every year, and was not far from forming a sort of permanent fair.

The fair at Lagny opened on the second of January and did not close until the nineteenth of February; the fair at Bar-sur-Aube opened on the Tuesday before mid-Lent (i.e. between Feb. 24th and March 30th) and lasted, according to the date of opening, until the last fortnight of April, or the first fortnight of May; the "May-fair" of Provins began on the Tuesday before Ascension Day (i.e. between April 28th and May 29th) and went on until some date in June or July; the "warm fair," or fair of St John, at Troyes, came next, from the middle of July until the end of August; then the fair of St Ayoul, at Provins, from September 14th until November 1st, and the cycle closed with the "cold fair," or fair of St Remi, at Troyes, from November 2nd until December 20th.

The organisation of these fairs was a model of good management. Each of them started with a week reserved for the reception of goods. Sales only began in the second week and were divided into three successive series: the sale of textiles, called "sale of cloth"; the sale of leathers and furs, called "sale of Cordovans"; the sale of spices, dyes and other small goods sold by weight, called "sale of weighed goods" (*vente des avoir de poids*).

For each of the three series the very meticulous rules of the fair provided a larger or smaller number of days, which were kept exclusively for the exhibition of all goods, so that the purchasers might compare them at leisure, and afterwards a period for buying and selling. This last period was limited to three or four days for the sale of textiles, leathers, or furs, which were sold in large quantities, but on the other hand was extended to twenty days or so for the much more minute and delicate operations of the "weighed goods," which necessitated a number of small weighings. Finally, a fortnight before the closing date of the fair dealings were stopped, and the remaining two weeks were kept for the settlement of accounts between buyers and sellers, purchases being paid for either by bills of exchange between one current account and another in banks (we shall return to the financial side of the great fairs of Champagne), or by direct payment. But, in every way, the fair was the meeting-place of all who were traders by profession, and consequently as almost every buyer was also a seller, settlements were most commonly made by balance of debits and credits.

The Counts of Champagne were directly interested in the maintenance of good order because of the fiscal dues which they levied on sales, and they organised a police service, which was entrusted to a special body of "guards of the fairs," whose duty was to maintain what was called "the peace of the fair," i.e.

the safety of the merchants and their precious freights, the strict observance of rules, and, finally, the exercise of justice between traders, in case of disputes.

The protective duties of the "guards of the fair" did not extend beyond the actual limits assigned to the grounds of the fair itself, but the risks of the journey to Champagne were averted by special organisations. Merchants of the same district, having to go at the same time to the same place, formed large commercial caravans. They arranged amongst themselves for the transport of goods or entrusted them to special carting contractors, who, in some cases, took over, in return for a price to be agreed on, all the risks and expenses of the journey, undertaking to attend to the custom-house transactions, and to deliver their loads at a fixed date (about twenty days were allowed for the journey from Marseilles to Troyes) to the merchant himself or to his representative.

Furthermore, as merchants of the same districts had common interests, they formed themselves into district associations. Thus the merchants of Montpellier formed at the end of the 13th century a "Society of Merchants trading in France" (by this must be understood in northern France as opposed to Languedoc), *Societas et communitas mercatorum in Francia utentium*. They appointed a common representative or "consul general" (*capitaneus consul*), sometimes more particularly designated "consul general at the fairs of Champagne and France" (*capitaneus consul in nundinis Campaniae et Franciae*), whose office was to defend their collective interests. The towns of Flanders, Artois, and Picardy had formed societies or "hanses," of which the most powerful was the famous "hanse of seventeen towns," exclusively composed of "cloth-weaving" towns, which, owing to further adhesions, had by the end of the 13th century become the association of twenty-four northern manufacturing towns. Foreign merchants were organised in a similar manner; the Italians, for instance, formed a powerful association, directed by an administrative council (the consuls), which was presided over by a consul general (*capitaneus consul*).

These associations enabled merchants attending the fairs to treat on equal terms with the feudal lords, or the towns whose territory had to be crossed on the way to Champagne; and we possess the text of agreements, in due form, assuring free passage for the goods of the merchants of a certain district, in return for duties fixed by tariff, or to be agreed on, and which under stated eventualities might be cancelled.

For nearly a century the Champagne fairs filled their place as the great market of the commerce of western Europe with success. The Italian merchants, in particular, came thither in crowds and as they had long practice in commerce on a great scale, and as the transactions concluded at the Champagne fairs involved large monetary payments, their bankers, or "money-dealers," soon occupied a very important place there, all the more because the Jews, who also had for long been well versed in banking affairs, preferred to pursue their operations in the great ports of Provence and Languedoc, where they were less exposed to persecution and to confiscation than in the north of France.

The most important banks of Asti, Siena, Florence, Lucca, Pistoia, Roma, Piacenza, and Bologna, the Perruzzi, Frescobaldi, Bardi, Anguisciola, Certaldi, Bindi, Ammanati, Albizzi, and Buonsigni, sent thither their representatives to "hold" the "money-changers' tables," as they were called, which were supported by the lord of the place.

These agents of Italian banks, or to give them the generic name under which their contemporaries grouped them all together, these "Lombards," devoted themselves to the ordinary business of money-changing for the traders who came from all the points of the compass, and to the operations connected with the credit necessary for the smooth course of business, especially to loans at interest (which at the fairs of Champagne was not theoretically supposed to be higher than 15 per cent.), to the issue, discounting, and payment of bills and of letters of credit, finally to the opening and clearing of current accounts. For most of the business to be settled between traders was, as we have said, chiefly by the exchange of bills payable to order or to bearer, in order to avoid the risks which would have been run by the carrying about of large amounts.

## § VIII. THE DECAY OF FRENCH COMMERCE IN THE 14TH AND 15TH CENTURIES. THE FIRST SYMPTOMS OF ITS REVIVAL

The extraordinary commercial prosperity, of which the development of the fairs in Champagne is the most striking proof, unfortunately only lasted for a time. The tempest of the Hundred Years' War swept away French commerce as it did French industrial life.

By land, the earliest result of the struggle between the house of Capet and first Flanders, then England, was especially the ruin of the fairs of Champagne. Being no longer the great market for English wool and Flemish cloth, they quickly lost their European importance: it has been calculated (but these figures require verification) that the amount of dues received by the Comte de Champagne at the fair of St John at Troyes, fell from 1375 *livres* in 1296 to 250 *livres* in 1320. The authorities tried to give them an appearance of life by means of edicts and orders; but the damage was irretrievable. The Italian merchants gradually deserted these fairs, where they could no longer meet the great English wool-merchants, and, following the Genoese, the Venetians passed through the straits of Gibraltar and did not hesitate to sail direct to the Flemish port of Sluys, to Bruges, or to London, thus little by little leaving France out of their field of operations.

On the Atlantic and in the English Channel the consequences were not less grievous. The French navy was almost entirely diverted from its commercial activities by the privateering warfare and the military enterprises against England in which it was called to take part, and in which it lost many units. Almost the only vessels that dared to sail with cargoes of goods were the trading-vessels consigned from British Guienne to England or Flanders. Thus the control of the great maritime trade passed, on this side, almost entirely from the French shipowners to the hands of strangers, and especially to neutrals, Spanish or Portuguese. The ships belonging to these two nations began to invade the Channel and North Sea ports, and took the place of the French ships in the trade of exchange between these ports and those on the Atlantic coast. The French kings were obliged to grant them privileges and exemptions in French ports, notably at Rouen and Honfleur, and the Spaniards and Portuguese took to coming regularly to France to unload their leathers, their wool, their oil, their fruit, and to load cloth and linen, salt, dried fish from Brittany, and grain from French fields.

In the Mediterranean this decadence, which was made worse by the pillage of mercenaries and the difficulties of dealing, was accelerated by natural causes: in 1320, the bursting of the dam on the Aude, and the silting up of the pools, ruined the port of Narbonne; the efforts of the population to repair the dykes, the deepening of the river-bed, the struggle against the mud, the establishment of an outer port at Leucaste, all were powerless to avert the disaster. From 6229 households in the 13th century, the town fell to 2500 in 1366 and to 250 only in 1378. The channel at Aigues-Mortes became so silted up that after 1336 the port was unnavigable. Montpellier, decimated by epidemics, saw her population decrease from over 10,000 households to 4520 in 1367, 2300 in 1373, 1000 in 1379, 800 in 1390, and finally to 334 in 1412! This spelt ruin.

In Provence too, we watch the decay of Marseilles, dragged into the costly wars of the house of Anjou for the possession of the kingdom of Naples, cut off from communication by land with northern France, and, to crown all, rendered unable to compete with Genoa and, above all, with Venice in the sea-trade of the Atlantic.

At the end of the 14th century and the beginning of the 15th France seemed no longer of any importance from an economic point of view. Everywhere the suppression of fairs was proclaimed, on account of the insecurity of the roads, the decline in the population of towns, and the stoppage of looms; at Provins in 1399, only 30 were counted, where formerly 3200 had been in full work; at Troyes, the number of workmen and apprentices fell from 500 in 1317 to 10 in 1419. The workmen, reduced to misery, were obliged to emigrate in order to find work: in 1417 the cloth-workers of St Lô in Normandy thus migrated to Brittany; at the same time Rouen lost almost all her working population. The roads were no longer kept in repair; some rivers, such as the Loire, became impossible to navigate for want of cleansing.

But France was to recover from her state of ruin with that astonishing rapidity, that powerful vitality, of which she has given so many proofs in the darkest moments of her history and at all periods. The Hundred Years' War was not yet over, the national territory was not yet liberated, when already at those places where danger no longer threatened, economic activity revived.

In Languedoc especially the speed of this recovery was almost miraculous. In the town of Montpellier, almost reduced to extinction at the end of the 14th and beginning of the 15th centuries, a man of great energy, the world-renowned Jacques Cœur, took the step of opening a business house about 1440. The port recovered itself; the merchant became a shipowner; he founded a branch at Marseilles, revived the old tradition of trade with the Levant, re-established counting-houses in Syria, Egypt and in North Africa; he exported to the East, cloth, linen, precious metals, or copper from France, brought back silks from Alexandria and Beyrout, carpets from Syria and Persia, spices from India, scents from Arabia, sugar from Asia Minor. Moreover, in a few years' time the western basin of the Mediterranean was crossed by many of his vessels, and he even contemplated trading directly with Flanders, in imitation of the Venetians, when he was prosecuted and condemned to banishment after a famous trial (1453).

The story of Jacques Cœur has become a legend: but it was not an unique case, and his personal ruin was only an incident.

Similarly, inland the re-establishment of the fairs followed the liberation of the French provinces. In 1444 and 1445, the fairs of Champagne, that of Lendit at Saint-Denis near Paris, and those at Lyons reappeared.

The roads were repaired and put into good condition; navigation by river was resumed; on the coasts of the Atlantic and the Channel, the sea-ports were re-opened. The working population returned to their work; where needful, they were attracted to the old manufacturing centres by the abandonment of various superannuated rules. In a word, before peace was even signed, France had already partly regained her equilibrium and re-conquered a place in the business world.

There were still however many shadows in the picture. The king, for instance, might decree the re-establishment of the fairs of Champagne, but the fairs were utterly dead, because, as we have seen, the great commercial routes no longer passed through the Troyes country. At the same time, the Turkish victories completed the ruin of Mediterranean commerce at the very moment when in France men were trying to revive the old traditions. On the other hand, Atlantic navigation took a place in commercial activity which it had never yet taken, and here the Spaniards and Portuguese had secured such a start that there was a danger that the French would be ousted from the markets of the world. Finally, French industry had henceforward dangerous rivals: after the 14th century, the woollen trade made such great strides in England, in Italy and other countries, that France could no longer hope to reconquer for her own manufactures the semi-monopoly which she had formerly exercised in western Europe.

Briefly, from whatever point one views it, the industrial and commercial position of France appeared gravely compromised; the vitality of the country might well justify hope, but the struggle was to be hard and long.

## BIBLIOGRAPHY

G. Fagniez, *Documents relatifs à l'histoire de l'industrie et du commerce en France*, 2 vols. 1898–1900; H. Pigeonneau, *Histoire du commerce de la France*, I. 1885; E. Levasseur, *Histoire des classes ouvrières et de l'industrie en France avant 1789*, I. 2nd ed. 1900, and *Histoire du commerce de la France*, I. 1911.

K. Th. von Inama-Sternegg, *Deutsche Wirtschaftsgeschichte bis zum Schluss der Karolingerperiode*, Leipsic, 1909; L. Halphen, *Études critiques sur l'histoire de Charlemagne* (VII. *L'agriculture et la propriété rurale*, VIII. *L'industrie et le commerce*), in *Rev. historique*, 1920.

Martin Saint-Léon, *Histoire des corporations de métiers depuis leurs origines jusqu'en 1791*, 2nd ed., 1909; G. Espinas and H. Pirenne, *Recueil de documents relatifs à l'histoire de l'industrie drapière en Flandre aux xiii^e et xiv^e siècles*, 2 vols. Brussels, 1906; G. Espinas, *La vie urbaine de Douai au moyen âge*, 4 vols. 1913 (contain documents of the greatest interest); G. Fagniez, *Études sur l'industrie et la classe industrielle à Paris au xiii^e et au xiv^e siècles* (*Bibl. de l'École des hautes études, sciences hist. et phil.* fasc. 33); H. Pirenne,

*Histoire de Belgique*, II. 2nd ed. Brussels, 1908, and *Les anciennes démocraties des Pays-Bas*, 1910; G. des Marez, *L'organisation du travail à Bruxelles au xv[e] siècle*, Brussels, 1904.

A. Schaube, *Handelsgeschichte der Romanischen Völker des Mittelmeergebietes bis zum Ende der Kreuzzüge*, Berlin, 1906; W. Heyd, *Histoire du commerce du Levant au moyen âge*, 2 vols. Leipsic, 1885–1886; A. Germain, *Histoire du commerce de Montpellier*, 2 vols. Montpellier, 1861; L. Blancard, *Documents inédits sur le commerce de Marseille au moyen âge*, 2 vols. Marseilles, 1884–1885.

Fr. Michel, *Histoire du commerce et de la navigation à Bordeaux*, 2 vols. Bordeaux, 1867–1870; E. de Fréville, *Mémoire sur le commerce maritime de Rouen*, 2 vols. Rouen, 1857; F. Lennel, *Histoire de Calais*, I. Calais, 1909.

F. Bourquelot, *Études sur les foires de Champagne*, in *Mém. présentés par divers savants à l'Acad. des inscr. et belles-lettres*, 2nd series, vol. v. 1865; Huvelin, *Essai hist. sur le droit des marchés et des foires*, 1897; E. Bassermann, *Die Champagnermessen*, Tübingen, 1911.

P. Clément, *Jacques Cœur*, 1853; Mlle L. Guiraud, *Recherches et conclusions nouvelles sur le prétendu rôle de Jacques Cœur*, Montpellier, 1900.

# CHAPTER VI

## SCHOLASTIC PHILOSOPHY AND UNIVERSITIES

THE history of Scholastic philosophy falls naturally into two main periods; the first extends from the 9th to the latter part of the 12th century; this is the period of formation, and culminates in Abélard: the second extends from the latter part of the 12th to the 15th century; this is the period of full development and decline, and reaches its most complete expression in St Thomas Aquinas. The first is the pre-university age, the second the age of Universities.

Scholastic philosophy means literally the philosophy taught in the schools: in this sense it embraces all systems of mediaeval philosophy. Some writers confine the term to the most prevalent system or groups of systems, and exclude all theories which deny the spirituality of the soul, or the personality of man, or the distinction between God and the creature, as subversive of the fundamental positions of scholasticism. Thus according as one or the other point of view is adopted, John Scotus Erigena, the boldest and most original of all mediaeval philosophers (*fl.* 860), has been called the first scholastic or the first anti-scholastic philosopher. In any case it is important to bear in mind the great varieties of thought existing in the Middle Ages, in spite of the subordination of philosophy to theology.

That philosophy was the handmaid of theology was a commonplace throughout the Middle Ages, and it was the realisation that dialectic could be applied to problems of theology that gave zest to the study of logic and raised logic to the leading position in the curriculum of secular studies.

In his educational reforms Charles the Great was necessarily guided by ecclesiastics and made use of the organisation of the Church. The Palace School, it is true, for more than a century gave an impetus to the new revival of learning, set a standard and an example to Europe, and even resuscitated a certain measure of classical culture. But the more permanent part of

Charles's legislation was the capitularies which enacted that every monastery and every cathedral should have a school for the education of young clerks.

The ultimate object of education in these schools was to enable the future ecclesiastic to understand and expound the scriptures and the patristic writings. But a certain amount of secular knowledge was held to be a necessary preliminary, and instruction was professedly given in the traditional Seven Liberal Arts. These were divided into two groups, the "Trivium," comprising grammar, rhetoric and logic, and the more advanced "Quadrivium," comprising music, arithmetic, geometry, and astronomy. The "Quadrivium" was never much more than a scheme on paper: it was superseded before it had been fully elaborated. The real secular education of the early Middle Ages was confined to the "Trivium." In grammar was included not only the technical rules of Latin grammar, as given by Priscian and Donatus, but the study of some Latin classics. Rhetoric included the study of some Ciceronian treatises, practice in composition, and some elements of Roman Law. But by far the most important subject was logic.

The principal works used in teaching logic were Aristotle's *De Interpretatione* and (from the end of the 10th century) the *Categories*, both in translations by Boethius. These were later known as the "Logica vetus," as distinguished from the "Logica nova" which embraced the other logical treatises of Aristotle (*Prior Analytics*, *Topics*, and *Sophistical Arguments*), which became known in Western Europe about 1141. The earlier Middle Ages knew Aristotle only as a logician. Next there were certain commentaries on Aristotle: of these the most influential was a translation of Porphyry's *Isagoge* or Introduction to the *Categories*. In this he deals with the five predicables (genus, species, difference, property, accident) in their logical aspect: a sentence, in which he hints at, but declines to discuss, the real or ontological significance of genera and species, became the starting-point of the controversy on universals which formed the central theme of scholastic debate in the earlier period and divided the schools of thought throughout the Middle Ages. The sentence runs: "Now concerning genera and species, the questions whether they have a substantial existence or are mere products of the intellect, whether (if they are things apart from the mind) they are corporeal or incorporeal, whether they exist outside the individual things of sense or are realised in the latter, I shall refuse to answer: these are problems of the highest importance and require more thorough investigation." The early scholastics limited themselves chiefly to the first question: do the objects of our concepts—genera and species—exist in nature (*universalia ante rem*) or are they mere abstractions (*universalia post rem*)? Those who adopted the first alternative were known as Realists, those who adopted the second as Nominalists. Extreme realism ends in pantheism, extreme nominalism in individualism.

The disputes in the schools acquired a new importance when the applicability of dialectic to theological questions began to be seen. The system of John Scotus Erigena, with its extreme realist basis, was too much in advance of his time to exercise much immediate influence, and the pantheistic conclusions to be drawn from it were not condemned by the Church until the beginning of the 13th century. Realism was in the ascendency in the 9th and following centuries, partly because it asserted a correspondence between the things of nature and the representations of them made by the intellect, partly because it offered an intelligible explanation of some dogmas of the Catholic faith. Thus Odo of Tournai explained the transmission of original sin by the theory that the human race is one substance. But the tendency to assert the real objectivity of general concepts always called forth opponents. Two of these at the latter half of the 11th century brought nominalism into bad odour by attacking received doctrines of the Church.

Berengarius of Tours, a pupil of the Abbey school of St Martin and of the Cathedral school of Chartres, spent his time, according to his fellow-pupil Lanfranc, in "collecting authorities against the Christian faith"; in particular he disputed the dogma of transubstantiation on the ground that the substance of bread and wine could not be changed without a corresponding change in their accidental qualities (taste, colour, etc.); hence the Gospels cannot have meant to teach real, but only ideal transubstantiation. He was compelled at a Synod of Rome, in 1059, to declare that the body and blood of Christ were "sensualiter, non solum sacramento sed in veritate" eaten by the faithful.

Roscelin, canon of Compiègne, and like Berengarius a member of the Chartres school († *c.* 1121), was regarded by contemporaries as the first champion of nominalism: his views have probably been exaggerated by his opponents and critics, who accuse him of holding all general concepts as "mere words," but he was, at any rate, all through his life and in spite of persecution the outspoken enemy of realism, and he put forward his opinions with an incisiveness which compelled attention. He fell foul of ecclesiastical authority by applying logic to the doctrine of the Trinity: if the three divine persons are one God, then (he argued) all three must have become incarnate, which is absurd: there are therefore three divine substances, three Gods ("if usage allowed us to speak so"), because each substance constitutes an individuality.

The suspicion and anger roused among theologians and the populace by these incursions of the philosophers into the domain of faith threatened to lead to a complete divorce between philosophy and theology. The danger was for the time averted by the intervention of Anselm in the controversy against Roscelin. Anselm, "the last of the fathers of the church and the first scholastic theologian," while asserting that reason must submit to authority, aimed at giving a rational justification of dogma—even of the Trinity and Incarnation, which were later a prohibited area to philosophers as mysteries beyond the reach of the human intellect. His motto "Crede ut intelligas" implies the belief that "religion is rational and reason divine"—the belief which inspired scholastic theology. In refuting Roscelin, Anselm uses the arguments of exaggerated realism. "How shall he who has not arrived at understanding how several men are in species one man comprehend how in that mysterious nature several persons, each of which is perfect God, are one God?" Philosophic language had not in the 11th century the precision it acquired later, and must not be taken too rigorously. But the use of doubtful arguments by a champion of orthodoxy would strengthen the reaction against philosophy of any kind. Bec, under Anselm, was the last monastic school to exercise a wide influence. Henceforth the monasteries closed their schools to outside students, and education passed exclusively into the hands of the seculars.

The principal secular schools in France at the beginning of the

12th century were Laon, Chartres, and Paris. Laon under Anselm of Laon († 1117) acquired fame as a school of theology. Chartres under Bernard and Theodoric of Chartres (*fl.* 1130) and Guillaume de Conches († 1153) was the home of a vigorous, if short-lived, classical revival, of which John of Salisbury has left an account. But Chartres contributed powerfully to the growth of that dialectic which was to strangle the infant humanism. The new logic was taught at Chartres before it was known in Paris, and the *Liber Sex Principiorum* (a completion of Aristotle's study of the *Categories*) of Gilbert de la Porrée, for twelve years lecturer at Chartres, was universally adopted as a text-book in the schools and retained its popularity to the end of the Middle Ages.

Before the 12th century, Paris had made little mark as a centre of study. The first known master of the Cathedral school of Notre-Dame was Guillaume de Champeaux, and Guillaume would hardly have been remembered had he not served as a target for the sarcasms of his famous pupil, Abélard.

PIERRE ABÉLARD (1079–1142) was, like many other early scholastics, such as Roscelin, a Breton by origin. The eldest son of a noble house, he preferred to fight with his brains rather than with his hands, and wandered from school to school, attending the lectures of Roscelin of Compiègne and those of Guillaume de Champeaux (*c.* 1100) at Paris. The latter recoiled from the nominalism of his former master, Roscelin, to extreme realism: individuals were merely accidents of one and the same substance. His recoil was so violent that he almost reached a kind of inverted nominalism from the other side. His doctrine, according to Abélard, was that the same thing or substance was simultaneously present in its essence and entirety in every individual. Unless this meant that every individual was a genus and species by himself—a separate universal—it was absurd, and Abélard destroyed it by ridicule: if humanity is wholly present in Socrates, it is absorbed in Socrates and cannot be in any other individual. The ridicule of his pupil drove Guillaume de Champeaux from his chair at Notre-Dame (1108): he retired to the Abbey of St Victor, where he renewed his lectures but modified his theories.

As permission to teach was dependent on the will of the ecclesiastical authorities, Abélard was unable to lecture in the

Cathedral schools of Paris, and set up schools in other places, either with or without authority. For a short time he succeeded in obtaining the master's chair at Notre-Dame, but being ousted thence he obtained a licence to teach from the Abbey of Sainte-Geneviève, then a house of secular canons, and the "Mountain," as it was called, remained for some years the headquarters of philosophical teaching in Paris. Next he went to study theology under Anselm of Laon, of whose capacity he formed a very low opinion: at the instigation of his fellow-students he lectured himself on the Bible to show how it should be done. About 1115 he returned to Paris as master of the schools of Notre-Dame and was now at the height of his fame. His triumph was short-lived; and after many vicissitudes and two condemnations of his opinions he ended his life in disgrace and broken in spirit at Cluny in 1142.

Abélard has been claimed both as a nominalist and as a moderate realist, and also as a conceptualist. He taught that the individual alone has a substantial existence, but the universal exists in the individual (*universalia in re*) and elements common to different things can be abstracted by the mind: these mental concepts are thus not merely subjective but correspond to an external reality. His view was by degrees generally adopted and the problem of universals in its original form ceased to be the central problem of the schools.

Abélard was also a moralist and a theologian. In his treatise on ethics, *Scito te ipsum*, he lays stress on the subjective intention as the main factor in determining the moral value of human action, thus making the individual conscience the supreme judge. His text-book on theology, *Sic et non*, exercised a profound influence. In this each question is followed by a series of extracts from the fathers giving conflicting views and arguments, and no solution is attempted. The method consists in facing the difficulties before attempting an answer. Abélard's pupil, Peter Lombard, adopted the same form in his famous *Sentences*, but tried to avoid the dangers of free inquiry by appending to each set of extracts the accepted solution or by an attempt to harmonise divergent views. The *Sentences* quickly became, and remained throughout the later Middle Ages, the universal text-book of theology in the schools.

It was not so much for any particular views which he enunciated as for his general attitude of mind that Abélard was persecuted through his later life by St Bernard and his followers with unrelenting ferocity. "The fathers of the church (he maintained) are to be read, not with the necessity of believing them but with the freedom of judging them." "Doubt is the road to inquiry, and by inquiry we perceive the truth." "A doctrine is believed, not because God has said it, but because we are convinced by reason that it is so."

Abélard attracted unprecedented numbers of students of all ages and all nations to Paris and made Paris the centre of the intellectual movement of Europe. There were many schools and many teachers. The materials for a university were to hand. But as yet there was no central and permanent organisation. The schools of Paris might have been, if not as ephemeral as Anselm's school at Bec, or Abélard's at the Paraclete, not more long-lived than those of Laon or Reims. The intellectual impulse, if it survived the bitter hostility of the most active section of the Church, might have succumbed from lack of material. But on the one hand, Paris now became a natural centre of attraction as the capital of the expanding kingdom of France; on the other hand, the recovery of the lost works of Aristotle gave the mediaeval mind all the material it required. Paris became the home of the first University in northern Europe.

The word university in the Middle Ages meant any organised body of persons. It could be applied to a town or a guild of merchants or a college of canons as well as to an organisation of masters or scholars. The word is first used in connexion with the University of Paris in a letter of Innocent III about 1208–9. The usual phrase is University of Masters or University of Masters and Scholars. It has nothing to do with a "universality of knowledge." The term generally used to denote university institutions or the town in which they were situated was *scholae* or *studium*. Early in the 13th century a distinction arose between a *studium generale* (or more rarely *universale* or *commune*) and other kinds of *studia* designated in contrast as *particularia*. A *studium generale* meant in the first instance a place of study for all, a university which was open to students of all parts (cf. general chapter in the religious orders). A further meaning was sometimes incorporated with this: a degree in any *studium generale* was held to give the *jus ubique docendi*, the right to teach in the same faculty in any other university without further examination. This privilege was expressly conferred on Toulouse by Gregory IX in 1229, and the idea grew up that the foundation of new *studia generalia* belonged only to popes and emperors. Even the old universities of Paris and Bologna obtained papal bulls in 1292 conferring on them the *jus ubique docendi*. In practice the right was only partially admitted by other universities. Paris refused to recognise Oxford graduates without fresh examination, and Oxford retaliated in like manner on Paris, the papal bull notwithstanding.

The University of Paris grew out of the Cathedral school of Notre-Dame. There were other schools in Paris, but these had an intermittent existence: thus, the school of St Victor had a short life; the Abbey of Sainte-Geneviève passed about 1150 from secular to regular canons, and the schools of the "Mountain," where Abélard had for a time taught, had fallen into comparative obscurity by the end of the 12th century. At this period the Chancellor of the Cathedral alone conferred licences to teach upon the masters.

In some Cathedral schools the duty of teaching was conferred on a specially appointed officer, the Scholasticus: in others the office of the Scholasticus was united with the office of Chancellor or secretary of the Chapter. As his secretarial duties increased, or as students multiplied, the Chancellor delegated his teaching functions to others, sometimes (as was usually the case in England) retaining for himself the lectureship on theology and entrusting the lectures on grammar and arts to subordinates. In Paris, the Chancellor of Notre-Dame seems soon to have become merely a supervisor of education, licensing others to do the teaching work. A curious piece of evidence of the intimate connexion between the Church and the University survived till the 14th century in the custom which allowed any canon of the Cathedral to occupy a chair of theology without graduation. The arbitrary power of the Chancellor was limited in 1179 by a decree of the Lateran Council. The decree provided (1) that every Cathedral should endow a master to teach the clerks of the

Church and poor scholars gratis; (2) that "no one should exact any fee for the licence to teach, or demand anything from those who are teaching under colour of any custom, or deny the licence to any suitable applicant." The last clause evidently applied to schools where numbers of students congregated and numbers of teachers were required—above all, at this period, to Paris. The decree would hardly have been issued except on the petition of some body of persons interested: it suggests the existence of some association or guild of licentiates.

There is more direct evidence of a guild of teachers at Paris about 1170: about this time John de Cella, then a student at Paris, afterwards Abbot of St Albans, was admitted into "the fellowship (*consortium*) of elect masters." This association or guild of masters must, at its origin, have been little more than a private club: as in other guilds, the admission of a new member was accompanied with certain ceremonies and formalities; he "incepted" or entered on his new duties under the presidency of his master and paid his footing by feasting his colleagues and giving them presents. The important point is, that, as the guild admitted members, so it could impose conditions of membership, refuse admission to any who were unwelcome, and even expel any who disregarded the conditions of membership or the customs of the society. A man might be licensed to teach by the Chancellor of the Cathedral, but he could not become a master, and would find his licence of little value, unless he were approved by the "University" of Masters. Another valuable privilege which is said to have been granted by Louis VII, was the right to strike: the masters were authorised to suspend lectures as a protest against any injury done to teachers or students and as a means of enforcing redress of grievances: this was also held to justify the removal of the *studium* to another place.

From these vague beginnings the University grew in definiteness and power through its contests with its natural enemies—the townsfolk and the Chancellor.

The first extant charter of privileges was granted by Philip Augustus in 1200 as the result of a "town and gown row" and in consequence (it was said) of a threat to strike. The right of the scholars to protection of their persons and chattels (*capitale*) by ecclesiastical law was asserted, and the Provost of Paris on assuming office was compelled to swear to maintain the privileges of scholars in the presence of the assembly of masters.

About 1209 the first statutes were reduced to writing: these required uniformity in the dress of the masters, the observance of "the accustomed order in lectures and disputations," and attendance at the funerals of deceased clerks. A master who refused to swear to observe these statutes was expelled from the society of masters until he submitted.

About the same time Innocent III recognised the corporate character of the university by allowing the appointment of a legal representative or proctor at the Roman Court. Such an official was necessary to enable the university to carry on a long struggle which had already begun against the Chancellor. The Chancellor and canons of the Cathedral church of Paris denied the right of combination to the new trade union as inconsistent with the obedience which every individual master owed to the Chancellor and as subversive of the authority of the local ecclesiastical body over the schools which had sprung up under its protection. Innocent III in 1212 supported the masters: he forbade the Chancellor to exact an oath of obedience from them and prohibited him from refusing the licence to any candidates duly recommended by the masters in the various faculties. The Chancellor's powers of imprisoning or fining scholars were curtailed or abolished. Most of these provisions were embodied in a code of statutes imposed on the university by Cardinal Robert de Courçon, and the right of the university to make statutes for its own government was recognised within certain limits. The Chancellor, far from submitting to the papal decisions, excommunicated the university *en masse* for conspiracy and denied its right to make statutes, except with the approval of the bishop, chapter or chancellor.

In the course of this litigation the university found it necessary to have a common seal and to raise money for expenses. For the latter purpose the university elected certain officers known as proctors "according to their nations." The first indication of the existence of the organisation into nations occurs in a bull of 1222, when the election of such proctors was temporarily forbidden. A few years later the institution of proctors and nations appears as fully established.

The conflict with the Chancellor of the Cathedral was carried on mainly by the Faculty of Arts: in the course of it the artists set up a rival to the Chancellor; they withdrew from the island to the south side of the river, set up schools in what became known as the Rue de Fouarre (from the straw littered on the floors of the schools) and obtained their licences to teach from the Abbot of Sainte-Geneviève. The Faculty of Arts, besides being the youngest and most unruly section, was by far the largest body in the university, the chairs of theology being limited by Innocent III to eight. So the junior faculty, bearing the brunt of the fight, developed its organisation earlier than the superior faculties and acquired a preponderant influence in the growing university. The four nations which came into existence between 1219 and 1222 were divisions of the Faculty of Arts. They were not, like the Universities of Bologna, student organisations, but organisations of Masters of Arts, who alone had full voting powers and who were probably supposed to represent their students. It must be remembered that the Arts students were generally boys (unlike the law students at Bologna) and could become masters at the age of twenty years. The nations were the French, Norman, Picard, and English nations—a classification which may have been fairly representative at the time of origin, but which certainly in course of time ceased to correspond to the facts. Each nation elected a proctor When, some time before 1245, the need for a single head or president became apparent, the four proctors elected a rector. Though the Rector was head only of the Faculty of Arts, he was the only official who could preside at meetings of all the faculties. The superior faculties had not yet appointed heads of their own, the deans being a later institution, first heard of in 1264: the Chancellor of the Cathedral claimed to be *ex officio* head of the theological faculty, and he was clearly impossible as head of the university. In 1259 the pope addressed the Rector as "Rector of the University." Every Bachelor of Arts was required to take an oath of obedience to the Rector "as long as he should profess the Faculty of Arts": this was altered before the end of the 13th century to the phrase "to whatever state you shall come." Every member of the superior faculties, who had been a B.A., was therefore bound to obey the Rector by a permanent oath.

The position of the Rector as head of the university was occasionally disputed to the middle of the 14th century, but it was never overthrown.

In the "town and gown" rows again it was the Masters of Arts and their scholars who were the aggressors and the sufferers, and who felt the need of a strong organisation to defend themselves and avenge injuries. A tavern brawl in the spring of 1229 resulted in the death of a number of scholars. So bitter was the feeling of the Cathedral authorities against the rebellious university that, instead of vindicating clerical privileges, they encouraged the civil power to suppress the unruly students with a strong hand. The university ordered the suspension of lectures, and, when this failed, the dispersal of the university for six years was decreed. Many other schools and universities in France and England profited by this measure. Some two years later the masters and scholars again returned to Paris on terms which were embodied in a series of papal bulls. The terms show how closely the two struggles—against the town and the Chancellor—were intertwined. The right to order a suspension of lectures received papal sanction. The offending townsmen were punished and measures taken to protect the rights of scholars. The Chancellor was deprived of his prison and his criminal jurisdiction. At the same time in one important respect the Chancellor's powers seem to have been enlarged. In granting licences he was henceforth bound to act according to his conscience after consultation with masters, instead of—as heretofore—being bound to grant a licence when it was demanded by a majority of the faculty or examiners. The concession would be more likely to affect the theologians (especially in their coming struggle with the Mendicant Orders) than the artists who now had a second string to their bow in the Abbot of Sainte-Geneviève. The privileges acquired were specially calculated to benefit the artists; the dispersal of the university was their policy and their triumph.

The predominance of the inferior faculty in the constitution and government of the university was the result of a historical process, not of any theory. The masters of the superior faculties were, like the artists, members of the university. In the earliest corporate act of the university preserved to us—the deed by which, in 1221, the "University of masters and scholars" transferred to the Friars Preachers its rights over the Place Saint-Jacques as a site for their convent—the masters of theology append their seals as representatives of the university, and the highest faculty might have taken its natural place as leader of the university, had it not been crippled by the claims of the Chancellor.

The branches of study recognised in the University of Paris from the end of the 12th century were Theology, Law, Medicine, and Arts—the last being regarded as in some sort preparatory to the other three. The regent masters—i.e. the masters actually engaged in teaching in these four branches—met in separate assemblies to decide courses of study and times of lectures, and to pronounce on the claims of candidates for degrees, and so gradually formed four distinct corporations known as faculties. Assemblies of all four faculties, known as congregations, were held to decide on the adoption of statutes for the whole university.

In these congregations the Rector, i.e. the head of the four nations of the Faculty of Arts, presided and announced the proposals. Each faculty then retired and discussed the proposals apart and decided on its vote by a majority—the vote of the Faculty of Arts being decided by a majority of the nations. On reassembling the votes were given by faculties. During the 13th century unanimity of faculties was required for the passing of new statutes: in the 14th century the majority of faculties bound the minority. Each faculty—and in the Faculty of Arts each nation—had equal voting power, irrespective of the numbers composing it. None but masters had the right of taking part in the deliberations and voting. Every master was bound to give ordinary lectures for two years from the time of his graduation; this was the period of necessary regency; he might continue to lecture after that period. In the 14th century it became more and more the custom for the Rector to summon non-regents, i.e. masters who were no longer engaged in ordinary university teaching, to congregations, though it does not appear that they ever established a right to be consulted. Normally the decision rested with recent graduates.

It may be noted that grammar was not a faculty, and that in

1219 Honorius III forbade the teaching of Civil Law in Paris in the interests of theology, so that the Faculty of Law meant Canon Law or Decrees.

The period of study in the different faculties varied from time to time. In the Faculty of Arts Robert de Courçon (1215) fixed it at six years and decreed that no one should receive the licence (as master) before he was twenty years of age. The period was reduced in the 14th century to four and a half years or less. For the doctorate of theology eight years of theological study were required in 1215 and the candidate must have reached his thirty-fifth year: the period was lengthened in 1366 to sixteen years. The Faculty however possessed a power of dispensation which was liberally used.

A great change in the course of studies—a change which added greatly in the first instance to increase the prestige, popularity and vigour of the Faculty of Arts—resulted from the recovery at the beginning of the 13th century of the lost works of Aristotle.

Down to the end of the 12th century the only works of Aristotle known to the Latin world were the treatises on logic. At the beginning of the 13th century many of the other works were translated from the Arabic by a school of translators, established at Toledo by Archbishop Raymond († 1151). The best known of the translators were Gundissalinus, Johannes Hispanus (a Jew), Gerard of Cremona, and Alfred the Englishman of Sareshel, and somewhat later Michael Scot and Hermann the German. Their translations of the *Physics*, *Metaphysics*, *De Anima*, *De Animalibus*, *De Coelo et Mundo*, *Meteorica*, and the pseudo-Aristotelian *Liber de Causis* and *De Vegetabilibus*, were made from Arabic versions, which had generally in their turn been made from Syriac translations of the original Greek. The commentaries of the Arabian philosophers were translated and introduced to the West simultaneously with the Aristotelian text. When the Fourth Crusade and the foundation of the Latin Empire of Constantinople brought the West into closer contact with the near East, translations began to be made direct from the Greek. Among the early promoters of this movement Robert Grosseteste holds an honoured place. The most prolific of the translators from the Greek was the Dominican William of

Moerbeke, later archbishop of Corinth, who, with Henry of Brabant, at the request of Thomas Aquinas undertook the translation of all Aristotle's works into Latin. But the new Aristotle was first introduced to the West through translations from Arabic and through the interpretations of the Arabian commentators, especially Averroes, called "the Commentator" *par excellence* in the later Middle Ages.

The Arabs emphasised and exaggerated the anti-Christian elements in Aristotle, asserting the eternity of matter and denying the immortality of the soul. The outbreak of heretical teaching in Paris led not only to the burning of the heretics but to the condemnation of Aristotle. In 1210 an ecclesiastical synod forbade the reading publicly or privately of "the books of Aristotle on natural philosophy and his commentaries" in Paris. In 1215 the statutes drawn up for the university by the papal legate again forbade the reading of the *Physics* and *Metaphysics*, while allowing the *Ethics*. The prohibitions seem to have remained in force in Paris until after 1231, but did not apply to other universities. The masters of Toulouse in 1229, when enumerating the special advantages which their university offered, boasted that students could hear there the "libros naturales" which were prohibited at Paris. In 1231, after the return of the scholars to Paris, Gregory IX appointed a commission of theologians to revise and correct the condemned books; meanwhile he renewed the prohibition "until the books shall have been examined and purged of all heresy." The papal prohibition still remained and was repeated as late as 1263 by Urban IV, but it was a dead letter. Alexander of Hales († 1245) and Guillaume d'Auvergne († 1248) made use of all the suspected books, and a statute of the Faculty of Arts in 1255 prescribed all the genuine and some spurious works of Aristotle as textbooks for the masters' lectures.

The reconciliation of Aristotle with Christian theology was the work not of papal prohibitions or alterations in the text but of the Mendicant Orders.

The Dominicans were from the first a learned body of preachers, trained in theology to combat heresy. Secular learning was at first discouraged among them, but this attitude was soon changed and philosophy was studied at the "studia generalia" and "studia sollemnia" and "particularia" of the Order with as much thoroughness as at the universities. The Franciscans, though aiming originally at influencing men rather by example than by preaching, quickly followed suit and organised their educational system on much the same lines as their rivals.

The Dominicans established themselves in Paris in 1217, and in 1221 obtained part of the site for the famous monastery of the Jacobins from the university itself. The Franciscans came to Paris in 1219.

The friars at first attended the lectures of the secular masters in theology but also had schools in their own convents. These schools were not affected by the great secession in 1229, and the Dominican school under the Italian canonist, Friar Roland of Cremona, was now opened to such secular students as remained. In 1231 John of St Giles, when regent master of theology, preached in the Dominican Church on voluntary poverty, and "that he might confirm his words by his own example" descended from the pulpit in the middle of his sermon and received the habit of the friars. In the same year another Englishman, Alexander of Hales, then regent master in theology, joined the Franciscan Order, and continued as a friar the course he had begun as a secular. In the next year a second Franciscan school was opened under Jean de la Rochelle. Other friars began to incept under masters of their respective Orders, and as it was considered improper for humble professors of poverty to apply for licences, a papal bull in 1250 enjoined the Chancellor to confer the licence upon as many religious as he should, after examination, according to his conscience consider qualified. The rights of the other doctors of theology to a voice in the admission of candidates were ignored. The university had no control over the schools in the convents, and the Faculty of Theology found their ranks being filled by men whom they had not admitted.

Early in 1252 the Faculty of Theology issued their first written statute. This decreed that "no religious not having a college in Paris" should be admitted to the Society of Masters, that each religious college should be restricted to one master and one school, and that no bachelor should be promoted to a chair unless he had already lectured in the schools of an actually regent master. Any master refusing consent to this statute was "deprived of the Society of Masters."

In the struggle the secular theologians received the support of the Faculty of Arts who used their organisation to raise funds for the expenses. The Masters of Arts refused to admit the regulars to their society. This however was in accordance with the customs of the Mendicant Orders, whose members were not allowed to take degrees in Arts. It is singular that the seculars did not raise the point that a degree in Arts was a necessary preliminary to a degree in Theology—a position maintained in the contemporary dispute between regulars and seculars at Oxford. It must be inferred that the rule did not hold good in Paris at this time.

In the course of the controversy it appeared that the seculars were partly moved by jealousy of successful rivals. The Franciscans at an early stage surrendered their claim to a second chair; when there seemed a chance of the Dominicans doing the same, the seculars are said to have replied that this would do no good, as the friars would merely knock two schools into one and have as many students as ever. The secular masters complained to the Pope that they were left without an audience "like solitary sparrows," while the class rooms of the Mendicants were crowded. It is not stated whether a difference in the fees charged had any influence on this result. We need not accept the Dominicans' taunt that the secular masters were stupid and lazy from eating and drinking too much, but it is certain that the Mendicant Orders attracted the finest minds of the time, and that the friars came to the university better prepared than the secular students. Among the licentiates whom the Faculty of Theology refused in 1256 to admit to their fellowship were Thomas Aquinas and Bonaventura.

The leader of the secular doctors was Guillaume de Saint-Amour, who showed great ability in linking the university question with the general struggle of the secular clergy against the encroachments of the Mendicant friars, and thus enlisting the support of bishops and parish priests throughout Europe. The university was not always scrupulously accurate in its statements. In a public manifesto issued in 1254 they asserted that (apart from some canons of the Cathedral who had an *ex officio* right to teach as masters) the chairs of theology were confined to twelve, that nine of these were already held by regulars, and that the seculars were in danger of being altogether excluded. The truth of all these statements is doubtful, and Guillaume de Saint-Amour was guilty of a deliberate misstatement in trying to tar the Dominicans with the brush of Joachite heresies. The appeal to the secular clergy was, however, so successful, that Innocent IV, who had hitherto supported the friars, restrained their encroachments against the parish priests and gave signs of an intention to support the secular party in the university. His death in 1254 was attributed to the prayers of the Dominicans, and the next Pope, Alexander IV, reversed his predecessor's policy and supported the friars heart and soul. The Bull *Quasi lignum vitae,* 1255, asserted the right of the Chancellor to license any regulars whom he considered fit and ordered the university to admit all such to the privileges of fellowship: the power of suspending lectures was made dependent on the vote of a majority of two-thirds in every faculty. As the regulars were always certain to number more than a third of the Faculty of Theology, it was in the power of a body of men who owed allegiance rather to their Orders than to the university to render this weapon useless. The university declared the bull was a *lignum mortis* to them and resisted it vigorously, but they were eventually forced to yield. The result was that the Faculty of Theology was deprived of all influence over the granting of degrees to regulars, which remained in the hands of the Chancellor. On the other hand, from 1318 the university succeeded in making admission of the regular doctors to congregation conditional on the latter swearing to obey the statutes of the university. The longstanding alliance between the papacy and the university was broken, and the beginning of the "Gallicanism" which characterised the university in the later Middle Ages is seen in the attempts to appeal from the Pope to a council of the French Church.

A direct outcome of this controversy and of the example of the Mendicant houses was the establishment of a residential college for secular theologians by Robert de Sorbonne, Chaplain of Louis IX, in 1257. A few endowed hostels, chiefly for the support of poor grammar students, had already been founded, but the College of the Sorbonne was the first institution of the kind in Paris to rival the houses of the Student Orders of Dominicans and Franciscans. It was designed originally for sixteen students of theology—four from each nation—who were already M.A.s, and the number of fellows was soon increased to thirty-six. Other theologians, who were not on the foundation, were subsequently admitted as *hospites*; honorary membership with the Sorbonne was usually sought by most of the secular doctors of theology, and as meetings of the faculty were held within its walls, the Sorbonne became, in popular speech, identical with the Faculty of Theology. The government of the college and right of filling up vacancies were entrusted to a body of external governors, while the president of the college was an annually elected prior. Another larger college was founded in 1304 by Joanna of Navarre, Queen of Philip the Fair, for 20 grammar students, 30 arts students, and 20 theologians, each class having a separate master, while the government and patronage of the whole belonged to the Faculty of Theology. More than fifty colleges were founded in the course of the Middle Ages, and college instruction, which at first was supplementary to university lectures, superseded them in the 15th century.

Roger Bacon, writing in 1271, declared that for forty years the seculars had not composed a single treatise on theology or philosophy, but relied wholly on the books and lectures of the Mendicant Friars. Though somewhat exaggerated, the statement represents not unfairly the intellectual supremacy of the Dominicans and Franciscans in the middle of the 13th century.

The first teacher of primary importance who comes to the fore after the return of the university in 1231 was the English Franciscan, ALEXANDER OF HALES, whose *Summa Theologia* was left unfinished at his death (1245) and continued later by other hands. Alexander adopted in the main the divisions of Peter Lombard's *Sentences*—an example which was followed in many of the later *Summae*. He perfected the teaching method introduced by Abélard, giving the reasons for and against a particular opinion, and then discussing the arguments on either side and stating his conclusion. He adduced Greek, Arabic, and Jewish writers besides the traditional authorities and was the first to make use of all the newly discovered works of Aristotle. He attempted to reconcile the doctrines of Augustine with those of Aristotle—e.g. on the nature of the soul—but his work is of more interest as that of a pioneer than for any particular results.

BONAVENTURA was born in 1221 and entered the Franciscan Order in 1238: he was sent to Paris in 1242: he lectured on the *Sentences* as bachelor in 1245 and received the Chancellor's licence and became master of the Franciscan school in 1248, but was refused admission to the guild of masters till 1257: three years later he became Minister General of the Order. He was rather a mystic theologian than a philosopher and wrote no commentaries on Aristotle. In the main he represented the Augustinian standpoint—e.g. the supremacy of the will over the intellect—and regarded St Augustine as embracing both the *sapientia* of Plato and the *scientia* of Aristotle.

ALBERT THE GREAT had little direct connection with Paris but much indirect influence. Born about 1200 of a noble German house, he took the Dominican habit in 1223 and lectured at the chief Dominican *studia* in Germany. In 1245–6 he taught as Master of Theology in Paris, where he had Thomas Aquinas as a pupil. He then returned to Cologne, visiting Paris again in 1277, shortly before his death, to defend the doctrines and memory of his famous pupil. His knowledge was enormous, and extended to the physical sciences which met with scant recognition in Paris. His great aim was to make the works of Aristotle, as he put it, "intelligible to the Latins." After the manner of Avicenna he wrote paraphrases of all Aristotle's works, borrowing largely from his commentators, Arabian and other, and adding opinions and criticisms of his own. While in the main following Aristotle he modifies the latter's views in accordance with Christian doctrine—substituting e.g. the notion of the Infinite Being for that of the Prime Mover—and he was the vigorous opponent of Averroism. But he did not evolve a consistent and coherent system of philosophy. This was the work of his pupil, Thomas Aquinas.

THOMAS AQUINAS, a son of the Count of Aquino, was born about 1225 and studied first at Naples where he joined the Dominican Order in 1243; he studied at Paris from 1245 or 1246 to 1248, and returned again in 1252 to lecture as bachelor and master of Theology, being finally admitted as master in 1257:

about 1260 he became Master of the Schools of the papal court and was again lecturing in Paris 1268 to 1272: he died in 1274 at the age of forty-nine.

Thomas Aquinas had not the vast knowledge and enormous range of interests which marked Albert the Great, but in clearness of thinking he is far above his master. His commentaries on Aristotle—*Physics*, *Metaphysics*, *Ethics* and parts of the *De Coelo et Mundo* and *Politics*—were not paraphrases but careful expositions of the meaning of the text. The *Ethics* of Aristotle were now incorporated in Christian theology. Aquinas defined more clearly the spheres of philosophy and theology, excluding from philosophy the mysteries of revealed religion—such as the Trinity and Incarnation—as being not contrary to reason but above reason. "Credere debet homo ea quae sunt fidei, non propter rationem humanam, sed propter auctoritatem divinam" (*S.T.* II. ii., quaest. II. art. x): but in matters of philosophy he maintained that "the argument from authority is the weakest kind of argument."

Aquinas was recognised by his contemporaries as an innovator, and the fundamental change which he introduced into scholastic philosophy was the assertion of the primacy of the intellect over the will, of the true over the good, in opposition to the hitherto prevalent Augustinian doctrine of the primacy of the will (*S.T.* I. q. XVI. 4). But the theory which attracted most attention and roused most opposition, as being the most vulnerable, was the Thomist theory of individuation. What is the principle of individuation? Is it matter or form or the union of both? Aquinas maintained it was matter, but determinate matter, *materia signata*. In that case, argued his opponents, does it not follow that individuality is extinguished after death and that in the non-material world only the universal remains? This was the heresy of Averroes, which Aquinas combated vigorously, maintaining the separate origin of every human soul, but his own principles seemed to lead to the same result. And his opponents succeeded in getting the Bishop of Paris to include among 219 propositions condemned in 1277 this and other opinions of Aquinas. The condemnation was repudiated by the Dominican Order; it was never regarded as authoritative and had no lasting effect, except to produce great literary activity. His views were so generally accepted in the University of Paris that he became known there as the "doctor communis."

Two other movements in the intellectual world have to be noted—the Averroistic and the scientific.

The Averroists were specially strong among the Parisian artists from about 1250 to the end of the 13th century. They attributed to Aristotle and his commentator, Averroes, an infallibility far more absolute than was allowed to them by the leading scholastic philosophers and theologians, and the principles on which they laid stress were distinctly anti-Christian. These principles were (1) the unity of the human intellect, which involved the denial of individual responsibility—a doctrine which spread among the students of Arts and even outside University circles: (2) the denial of personal immortality, which was a corollary of the former thesis: (3) "Human actions are not governed by divine providence": (4) "All that happens on earth is necessarily subject to the influence of the heavenly bodies," and the will is not free. To protect themselves the Averroists advanced the theory of "the two truths" and maintained that what is true in philosophy may be false in theology and *vice versa*. The principal champions of these views were Siger of Brabant and Boethius of Dacia: their principal opponents were Albert the Great and Thomas Aquinas. Their tenets were condemned in Church Councils at Paris in 1270 and 1277. It was fortunate for them that the university exercised its own theological censorship and was able to keep in check the Inquisition.

The mediaeval philosophers held in theory that philosophy was the quintessence of all the sciences and was based on and abstracted from them. But a careful observation of phenomena was as alien and repellant to the mediaeval mind as an investigation of the nature of angels would be to a modern scientist. The result was that the particular sciences were generally neglected, and this was especially so at Paris. Even the medical course at Paris was little more than a training in disputation. Scholasticism was built on narrow and insecure foundations. Thomas Fuller compares the schoolmen to persons living in populous towns, who, having very little ground to build upon, run their houses high up. "So the schoolmen in this age, lacking the latitude of general learning and languages, thought to enlarge their active minds by mounting up."

A movement to widen the bases of knowledge was set on foot early in the 13th century by Grosseteste at Oxford: the most famous student of Grosseteste's school was Roger Bacon, whose researches into the science of optics might have formed the beginning of a new and fruitful era. But though Bacon spent many years of his life at Paris, his advocacy of the claims of positive science and of the consequent reforms in the educational system met with scant sympathy in the chosen home of dialectic and theology. The same group or groups of men who advocated the study of science advocated also the study of languages, especially Greek, Hebrew, and Arabic: their interest, however, was not primarily linguistic or literary: a knowledge of these languages was desired firstly for the better understanding of the Bible and Aristotle and his commentators, secondly, for the conversion of schismatics and infidels. They succeeded in getting Chairs in Greek and Oriental Languages established at Paris and elsewhere by the Council of Vienne in 1312, and there are references to a teacher of Hebrew and a teacher of Greek living in great poverty in Paris between 1421 and 1430.

Scholasticism was not overthrown either by Averroist heretics or by the champions of positive science, but by its own weakness. The system of Thomas Aquinas seemed for the moment to have reconciled the most advanced thought of the time with the doctrines of the Church and to have established harmony between reason and faith. It was, however, subjected to severe and damaging criticism especially by the Franciscans, William de la Mare, Richard of Middleton, and above all John Duns Scotus.

DUNS SCOTUS was born about 1270, and studied and taught at Oxford till 1304: here his greatest works were written—commentaries on various books of Aristotle and on the *Sentences*: from 1304–8 he was at Paris where his *Quodlibetica* secured him the degree of Doctor of Theology: in 1308 he was sent to Cologne and died the same year at the age of about thirty-eight.

Duns Scotus was the destroyer of systems. In the "Subtle

Doctor" the critical element was more pronounced than the constructive. He attacked, generally without naming them, most of his contemporaries and immediate predecessors, Bonaventura, Thomas Aquinas, Roger Bacon, Henry of Ghent, and others. The contrast between him and Aquinas has been well put in the words: "Aquinas takes the *doctrines* which are to be proved, while Duns Scotus takes the *proofs* for those doctrines, as the peculiar subject of study." Arguments, when they are arranged to lead up to a fore-ordained conclusion, have a way of looking much more convincing and inevitable than when they are examined for themselves and followed up to their natural conclusion. Hence Duns Scotus showed that the apparent harmony between theology and philosophy established by Thomas Aquinas was largely illusory. Thus the immortality of the soul and the existence of an Omnipotent God were incapable of rational proof. The result was that the gulf between the two was again widened. Duns Scotus even asserts that a proposition may be true for the philosopher but false for the theologian, but in general he avoids the error of the "two truths" by proclaiming the subordination of philosophy to theology and by excluding from the domain of philosophy more and more of the doctrines of the Church. The acutest thinker of his age, he was sceptical of the unaided powers of the mind and tended unduly to limit its scope. To theology itself he was inclined to deny the title of science (as its propositions could not be proved)—maintaining that it was not speculative (against Aquinas) but practical or moral. He rejected the Thomist theory of the primacy of the intellect and reverted to the Augustinian theory of the primacy of the will, which he asserted in its extremest form. The will is absolutely free to choose good or evil—not subject to a rational determination. God does not choose a thing because it is good—rather what God wills is good, and it is good because He wills it. This was in direct opposition to the theory of Aquinas that good is good *per se* and not *ex institutione*.

Duns Scotus rejects the theory of Thomas that the principle of individuation is *materia signata*, not only on the ground that it is heretical but also on philosophical grounds. Matter, in St Thomas's view, was a limit and defect: hence it would be an imperfection for a thing to be this or that—to attain its perfection. For the individual is the true end of nature. According to Duns and his followers *haecceitas* is the principle of individuation, which does not seem to amount to more than the statement that individuality constitutes the individual: "ergo," he concludes, "frustra quaeritur ratio singularitatis."

According to Duns, primitive matter—*materia primo prima*—is the element of all contingent things—the ground in which they are sown and in which they strike root. Thus all created things—animate and inanimate, spiritual and corporeal—have a homogeneity, a community of essence. This primitive matter is impressed with different forms or principles of determination: each composite of matter and form may serve as the matter or potentiality for an ulterior form until we reach the final form, the individual. "In toto opere naturae et artis etiam ordinem hunc videmus, quod omnis forma...semper est de imperfecto et indeterminato ad perfectum et determinatum." Even primitive matter (which is without form) and all composites of form and matter have an objective reality, a unity of essence, but unity of essence is less than individuality. The concepts of the intellect were in a sense as real as, or even nearer reality than, the phenomena of the external world. The tendency to multiply realised abstractions led to the reaction associated with the name of Ockham.

Ockham is known as the "prince of nominalists." This does not mean that he "made universals nothing more than names." Rather what he insists on is that our conceptions are not the realities: however much we may describe things, the things are not the description. "Prince of individualists" would be a fairer title than that traditionally given to him. In many ways he is in close agreement with Duns Scotus, e.g., in his extreme voluntarism and in his denial of the capacity of the reason to reach certitude in matters of the faith. In all these respects his influence was in the direction of intellectual scepticism.

The usual account of William of Ockham's early life is erroneous. He lectured on the Sentences at Oxford and as *baccalareus formatus* took part in disputations (*c.* 1320–4) but he does not seem to have been promoted D.D. In 1324 his academic career was cut short by a summons to Avignon to answer charges of heresy. In 1328 he fled from Avignon and joined the anti-papal party of his Order. Thus he had no direct connexion with Paris. The first mention of Ockham in the University of Paris is a statute of the Faculty of Arts in 1339 forbidding the exposition of his writings either in public lectures or "private conventicles": the prohibition was renewed next year: these novelties are declared to be full of dangers and to reduce science to a study of concepts and words not of things. In 1346 the Pope intervened to repress these foreign doctrines. Notwithstanding all these efforts at suppression, Ockham's views gained ground, and the most distinguished Parisians of the later 14th and earlier 15th centuries were avowed nominalists—Jean Buridan, Rector of the University, Marsilius of Inghen, Pierre d'Ailly, and Gerson. Perhaps the growing anti-papal feeling at the time of the Great Schism and the conciliar movement helped to make the great anti-papal champion popular in the schools. It may be noted that the leadership in thought had now passed from the friars to the seculars. But during all this period there was very little independence of thought at the university. The great age of scholasticism had passed: new ideas grew up outside the universities. The energies of the University of Paris were diverted from what Gerson called the "useless speculation without fruit or solidity" to practical questions of ecclesiastical reform.

The Great Schism and the means of ending it became at the end of the 14th century the absorbing subject of discussion in the university, and a kind of plebiscite of its members was taken in 1394 as to the best way of restoring peace and unity. The university tried at first to force a simultaneous resignation on the rival Popes, and when this proved hopeless it adopted the plan of a General Council, in which representatives of the universities sat by the side of bishops and abbots and ambassadors of kings and cities. The ambassadors of the University of Paris travelled all over Europe in order to organise a concert of the powers of Church and State: the *Studium* was still an international power and was, at this time, a truer representative of the international idea than either the empire or the papacy. One difficulty in the councils was the question of voting: if voting were by heads, the number of small sees in Italy would give to that country a preponderance altogether in excess of its real importance. At Constance the problem was solved by the adoption of the university custom of "voting by nations." As in the

Faculty of Arts, so in the Council, the four nations (Italian, French, German, and English) were organised separately, deliberated apart, and had equal voting power.

With the failure of the conciliar movement and the nationalisation of churches the University of Paris lost its prestige and position. Louis XI deliberately aimed at destroying its international character by expelling foreign students and forbidding the election of aliens to the rectorship. The university became the home of Gallicanism, but Paris ceased to attract foreign students. In the history of the university one of the most remarkable facts is that almost all its teachers and thinkers of the first rank were either Bretons or of foreign origin.

It remains to say something on the life and academic career of the students. A boy generally came to the university about the age of fourteen. He lived in a hostel with a party of his compatriots, one of whom was chosen as head. Rents were supervised by the university authorities. The young student either joined the class of a grammar master, or, if he already possessed a sufficient knowledge of Latin (and apparently not much was required), he entered at once on the Arts course; there seems to have been no matriculation examination. The first years were spent in attending lectures. Every student had to have his own master: at the University of Orleans he had to attend his master's lectures at least thrice a week, and some similar rule prevailed at other universities. The students sat on the floor round the lecturer's desk: the luxurious habit of sitting on benches was gradually coming into fashion in the middle of the 15th century in the face of much opposition from the constituted authorities. The serious mediaeval student had a passion for taking notes and tried to take down the whole lecture. This habit of writing from dictation was not encouraged, and many regulations were made prescribing the exact rate at which a lecturer should speak and forbidding him to read from a manuscript. The rules proved useless, and reformers in the middle of the 15th century contented themselves with requiring that a lecturer should deliver the lecture himself and not hand his manuscript to a student to read out. As part of a lecture was always devoted to reading out the text commented on, there was a good deal to be said for the student writing it down and making his own text-book: the purchase or (more usually) the hire of manuscripts from booksellers, even at the low rates fixed by the "taxatores" of the university, would make a big hole in the average student's purse.

The Arts curriculum included a certain amount of grammar. The student had to attend two ordinary courses and one cursory course on the two Priscians and the same number on the *Barbarismus* of Donatus: further, two or three courses on each of the logical works of Aristotle and one on the *De anima*. The difference between ordinary and cursory lectures was largely one of time; ordinary lectures being given by masters early in the morning, cursory lectures being given by bachelors, as well as masters, at other times. Further it was customary in most universities and probably at Paris for lectures to be "repeated" or gone over again: the repetition was generally conducted by a bachelor or senior student after the midday meal. These were the requirements for the B.A. degree. But before "determining," the candidate for the B.A. had to "respond," i.e. to dispute in grammar or logic with a master. This exercise, which took place in December, was in the nature of a test, in which the candidate had to satisfy the examiners before proceeding further. Having passed this, the candidate was examined by a board of examiners appointed by his nation: their duty was both to certify that he had heard the prescribed lectures and "had diligently attended the disputations of masters for two years," and to test his knowledge of the prescribed books. He was then admitted by the proctor of his nation to determine, and took rank as a bachelor. The Chancellor had nothing to do with the conferment of this lower degree. Determination took place in Lent and was a disputation in which the candidate maintained a thesis against an opponent. The determiner had to pay his master for the use of a school, and secured a large audience by providing free drinks: the day ended with a feast. A successful determination was a help to subsequent preferment. The bachelor was a kind of pupil teacher—hearing lectures, taking part in disputations, and himself delivering cursory lectures on logic.

After five or six years' study, counting from matriculation, and due performance of the necessary exercises, the bachelor, on reaching the age of twenty, might apply for the M.A. degree. For this there were several examinations and exercises; first an examination held by the Chancellor of Notre-Dame or Sainte-Geneviève, and four examiners chosen by the Chancellor and accepted by the Faculty of Arts (the rejection of candidates seems to have been rare but was not unknown); secondly a disputation among the *licentiandi* on some subject chosen by themselves and known as *Quodlibetica*: thirdly the formal conferment by the Chancellor of the licence to "incept" or begin to teach in the Faculty of Arts, the ceremony being accompanied with a further examination known as collations; and lastly the inception. About half a year intervened between the licence and the inception. In this interval the candidate had to obtain the approval of his nation to his promotion and swear to obey the Rector and his Faculty and nation: on the day before inception he took part in a solemn disputation known as Vespers. The inception itself consisted of an inaugural lecture or disputation by the licentiate, the reception of the master's cap from the presiding regent, and admission to the fellowship of masters. The proceedings concluded with a feast given by the inceptor, or group of inceptors, to the masters and others. The expenses at inception were so heavy that many were burdened with debt and others were unable to proceed to the master's degree: Clement V, in 1314, limited the expenditure to 3000 silver groats of Tours.

The new master was, in early times, bound to dispute for forty days continuously after inception and to give ordinary lectures as regent for two years. Necessary regency, as it was called, implied either a limitation of the number of graduates or an unlimited number of schools, and became impracticable in the 14th and 15th centuries, when each nation owned or rented schools in which alone masters must lecture, and still more when college lectures took the place of university teaching. In 1348 over 500 Masters of Arts described as "actu legentes" at Paris applied to the Pope for benefices. It is clear that at this time the phrase had ceased to bear its literal meaning and that many men took degrees at Paris without any intention, and without any real obligation, of teaching in the university.

If the Master of Arts wished to take a theological degree he would have to attend lectures for six years—the first four on the Bible, the next two on the *Sentences*. After this, and on reaching the age of twenty-five, he would after examination by four doctors be admitted by the Dean of the Theological Faculty to the reading of his first course and would rank as a bachelor or cursor. The first course consisted, in the case of a secular, of "cursory" lectures on two books of the Bible extending over two years: "ordinary" lectures on the Bible were given by regulars, especially mendicant friars. In his ninth year the bachelor was required to respond in a disputation with the senior bachelor, who decided in consultation with the master whether the exercise should be accepted by the faculty. The bachelor then became a *Sententiarius* and proceeded to deliver ordinary lectures, varied with disputations and "honest and moderate beer-drinking," on the *Sentences*. After completing the course on the *Sentences* the bachelor became a *baccalareus formatus*, and as such was supposed to reside in Paris for three or four years before he received the licence, and to take part in various disputations. The most famous of these was the "Sorbonic," when as respondent he had to reply, standing, to a succession of opponents who relieved each other at intervals from 6 a.m. to 6 p.m.

The length of time and the complicated series of exercises prescribed for the degree of D.D. were probably designed to maintain the prestige of the degree after the restrictions on the number of doctors had fallen into disuse. One result was that nearly all the ordinary teaching in the faculty came to be given by bachelors—and in the conferment of the bachelor's degree the Chancellor had no voice.

Secular bachelors were presented to the Chancellor for the licence after an examination in which all doctors of theology, non-regent as well as regent, might take part. The examination was confined to the questions whether the candidate had performed the acts required by statutes and whether he was of suitable reputation. The importance of it probably was that it gave an opportunity of granting dispensations or graces for the non-fulfilment of the nominal conditions. In 1426 a candidate who was rejected at this stage, though he had fulfilled the conditions, claimed the licence as a right, and brought an action against the faculty for exceeding their powers. In the Faculty of Theology the bachelor not only received the licence from the Chancellor but was admitted into the fellowship of masters by him—a survival of the time when the Chancellor was the principal master of theology in the Cathedral school.

The mediaeval University of Paris did not produce an endowed or salaried professoriate. The masters, unless they were fellows of an endowed college, depended on fees and perquisites from their students and bachelors, and on ecclesiastical benefices. Experience showed that the papacy was a more liberal patron of learning than diocesan bishops or private patrons, who were more subject to local influences. In the 14th century it became the regular practice for each faculty to send to the Pope *rotuli beneficiandorum* or lists of scholars who supplicated for benefices; and beneficed clergy habitually obtained dispensation from residence for the purpose of study at a university.

Mediaeval France contained thirteen universities besides Paris, or seventeen if we include four—Avignon and the insignificant *studia* of Orange, Aix, and Perpignan—which were in territory of which the King of France was not even suzerain. Most of them were founded in the 15th century and require little or no mention here. With the single exception of the Medical School at Montpellier, they were all more or less local universities: in all of them Law occupied a more prominent position than Theology or Arts, and in their organisation the influence of Bologna was at least as strong as the influence of Paris.

When in 1289 Nicholas IV formally established a *studium generale* at MONTPELLIER, there already existed three separate universities there—those of Medicine, Arts, and Law—and a fourth, of Theology, was subsequently added. The Bull of 1289 made no change in the School of Medicine, which had long enjoyed all the rights of a *studium generale* by prescription. Montpellier was closely connected by racial, political, ecclesiastical, and commercial ties with Aragon and Italy. In the 12th century it comes to the fore as a school of medicine. The origin of the school is obscure. It is sometimes ascribed to Arab or Jewish, sometimes to Salernitan influence. John of Salisbury mentions Salerno and Montpellier as places to which Parisian students tired of dialectic might go to study medicine in the works of Hippocrates and Galen. Though these works were probably known through Arabic translations, the earlier tradition of the school seems to have been Greek, and no definite trace of independent Arabic influence appears before the end of the 13th century: the later introduction of Avicenna and the Arabs may probably be ascribed (so far as it can be ascribed to any individual) to Arnaud de Villeneuve, who is said to have known Arabic and Hebrew, and was certainly much influenced by Roger Bacon.

The medical school seems at first to have been free from any direct ecclesiastical control, as in the 12th century we find the Lord of Montpellier conferring the *licentia docendi*. His rights were successfully resisted by the bishop of the neighbouring city of Maguelonne, who claimed the authority over the schools which was everywhere enjoyed by the Church north of the Alps, and by the guild of masters. A long conflict between the bishop and the guild resulted, in accordance with the decrees of Clement V in 1309, in the practical victory of the latter. Henceforth a two-thirds majority of the masters was required for the conferment of degrees and the election of the Chancellor. Montpellier in the Middle Ages was not an episcopal city and the Chancellor was not connected with any capitular body. He was the representative of the bishop and the masters, and in this respect resembled the Chancellors of the English universities rather than the Chancellor of Notre-Dame at Paris.

Hitherto the university was a university of masters. In the 14th century the students began to assert themselves, and to the two proctors of the masters a third proctor appointed by the students was added. In 1340 they successfully established the claim that any alteration of the statutes which affected the students should have their consent. Twice a year assemblies of the whole university were called, at which students could ventilate their grievances and have some share in deciding what lectures should be given. The students' proctor could at any time protest against neglect of duty by any doctor: but the students had not the power, exercised by the students of Bologna, of fining a doctor or suspending him from his office.

The degree of doctor in medicine was obtainable by a master

of arts after five years, by other candidates after six years. Twenty-four months of actual attendance at lectures was required. As lectures ended at Easter bachelors and students spent the summer in practice at Montpellier or elsewhere. The candidate for the bachelor's degree was taken round by his master to visit the sick; each master could appoint his own bachelor.

The candidate for the licence (or degree of Doctor) had to possess (in 1309) a number of the works of Galen, and those of Avicenna or Razes, and some others. As bachelor he must have "read" three books, one with and one without comments, selected from a list in which Galen predominates. In the subjects for lectures prescribed in 1340 Galen also occupies the largest place: next in importance comes the canon of Avicenna.

Among famous doctors of Montpellier may be mentioned, besides Arnaud de Villeneuve, Petrus Hispanus (afterwards Pope John XXI, † 1277), Bernard de Gordon, the author of *Lilium Medicinae*, *c.* 1305, and Gui de Chauliac (1367) whose work marked a great advance in surgery. The number of students varied, and was small in 1368, when Urban V founded out of church property the College of Twelve Physicians—apparently the first medical college founded in Europe. The medical school maintained its reputation and popularity to the end of the Middle Ages.

A school of law was founded at Montpellier (1160–1192) by Placentinus who had been driven out of Bologna by the jealousies of his colleagues. About 1230 there was some increase of doctors and students of law—due perhaps partly to the prohibition of the study of civil law in Paris, to the great dispersal of the University of Paris, and to troubles between the city and University of Bologna—and the bull of Nicholas IV in 1289 added to the prestige of the legal university. The doctors about this time had formed themselves into a college and claimed to limit the arbitrary power of the bishop. The students soon began to assert their rights and to form themselves into nations or student universities under a Rector, on the analogy of Bologna. In 1339 a new set of statutes was drawn up by the papal legate and a constitution established in which the students were given more power than at Paris or Oxford, less than at Bologna. The doctors were included in the university and apparently in the nations. The governing body was a Rector and twelve councillors. The Rector must be a doctor and was chosen by the outgoing Rector and councillors from each nation in turn. One councillor was elected from the Cathedral Chapter, another from the town (town students?), the rest by the three nations, Provence, Burgundy, and Catalonia. The Law School, like the Medical School, was depopulated in the middle of the 14th century; the masters declared to Urban V in 1362 that "where there used to be 1000 students there were now scarcely 100." It was evidently recovering by 1378, when the applicants for papal favours included 176 doctors, licentiates, and bachelors in civil or canon law (most of whom were *actu legentes*), besides over 200 scholars.

A University of Arts existed here as early as 1242, but in course of time it became little more than a town grammar school with a single regent of logic and grammar, who was in receipt of a municipal salary.

Montpellier was a centre of orthodoxy in an Albigensian country and the starting-point of mission work. Both Dominicans and Franciscans early founded houses and schools of theology here, and the Dominican house ranked as a *studium generale* in the Order. The Carthusians in 1263 founded a college at Montpellier and other religious Orders were represented. There thus grew up a school of theology in the hands of regulars, but no theological faculty or theological degrees existed until Martin V founded the University of Theology in 1421 with the bishop as Chancellor. The masters then formed a college, but students still remained members of the University of Law. It is noteworthy that at Montpellier regulars were not excluded from the rectorship.

The University of TOULOUSE is interesting and peculiar as being an artificial creation, not a natural growth. Toulouse had been the centre of the various religious anti-ecclesiastical, intellectual, and artistic movements which led to the Albigensian Crusade. After the forcible suppression of heresy, Gregory IX determined to plant in the heretical country a great centre of orthodox learning. In the final treaty of peace, 1230, Count Raymond of Toulouse promised for ten years to pay salaries, amounting to 400 marks per annum, to fourteen professors—

namely to four doctors of theology (50 marks each), two doctors of canon law (30 marks), six artists (20 marks) and two grammarians (10 marks)—probably the earliest instance of salaried Chairs. The University of Paris had recently decreed dispersal, and a circular was issued in the name of the masters and scholars of Toulouse setting forth the attractions of the new university: prominence was given to the fact that the works of Aristotle, forbidden at Paris, were taught at Toulouse. Some teachers and students were undoubtedly attracted: thus John de Garlandia was already teaching grammar at Toulouse in 1230. Dominicans were entrusted with the theological instruction. But the re-opening of the University of Paris, the refusal of the court to pay the salaries, the resistance of the town to the burning of heretics by Dominican inquisitors, combined to empty the new university. In 1233, therefore, Gregory IX issued a bull conferring on Toulouse the *jus ubique docendi*, dispensation of beneficed students from residence in their cures, and all the rights enjoyed by Paris. It was the first assertion of the papal claim to found a university, and a step towards building up the theory, accepted later, that to the Pope (or to his secular counterpart the Emperor) alone belonged the right to found *studia generalia*.

From the first all faculties, including the faculty of grammar, which was not usually recognised as a faculty, were at least nominally represented at Toulouse. Evidently grammar was held in higher repute at Toulouse than at Paris. The students were numerous; degrees were granted in grammar and the masters of grammar had privileges and an organisation of their own. The teaching, however, was confined to such works as the *Doctrinale* of Alexandre de Villedieu and a few elementary reading books and did not include the ancient classics. But the prestige of Paris was so great that the older university was able to retain a practical monopoly in theological degrees until Innocent VI, in 1360, authorised the conferment of degrees in theology at Toulouse. Both students and teachers of theology were almost, if not entirely, confined to the regulars. The most flourishing faculties were those of Canon and Civil Law, especially since the establishment of the Parlement of Languedoc in 1273 opened up new and lucrative careers to jurists. In this year,

Accursius was lecturing in Toulouse, and it is a remarkable fact that Philip IV obtained his chief legal assistants in his struggle against Boniface VIII from Toulouse: Guillaume de Nogaret was a product of the papal university.

The total number of students in 1335 was estimated by a contemporary chronicler as 3000. A roll of clerks seeking preferment sent to Clement VII in 1378 gives some clue to the numbers at the university at this time. The list contains the names of 5 regent masters of theology (all regulars), 6 of canon and 1 of civil law, 1 of arts and 2 of grammar, 5 non-regent doctors, 29 licentiates of various faculties, 154 bachelors of decrees, 62 bachelors of civil law, 40 scholars of decrees, 130 scholars of civil law, 47 bachelors of arts, 246 scholars of arts, and 295 grammarians.

The Scholasticus of the Cathedral was the Chancellor. The Rector must be a master and was chosen from each faculty in turn by congregation, which consisted of the professors of all faculties and the students of law—a concession to the Bologna tradition. The ordinary administration was in the hands of the Rector and a council composed of some elected and some nominated members and all the lectors in theology. Subsequent changes in the constitution were made in 1313, but all through student influence was of the slightest, and ecclesiastical and especially papal authority was prominent.

A school of law existed at AVIGNON in the 13th century, and was raised into a *studium generale* by bull of Boniface VIII in 1303. The chief power was in the hands of the bishop, who conferred the licence and for some time appointed the ordinary doctors. The College of Doctors, however, later co-opted its own members and formed (under the bishop) the governing body of the university. The exclusion of students from all power was unusual in legal universities and led to a series of revolts, including the boycotting of doctors' lectures. In the 15th century the students acquired certain rights. A faculty of theology was created by the Pope in 1413, and the insolence of "lay polygamous jurists" in claiming precedence over masters of theology induced Pius II in 1459 to impose constitutional reforms which limited the authority of the doctors of law and gave the students a modest representation on the governing body. The law students had recently organised themselves into a guild, the confraternity of St Sebastian; this was a voluntary organisation, but recalcitrant students were compelled to submit to it by such means as the "subtraction" of their books. The guild received papal recognition, and was able as a students' council to negotiate on equal terms with the governing body of the university.

During the stay of the Papal Court at Avignon the university was much frequented, partly owing to the special facilities enjoyed by its members for obtaining papal provisions. The professors were entirely dependent on fees, but they had the right to fix fees and could fix them high owing to the bright prospects of the students. The removal of the Papal Court was followed by a period of decline. The university was saved partly by the endowment of a number of colleges, but mainly by the bounty of the papacy. Sixtus IV in 1475 granted from papal revenues in Avignon annual salaries to eight doctors of law. In this policy he was acting under the advice of his nephew, Cardinal Giuliano della Rovere, Archbishop of Avignon, afterwards Pope Julius II, who was the chief benefactor of the university.

In the same year in which he endowed Avignon, Sixtus IV issued a bull against those who took degrees at the neighbouring town of ORANGE, "where no *studium generale* existed." A school of law and grammar existed here in the 13th century, and the curriculum was of such an advanced type that Urban V in January 1365 granted an exceptional privilege authorising students who had studied at Orange to take degrees in other universities. Orange belonged to the Empire, and in June of the same year Charles IV raised the school into a *studium generale* in all faculties. The action of Sixtus IV is however explained by an edict of Charles VIII in 1485, from which it appears that the university had dwindled to a single master in grammar, who constituted himself Rector of the university for the purpose of conferring degrees in all faculties upon "vagabond, ribald, unprofitable and ignorant scholars," who had been refused degrees elsewhere.

ORLEANS was famous as a school of law in the 9th century, as a school of grammar, rhetoric, and classical literature in the 12th and early 13th centuries. As a school of letters it ranked in popular opinion at the beginning of the 13th century with Salerno, Bologna, and Paris, the schools respectively of medicine, law, and logic. Yet by the middle of the 13th century it was essentially and solely a school of law. The connexion between literature and law was close: one of the chief branches of rhetoric was the art of writing official letters, and *dictamen* (as this art was called) was almost a distinct faculty in the University of Orleans. The revival of the study of canon and civil law at Orleans was due to the prohibition of the study of civil law at Paris in 1219 and the migration of jurists to Orleans. From this time it may be regarded as a *studium generale* by custom, and it remained the greatest law university in France throughout the Middle Ages. Orleans was a cathedral city and the Scholasticus or Chancellor of the Cathedral exercised over the masters of law the same authority which he had exercised over the masters of grammar; and behind the Scholasticus was the bishop. The first extant statute was enacted in about 1290 by the Scholasticus after deliberation with the doctors and the chapter and with the consent of the bishop: it limited the staff of the university to five doctors in canon law and five in civil law. At the beginning of the 14th century the bishop claimed the right of adding other professors by his own authority. Appeals to the papal court resulted in a series of bulls from Clement V granting the university the right to make statutes for certain purposes and to elect a Rector. The Rector now became head of the university, superseding the Scholasticus, whose duties were limited to the conferment of the licence. As in most law universities the students acquired considerable influence in the government. The affairs of the university were administered by the Rector, the college of ordinary doctors, and ten proctors of the nations. The ten nations were France, Germany, Lorraine, Burgundy, Champagne, Picardy, Normandy, Touraine, Aquitaine, and Scotland. They were student organisations and elected both Rector and proctors. The Rector was generally a doctor, and the proctors had to be licentiates or bachelors whenever possible. There was probably a connexion between the ten regent masters and the ten nations. Orleans is the only university of note which was confined to a single faculty. It is also remarkable as having no endowed colleges. In spite of this fact its reputation remained high beyond the limits of the Middle Ages, and it counted among its students in later times Reuchlin, Calvin, and Beza.

The Cathedral school of ANGERS enjoyed considerable fame at the end of the 11th and beginning of the 12th centuries under successive Scholastici. It is probable that the prohibition of the teaching of civil law in Paris, 1219, resulted in an increase of students and the organisation of a school of law, as Angers was later specially noted as a school of civil law. It was however still at this time a *studium particulare.* Its recognition as a *studium generale* dates from the migration from Paris in 1229, when the majority of the students, according to Matthew Paris, chose Angers "ad doctrinam universalem." It was one of the few universities which never obtained a papal confirmation of its *jus ubique docendi,* which however was never questioned. The university long retained the constitution of a Cathedral school. The Scholasticus of the Cathedral was as late as 1350 sole head of the university; he was *ex officio* a regent doctor and head of the College of Doctors. Statutes were made in 1373 by the Scholasticus with the consent of the doctors: by these statutes the staff of regent masters was limited to a small number, seven or nine doctors of both laws. The students were probably early organised into nations, but it was not till the end of the 14th century and after several revolts that they acquired any voice in the management of affairs. It appears to have been the question of raising and administering a tax to defray the expenses of sending the *rotuli beneficiandorum* to the Pope that gave them their opportunity. They brought their grievances before the Parlement, which in 1398 reorganised the university mainly on the model of Orleans. A Rector now became head of the university, but the doctors were to hold the rectorial office in the rotation: and a general congregation was definitely recognised as the supreme governing body. Further democratic changes were made in 1410, when it was decided that the Rector should not be a doctor but should be chosen from the licentiates by electors named by the nations. The nations, in order of importance, were Anjou, Brittany, Maine, Normandy, Aquitaine, and the recently added nation of France, which had very few students. A reaction against the democratic movement appears at the end of the 15th century in a decree of the Parlement of Paris, that no one in future should have a vote in congregation or in any of the nations who was below the degree of Master of Arts or Bachelor in one of the superior faculties. Faculties of theology, medicine, and arts were established at Angers by bull of Eugenius IV in 1432. It does not appear that any preliminary training in arts was required from students of law. The number of graduates and students in law mentioned in the papal roll of 1378 is 578—more than at Montpellier, but far fewer than a few years later at Orleans.

The Cathedral school at AIX in early times is interesting, because the syndics of the town had a share in the appointment of the Scholasticus of the cathedral—a possible survival of Roman civilisation. But it is doubtful whether Aix could claim to be a *studium generale* before the papal bull of foundation in 1409. The degree of Doctor in Civil Law was conferred here on a jurist of some note in, or before, 1303, but it was conferred "in the king's court and in the king's presence," and may merely be an attempt of the temporal power to place itself on a level with the papacy in the conferment of exceptional degrees. Though formally founded by the Pope with the privileges of Paris and Toulouse, Aix was made by the Count of Provence into a national university, where all students of Provence were compelled to study, and was given a constitution entirely of the student-university type.

Several universities owed their origin to the rivalry between France and Burgundy and the Hundred Years' War. DÔLE in Franche Comté was founded by papal bull in 1422 on the petition of Philip the Good and was endowed from public funds by the Estates of Burgundy. The foundation of a university at POITIERS in 1431 was due to the English occupation of Paris and was supported by municipal grants. CAEN was founded in 1431 as a legal university—first as rival to Angers and Orleans—by the Duke of Bedford: after the expulsion of the English from Paris a papal bull was obtained extending the scope of the University to all faculties; the influence of the Renaissance may perhaps be traced in the fact that the endowed chairs included rhetoric and poetry as well as theology, canon law, and medicine. Among the sources of revenue was a tax on beer and wine. The University of BORDEAUX, which never became prosperous, was founded in 1441 chiefly by the municipality with English support. The right of teaching was limited to a small number of regent masters, who were not endowed but were dependent on the fees of students. The statutes enjoined examiners to treat candidates "with all tenderness and charity" so as to "increase the University rather than diminish it," and special exemptions were granted to nobles and some other classes of students.

In conclusion it would be interesting to conjecture what would have happened if the Sibyl of the Renaissance had offered more of her books to the Western World when the tide of philosophic speculation was at the flood—if Plato had become known at the same time as Aristotle—if the age of Dante had read the tragedies of Aeschylus. In that case it is probable that Catholic theology would have taken a somewhat different—perhaps more progressive—form than it assumed in the hands of St Thomas Aquinas, and that the study of the classics would have been saved from that exaggerated devotion to grammatical minutiae which has prevailed down to our own time.

## BIBLIOGRAPHY

B. Hauréau. *De la Philosophie Scolastique*. 2 vols. 1850.

M. de Wulf. *Histoire de la philosophie médiévale*. 2nd ed. 1905; E.T. by P. Coffey. 3rd ed. 1909.

J. E. Erdmann. *Grundriss der Geschichte der Philosophie*. 3rd ed. 2 vols. Berlin. 1878; E.T. ed. by W. S. Hough, I. 2nd ed. 1891.

*Encyclopaedia Britannica*, esp. art. on "Scholasticism" by Pringle Pattison.

P. Mandonnet. *Siger de Brabant et l'Averroisme Latin au xiii^me^ siècle*. Louvain. 1911.

F. Picavet. *Esquisse d'une Histoire générale et comparée des philosophies médiévales*. 1907.

H. Denifle. *Die Universitäten des Mittelalters*. Berlin. 1885.

H. Denifle et Æ. Chatelain. *Chartularium Universitatis Parisiensis*, vols. I–IV. 1889–97, and *Auctarium Chartularii*, etc. 2 vols. 1894–7.

M. Fournier. *Les Statuts et Privilèges des Universités françaises*. 3 vols. 1890–2.

H. Rashdall. *The Universities of Europe in the Middle Ages*. 2 vols. Oxford. 1895.

L. J. Paetow. *The Arts Course at Mediaeval Universities*. Illinois University Studies, vol. III. No. 7. 1910.

# CHAPTER VII

## LANGUAGE AND DIALECTS

We know very little about the linguistic conditions of Gaul previous to the Roman conquest (58–51 B.C.). We know that the Ligurian and Iberian dialects belonging to the races driven out by the Gauls were still spoken in the south-east and south-west, but we know absolutely nothing about these dialects. Even about the language of the Gauls, who occupied the rest of the country up to the Rhine, our knowledge is very scanty; the inscriptions in languages other than Latin, which are few in number, have only supplied us with some proper names; ancient writers have collected and translated some two hundred and fifty words, which they record as Celtic, but perhaps not always correctly; a comparison of the various existing Celtic dialects has enabled us to reconstruct about a hundred and fifty more, almost all substantives; as to the rest of the Celtic vocabulary, it is composed only of names of persons, divinities, and places.

The Gauls, who had not succeeded in developing the germs of a national spirit, submitted to the domination of Rome after fleeting attempts at resistance. Most of them even welcomed a well-regulated government, which put an end to local quarrels, a state of culture which they felt to be superior to their own, and two successive religions; they devoted themselves with ardour to the study of Latin, which was not only the organ of government, culture, and religions, but the knowledge of which rendered them eligible for public offices. Celtic was relegated from the outset to the depth of the country, and when the barbarian invasions occurred it had completely disappeared.

Of this contact of three or four centuries the victorious language bore some traces, but fewer than might have been expected; the words introduced into the Latin spoken in Gaul belonged to the lowest stratum of the vocabulary; they are words used by the peasant to denote plants (*bétoine* betony, *bouleau* birch, *vergne* alder), animals (*alouette* lark, *vautre* boar-hound), clothing, tools, and common objects (*banne* a basket, *bouge* a pocket, whence *bougette,* which has formed the English budget, *braies* breeches, *cervoise* beer, *char* cart, *charrue* plough, *tarière* auger, *vouge* bill-hook); no adjectives are found and only one verb (*changer* to change)[1].

It is in the names of inhabited places that the most numerous traces of Celtic origin have been preserved—the names of rivers, mountains, etc. may have been derived from earlier languages Some are formed from the name of a people: Amiens, Cahors, Le Mans (instead of Celmans), Nantes, Paris; others by the addition of suffixes: (*a*) *dunum* (a height), (*b*) *magus* (a field), (*c*) *durum,* (*d*) *oialum,* etc. (the former class generally denote fortified towns, the second, commercial places). Examples are (*a*) Laon, Lyon, Verdun; (*b*) Caen, Noyon, Rouen; (*c*) Auxerre, Briare, Issoire; (*d*) Arcueil, Verneuil.

The commonest of these suffixes, in the Roman period, was *-acus,* which added to family names in *-ius* gives very divergent forms in different regions; *ac* in the south, *at* in the Central Plateau, *ieu* in the east, *y* in the centre (from Normandy to Lorraine), *ey* in the north-east, *é* in the west (Savignac, Lignat, Lagnieu, Lagny, Sévigné).

Latin, as transplanted into Gaul, was not Latin as written by Cicero or Virgil. We know that there was in Rome side by side with the literary language, which had been profoundly influenced by Greek, a popular language (*sermo plebeius, vulgaris*); it must not however be thought that these were two absolutely different languages; rather they were the same language differentiated by shades of meaning, due either to individuals or to circumstances. This may be seen if in the comedies the parts of the noble personages and the slaves are compared, or if we compare the discourses of Cicero with his private letters; ancient writers, in fact, refer not only to a *sermo plebeius,* but to a *sermo usualis* or *quotidianus.* Moreover, similar differences are to be found in all races where there is a great difference of culture between classes, as there was in Rome.

[1] This and the subsequent lists are purposely incomplete; an exhaustive list of the words borrowed by French from other languages has been compiled in the *Traité de la formation de la langue française,* mentioned in the Bibliography.

It was naturally this popular Latin which was brought to the conquered countries by soldiers, merchants, and petty officials, who were the earliest colonists; it is only known to us by rare documents, such as certain inscriptions, certain technical treatises of a late period, the comments of grammarians and the list of incorrect forms entitled "Appendix Probi" (the date and origin of which are unfortunately not known); but the comparison of Romance languages with each other has revealed its chief characteristics, and, above all, has enabled us to reconstruct a great part of its vocabulary.

This vocabulary, less rich and less varied than that of classical Latin, was abundant in expressive terms, many of which were derived from humorous or ironical metaphors, like so many words in our popular speech; *os* for example was replaced by *bucca* (swollen cheek), *gena* by *gabata* (bowl), *caput* by *testa* (earthen pot), *crus* by *gamba* (hock of an animal), *equus* by *caballus* (screw), *domus* by *casa* (hut), *magnus* by *grandis*, *parvus* by *pusillus*, *pisinnus*, *paucus*; *edere* by *manducare* (to devour), *ferre* by *portare*, *ire* by *andare* (of very obscure origin). Excessively short words were replaced by derivatives (*mentonem*, *talonem*, *genuculum*, *soliculum*; *ausare*, *cantare*, *fixare*, *figicare*). The system of inflexions, which was too complicated, was simplified; the system of declensions was replaced by the use of prepositions used with a few cases (which soon became reduced to a single case), that of conjugations by the extension of analytical tenses and the total suppression of passives and deponents; finally, syntax became simpler and inversions rarer.

A borrowed language becomes modified in different ways, according to the habitual pronunciation of those who adopt it. Consequently the Latin of Gaul at the end of two or three centuries already differed perceptibly from the Latin of Italy or Spain. The invasions of the 5th century could not fail to hasten this evolution, at first by causing a new mixture of races, and perhaps, above all, because the grammatical and literary traditions were broken by the closing of most of the schools. Of all the countries conquered by Rome, Gaul was the most thoroughly Germanised, above all from the Rhine to the Loire; it is for this reason that of all the Romance languages French is the furthest away from Latin.

It was in 407 that the Germanic hordes crossed the Rhine and swarmed into Gaul. The Burgundians established themselves in the valley of the Saône and the Upper Rhone, the Visigoths between the Loire and the Pyrenees, the Franks to the north-west, at first only as far as the Scheldt, later up to the Somme. The Franks had originally formed an alliance with the Romans to resist the formidable invasion of Attila, but ended by supplanting their allies; Clovis, the greatest of their leaders, having conciliated the clergy and the people by his conversion to Catholicism (496), settled himself in Paris, conquered the Burgundians, drove back the Visigoths beyond the Pyrenees, and founded a powerful empire, which became dismembered under his feeble successors; nevertheless the Franks remained masters of all the northern part of Gaul and became thoroughly blended with the population, while in the south-east and south the Gallo-Roman element regained the ascendant.

The language spoken by the Burgundians and the Visigoths, of which we really know very little, has certainly left some traces in the dialects of the south and the south-east, which possess certain characteristic words of Germanic origin, and these traces would doubtless appear more evident, were these dialects better known.

But it was above all the language of the Franks (Low German), spoken by the aristocracy until the time of Charles the Bald, which has exercised a profound influence on the dialects of the north and north-east, one of which has become, as we shall see, the literary language. The borrowed words prove how closely and profoundly the two languages and the two civilisations had become intermingled. The Germanic words incorporated in the Latin of this region do not merely describe common objects, clothing, arms, engines or actions of war, political or juridical institutions, but also abstract ideas, as will be seen in the following lists, wherein are also shown some words which have disappeared since the Middle Ages (these are marked by an asterisk).

Plants, animals, nature: *agace* magpie, *alise* rowan, *braque* brack, **brachet* little dog, *chamois*, *cresson* cress, *épervier* sparrow-hawk, *esturgeon* sturgeon, *gerfaut* gerfalcon, *groseille* gooseberry, *haie* enclosure, **herde* herd, *hallier* thicket, *houx* holly, *jardin* garden, *marsouin* porpoise, *mousse* moss, *roseau* reed, *troène* privet.

Human body: *échine* spine, *hanche* haunch, **quène* tooth (whence *quenotte* a child's tooth).

Clothing, utensils, agricultural life, food: *alêne* awl, *banc* seat, *bille* trunk of a tree, *bloc* log, *bord* board, *braise* embers, *bride* bridle, *brosse* brush, *canif* penknife, *clenche* latch (whence *déclencher* to unlatch), *cotte* petticoat, *cruche* jug, *danser* to dance, *échoppe* shop, **espringuier* (dance), *fauteuil* armchair, *feutre* felt, *gagner* to gain, *gant* glove, *garnir* to trim, *gâteau* cake, *gaufre* honey cake, **guimple* (*guimpe* wimple), *hache* hatchet, *hanap* goblet, *houe* hoe, *houseaux* gaiters, *huche* bin, *latte* lath, *loge* lodge, **mite* a small coin (whence *mitraille* grape-shot), *quille* skittles, *regain* second crop, *robe* gown, *rôtir* roast, *salle* hall, *souper* supper, *taudis* hovel, *trappe* trap-door.

Armament, equipment, war: *bannière* banner, *baudrier* shoulder-belt, *blesser* to wound, **brant* sword, **broigne* cuirass, *éperon* spur, *épieu*, heavy spear, *garder* to guard, *gonfanon* gonfalon, *guetter* to lie in wait for, *heaume* helmet, **herberge* camp (whence *héberger* to harbour), **hourder* (to board), *navrer* to wound, **targe* a shield (whence *targette* a flat bolt).

Institutions and social terms: **adouber* to arm, *alleu* freehold, **arramir* to fix by a convention, *bannir* to banish, *échevin* sheriff, *fief* fief, *gage* pledge, *garantir* to warrant, **guerpir* to abandon, *guerre* war, *lige* liege, *maréchal* marshal, *nantir* to provide with, *sénéchal*.

Abstract words. A. nouns: *guise* manner, *hâte* haste, *honte* shame, *orgueil* pride, **sen* (wisdom, whence *forcené* out of his senses), *soin* and *besoin* care and need. B. adjectives: *blanc* white, *bleu* blue, *brun* brown, *fauve* tawny, *frais* fresh, *joli* pretty, *laid* ugly, *riche* rich, *sale* dirty, *sur* acid. C. verbs: *flatter* to flatter, *fournir* to furnish, *guérir* to heal, originally to protect, *guider* to guide, *haïr* to hate, *honnir* to dishonour, *marquer* to mark, *regretter* to regret, *tirer* to pull, *tomber* to fall, *toucher* to touch.

From Germanic sources also are derived a number of names of places, formed of a personal name and the substantives *cour* or *ville* (or *villers, villier*), instead of the German *heim* or *burg*; these names, which are very frequent in the north and north-east, specially denote rural localities of recent formation, the towns having kept their old names. Almost all personal names are also of Germanic origin, especially in the aristocratic class, where they long survived (*Bernard, Eude, Ferri, Garnier, Gautier, Geoffroi, Guillaume, Henri, Hue, Louis, Renaud, Richard, Thierry*); Scriptural names, especially those of apostles and evangelists, were more common in the lower classes (*Jean, Jacques, Martin, Remi*).

The Germanic influence also introduced the aspiration of the initial letter in certain words of Germanic origin (*hache, haie*) and others (*haut, hennir* to whinny, *herse* a harrow), and in others replaced the Latin initial letter *v* by the sound *g* (*gaîne* a sheath, *gâter* to spoil, *gué* a ford). Finally to this influence are owing the suffixes *ard* and *aud*, generally uncomplimentary (*bavard* chatterbox, *criard* a scold, a grouser, *pillard* a pillager, *finaud* an artful dodger, *lourdaud* a lout), *enc* modified by analogy into *ent, an, and* (*merlan* whiting, *tisserand* weaver), *ois* from *esc*, which was later confused with *ois* from *ensem* (*anglois*, fem. *anglesche, griois* Greek, fem. *griesche*).

In the course of this very troubled period, Latin lost ground; in the east the Germanic dialects spread to the left bank of the Rhine; in the west, part of Brittany, peopled in the 6th century by emigrants from England, returned to Celtic speech.

The very rapid phonetic evolution completely changed the appearance of Latin; the principal characteristics of the new language in the time of Charlemagne were as follows: the predominance of the accented syllable contracted the word round it; the penultimates were dropped in proparoxytones (*cal'du, duod'ce*), as also the syllable before the accented one, when not the first, except *a* (*rad'cina, mand'gare*); the accented vowels were lengthened; *u* became *ü*; open *e* and *o*, under the influence of *y* and of *u*, passed into *ie, uo* (*pieytu* for pectus, *nuoyte* for noctem, *fuogu* for focum); closed *e* and *o*, which remained as they were in the south, tended to *ei* and *ou* in the north; *a*, persistent in the south, became *ae* in the north; final vowels tended to become confused and all of them, except *a*, were about to disappear; initial *c* before *e* and *i* became modified to *ts* (*tsera* instead of ceram, *tsenere* for cinerem); *c* before *a* had become *tch* in the north (very soon *ch*) (*tcharn* from carnem); *ty*, *cy* in the middle of words also became *ts* after a consonant (*cantsone* from cantionem, *poltsino* from pullicenum) and *ds* after a vowel (*paladso* from palatium, *vedsino* from vicinum), the hard plosives between vowels became soft, *t* at a very early date (*mudare*), then *p* (*riba*), then *c* (*seguru*); final *m* and *n* were dropped. The declensions were reduced to two cases; the demonstrative *ille* began to be used as an article, the conjugations were reduced in number and exchanges between different types occurred; formations with the help of suffixes increased and compensated for the losses suffered by the vocabulary[1].

At the end of the 8th century, Charlemagne made a great effort to restore the knowledge, and even the use, of classical Latin in schools. This attempt resulted in demonstrating the changes undergone by Latin, or, to speak more correctly, showed that a new language had been born. In fact it is after this period that various texts set in clear opposition the three languages spoken in Gaul, described as *lingua theotisca* (German), *lingua latina* (classical Latin) and *lingua romana* (a name sometimes explained as *rustica*). At this time also the third of these languages received the approval of the Church; in 813, the Council of Tours (whose recommendations were renewed by other councils) directed priests to use it for the instruction of the faithful, which is an evident proof that the latter no longer understood Latin. This text, often quoted, is, so to speak, the official birth certificate of the French language. The *Homelie sur Jonas* (a Valenciennes fragment, at the beginning of the 10th century) is a curious specimen of these preachings; unfortunately the author, carried away by his habits, has mixed many Latin words with the *lingua rustica*.

The new language was not long in making further conquests; soon the scholars made use of it, under versified forms, to translate passages of Scripture, or lives of the Saints intended for the instruction and edification of their hearers (*Cantilène*

[1] Of this language, which was not written and which is called Low Latin, we have no authentic specimen; we can however form some idea of it by the mistakes which have escaped the notice of writers and by a very small number of texts: the *Serments de Strasbourg* (843); the *Gloses de Reichenau* (written in Gaul towards the end of the 8th century, in which Biblical Latin words are translated by words then in use); the *Gloses de Cassel*, a small Germano-Roman lexicon, including words and some common phrases.

*de Ste Eulalie* in the 9th century; *Passion du Christ, Vie de St Léger* in the 10th; *Vies de St Alexis, de Ste Foi* of the 11th or 12th); finally some writers, either clerical or lay, used it to instruct or amuse the aristocratic or popular public (*Chansons de Guillaume IX* at the close of the 11th century, *Chanson de Roland, Pèlerinage de Charlemagne* of the 12th century).

A language has a greater tendency to fall into dialects if the territory which it occupies is politically subdivided, if communications are difficult, and literary culture feeble. Such were precisely the conditions prevalent in Gaul (if we ignore the short renaissance of studies under Charlemagne) from the 5th to the 12th century. Accordingly the two linguistic divisions, which were already to be distinguished at the time of the *Serments* (mentioned above), had a tendency to break up into a number of varied dialects, which are represented very unequally and imperfectly in literary texts, and which can only be studied in administrative documents, unfortunately all rather late, none of them being earlier than the beginning of the 12th century.

It would be out of place here to enter on the question of the reality of dialects, which has given rise to so many discussions and researches during the last thirty years. Two facts at least have emerged clearly: on the one hand, it is true that the different features which characterise the speech of a district have never exactly the same geographical limits, so that at certain places the lines which mark the different boundaries intersect and become entangled; but on the other hand, the common features coincide on a sufficiently large number of points for the inhabitants of the district to have a very clear feeling that they belong to the same linguistic group. In this sense it is legitimate to speak of dialects and to contrast them one with the other.

Of those which divided France in the 13th century only the principal are here enumerated and only their most characteristic points are mentioned.

The group of the *oc* language (i.e. where the affirmative particle is borrowed from the Latin *hoc*) occupied all the south of France, except the present department of Basses-Pyrénées, where Basque, a language of unknown origin, foreign to the

Indo-European family was (and still is) spoken. The line which bounded this group to the north started very nearly at Blaye, cut Angoumois in half (from south to north), then, bending to the east, passed to the north of Marche (Creuse), to the south of Bourbonnais (Allier), crossed Forez (Loire, Rhône), rejoined the Rhône near Lyons, and reached the Alps, leaving to the south the departments of Drôme and Hautes-Alpes. The actual boundary is still noticeably the same.

The features common to the whole group were the preservation of several of the Latin tonic vowels, *a*, close *é*, close *o*: *amar, ser, flor* (as opposed to *amer, soir, fleur*), the fact that open *e* and *o* remained without a diphthong, when uninfluenced by *y* or *u*; *pe, mor* (as opposed to *pied, meurt*), the retention under the form of soft consonants of the former hard consonants, which have been dropped elsewhere: *pagar, mudar* (instead of *payer, muer*), the change of *p* to *b*: *saber* (Fr. *savoir*), of *d* to *z*: *fizar* (Fr. *fier*).

The principal varieties were as follows:

Gascon, spoken approximately from the Atlantic to the Garonne, showed such peculiar features that it might be considered a separate language; *f* at the beginning of a word becomes *h*: *hemna* (femina); *ll* between vowels become *r*: *bera* (bella); *n* between vowels is dropped: *lua* (luna); final *ll* become *t*: *castet* (castellum); final *l* becomes a vowel sound in *u*: *nadau* (natalem).

At the other end of the Pyrenees, Catalan occupied a vast region on either side of the ridge; on the French side it was spoken throughout the old province of Roussillon. It retains the Latin sound of *u*: *mur*, and *qu*: *quatre*; does not turn open *e* followed by *y* into a diphthong: *mitj* (medium); changes *z* in the middle of a word into *h*: *rahó* (rationem); final *tz* into *u*: *creu* (crucem); and the suffix *-arium* into *er*: *primer*.

In the Centre, from the Garonne to the Rhône (or nearly so), and from the Pyrenees to the Central Plateau, the group of Languedoc languages included Quercy, Albigeois, Rouergue and Auvergne; these dialects, which have since diverged, then formed one group, the most striking feature of which was that they were more conservative in their phonetics than any of the others.

To the south-west, the dialects of Provence proper retained a final *n*, when not followed by a consonant, which was dropped in the Central region: *razon* (Lang. *razo*); weakened final *tz* to *s*: *cros* (Lang. *crotz* from crucem); and, like Gascon, turned the final *l* into a vowel (*nadau*).

From the north of Provence to Franche-Comté, going beyond the Rhône in several places, stretched the Franco-Provençal dialects, so-called because they unite southern and northern characteristics: tonic free *a* persists as in the south: *clar* (clarum); but when influenced by *y* it changes to *ié*, then *i*: *payi* (pacare); as in the north, initial *c* and *g* before *a* become *ch*, and *j*: *chambra, jardi*; *c*, and *t*, between vowels, are dropped: *louy* (locare), *poeir* (potere), *p* between vowels changes to *v*: *chièvro* (capram); *o* after the accented syllable remains and extends: *autro* (alterum), *fraro* (fratrem).

To the north of the Central Plateau, Limousin (Haute-Vienne, Creuse), although frankly southern, shows some northern features: *c* and *g* at the beginning of a word become *ch* and *j* (*chambra, jardi*); *d* between vowels is dropped and is often replaced by *v* (*jauvir* from gaudere).

On the contrary, the dialects of the south-west (west of Angoumois, Saintonge, Aunis, Poitou), although definitely northern, resemble the *oc* group in some of their phonetic features: *p* between vowels changes to a *b*: *saber* (sapere); *tr* to *ir*: *paire*; close tonic *o* remains: *espos*; *ié*, as in all the west, tends to become *e*.

In the region of *oïl* (i.e. where the affirmative particle is *hoc-illi*) the boundaries are even less clearly defined and the dialects intermingle by overlapping in several particulars. In the centre, the dialect of Ile de France (or *francien*), which soon prevailed over those of Orléanais and Western Champagne, had as distinctive features: the development of close *e* into *oi*, pronounced *wé* after the 13th century (*soir*), of close free *o* into *eu* (*seigneur*), of close stopped *o* into *ou* (*tour*), of short *e* followed by *y* into *i* (*lit*), the confusion of *an* and *en*, *ain* and *ein*.

In the outer provinces of the region of *oïl* the principal dialects were Burgundian (Burgundy and the east of Franche-Comté), Lorrain (from the Vosges to the Ardennes, including the three bishoprics of Metz, Toul and Verdun), Walloon (from the eastern district of the Meuse to Flanders and Artois, i.e. Hainault and the south of Brabant), Picard, which is very like the dialect of Artois (with Amiens and Arras as centres), Norman, which extended into Brittany at some points, and the dialects of Touraine and Berry, which were soon overpowered by the influence of Ile de France.

The following features are common to the dialects of Lorraine and Picardy, and part of the Walloon district: the change of tonic *a* to *ei* (*ameir, bontei*), the retention at the beginning of Germanic words of the letter *w* and its insertion in some others (*warir* for *guérir, wespe* for *guêpe*), the persistence of final *t* up to a late date (*aimet, vertut*).

Common to the Lorrain and Walloon dialects: the imperfect of the first conjugation in *éve* (*améve*).

Common to Walloon and Picard: the distinction between *an* and *en*, the shrinking of *iee* to *ie* (*fie* from vicatam, *ploiie* from plicatam), the change of short *o* followed by *l* and a consonant to *au* (*cauper* from colpare, *caure* from corylum), the feminine article *li* in the subject case, *le* in the object case.

Common to Picardy and Eastern Normandy: the development of the suffix *-ellum* into *iau* (*castiau*), the retention of *c, g,* before *a* (*camp, kien*), the transition from *ce, ci* to *ch* (*chire* from ceram, *chest* from ecce-istum).

Features peculiar to the Burgundian dialect: the change of *ein* to *oin* (*poine, avoine*), of *e* derived from close *é* to *a* or *o* (*matre* from mittere, *vaslot* for *vaslet*), and the shrinking of *oi* to *o* (*valor* for *valoir*).

Peculiar to Lorrain: reduction of *au* to *a* (*atre*), of *els* to *és* (*chastés*), of *a* to *ai* (*ai* from habet, *pairt* from partem).

Peculiar to Picard: change of *ty* and *cy* to *ch* (*canchon, fache*), the omission of *b* and *d* in the groups *ml, nr* (*sanler, tenre*).

Peculiar to Norman: the development of close *e* to *ei* (*teile*), the shrinking of *ie* to *e* (*desraisner*), the late survival or change to *u* of close *o* (*flor, flur*). The Norman dialect, transplanted to England, underwent a special evolution, as we shall see.

It is only very slowly and as a result of circumstances difficult to analyse, that a common language comes into being beside dialects, or takes their place. Moreover this language may be either of every-day use and really a living one, or merely a literary instrument.

It was a language of this latter kind which in the south very soon emerged from the dialects, but without superseding them. At the beginning of the 12th century, we see this language perfectly formed in the work of Guillaume of Poitiers; it was this language which, up to the end of the 13th century, was written by all the troubadours who cultivated lyrical poetry, even those outside France (Northern Italy and Catalonia). It may even have been spoken in the centres frequented by courtly society, which was of very composite and varied origin. It was, in fact, the extent and variety of this public which explains its formation; the wandering troubadour-poets, wishing to make their works popular to a very wide circle, were obliged to have recourse to a language with as few words of dialect as possible. The same characteristic has been noticed in the Homeric poems, and is explained by the same causes.

The basis of this language was not, as was long believed, the dialect of Limousin (if this name is often attached to it, it is because the most accomplished troubadours came from this province); it was the speech of Languedoc, the most central, the least developed of these dialects, consequently that which contained most common features and was the most easily understood throughout a wide region.

Born of circumstances and of a tacit agreement, it had never been trammelled by the narrow rules of grammarians and did not exclude some foreign elements; one of its most characteristic terms (*joi*) is of northern or eastern origin and others (*chanso, chantar, chausimen*) appear most frequently under these forms, which are of Limousin; finally, double forms are not infrequent (*tener* and *tenir*, *paes* and *pais*, *amic* and *ami*, *fach* and *fait*, *merce* and *merci*).

In spite of its aesthetic qualities and the masterpieces which adorned it, it did not survive the circumstances which gave it birth and perished with courtly society and poetry. After the end of the 13th century, local forms reappeared amongst the last troubadours, who were attendants at small courts; these forms were more numerous amongst the "Maintainers of the

Gay Science" of Toulouse, who nevertheless boasted that they revived the old traditions, and more numerous still in the religious, scientific, and moral works, which followed each other in the course of the 14th century, and in dramatic works, of which we have only late examples.

But at this period the predominance of French was making itself felt to the farthest limits of the kingdom, and all the southern authors who cultivated a lofty style or addressed themselves to a wide public wrote in French. The Southern dialects fell to the level of *patois* and did not re-appear in literature until towards the end of the 16th century, and then at first very feebly; but they still live to-day in popular use and they are much better preserved and much less intermixed with French than those of the north.

In the north, a literary language did not become noticeable until much later; but its slower progress was uninterrupted and it is possible to foresee the moment when it will take the place of all the dialects. For reasons too long to enumerate, the conditions here found by writers were quite different; literary centres were very soon formed, at first exclusively aristocratic, which were each quite independent and, in a certain measure, characteristic; those of Normandy were chiefly interested in serious literature, historical, scientific, or religious; those of Brabant, Hainault, and Champagne in lyrical poetry; romantic poetry was everywhere well received. Soon some kinds of literature were welcomed by the middle-class public, for whom were written, especially in the northern and north-eastern provinces, many heroic poems, and witty or satirical tales (*fabliaux, contes de Renart*, etc.).

Thus, until about the middle of the 13th century, all provinces were represented in literary production, but in very unequal proportions. To Normandy belong the *Vie de St Alexis*, the works of Marie de France, the romance of Aeneas, and a large number of chronicles (almost all translated from Latin); to Brittany and Anjou, the *Livre des Manières* by Étienne de Fougères, and the *Chanson d'Aquin*; to Touraine the romance of Thebes and Troy; to Orléanais the *Miracles de Notre-Dame* by Jean le Marchand; to Franche-Comté a collection of fables

(Ysopet de Lyon); to Burgundy and to Lorraine *Floovant* and a prose translation of the Psalms; to the Walloon country, a translation of the dialogues of St Gregory and of the sermons of St Bernard, the *Poème Moral*; to Saintonge and Poitou, an *Épître de St Étienne*, the *Mystère des Vierges Sages* (*Sponsus*), a translation of the *Chronique de Turpin* and of the sermons of Maurice de Sully.

A singular fortune was reserved for Norman, which, transported to England after the Conquest (1066), enjoyed the prestige of all aristocratic languages. But its evolution was so rapid that at the end of a century it had assumed a very original form, the principal characteristics of which were the shrinking of *ié* to *é*, the evolution of *an* and *on* to *aun* and *oun*, of close *o* into *ou* and *u*, the dropping of the unaccented *e*, the complete disappearance of declensions, the confusion of the different types of conjugation, especially to the advantage of the first. As in Normandy, its mother-country, this language became the medium of expression of a very rich literature, historical, moral, and religious. As it was the official language of justice, of government, and of schools, it might have been expected to supersede Anglo-Saxon, as Latin had superseded Gallic, but from the 13th century onwards the middle-class element played an ever greater part in public life, the two races became more closely blended, and every day the Norman language lost ground. After the 14th century it was only a half-artificial language, maintained by aristocratic or literary snobbishness, and its correctness depended on the culture of those who spoke or wrote it. It is, for instance, much less altered in the works of Gower (end of the 14th century) than in the sixty years older works of the Franciscan, Nicholas Bozon, or even in the letters, written even earlier, by members of the highest aristocracy[1].

But before this language disappeared, it had thoroughly permeated and greatly enriched Anglo-Saxon, and its literature had awakened and given life to the national literature.

The language of Ile de France had been spread by reason of its administrative and judicial use throughout the royal

[1] See *Recueil de lettres anglo-françaises* (1265–1399), ed. F.-J. Tanqueray, 1916.

dominions, which extended to Orléanais in the south, and to Vermandois (Saint-Quentin) and Ponthieu (Abbeville) in the north Soon it exceeded these limits. Its progress was facilitated not only by the existence of a literature (which included *Fierabras*, the *Pèlerinage de Charlemagne*, the romance of *Alexandre*, and the "Chansons" of the Châtelain de Couci), but in the highest degree by the presence of two flourishing universities, Paris and Orleans, to which from all parts there flocked students, who adopted this language, enriched it, and carried the knowledge of it back to their homes. Hence, from the end of the 12th century, it was in a certain sense imposed on all writers cultivating a lofty style and addressing themselves to a wide public, and it increasingly restricted their use of local forms. The latter are already very scanty in the romance of *Troie*, written by a native of Tours for the Norman court, in the works of the writer of Champagne, Chrétien de Troyes, and his imitators, and in the songs of the lyrical poets, even those who were natives of very distant provinces, such as Lorraine or Anjou.

Moreover this language was no more exclusive than literary Provençal and it admitted some foreign elements; thus we find phrases very characteristic of Picardy used by writers born in the heart of the Ile de France, such as the Châtelain de Couci or Helinand.

The Picard dialect, in fact, was no less widely cultivated than French and was spread by some very popular works; it was more or less mixed with Walloon and tended, in its turn, to become a literary language. In the 13th century there were written in Picard numerous works addressed to a middle-class public, chiefly local—songs, *jeus partis*, *fabliaux*, sacred and secular dramas. Picard even held its own as a court language and, up to the end of the 14th century, was adapted to the most lofty themes in Brabant and Hainault, in spite of the close relation between these provinces and their nobles with the monarchy; the authors of the lengthy cycle of the Crusades and of other romances—Adenet le Roi, Baudouin and Jean de Condé, Jean le Bel, and Froissart—wrote in Picard. It was the last of the dialects to yield to the pressure of the French of Ile de France.

From the end of the 12th century there are abundant proofs

of the diffusion of French and of the estimation in which it was held abroad. Soon it tended to become the language of polite society throughout Europe, as it did in the 18th century. The German nobles summoned French tutors to their homes; an educational treatise compiled in Norway at the end of the 13th century compared the diffusion of French to that of Latin. The Venetian, Martino da Canale, and the Florentine, Brunetto Latini, declared that it was "la langue la plus delitable, la plus commune à toutes gens," and prided themselves on writing it. It spread in Northern Italy and it was only on account of their ignorance that the Venetian jongleurs, far away ancestors of Boiardo and Ariosto, wrote it so incorrectly. It was also in common use in Constantinople, Cyprus, and the Holy Land, among the very mixed Christian populations of these countries. French words, particularly those borrowed from military and courtly life, invaded German and Italian.

The success of French was justified by its qualities of unity and harmony, which have since diminished to an ever greater extent. The very varied vowel system alternated vowels, diphthongs, and triphthongs; nasal sounds had so far only made their appearance in *a* and *o*; no combination of consonants presented a harsh sound; in the conjugations, the alternation of strong forms (*aime, vient*) with weak (*amons, venons*) introduced a harmonious balance; the two cases of the declension facilitated the liberty and variety of construction; the more restricted use of the article, the shorter form of the pronouns, rendered the clauses less ponderous; finally the vocabulary, thanks to the freedom with which words were borrowed and to the numerous double forms (*tristece* and *tristor*; *richece* and *richoise*; *arestance* and *arestison*), was extremely rich, even more so than was necessary for the expression of thought.

What was lacking to the French writers was a technical vocabulary suitable for philosophical and scientific speculations and the art of constructing the sentence and co-ordinating its elements. Syntax was too often haphazard. "Modern French," says M. Lucien Foulet, "is often logical without any apparent reason, without urgent necessity, for the pleasure of being so. Old French, with a few exceptions, is generally very clear. But it is a language which grew quite independently.

Grammarians and logicians have had no hand in its development; it says, indeed, all that it wishes to say, but does not always use the right forms. Spontaneous and simple, it is satisfied as soon as it has made itself understood[1]."

It was in these two directions that it perfected itself in the course of the 14th and 15th centuries, but not without losing much of its harmony, grace, and youthful lightness.

It was during this period, rightly called "Middle French," that the characteristics of the modern language began to show themselves clearly. The principal changes which came about were as follows:

In phonetics *ié* (from *a* influenced by *y*) was replaced by *é* (*léger, traiter*); *oi*, already pronounced *wé*, tended towards *wa* (popular pronunciation) and to *è*; a nasal sound crept into open *e* and *oe* (*ẽ, õẽ*); unaccented *e* was increasingly weakened, and was dropped before another vowel (*chance* from *cheance, rond* from *reond, mûr* from *meür*). The subject case disappeared in favour of the object case; in consequence, inversion became rare and the present order of the elements of the sentence (subject, verb, object) tended to become the rule. The use of the article and of personal pronouns extended; the first person of the present indicative took an *e* in the first conjugation and an *s* in the others. In the strong preterite, the variation between the differently accented persons disappeared and the unification was made sometimes in one way (*tu vins* like *je vins*), sometimes in the other (*je peignis* like *tu peignis*).

But it was the vocabulary which underwent the most important modifications, by the adoption of a number of learned words, almost all taken from Latin. This invasion has resulted in the alteration of the aspect of French and is regrettable from an aesthetic point of view. "It would no doubt have been desirable for the beauty and organic harmony of our language," says Gaston Paris, "that our civilisation should have developed spontaneously, like that of the Greeks, and that all our abstract and scientific terms should have been the product and the reflection of the personal work of our own thought. But this was impossible; Latin was the official language of a religion which was neither born on our soil, nor of our race, and

[1] *Petite Syntaxe de l'ancien français*, p. 271.

which reached us with a terminology which had been elaborated by foreign thought. Similarly philosophy, science, and high intellectual culture were transmitted to us by Latin books, and were maintained all through the Middle Ages by men who not only wrote but spoke Latin. It was these men who by their translations or summaries laid the foundations of serious literature in the common tongue; how could they describe in French words the objects which they were actually endeavouring to explain to people who spoke only French? It was all the more natural that they should use Latin words and add thereto French terminations, as all the world at that time knew that French was only Latin fallen into common use[1]."

This penetration began very early, even before the language had taken definite shape. In the Merovingian period, the clergy who spoke both classical Latin and the rustic language had carried words from one to the other; these words were adopted by the people, shared in subsequent evolution, and consequently wore a hybrid appearance. To this category of very old borrowed words belong almost all church and school terms: *aneme* (later *âme*, soul), *apostle* (*apôtre*), *epistle* (*épître*), *esperit* (*esprit*), *grâce*, *trinité*, *vice*.

These words are naturally very numerous in the texts translated or imitated from Latin: the twenty-nine verses of *Eulalie* contain a large proportion (*aneme*, *element*, *empedemenz*, *virginitet*), the translations of the Bible are overloaded with them; but though very numerous in scientific and theological works, they are on the contrary very rare in heroic poems or in *fabliaux*.

From the 14th century onwards, it became a veritable invasion. At this period, in fact, there appeared the first renaissance of ancient studies, one feature of which was the vogue for translations. Under the vigorous encouragement of John the Good, of Charles V, and a whole group of patrons, staffs of translators rendered into French not only Livy, Aristotle, and St Augustine, but the great encyclopaedias of the Middle Ages. The desire for accuracy, then quite new, led these translators at every turn to copy the Latin words for which they could find no equivalent in French. Oresme, mentioning this difficulty, declared

[1] *Mélanges linguistiques*, 1909, p. 205.

that one cannot explain a difficult science in popular terms, and he drew up a list of "foreign words" which he was obliged to use.

It cannot be said, however, that he Latinised to excess or that he did great violence to the language. In the following passage it is remarkable that all the new words have passed into use (except *fortitude*, which is nevertheless as correctly formed as *promptitude*, for instance):

"*Politique* est celle qui soustient la *cure* de la chose *publique* et qui, par *l'industrie* de sa *prudence* et par la balance ou pois de sa *justice* et par la *constance* et *fermeté* de sa *fortitude* et la *pacience* de son attrempance donne *medecine* au salut de tous, en tant qu'elle peut dire de soy meïsmes: 'Par moi les roys regnent et ceux qui font les loix *discernent* et *determinent* quelles choses sont *justes*.'...Et donques de toutes les *sciences* mondaines, c'est la tres *principale* et la plus *digne* et la plus profitable[1]."

In the course of the 15th century, on the contrary, the mania for Latinism became a positive curse; it raged first in the pedantic and pretentious school gathered round the Dukes of Burgundy, whose leaders were Chastellain, Le Maire, and Molinet; then it was not long in attacking the writers patronised by the kings or the queens of France, such as Cretin and Jean Marot. To get some idea of this nonsensical jargon, it is enough to read the celebrated chapter (*Pantagruel*, II. 6) in which Rabelais has given us, not a caricature, but a faithful picture.

The works of most of these "rhetoricians" are written in a jargon which to us seems intolerable; but even in the most moderate of them, those who were at the time masters of taste and arbiters of fashion, Latinism held a really overpowering place, as may be seen in the following passage from Lemaire de Belges, which gives us an approximate picture of his ordinary style (the author therein describes the apparition of a nymph to Paris):

"En son beau chief elle ne portoit or ne *gemmes*, mais seulement pour le *preserver* du hasle, un chapeau de branches de laurier. Sa belle face, sans fard et sans teinture autre que naturelle, *modeste* et *gracieuse* de blancheur sans *blandices*, pretendoit *autorité* non *austere* et *reverence* lointaine de *rusticité*.

[1] Quoted by F. Brunot, *Histoire de la langue française*, I. 517.

...Les ondes *multicolores* de cest habillement flottoient jusques a terre. Et le regard diceluy estoit de *variable* plaisance, semblable a la *superficialité* d'un ruisselet argentin....Au bas de ce vestement non pareil pendoient franges vermeillettes, avec petits *tintinables* et *cymbalettes armonieusement* sonnant quant elle marchoit[1]."

Fortunately, the writers did not only borrow copiously from the Latin vocabulary; they also tried to reproduce the noble breadth of the Latin period and, though in this direction there were many unhappy efforts, it may be said that such writers as Christine de Pisan and Alain Chartier were often successful.

It is remarkable that in this hybrid language, Greek should be very feebly represented; the works of the Greeks were in fact only known by Latin translations. Through the medium of these however, a fair number of words crept in, almost all technical words belonging to various sciences (*anarchie, aristocratie, démocratie; anthrax, cataplasme, diaphragme; économie, éphémère, étymologie, mathématique, métaphysique, monopole*).

In comparison with this influx of ancient words, modern additions are of little importance. The most important are derived from the dialects, which were not systematically condemned before Malherbe. At this period they added many words to French, either by means of authors, or more commonly, as a result of the exchange of products between different districts. From the South came *abeille* (bee), *aubade* (morning serenade), *ballade, bastide* (country-house), *câble, cadet* (younger son, a Gascon word), *camail* (hood), *cap* (cape), *ciboule* (spring onion), *cigale* (cicala), *escargot* (snail), *fat* (fop), *goudron* (tar), *gouge* (young woman), *goujat* (young man), *merlus* (dried cod), *muscade* (nutmeg), *salade*.

From Lyonnais, *dot* (dowry), *marron* (chestnut).

From Dauphiné: *crétin* (idiot), *mélèze* (larch).

From Norman-Picard: *caillou* (pebble), *cape* (cloak).

From Walloon: *houille* (coal).

Finally, slang words, which first made their appearance in the 13th century, became multiplied in the 15th in humorous works and in the comic parts of the Mystery plays, whence came most of the following: *blanc* (simpleton), *brocant* (ring),

[1] *Les Illustrations de Gaule*, 1528, book I, ch. 24.

*brouer* (to walk), *endosse* (a garment), *mate* (a haunt of thieves, whence *matois*, a gaolbird); most of these have disappeared, but some have survived, such as *gueux* (rogue), *matois* (cunning), *narquois* (chaffing).

Contributions from foreign languages are comparatively few in number. As a result of the Crusades, of the French settlements in the East, and the translation of Arabic works, a fairly large number of Eastern words had crept in, some at a very early date.

Borrowed from Greek: *besant, boutique* (shop), *chaland* (boat), *chiourme* (ship's crew), *dromon* (cruising ship), *émeraude, galée* (galley), *mangoneau* (mangonel), *timbre* (originally *tambour*, bell or gong).

From Arabic: *alquemie* (*alchimie*), *aucube* (tent), *calife* (at first *algalife*), *coton* and *hoqueton*, **drugement* (interpreter, dragoman), *échec* (check), *housse* (hammer-cloth), *nacaire* (trumpet), *orange, sirop, zéro.*

Up to the 14th century, the contribution from Italian was very small: the words quoted by a few philologists as borrowed at an earlier time occur in Italian authors or in works written in the Holy Land in an italianised *milieu.* From that time they became very numerous: *alarme, ambassade, bande* (troop), *banquet, baraque, bastion, brigade* (troop), *brigand, canon, câpre* (caper), *citadelle, citadin* (townsman), *courtisan* (courtier), *crédence, cassette* (chest), *crédit, douane* (custom-house), *embusquer, escadre* (squadron), *estampe* (print), *magasin* (a shop), *médaille, musique, niche, partisan, pavois* (shield), *perruque* (periwig), *régal* (entertainment), *représailles, se révolter* (to turn round), *salade* (helmet), *tercet, trafic, tribune.*

As will be seen, the chief words in this list relate to commerce and war; artistic terms, which were adopted so freely in the 16th century, are very rare.

Up to this time Spanish had only supplied a few words: *caparaçon, genet* (jennet), *mélasse* (molasses), *simarre* (a woman's dress).

From English also very few: *bigot, goudale* (good ale), *guerseiller* (to drink healths, from *wæs heil*, a drinker's salutation), *milord.*

There are considerably more words derived from German and Dutch; the former of these languages supplied many military terms, which is explained by the frequent employment of German and Swiss mercenaries; the latter is almost exclusively represented by sea-terms.

From German are thus derived: *bélitre* (originally a beggar, a vagabond, now a rascal), *blocus* (little fort), *boulevard* (an earthern rampart supported by boards), *crèche* (manger), *cric* (jack), *écrevisse* (crayfish), *foudre* (a large tun), *godendart* (a long pike), *lansquenet*, *rosse* (jade).

From Dutch: *aigrefin* (a fish), *amarre* (cable), *brodequin* (a boot, originally a kind of stuff), *cranequin* (arbalest), *digue* (originally *dique*, dyke), *drogue* (drug), *dune*, *équiper* (originally *eschiper*), *étape* (stage, originally *estaple*, warehouse for merchandise), *houblon* (hops, originally *houbelon*, *houbillon*), *laie* (a small case, hence *layette*), *lest* (ballast), *matelot* (sailor, originally *matenot*), *mannequin* (a little wooden figure), *mouette* (sea-gull), *quille* (keel of a ship), *vilebrequin* (brace, originally *wimbelkin*).

In the 16th century, words borrowed from modern foreign languages, especially Southern ones, were much more numerous, and those from ancient Greek more numerous still; hence our vocabulary became redundant, and the chief anxiety of the 17th century grammarians was, not to enrich the language, which did not require it, but to restrain and to discipline it.

## BIBLIOGRAPHY

A. Darmesteter, A. Hatzfeld and A. Thomas, *Traité de la formation de la langue française*, prefixed to vol. II. of *Dictionnaire général de la langue française du commencement du xvii^e siècle jusqu'à nos jours*, 1890–1900. Kr. Nyrop, *Histoire de la langue française* (*Grammaire historique de la langue française*, vol. I. 2nd éd., Copenhagen, 1904). F. Brunot, *Histoire de la langue française des origines à 1900*, vol. I. 1905. G. Paris, *Mélanges linguistiques publiés par M. Roques*, 1909. E. Bourciez, *L'ancien français et le provençal* (*Eléments de linguistique romane*, 1910, pp. 311–99). H. Suchier, *Le français et le provençal*, 1891, translation by P. Monet of a chapter (III. i. B. 5) in G. Groeber, *Grundriss der romanischen Philologie*, Strasbourg, 1888 ff., and *Les voyelles toniques du vieux français*, translated by Ch. Guerlin de Guer, 1906. G. Bertoni, *Testi antichi francesi, per uso delle scuole di filologia romanza*, Rome-Milan, 1908, introduction. H. Morf, *Zur sprachlichen Gliederung Frankreichs*, in *Abhandlungen Akad. Berl.* 1911.

# CHAPTER VIII

## LITERATURE

THE great invasions of the Barbarians during the 4th and 5th centuries, which brought about the fall of the Roman Empire, mark the end of the period of Antiquity and the beginning of what is called the Middle Ages. At that time Latin was the language of Gaul, and many hundreds of years passed before the Latin language developed, after numerous gradual changes, into the French language.

It was only in the 9th century in the celebrated *Serments de Strasbourg*—declarations made by Louis the German and the soldiers of Charles the Bald—that the French language appeared for the first time. A few rare texts of the 10th and 11th centuries show the rapid developments of this new language. Of the 12th century there are numerous texts which already afford evidence of the existence not only of authors but of a public.

Henceforth it is possible to speak of a Medieval Literature, which continues down to the end of the 15th century. The Renaissance, which was the beginning of Modern Times, started in Italy; the expeditions of the French kings into Italy introduced Italian influence into France. The end of the period of the Middle Ages may therefore be placed at the time when the first French army was preparing to pass over the Alps. If we look for equally important events at the beginning of our period we shall find them in the two great adventures of the 11th century: the Conquest of England by the Normans, and the First Crusade. The history of French medieval literature may therefore be said to be the history of the progress of this literature during the four hundred years and more between the Conquest of England by William of Normandy (1066) and the departure of Charles VIII for Italy (1494).

Within the limits of this period however great changes took place. The 12th and 13th centuries saw the triumph of feudalism and of the feudal spirit, but the Hundred Years' War broke the ancient framework of society; during the 15th century the royal power definitely predominated, while the *bourgeoisie* became more important than it had ever been before. To these historic and social changes correspond parallel changes in literary outlook and literary inspiration. So that we may say there were two definite periods in French medieval literature: the period before, and the period after the beginning of the Hundred Years' War. We shall examine each of them in turn, but at the outset it is worth noting certain characteristics, common to both periods, which clearly distinguish French medieval literature from modern literature.

The first thing to be noted is that the works of the Middle Ages have come down to us, not in the form of books, but in the form of manuscripts. Only a very few authors of the 15th century and a small number of successful works belonging to the preceding period were printed towards the very end of the 15th century. These exceptions may be ignored. On the whole we have to deal with work in manuscript form which has never been printed, and often not even discovered, until our own day. From this fact there are several conclusions to be drawn. It is obvious that everything that was written has not been preserved, but we are not even sure that all the important works have survived. One of the gems of early French literature, the charming romance of *Aucassin et Nicolette*, has come down to us in only one manuscript. Suppose that, by some unlucky chance, this manuscript had been destroyed long ago; we should have no means of ever suspecting our loss, since, so far as we know, no one during the Middle Ages has alluded to it.

Chance has served us here, but in other cases, perhaps, it has worked against us. However, there is reason for believing that our losses, though indisputable, have not been considerable. On the other hand, it is not always the best manuscripts that survive. Some, while not bad, are late and the language has evidently been modernised. The cases in which we have a work in the exact form given to it by the author are on the whole rare. But here again we must not exaggerate; very often the differences between the original work and the version that has come down to us are insignificant.

Another and a more important point is that a great number of works of the Middle Ages are anonymous, though it has by no means been proved that in most of these cases the anonymity was intentional. The names of the authors have apparently been lost, often in spite of the authors, and often through their own negligence. Those of them who trusted to the testimony of their own contemporaries were soon forgotten except when the latter left some written evidence. Names inscribed on the first sheet of manuscript must have disappeared without hope of recovery when the sheet was torn or stained. Some authors, more wary, enshrined their names in their own verses, and in this way many of them have succeeded in making themselves known to us; but even this precaution did not save them all from oblivion, as the scribe in copying a manuscript would often omit these indications, which were of no interest to him, or which perhaps were already by that time beyond his comprehension. Moreover, the majority of manuscripts are as innocent of all mention of date as of author. Doubtless after examining the characteristics of the language it is possible to suggest a date, but this, even under the most favourable conditions, can be only an unreliable approximation, and there is a risk of committing very serious errors. A rough chronology in divisions of fifty years has been practically established, but within these divisions the classifications are too often arbitrary.

One result of all this uncertainty is that the literature of the Middle Ages appears to the modern reader a confused mass of independent works, independent of each other, independent of all historical and social surroundings, and with no visible relation to any author. We seem to be transported into a world where literary production was a very different matter from what it is in our own world. But this is merely an illusion. If we knew all the names and all the dates we should be much better able to see that in medieval times there were such things as literary tradition, schools of poetry, influence of one author on another, technique, and even authors who were not perhaps essentially very different from those of to-day. Naturally, as we get nearer to modern times we see more clearly under what conditions literature developed, and what has just been said is more specially applicable to the 12th and 13th centuries.

## § I. FROM THE NORMAN CONQUEST (1066) TO THE BEGINNING OF THE HUNDRED YEARS' WAR (1337)

The beginnings of French literature are just as much hidden from us as are the beginnings of the French language. The earliest texts that have been preserved are written in a language infinitely nearer to the French of the 20th century than to the Latin of the 4th century. How the change took place from Latin to French we do not know; however, as we have the point of departure and the point of arrival it is possible to guess approximately and at times with certainty.

The fact is that languages develop continuously, so long as there are people to speak them; there is never a break in tradition, only a gradual transformation. A literature on the other hand is born and dies. We do not know exactly when French literature was born, nor under what influences it developed. We must not place its origin too far back, as it could only find expression in a language already formed. Furthermore there are certain periods of history so dark and so full of confusion that even the most rudimentary intellectual culture would hardly be possible.

Such a period was the 10th century in France. One is therefore inclined to fix the birth of French literature in the 11th century. But the development was so rapid that one cannot admit that it was spontaneous. There must have been models which fired the authors' imaginations, showed them the way they must follow, and prompted a fertile spirit of emulation. Latin literature alone, with its often threatened but unbroken tradition, could have furnished these models. In spite, however, of the extreme probability of the hypothesis that French literature springs from Latin literature, just as the French language is derived from the Latin, we cannot, up to the present, say that it has been fully proved. But what is certain is that the earliest literary texts show all the characteristics of an already established tradition. The language in which they are written is not the awkward, stammering speech of apprentices making their first effort in artistic composition, but a language apt, terse, harmonious, capable of expressing delicate shades of meaning and, at times, reaching real grandeur. It is free from provincialisms and generally avoids words and pronunciations that smack of any definite locality; evidently it is a language addressed not to the people of this or that district, but to all who speak French. Such a language implies frequent communication between the various provinces, a busy exchange of ideas and impressions, and indeed a real culture throughout the nation.

Another characteristic common to the early works is that they arrange themselves into distinct categories, in which one can hardly help recognising, even at this early stage, the various literary forms of a later day. In the Lives of Saints and the *chansons de geste* we find poems often instinct with a very personal inspiration, but expressed in a literary form for the most part imposed by tradition. Even as early as this we can recognise poetic schools and can see that the literary production has taken a definite direction. It is therefore not surprising to find that the very versification is governed by precise rules. There are several types of verse, but the most usual by far is the decasyllable, the rhythm of which is given by the recurrence of a fixed stress at the 4th and 10th syllables, the position of any other stress being left to the choice of the poet; the lines are grouped, either in stanzas of equal length, or, most frequently, in *laisses* or sections of verse of unequal length, by assonance—that is to say by the identity in sound of the last accented vowel of each line.

The universal language, the well-defined literary forms, the already skilful versification constitute an original literature accepted throughout all the territories where French was spoken. These territories did not include the southern provinces of France, where Provençal was spoken—a language also of Latin origin, but with peculiarities of its own. But, by way of compensation, England was included, where, though of course English still held its own, French took the first place from the time of the Norman Conquest. For a long time the Normans of England considered themselves as French as the Frenchmen of France, and they composed works which form an integral part of French literature. Later on they entered into closer relations with their Saxon neighbours and became more and more conscious of their new nationality. This evolution, traceable as early as the middle of the 12th century, and fostered by the long wars between the Plantagenets and the Capetian kings of France, is fully accomplished at the beginning of the 13th. For many years afterwards French still continued to be written and spoken in England, but such writings as were produced there in French after this time belong to the literary history of the English people.

Who were the writers of the 12th century? In what class are we to look for them? The feudal world consisted in the first place of the feudal lords, owners of the land, who, be they suzerains or vassals, possessed all sovereign rights in their own domain. Theoretically they were all equal, but in reality a few great lords held a predominant position on account of the vast extent of their possessions. The king was the most powerful of all, and his power gave him unique prestige. By the side of the petty courts of the French and English lords the royal courts of Paris and London already made an imposing figure.

In the country the villeins toiled and hardly counted at all. They were still practically at the mercy of their masters. In the towns there was more freedom, the citizens often succeeding in defining their rights and obtaining recognition of them. They formed an active, industrious class, which increased in wealth and bided its time. Lastly there were the clergy, who held a very great position. Not only were there a great number of bishops who were lords living on their own lands amidst their own vassals, but the Church as the heir of Christ and representative of God upon earth was the supreme moral power of the time; the keeper of divine truth as well as the possessor of human knowledge, for the Church knew Latin, and Latin alone gave access to the wonderful world of thought. During the whole of the Middle Ages the philosophers and learned men of all Europe wrote only in Latin; the vulgar tongues such as French and English were not considered capable of being the vehicles of thought. So that it was a great privilege to possess the key to universal knowledge; and the clergy were very proud of their learning. *Clerc* was the title given to all members of the clergy no matter what their rank in the hierarchy, and also to all those who at one time or another had tried to take holy orders and had either failed or given up the career—in a word to all those who had studied in the schools and knew Latin. They did not all profit by the teaching of their masters to the same degree, and it is clear that a great number of them had but a poor knowledge of Latin, but it is certainly amongst the "clerks" that we must look for the cultivated men of the period. They were the intellectuals of the Middle Ages. However, their social origin was too varied for them to form a separate class; they came from the nobility, from the *bourgeoisie*, and even from the despised hordes of the villeins. The Church had its own hierarchy, which did not correspond to the narrow classifications of lay society; on the contrary the Church was the only way by which the individual might escape from the conditions in which birth and the feudal world had placed him.

In the great army of clerks were gathered together, often on an equal footing, representatives of the whole nation; they were therefore best able to express the feelings and the ideals of the nation. It would not be surprising to find that it was above all from their ranks that the authors of the Middle Ages were recruited. The clerks turned into French a great number of Latin works, and their translations, though often of no great interest to us, rendered immense services to their contemporaries. They brought this rough and rugged society into contact with the great civilisation of Antiquity and to a certain extent prepared for the coming of the Renaissance. They also composed original works which reflect the point of view of their own time, and it is in this way above all that they are of interest to us.

Where did they look for their audience? In the first place, as might be expected, in the ecclesiastical world itself to which they were closely or distantly related. It must not be taken for granted that for this audience they wrote only moral treatises and pious histories. They often found the most sympathetic readers of their works of pure imagination, even of their romances, among the clergy. For example, at the beginning of the 13th century we find country priests, bishops, and cardinals vying with each other in their knowledge of and ability to quote from the poems of Renart; they did not all approve of these amusing tales, but they had all read them closely at one time in their lives. It is hard to believe that during the 12th century the clergy were any stricter. The feudal lord also, during the leisure left him from fighting, needed distractions, and there is no doubt that the works of the clerks succeeded in finding their way to his castle.

In what form were the works published? Manuscripts were rare and costly. The publication of a book at this time meant making five or six copies, perhaps more, perhaps less. There was no difficulty in this for members of the Church. The convent and the schools had their libraries, where one manuscript served for the instruction and recreation of many generations, but in the greater part of the lordly castles there was certainly nothing of the kind during the 12th century. Even when the owners possessed a few manuscripts they were rarely able to make use of them. They had neither the taste nor the time for poring over musty pages generally covered with illegible writing.

How many of them could even read and write at the beginning of the 12th century? Generally speaking therefore they did not read the works of their contemporaries, which were known to them, however, thanks to the *jongleurs* or strolling singers who came to the castle to recite the poems or sing them to the accompaniment of the viol.

Who were the *jongleurs*? In our day, poems, romances, tales, histories, all come to us in book form; the only exception is the drama, which we go to the theatre to see. In the 12th century it was quite different; books were the exception. The author's public was first and foremost an audience. To this fact is due the existence of a class of men whose trade it was to go about from château to château to make known new works or to repeat the old ones. These were the *jongleurs*. Where did they come from? They had a little learning, they could decipher a manuscript, and, if necessary, recopy it; they recited and they sang. All this they must have learnt somewhere, and they could only have learnt from the clerks; indeed it is not always easy to distinguish between the two. So far as literature is concerned, the clerks were the authors and the *jongleurs* the performers, but the line of demarcation is at times indefinite. Many a clerk earned his living by hawking his works about the country, many a *jongleur* had sufficient talent to add a work of his own composition to his ordinary repertory. As a rule we perceive that the difference between the *trouvère* (thus was the clerk who turned author called) and the *jongleur* was less one of culture than one of social position. Amongst the *jongleurs* themselves there were many grades from the performer who recited a noble *chanson de geste* to the merry clown who went in for buffoonery and conjuring. The *trouvère* may be compared to the man of letters of our day, while the *jongleur* may at times be likened to one of our great tragedians, at times to a music-hall comedian.

A literature made for clerks and nobles is an aristocratic literature; the villeins, it must be admitted, had little place in it, and when they do appear it is generally to be laughed at and held up to ridicule. However, although it was addressed above all to the *élite* of society, it cannot be said to be a literature for the initiated only and inaccessible to the rest of the nation. The ideas which it expresses and the sentiments by which it is inspired have something simple, large, and human, so that the whole of 12th century France could find itself reflected therein. And indeed the *jongleurs* knocked not only at the castle gate; they journeyed from town to town, and it was often enough in the market-place or at the fair that they found their most attentive audiences—rich citizens who had houses of their own or noisy groups of the lower class who already swarmed in the towns. This contact with the seething life of the cities was an advantage to the literature of the 12th century by widening its horizon and spreading its influence. Thus it became a truly national literature.

The most ancient text of a literary character that we have is *The Life of St Alexis*; this short poem of 625 decasyllabic lines, dating from the second half of the 11th century, is thus early a finished work of art. It tells how the son of a Roman noble on his wedding day leaves his wife, his family and his riches, to devote himself entirely to God; after a wandering life of poverty and privation he returns to the house of his father; and there, hidden away, on a wretched bed of straw, unrecognised by all, despised by nearly everyone, made mock of and persecuted by the servants, seeing his parents overwhelmed at his disappearance but unable to console them without betraying himself, he carries out to the end the bitter sacrifice he had imposed upon himself. He dies at last and his soul flies straight to heaven. Too late his family discover that the ragged wretch who lived for seventeen years under the stairs was none other than the son of the house. Father, mother and wife weep for the departed, but the city is filled with divine joy at the thought that a saint lived in Rome, that he has just died there, and been buried there. He will be a powerful intercessor with God and miracles will be wrought at his tomb. Many a one will come to pray there with tears and go away singing praises.

The lives of the saints are continued in the *chansons de geste*: *Roland* completes *Saint Alexis*; there is the same religious inspiration; both saint and hero are great servants of the Lord; but the one reaches heaven by asceticism and renunciation, the other by the practice of the manly virtues, energy, courage, generosity. Of the two Roland seems the nearer to ourselves, but it must be recognised that both were loved with an equal affection in medieval times; each presents a facet of the same ideal.

This ideal was both religious and warlike, for it is only in battle that the hero reveals and asserts himself. Obviously he could not show his mettle in petty quarrels; during a long period the knight of the *chansons de geste* will fight for his God and for his king in a holy war. Thus is knighthood justified and made glorious by the beauty of its mission; herein lies the true greatness of the Feudal régime; this is the secret of its enduring. And this mission, for the author of *Roland* and the ancient *trouvères*, is pre-eminently the mission of France. Not that they oppose their own country to others; on the contrary, they dream of a Christian Europe united through its length and breadth against the pagan assault, but what they wish is that their own people should be first in danger and first in glory. Now this dream of a Europe united against the infidel had been dreamed before and even realised under Charlemagne. The clerks had not forgotten the great Emperor of the West; their books were filled with his memory just as ours are with Napoleon's, and when the Crusade was preached his name and his example were often invoked with sincere fervour. Europe in the 12th century had no Charlemagne, but the Charlemagne of the past, magnified and idealised, was still capable of leading to victory the Franks of France. That was why the contemporaries of the First Crusade liked to locate their ideas, their dreams, and their ideals in those far off times of the 8th and 9th centuries.

The *Chanson de Roland* is our most ancient *chanson de geste*; it has been preserved for us in the famous manuscript of Oxford, dating from the end of the 12th century, but it was probably composed in the first quarter of that century. The first person who definitely mentions it was an Englishman, William of Malmesbury, and he tells us that it was sung at the battle of Hastings by the Normans before the combat. If this be true it could only refer to an older poem than the one we have, but probably William is repeating a mere legend, a beautiful legend, which relates how the *Roland* was thus sung to men about to fight in order to fire their courage with the example of a hero. Such was the high opinion the people of the 12th century had of the *Chanson de Roland*. They could choose no nobler exemplar than the knight who died at Roncevaux because he believed that courage and right should never give way before numbers. Roland with the twelve peers and 20,000 Frenchmen holds the pass of the Pyrenees, while Charlemagne and the main body of the army return to France. Suddenly the Saracens in countless hordes charge upon the rearguard. Roland could have sounded his horn and summoned Charlemagne back; this it was perhaps his duty to do, and Oliver advised it. But prudence might here be taken for cowardice, and Roland does not wish that after his death a song be sung to his discredit. He struggles desperately and does wonders with Durendal, his trusty sword; the infidels fall in heaps, but the French fall also, and the twelve peers likewise one after the other. Finally the Saracens take flight, and it was time they did. Roland's men have fought like heroes and died like Christians. Archbishop Turpin has given them the promise of heaven and they know they have deserved it. And now Roland, left alone and himself about to die, can sound his horn. He no longer fears a defamatory song, neither he nor any of his 20,000 valiant men whose bodies cover the plain. Such is the song, which a great poet, whose name was perhaps TUROLDUS, has sung for us in rich, admirable, and vigorous verse. It is in the *Roland* that we find the best of the soul of old France; it is the magnificent expression of the ideal of a great people at a glorious moment of their history.

Two other *chansons de geste* belong to the time of Roland, though perhaps of a little later date: the *Chanson de Guillaume* and *Gormont et Isembart*. In the *Guillaume* the Saracens have penetrated into France, but Charlemagne, the great emperor, with whose presence the whole of the *Roland* is filled, is no longer there.

His son Louis is a weak king, fond of his peace and quiet, who stays at home in his town of Laon. His good vassals defend his kingdom in his stead, and amongst these is a young man named Vivien. Overwhelmed by numbers, his companions all killed or put to flight, he himself must stand his ground, for he has made a vow never to fly from fear of death; surrounded by a few faithful men he fights against all hope. He longs for the presence of the valiant Guillaume, his uncle; were he but on the field of battle, victory might change sides. The despairing refrain is often repeated, "*Ah! si Guillaume était là!*" Vivien is a hero whose vow has marked him out for death, and who knows it, but Guillaume we feel is the hope of Christendom. He is a second Roland, but a Roland who has no Charlemagne. Instead he has Guibourc his wife, one of the finest figures in French epic. She is the conscience of Guillaume; he has but to look at her to see where his duty lies. Not that he needs this, but he delights in her uprightness, in her watchful jealousy for his own fame. One day after a terrible fight, pursued by hordes of Saracens, Guillaume reaches the gates of Orange; but Guibourc refuses to believe that it is her husband fleeing thus before the infidel and denies him admittance.

The curious thing is that Guibourc is a converted pagan; the *trouvères*, who pitilessly massacre the Saracens in hundreds of thousands, bear them no hatred; they paint them as brave as the Christians and, once they are baptised, freely grant them all the noblest virtues. Nothing shows better, not merely the Christian but the deeply human character of these old poems.

The Saracens have taken flight, but they will surely return, and Guillaume has lost his nephew Vivien, and all his barons. He must go to seek help from King Louis. In Laon they lead a peaceful life, and the fierce warrior arriving unexpectedly seems rather in the way and slightly ridiculous. The good vassal, thoroughly incensed, tells the courtiers what he thinks of them in terrifying tones; in his anger he spares no one, not even the

Queen, who is his sister. In the drowsy palace of King Louis it is as though the great voice of France, energetic, active, and conscious of her mission, thundered and boomed. The *Chanson de Guillaume* is not so well composed as the *Roland*, neither is it filled with the same rare spirit, but it has more variety and contains some passages of surprising beauty.

Of *Gormont et Isembart* we have only a fragment of a few hundred lines in octosyllables of an archaic type. The hero is a renegade Frenchman, who, whilst fighting in the ranks of the Saracens in a furious combat against the soldiers of King Louis, is mortally wounded. In his last prayers he returns to his God and dies in his native land, which he has never ceased to love.

Here again we feel a noble inspiration, but the *trouvères* did not always rise to the same heights. At times they unbent as may be seen from certain passages in the *Chanson de Guillaume*. But in the *Pèlerinage de Charlemagne* the heroi-comic strain finds full vent. The characters are well known to us: Charlemagne, Roland and Oliver, Guillaume and the other worthies. They go on a journey to the East and bring back to France relics of the Passion. But their reason for going was to see if Hugo, the King of Constantinople, wore his crown better upon his head than did Charlemagne; it was the wife of Charlemagne who said that he did, and the powerful emperor is much hurt and insists on seeing whether it is so or not. To a quarrel between husband and wife and a grotesque fit of vanity on the part of a great king France owed the possession of the shroud of Christ and a nail from the Cross. The author is obviously amused and wishes to amuse us; but he is a dry humorist and always keeps a serious face, so much so that at times we are forced to wonder if he is not making fun of his audience. This amusing work is not so old as *Roland*, *Guillaume*, or *Gormont*, but nevertheless it probably belongs to the first half of the 12th century. Anyhow we have no other *chanson de geste* which goes back to this remote period. There must have been others without the slightest doubt, but some were lost while others had to give place to newer versions of which we shall have to speak later. By a lucky chance the *Roland* and the *Guillaume*, those two masterpieces of medieval epic, were saved from the wreck.

Who was Roland? A prefect of the marches of Brittany in the 9th century. Who was Guillaume? A count of Toulouse of the same period. Why did these names live on into the 12th century? Just as the name of Charlemagne did, through the books of the clerks. But the fame of Roland and Guillaume had not been world-wide. Nevertheless in certain districts, where they had lived or through which they had passed, their memory had been piously preserved, associated with monuments that had endured, a cross, a chapel, or an abbey. The memory of Roland was kept at Roncevaux where he died, and at Blaye where he was buried. The monks of Aniane and of Gellone never forgot that Guillaume, a valiant knight who fought the Saracens in a great battle, had late in life retired to their midst and died in the odour of sanctity after having heaped upon them benefactions. Moreover, Blaye and Roncevaux on the one hand, and Gellone on the other, were stages on the great pilgrimage routes which led to the famous shrine of St James of Compostella in Spain. So that many pilgrims in this way heard of Roland and of Guillaume, and amongst these pilgrims there must have been many a *jongleur* whose business it was to amuse the tired pilgrims as they rested for the night and make them forget the fatigue of the journey. These *jongleurs* were welcomed by the monks, as they helped to attract the faithful to their sanctuaries, and the monks were in turn listened to greedily by the *jongleurs* when they related the glorious annals of their monastery. What vivid tales to take home with them! and these tales, many times told and retold in all parts of the land, were bound, sooner or later, to find their poet. What splendid subjects for spontaneous poetry if the *jongleur* himself happened to be a poet!

In this way birth was given to the religious and the martial legends, in this way were composed the *chansons de geste* in which at the side of the great Emperor of the West swarm a crowd of heroes of the past, whose glory now becomes greater than they had ever known when living. For what happened with the *Roland* and the *Guillaume* happened with many another contemporary and more recent *chanson de geste*. The work of monk and *jongleur* bore fruit. The collaboration may have been due to selfish interest, but it was ennobled by the grandeur of the legends and the sense of profound harmony with the ardent spirit of the age. For in these legends of the cloister and these poems of the *jongleur* we feel the heroic breath which filled the conquerors of Sicily, the victors at Hastings, and the Crusaders of 1099. In these poems a strong energetic generation expresses its faith in its own destiny, its confidence in the future.

This ideal was to be modified, however. The Second Crusade ended in failure. The First Crusade had resulted in the taking of Jerusalem and the foundation of the Christian kingdom of Palestine; but Louis VII returned to France (1149) without having accomplished anything; the massacre of Edessa (1144) had not even been avenged; hence a profound disappointment throughout Christendom and a falling off of enthusiasm for the Crusades. The great man of the Church was no longer St Bernard, the inspired apostle of the Second Crusade, but Thomas Becket, who, in his revolt against the English king, fought, not without a certain nobility, for purely human interests. It needed the fall of Jerusalem (1187) to stir Christendom once again to undertake a Third Crusade (1190).

The entire period from 1150 to 1190 was above all taken up by the quarrels of Henry Plantagenet with his sons, and by the struggle between England and the France of Louis VII and Philip Augustus. The immediate result was that the national interest centred round the kings. Certainly we have to admit that in these wars there was an obscure instinct which forced these two great nations to fight each other, and that in this very way they helped each other to take shape; but it is doubtful if the men of the time could see any great idea in these petty rivalries, which served rather to show up in high relief the personalities of the two kings. Hence the ever-increasing importance of their courts and their entourage. The great vassals in their provincial towns followed the example of Paris and London. In this way were formed centres of culture and learning. Latin poetry was in high honour at the court of Henry II. Knowledge and study were no longer left entirely to the clerks. Energetic feudal knights sought to learn fine sentiments and good manners; a society thus renewed obviously needed a new literature.

This need was at first filled by the Romances of Antiquity: *Thèbes* (*circa* 1150); *Énéas* (*circa* 1160); *Troie* (*circa* 1165), the latter written by BENOIT DE SAINTE-MAURE. They are very different works from those we know already. Their outward appearance is no longer the same. Assonance gives place to rhyme, the decasyllable to the octosyllable; sentences become longer and more complex. We no longer have a series of *laisses* meant to be sung to the accompaniment of a viol; instead we have poems meant to be read. This does not imply that everybody read directly from the manuscript, though, doubtless, many did so. The important point is that this elegant but rather thin poetry was not meant, and was indeed quite unfit, to dominate the noise of the riotous feasts in which the heroic decasyllable felt quite at home; it was written to be read aloud by a skilful reader in "my lady's chamber," before a select and small audience. We have here, then, works addressed rather to the individual than to a crowd; this was a great innovation at that time, but not the only one that these poems afford. In their very essence they differ from the *chansons de geste.* They are by no means faithful translations of classical epic poetry; the Middle Ages understood neither the Greeks nor the Romans; in all good faith they took them for men like the men of the 12th century. In the works of Statius and Virgil, of Dictys and Dares the *trouvères* looked for feudal knights, and found them there. They may tell us the story of the quarrel of Eteocles and Polynices, and the siege of Thebes; or the combats of Aeneas in Latium; or again the expedition of the Argonauts and the siege of Troy; but under the names of these classical heroes they only portray Frenchmen of their own time.

Such was their simplicity that they took with them into remotest antiquity the feudal system, of whose recent origin they had no suspicion. They saw clearly, however, that they could not put their Feudal Greece and their Feudal Rome at the service of the Church. They could not imbue these ancient heroes, whom they called back to an artificial life, with a modern soul, and they did not attempt to do so. What interested them in these ancient legends was the setting rather than the characters, the actions rather than the feelings which give birth to them. If the setting be strange and the deeds unexpected, all the more pleasant the surprise for reader and audience. In short these romances founded on the Latin epics introduced into France a taste for the exotic and the romantic.

We have travelled a long distance since the *Roland*. But some significance had to be given to these adventures, or else they would soon have tired the reader; and as a matter of fact these romances from the antique did bring in a new element which was their essential characteristic; this was Love.

*La belle* Aude, the betrothed of Roland, appears for an instant in the old poem, it is true, but only to die; and she obviously has little place in the mind of the hero. In *Thèbes*, *Énéas*, and *Troie*, on the contrary, love is one of the mainsprings of the action; its manifestations and influence are described with evident pleasure. This interest in love was due to the great importance which women had won in contemporary society. History mentions especially Eleanor of Aquitaine, who was first Queen of France, then Queen of England; her two daughters, Mary and Adela, who married two brothers, Henry of Champagne and Thibaut of Blois; and finally, the sister of these two princes, Adela, who became Queen of France after the divorce of Eleanor. Indeed it is hard to exaggerate the importance of the part played by these illustrious women in their sphere, and their example must have been imitated by a great number of women. It is therefore of interest to note that they patronised authors, and that the authors showed their gratitude by writing for them: *Troie*, for example, was dedicated to Eleanor, and many an author, who dared not aspire so high, hoped at least for such readers as she. We find here an influence which went far.

The love interest came into imaginative literature never to leave it again. But classical poetry as a source of romance was soon exhausted, and since the taste for the exotic was stronger than ever, other sources had to be found in order to satisfy a curiosity that was already exacting. It was at this time that the Celtic legends made their appearance. They take us into a wondrous Britain, full of marvels, where we still find knights who perform fine feats of arms, it is true, but we find also giants and dwarfs, fairies and enchanted palaces, a strange supernatural world in which everybody lives only for love and adventure. In this land of dreams Arthur is king; he is a sort of

British Charlemagne, the personification of the Welsh resistance against the Saxon invaders, becoming in the course of centuries a glorious ancestor for both victor and vanquished. His memory gives a wondrous halo of antiquity to the youthful past of Anglo-Norman England.

But in his magnificent court we shall find no Roland; his knights are brave, it is true, and their ideal is noble, but it is a personal ideal; they are not the champions of a great cause; they do not belong to real life. For this reason they pleased those who sought distraction and peace rather than inspiration. For this reason they delighted the brilliant society of London and Paris, which the austerity of the old *chansons de geste* was already beginning to repel.

It was a woman who first put into French verse these Celtic legends. MARIE DE FRANCE lived undoubtedly at the court of Henry II of England, to whom she dedicated her delightful book of stories, but there seems to be no reason for thinking that she was the king's sister. She was an educated woman, with a good knowledge of Latin; witness her translation of the *Purgatoire de Saint Patrice*; it is also probable that she utilised Latin sources for her *Fables*, which are the earliest specimens we have of this form in French. She is above all known as the author of *Lais* (*c.* 1165), which are a series of twelve tales describing adventures which took place long before in Brittany, Normandy, and England, and all presenting one feature in common: to wit that in order to perpetuate the adventure the "ancient Bretons," or Celts, made a "lay" out of it, that is to say, a lyric poem which the Breton *jongleurs* sang to the accompaniment of the harp. Hence the name of *lais* was finally given to the tales themselves.

Marie may perhaps have heard some of these *jongleurs* sing them; apparently at one time this sort of thing was the fashion and she ingeniously took advantage of it. But where did she get the adventures from? That is just what we do not know. All are not of Celtic origin, although she claims that each of them had given birth to a lay. Whence came those that are undoubtedly of Celtic origin? From Brittany or from the Welsh part of England? Perhaps from both. How did Marie get to know them? By hearing polyglot *jongleurs* sing them? Possibly, but more probably in most cases from earlier written French versions, since lost. In any case it was through her book that all the stories became favourites in French society of the 12th century. One of her contemporaries tells us how they were the delight of the court of Henry II and we know that they were welcomed with the same fervour soon afterwards in France. Some of these stories deserve mention: *Yonec*, or the lover who was changed into a bird in order to visit his lady; *Guigemar*, in which we find a hind which can speak and a boat that sails by itself on the waves; *Bisclavret*, the story of a were-wolf; *Lanval*, or the knight beloved of a fairy. In this last lay appears for a moment the figure of King Arthur.

As early as 1155 a Norman historian, WACE, in his *Brut*, which was a translation of the popular Latin work of the Welshman, Geoffrey of Monmouth, had made the French acquainted with Arthur; and in addition to the tales and legends of his original he even mentions the Round Table for the first time. Wace was a chronicler, and about 1170 he produced another work, the *Roman de Rou*, a history of the Normans, but even when he is telling us fables he still believes that he is relating history.

*Lanval*, which owes nothing to Wace, and which is meant only to charm the reader, is really the earliest Arthurian romance that we possess. In the fluent and graceful verse of Marie is preserved the flavour of the Celtic stories; she touches these legends with a light hand—no embellishments, the setting simply outlined, and in the foreground a love story told for its own sake into which Marie has put all her woman's heart.

One of her lays, entitled *Le Chèvrefeuille*, brings upon the scene two lovers celebrated in medieval literature: Tristram and Iseult. Marie knew their story from having read it "in writing," as she herself tells us; we no longer possess the older poem to which she refers, but we have two imitations or adaptations of it—one by THOMAS and the other by BÉROUL (*circa* 1170)—which allow us to form an idea of it, and which also have all the interest of veritable originals. Because they have drunk of a potion which was not intended for them Tristram and Iseult are henceforth united; driven from court, urged on by a fate stronger than their will, feeling at once both innocent and guilty, tormented with remorse and happy in their misery, pursued by their enemies, meeting ruse with ruse and violence with violence, they live a wandering and painful existence in the forest until the day they are separated never to be re-united save in death.

Thomas lived in England and doubtless wrote for the same public as Marie; he tried to adapt to the taste of an elegant and cultivated court a fierce and almost barbaric legend. He softened it, gave it a veneer of civilisation, and made it palatable to a society for which it was never meant. Béroul, probably a Norman *jongleur*, has not touched up his original to the same extent, so that his poem, rough and without any delicate shading, gives us perhaps a better idea of the original work, which we no longer possess. This probably was a strong and brutal *chanson de geste*, as powerful as the *Roland*, glorifying passion as *Roland* glorifies duty. It was a Celtic legend, the elements of which were doubtless furnished by the Welsh, but it was a French poet who made it immortal.

Like Marie and Thomas, CHRÉTIEN DE TROYES, a native of Champagne, wrote for the court; one of his romances is dedicated to Countess Marie of Champagne, another to Count Philip of Alsace. And he too takes us into the land of enchantment in which complicated adventures happen one after the other without order or sequence—foreign inventions which come from the same mysterious Britain as some of the lays of Marie and the first outlines of the Tristram legend. How did they reach Chrétien? We do not know. At any rate it is clear that they did not interest him for their own sake, for the meaning they may have held; what delighted him was their picturesqueness. In these Celtic traditions he saw only a piquant mythology, of which he made full use like the clever writer that he was, but without being so absurd as even to appear to believe in it. For the originality of his work lies elsewhere. In this brilliant setting his characters play their parts, but, under their borrowed names and for all their fantastic adventures, they are really nothing but French knights of the 12th century, of whom we see the best side; they are all brave, generous, human, sensitive on the point of honour, and, as the fashion demands, all lovers ready to fight for their lady. Their arms, their dress, and their castles are those of the period, and their manners also. Chrétien obviously took great delight in painting this world which he knew at first hand, and his readers were grateful to him for it. A great part of his success was due to this; but he tried to penetrate below the surface; he liked to analyse the feelings, to mark especially the different phases of love, and each of his romances introduces a problem of the heart which his characters must solve by their conduct. How far has a lady the right to doubt him whom she loves? and the lover, in such a case, how far should he carry his resentment, and what proofs must he have, in turn, to be sure of the constancy and fidelity of his lady? This is the theme of *Érec* (*c.* 1168). Should a knight sacrifice even the most legitimate self-esteem if his lady demand it? This is *Lancelot* (between 1170 and 1190). The problems are similar in his other romances: *Cligès* (*c.* 1170), which is a reply to the *Tristan* of Thomas, *Yvain ou le Chevalier au Lion*, *Perceval* (between 1170 and 1190). The supple, alert octosyllabic line, which is also the verse of Marie and of the Tristram poems, is admirably suited to the manner of Chrétien, lending itself to all the modulations of a subtle witty language full of fine shades. Chrétien is not a very great poet, but in the matter of style he is a master-craftsman, the first of his kind in French literature. He gave his contemporaries a lesson in art, which was not wasted.

The poems of which Renart is the hero were not written for the court; they were addressed to a larger, but still a cultivated, public. Fundamentally they answered the same need as *Troie*, *Tristan*, or *Érec*; except that they had recourse to another kind of exotic, a new source of romance. PIERRE DE SAINT-CLOUD, the author of *Renart et Ysengrin* (*c.* 1177), first had the very novel idea of putting characters taken from the animal world into a setting similar to that of the contemporary epics. Already Marie had given the French readers of the 12th century the wolf, the fox, the bear, and the cock, but only in short fables independent of each other; a Latin poem of 1152 shows us all these animals pitted one against the other, but the setting is very vague and Reinardus and Ysengrinus pass the greater part of their time in making speeches which express chiefly the ideas and the malice of the author. Pierre de Saint-Cloud, who knew his predecessors, effaces himself behind Renard and Ysengrin, and he turns them into feudal knights; not for an instant however does he allow us to forget that we have to do with a fox and a wolf. King Noble, the lion, has all the majesty of Charlemagne, with the courtliness of King Arthur, but he lives in his lair and is surrounded by animals of the forest. From this contrast, subtly portrayed and well-sustained, is derived an irresistible spirit of comedy. It is a very happy parody of the contemporary epics. The method is less crude than in the *Pèlerinage de Charlemagne* and implies a more refined art.

In the *Jugement de Renart* (*c.* 1179), which was a direct imitation, we find the same qualities of wit, proportion, and precision, with a keener sense of the dramatic. About the same period and following in the steps of Pierre de Saint-Cloud other works full of merry conceits relate the cunning tricks of Reynard the fox: *Renart Moine, Ysengrin dans le puits, le Pèlerinage de Renart.* They were all produced just at the right time and enjoyed immense success.

All these works, epics after the antique, lays, Celtic romances, have this characteristic in common—that love plays in them a great part, and even the Renart poems are no exception. It was only natural that love should sooner or later be treated for its own sake, and instead of being placed in the framework of a continuous narrative should furnish the whole matter of short lyrics. The fertile period from 1150 to 1190 saw the beginnings of lyric poetry in France. The direct inspiration came from the south of France, where the songs of the troubadours had been held in high honour ever since the end of the 11th century.

It was probably during the Crusade of 1147, when the men of France mingled with the men of Provence, that the barons of the north became acquainted with the lyric poetry of the south. But above all it was the influence of Eleanor of Aquitaine, of her two daughters, and of Adela of France which made itself felt again in this instance.

Eleanor was the grand-daughter of the earliest known troubadour, William IX; by encouraging the *trouvères* of the north she followed a family tradition. This tradition became acclimatised in France all the more readily because the social conditions were at that time very similar to those of Provence. In the baronial courts of the north there was the same ideal as in those of the south, an ideal in which the knightly virtues united with the social qualities and became what is known as "Courtesy."

Courtesy was learnt from the ladies; it was they who formed fine manners and inspired courage; it was in order to merit their love and esteem that the knights performed their greatest exploits. Hence the sovereignty of the lady and the cult with which she was worshipped by her humble and grateful knight. The *chanson courtoise* was one of the rites of this religion, which explains the monotony of this poetic form. We rarely find the personal note: "the knight" sings the praises of "his lady"; we never know who the lady is, and if the manuscript does not tell us we could never guess who was the knight; it is all in the abstract. Love is here entirely intellectual, an affair of the mind and the will. The idea being always the same, the art consisted in varying the expression. All the poets did their utmost and several succeeded, but the song itself became after all a mere exercise in style, in a word a sort of sport, in which each strove to show off his skill, as in a tournament. Knowledge and study were necessary, for each song had to have some novelty in its technique—in the number of lines, the arrangement of the rhymes, or the grouping of the stanzas; it was not permissible to use a combination of rhythm invented by a predecessor. Again, each song was sung to an original air composed by the author of the words, and the musical accompaniment was probably the chief centre of interest and the chief cause of success.

The earliest lyric *trouvères* were HUE D'OISY, CONON DE BÉTHUNE, the CHÂTELAIN DE COUCY, and RICHARD CŒUR DE LION, King of England. Their work seems rather artificial to-day. Still, we must recognise the nobility of the ideal which inspired it, and which was to be the ideal of Dante and Petrarch. Side by side with these *chansons* which held first place in contemporary opinion, the manuscripts have preserved for us lyrics of a rather different kind which are more interesting to us to-day. They differ in that they bring characters upon the scene; conventional praise of a perhaps imaginary lady gives place to a little love drama which happens before our very eyes. The earliest of these, of which the stanzas are still in assonance, were called *chansons d'histoire* (because they were partly narrative) or *romances*. The best known portrays two sisters who go to bathe at a spring; only one comes back and she sighs and weeps because Gaiete has left her to go with Gérard, her future husband, to the town.

In the *pastourelle* the author intervenes, generally to relate some little rustic love scene of which he has been the spectator. Never have shepherd and shepherdess been made to speak so charmingly. Both *pastourelles* and *romances* (sometimes called *chansons de toile* or spinning songs) generally have a refrain and they undeniably bear the stamp of artlessness and simplicity. But we must not be deceived; there is nothing popular about them; the *jongleurs* who composed and sang them wrote for the same public as their noble colleagues, the lyric *trouvères*.

If this rapid survey of the productions of the period from 1150 to 1190 were to end here, it would give the impression that in the second half of the 12th century literature had become a much more exclusive thing than it had ever been in France. The fact is that we have hitherto ignored the one form which, during this period, was really popular—the *chanson de geste*. It was, in fact, the time when the *chanson de geste* reached its greatest development. It is true that it no longer had quite the same success as of old in the baronial halls, where "courteous poetry" competed with it more and more successfully, but in amends for this it found a cordial welcome among the middle classes of the towns; in this direction its domain was widely extended.

The earliest *chansons de geste* of this period are connected with the legends of Guillaume: *Le Couronnement Louis, Le Charroi de Nimes, La Prise d'Orange, Le Chevalier Vivien,* and *Le Moniage Guillaume.* About 1170 appeared *Aliscans,* which is only a very free rehandling of the *Chanson de Guillaume,* but which is almost as fine as the original. We are generally unable to detect whether the text preserved is the original text, or the refashioning of an earlier version. The object of the rehandling was to adapt a form that had grown out of date to the taste of the day. Poems in assonance were transformed into rhyming verse, which is what happened, a little later perhaps, to the Oxford *Roland.* Or again there was an attempt to make more interesting a poem which seemed monotonous.

In the first part of *Raoul de Cambrai* we witness the struggles and death of fierce warriors in scenes of wild grandeur, but the second and later part introduces love scenes into this barbaric epic. This is important; it means that romance which had long dominated "courteous" literature had finally found its way into the *chansons de geste*, and that their old public had also been won over to the new fashion. The old ideas were no longer understood; the ancient forms seemed old-fashioned. *Roland* was still read about 1190, probably in rehandled versions, but at that time no Turoldus could have created a second Roland

The men of the Third Crusade were never animated by the same spirit as the Crusaders of 1099. The two chiefs, the kings of France and England, were unable to agree; they came back separately, each one when he thought fit, and were henceforth irreconcilable enemies. This put an end to the dream of a Europe united against the Infidel. The Crusades soon became private enterprises directed by a single nation, rather than a general effort on the part of Christendom. The last of all, the Crusade of 1248 (for we can ignore the Crusade of Tunis), was a purely French undertaking. After that, though people still thought sometimes about the Orient, they hardly ever took the trouble to go there. We can therefore fix 1248 as the limit of the period we are about to study. It was the period when the modern nations began to take on an individual character. England lost Normandy (1204) and the greater part of her continental possessions, and became completely detached from France; henceforth each country had a separate nationality and a distinct literature. In France the tendencies of the preceding period became more marked; the victory of Bouvines firmly established the prestige of the Capetian kings. There began to be a public opinion which had to be reckoned with and which was favourable to the king. The narrow self-contained feudal institutions broadened into a national system. The *bourgeoisie* of the towns played an important part in this great movement, and its influence was much increased. When Philip Augustus went on the Crusade of 1190 he left the burgesses of Paris in control of the finances and administration of the kingdom; the militia of the towns took part in the battle of Bouvines. So that it is only to be expected that the literature of this period, from 1190 to 1248, should be, to a great extent, addressed to the public of the towns, which insisted on its share of amusement. We must expect also to find that the literary forms handed down from the preceding period were subjected to certain modifications. Created for a society of which the select few were the life and soul, these literary forms could hardly survive exactly as they were after the disappearance, not indeed of the society as a whole, but, at any rate, of its most eminent members. This we are now about to demonstrate in as few words as possible. In order not to break the continuity we must first mention a few works belonging to the preceding period.

The success of the poems of Marie caused a number of *lais* to appear, the earliest of which are probably *Le Cor* and *Guingamor* (between 1165 and 1170), the latter equal in freshness to the best of her tales. Then come *Havelok, Desiré, Graelent* (which takes up the subject of *Lanval*); still later in the last decade of the century, *Tydorel, Doon, Mélion*, and *Tyolet*, in which subjects or themes already treated by Marie reappear; and finally during the first years of the 13th century *Ignaure* and *Le Trot*. A proof of the esteem in which these works were held is that the word *lai*, which had long been inseparably followed by the epithet *breton*, comes to be applied, as we shall see, to works which are in no way Celtic, but which have a certain distinctiveness of thought and of language. The lay long remained caviare to the general. The romance of *Tristan* did not lend itself easily to imitation or continuation; nevertheless we have two small episodic poems of the *Folie Tristan*, one of the last quarter of the 12th century (Oxford MS.), the other of the commencement of the 13th century (Berne MS.), in which something of the penetrating charm of the works of Thomas and Béroul survives. It was the romances of Chrétien de Troyes which had the most numerous posterity, and the reason of this is easily understood.

Chrétien was the founder of a real school; he discovered a path and furnished the means of following it: a love intrigue with sentimental complications in a setting borrowed, though not ostensibly, from contemporary life, a few characters intensely alive, and a description of the society of the time—this was the formula he supplied; a fertile formula capable of the most varied application, and which is still very largely the formula of the modern novel. In addition to the attraction of novelty there was the charm of a language which had never yet been handled with such a subtle and delicate art. There was no lack of disciples, as may be imagined, and more than one of them surpassed the master. About the time of Chrétien, or perhaps a little earlier, GAUTIER D'ARRAS wrote *Ille et Galeron* (1167 or 1168), related to a lay of Marie, but very inferior to Marie and to Chrétien. Imitating Chrétien, RENAUD DE BEAUJEU, a knight, composed *Le Bel Inconnu* (*c.* 1210) in the manner of *Érec.*

But the true successors of Chrétien were those who boldly discarded all the Celtic frippery of his work, and retained only his essential teaching. They saw that the picture of the life of their time would gain in fidelity, the analysis of feeling in persuasive force, if they abandoned the background of the supernatural Celtic world. They never gave up relating "adventures," which they borrowed on all sides, but they tried to bring them nearer to reality. The best representative of this school was JEAN RENART, author of *L'Escoufle*, of *Guillaume de Dôle* and of the *Lai de l'Ombre* (between 1195 and 1210). *Guillaume de Dôle* paints a brilliant world of knights and ladies, busy only with tournament, dance, and song, and teaches us what were the tastes of elegant society at this period. The *Lai de l'Ombre* is almost entirely made up of the conversation of the people of this world; it is all very pretty and delicate, but the effort to express fine sentiments is forced and at times amounts almost to preciosity. They borrowed from Chrétien some of his faults, as well as his qualities. *Galeran* by RENAUT (first quarter of the 12th century) is fresher and more natural, though recalling very closely the manner of Jean Renart. We may also mention the romance of *La Violette* by GERBERT DE MONTREUIL.

But in all the posterity of Chrétien the most remarkable works were *Floire et Blanchefleur* (end of 12th century), *Aucassin et Nicolette* (first years of 13th century) and *La Châtelaine de Vergi* (first half of 13th century). Here the "adventure" is of secondary importance, and the picture of society has less place than the idyll or the love tragedy.

*Aucassin et Nicolette* treats almost the same subject as *Floire et Blanchefleur*: it tells of a youth, Aucassin, and a maid, Nicolette, whose love is thwarted, and who after many obstacles and wanderings are at last united. The form is unique in medieval literature—prose and lyric verse are used alternately, whence the name of *chantefable* given to it by the author. He was a rare poet; he created two lovers who by their youth, their freshness, and their simplicity, belong to all time; he was too a very subtle humorist who can occasionally smile at his hero and heroine without robbing them of their charm, a man of independent mind who behind the brilliant apparel of chivalry seeks a more real humanity, and who is not afraid to make even the villein, the laughing-stock of the preceding age, assume an attitude of pride; last he was a consummate artist whose sparkling prose can still delight the most refined reader. Had *Érec* not been written we might never have had this *chantefable*, but Chrétien could never have written *Aucassin et Nicolette*.

*La Châtelaine de Vergi* likewise presupposes the work of Chrétien, and it also surpasses it; it is a beautiful and tragic love-story, in which the feelings and passions are analysed with infinite delicacy and in just the right tone.

Reading such works as these, one might imagine that the Celtic legends had already lost all attraction for the public of the period. Nothing of the kind. This part of the legacy of Chrétien was continued by other followers, not such great artists as those we have just discussed, but quite as original in their own way. In this case *Perceval* was the starting-point. The hero of this romance is a youth who has all the knightly virtues, but who is also almost a simpleton, and of this contrast Chrétien has made very clever use. But the strange adventures in which Perceval was engaged were far more interesting to some readers of the period than the hero's psychology. The weirdest adventure is the one in which appears, under peculiar circumstances, a mysterious "graal," or dish, about which Perceval ought to have asked, but did not ask, a question; and we hear nothing more about it; the author excites our curiosity without satisfying it. We probably have here a relic of very ancient pagan traditions which reached Chrétien in a perverted and unintelligible form—hence his reticence.

But his successors wanted to know more than he did. His *Perceval* was left unfinished. It was continued after his death, sometimes in widely diverging directions, by a whole series of writers: WAUCHIER DE DENAIN, GERBERT DE MONTREUIL, and others. Finally ROBERT DE BORON composed (*circa* 1206–1210) a trilogy of romances: *Joseph d'Arimathie*, *Merlin*, and *Perceval*, making use of both Chrétien and Wauchier de Denain, and adding a good deal of his own. The most striking novelty was that he turned the "graal" into a Christian relic; for him it was the dish, afterwards taken to Britain, in which Joseph of Arimathea had caught the blood of Christ crucified, and Perceval was the knight who was destined to win the precious relic. Very soon afterwards this idea was taken up and developed in an immense romance, perhaps the most characteristic work of the feudal Middle Ages, and possibly composed entirely by one powerful mind. It consists of several parts: *Histoire du Saint-Graal*, *Lancelot*, *Quête du Saint-Graal*, and *Mort d'Arthur*, but for the sake of brevity it may be called *Lancelot*.

Perceval had to give way before a more favoured hero; it was not Lancelot however who was to have the honour of winning the Grail, but his son, Galahad, the knight of perfect purity. The moral intentions of the author are obvious, and they dominate the entire work. He has given us a magnificent picture of Feudal Chivalry, brilliant, worldly, not without faults and weaknesses, but ennobled by the quest after a rare and difficult ideal. The idle legends of Britain take on a profound meaning now that they are illumined by the light of the Gospel. It seems as if, just when the *chanson de geste* was losing the austere tradition of *Roland*, a group of 13th century clerks tried to hand on to the Celtic Romance the great function of being the nation's spiritual guide and fountain of energy. But while about 1120 the *Roland* was in harmony with the soul of the nation, *Lancelot*, a century later, represented the noble dreams of a few fine spirits. These dreams, however, pleased many readers and were not without a certain influence on real life.

By its external form also *Lancelot* deserves attention. It is in prose. Robert de Boron had already led the way, but it was the success of the *Lancelot* that established this new fashion.

It originated no doubt in considerations of convenience. The authors of such vast compositions would have found it hard to bear patiently the constraint of rhyme and metre. Moreover, their religious sentiment would make them shrink from employing the disturbing and questionable charms of poetry. Prose, being more dignified, more severe, was better fitted to give to the fantastic Celtic legends the air of reality they so much needed. Similarly it was an effort after realism that made the author of *Aucassin et Nicolette* write part of his "romance of adventure" in prose; but this is the case of an artist who aims at a less conventional, a more direct, representation of life. Thus, by different paths, prose won a more important place in literature, and this was one of the most significant novelties of the time.

As early as 1212, or thereabouts, GEOFFROY DE VILLEHARDOUIN, marshal of Champagne, had written in prose his history of *La Conquête de Constantinople*. It is a history of the Fourth Crusade (1204) which, like the earlier crusades, was undertaken in order to deliver the Holy Land, but which resulted actually in the foundation of the Latin kingdom of Constantinople. It was, doubtless, in order to explain this extraordinary change of objective that Villehardouin wrote his book. Admitted to the Council of Chiefs he saw everything at close range, and if he has not told all he knew, he has at least made us understand what a Crusading Army was like at the beginning of the 13th century. There was no longer the religious fervour of the time of the First Crusade, but these knights of 1204 with their courage, their disinterestedness, and their indomitable energy, were fine types of men. Villehardouin, who was one of them, has related their exploits in simple, grave, and strong language. Reading his book one feels that the ideal of *Lancelot* was not without all relation to reality.

The *chanson courtoise* continues to show us the feudal nobility under its other and more worldly aspect. Its best representative was THIBAUT DE CHAMPAGNE, King of Navarre (second quarter of 13th century). A few *jongleurs* also composed songs, for instance COLIN MUSET (*circa* 1235), who in an easy and delightful fashion treats us to some picturesque episodes of his vagabond life.

Renart is still a popular hero: between 1195 and 1205 appeared

*Renart et Liétard* by a priest of La Croix en Brie, a keen observer of peasant life, *Les Vêpres de Tibert* by RICHART DE LISON, and *La Procession Renart*, the subject of which was often reproduced on the walls of the castles and even of the churches. Later came still more tales of Renart, but these have not the same freshness; this kind of literature was visibly approaching its end.

The *chanson de geste* enjoys the same success as in the preceding period. *Renaud de Montauban* (beginning of 13th century) is a very good example of the subjects which pleased the populace at this time. Four brothers in revolt against Charlemagne continue the struggle against the Emperor for many years, sometimes protected by the stout walls of their castle, sometimes wandering in the forests; they are aided by a marvellous horse, Bayard, and by their cousin Maugis, a wizard. Charlemagne both fears and esteems them, and they respect Charlemagne even though they fight against him. These noble rebels surely have the poet's sympathy, but he preaches no revolt against the King of France; it is obviously all mere imagination. *Renaud de Montauban* is fundamentally a "romance of adventure," but love plays no part in it, and some episodes reach a height of grandeur never found in the courtly productions of the time. Sometimes, the *chansons de geste* of this period strike a note which recalls the *Roland* or the *Guillaume*; for example *Girart de Vienne* and *Aymeri de Narbonne* by BERTRAND DE BAR-SUR-AUBE (first quarter of 13th century).

During this period the *chanson de geste* was not the only kind of literature written for the burgesses of the towns. We must note the appearance at the end of the 12th century of the *fabliau*, which for roughly a century had a great vogue. Essentially it is an amusing story, a tale to make one laugh. It is written in octosyllabic verse; this being the only possible form at the time for narrative poetry other than the *chanson de geste*. But the *fabliau* does not seem to have been influenced by the courtly romance, from which it is distinguished by its brevity (never containing more than 300 or 400 lines) and still more by an artlessness which is sometimes very striking. The language is often easy, clear, even elegant, but these qualities belong rather to the period than to the literary form. The chief interest is obviously the subject. The "adventures" were undoubtedly old and had long been repeated throughout the countryside, but the setting was quite new.

Instead of giving us scenes of contemporary high life, the *fabliau* takes its characters from town and village, from villein and *bourgeois*; the clergy appear also and even the knights, but we are shown the latter in their relations, not with the feudal aristocracy, but with their humbler neighbours, by whom they are sometimes feared and detested. The *fabliau* often makes the powerful lord look ridiculous. Not that it always takes the part of the humble. On the whole it tends to laugh at everybody, and it is not too fastidious about the quality of its laughter. Cynical, brutal, too readily obscene, the *fabliau* often takes us into very bad company, and it parades a complete contempt for women. We are far removed from the atmosphere of the *chanson courtoise* and the romances of the Round Table. It is the reaction of the spirit of coarseness from the spirit of refinement. The *jongleurs*, who composed the majority of the *fabliaux*, had fallen more and more into utter disrepute, and their work often gives the impression that they are practically outcasts of society.

The *bourgeoisie*, then, has its own literature and one that hardly redounds to its credit, but we must not forget that it also formed more than ever during this period the habitual audience of the noble *chanson de geste*. In justice to the *bourgeoisie* it must be further admitted that court and castle did not always look coldly upon the *fabliaux* from the town. And in justice to the *fabliaux* it must be admitted that some of them are very well told, with a fine sense of proportion, and sometimes wit: for example *Les Trois Aveugles de Compiègne*, *Le Prêtre qui dit la Passion*, *La Bourse pleine de Sens*, *La Housse Partie*, *Le Vilain Mire*, and *L'Oiselet* (a very pretty and graceful story). Sometimes the author makes a point of showing from the outset that he prefers the tone of good company by calling his tale a *lai*: for example the charming *Lai du Vair Palefroi*, which is perhaps a little later than our period. It is a pity that the work of the 13th century *jongleurs* did not contain more *lais* and fewer *fabliaux*.

The period from 1248 to the beginning of the Hundred Years'

War (1337) saw the last Crusades end in failure. Feudalism lost one of the chief justifications for its existence, and the kings of France profited by this. They made a determined attempt to increase their power. In this endeavour they found great assistance in the new class of jurists, who, sprung either from the *bourgeoisie* or the petty nobility, did their utmost to make the memories of the Roman Empire triumph over feudal traditions.

It was the jurists who constituted the "Parlement" or high court of justice of the kingdom, which held jurisdiction over even baronial domains, thanks to the institution of the "king's burgesses." The communes took a secondary place, and a no longer local, but national, burgess class came into being. This included also members of the university, who were to play an important part. These were priests and clerks, who, in temporal matters, sided readily with the King against the Pope. They were in opposition to the members of the religious orders, who also had great influence, but who were active agents of the Papacy. The rivalry between Pope and King resulted in the struggle between Philippe le Bel and Boniface VIII, which ended in the triumph of the monarchy. All this meant an absolute upheaval in the old feudal world. Literature was bound to reflect this new aspect of society. It was less intent on pleasing the classes whose influence was waning, and sought rather to criticise the events of the time and to influence opinion. It ceased to be a literature of entertainment, and became a literature of satire and argument.

The literary forms of the preceding period did not suddenly disappear. *Chansons de geste* were still written, such as *Oger* and *Berte* by ADENET LE ROI (*circa* 1270); romances of adventure such as *Le Chatelain de Couci* (end of 13th century); *fabliaux*, of which the best known are those written by BAUDOUIN DE CONDÉ (1245–1275) and JEAN DE CONDÉ (1310–1340). There were also Renart poems: *Renart le Bestourné* (between 1261 and 1270) by RUTEBEUF, *Le Couronnement Renart* (*circa* 1270), and *Renart le Nouvel* (*circa* 1288) by JACQUEMART GELÉE, but they are quite unlike the work of the ancient *trouvères*, who told their stories for the sake of the story. All these works are satirical allegories, which aim especially at attacking the Mendicant Orders. *Chansons courtoises* were still composed, but their authors are citizens of Arras, who have more interesting compositions to their credit. All this production is either a mere reflection of the preceding period or is animated by a new spirit which found more perfect expression in other works. The real originality of the period must be sought elsewhere.

The chief work of the second half of the 13th century and one of the most significant works of the Middle Ages is the *Roman de la Rose*. The author of it was JEAN DE MEUN, one of the most learned clerks of his time and certainly one of the most independent. One does not know why so vigorous a mind did not condescend to choose his own subject and his own plan. He preferred to continue an incomplete poem dating roughly from 1225 and consisting of 4000 lines, while his addition was of 18,000 lines. The author of the first part was GUILLAUME DE LORRIS, who imagined a world of allegorical abstractions in which the lover strives to win the Rose, i.e. his beloved. His poem has a certain amount of grace and charm, but Guillaume de Lorris would doubtless have remained quite unknown had not Jean de Meun done him the posthumous honour of collaborating with him in this work (*circa* 1270). Never however were there two minds more unlike. The first was a disciple of Chrétien, the second inherited the lively mockery of the *fabliaux*. The poem which began as a glorification of woman continues and ends as a bitter satire of women. But the book is much more than an overgrown *fabliau*.

In the first place it is an encyclopaedia of the knowledge of the time. Jean de Meun put into it all his learning and all his knowledge. He pays no attention to composition, but passes from one digression to another, often forgetting both lover and Rose, so that the whole work would be rather difficult to digest had not the author written in a firm, clear style which makes acceptable much that is tedious and much that is faulty. But the chief interest of the work, the cause of its success and often of the indignation which it roused, was the astonishing new spirit of free enquiry and free criticism. For Jean de Meun there is no such thing as a question which cannot be discussed. He dares to examine into the origins of the monarchy and to question the titles of the nobility. He is no respecter of the powers that be. And, a more serious matter, he shows the same independence in regard to the Church and even religion. Not only does he attack the Mendicant Orders, and various abuses and institutions; his criticism goes further: he exalts Nature and Reason in terms which at times suggest a smouldering revolt against the principle of authority. It was the beginning of the movement which led later to the Reformation of the 16th century and to the Rationalism of the 18th century. Doubtless Jean de Meun did not see so far ahead, but for centuries his book remained the *vade-mecum* of all those who felt shut in by the narrow limits of rigid tradition.

Jean de Meun was a vigorous thinker and a writer of talent, but although he wrote in verse he was no poet. His contemporary, RUTEBEUF, on the contrary, so like him in spirit and in inspiration, often attained real poetry. He also found much to blame in the society of the time; religion was losing ground, the Holy Land had been abandoned, while nobles and prelates thought only of their own enjoyment; the king himself, the future St Louis, handed the kingdom over to the monks. These burning subjects are not treated at great length by Rutebeuf, but in his short poems, in a few vigorous and forceful stanzas, he hits out unsparingly. We have already spoken of the formation of a public opinion; for the first time it expresses itself, loud and clear, by the mouth of Rutebeuf. Curiously mingled with much good humour, there is often a certain bitterness. The fact is that this humble *jongleur* often went hungry, and suffered not only mentally, like Jean de Meun, but also in the flesh. Hence the personal note which had not hitherto appeared in French lyrical poetry, save perhaps for a short outburst or so in the work of Colin Muset.

The frankness of Rutebeuf, his satirical wit, searching self-criticism, and spontaneous poetry, are found again in the work of ADAM LE BOSSU or ADAM DE LA HALLE, the author of two plays: *Le Jeu de la Feuillée* (*c.* 1255) and *Le Jeu de Robin et Marion* (*c.* 1280). The Parisian *jongleur*, however, had a larger horizon, and was concerned for the national interests, while Adam, a citizen of Arras, was above all a man of his own town. The *dramatis personae* of *Le Jeu de la Feuillée* are inhabitants of Arras or the neighbourhood: a doctor, a monk carrying relics, a potter and his crazy son, an innkeeper and his customers, Adam himself and his father Master Henry. All these people talk, laugh, and quarrel for our benefit, gossiping about their neighbours and sparing no one. Their humour, sometimes subtle, sometimes coarse, is always gay. One side of the turbulent and picturesque life of the great Picard town is shown before our eyes. The picture is attractive except for one or two details. We feel that the hand of authority could not have been too heavy in Arras; the play lives in an atmosphere of freedom; there is an entire absence of bitterness and full play is left to the poet's imagination. Towards the close, fairies appear without causing surprise. This mixture of realism and fantasy, of keen satirical observation and delicate grace, makes *Le Jeu de la Feuillée* one of the most original works of the 13th century.

*Le Jeu de Robin et Marion* is a *pastourelle* put into dramatic form. A knight tries to carry off a shepherdess, Marion, but she escapes from him, and it is Robin who marries her; shepherds and shepherdesses sing songs; it is a regular opéra-comique, and the first, but our modern libretto writers have not the talent of Adam de la Halle. In these two plays Adam gives us an epitome of the comedy of the first half of the Middle Ages; apart from him there is hardly anything worth mention, except perhaps the amusing play *Du Garçon et de l'Aveugle* (*c.* 1280), which is the earliest known farce. As for serious drama, there is even less at this period; we shall say a few words about it later.

All the works we have studied so far are in verse. What about prose? Prose followed up the career so well begun in the preceding period. About 1255, PHILIPPE DE NOVARE, Italian by birth, but French by speech and environment, wrote *Mémoires*, in which he relates an episode in the wars of Cyprus between feudal barons. Philippe himself fought in these wars, and, to a greater extent than the book of Villehardouin, his vivid narrative allows us to penetrate into the life of the French knights of the 13th century and even their private quarrels; so that we are able to see why it was that the Latin Empire of the East did not endure.

PHILIPPE DE BEAUMANOIR was one of those jurists of the 13th century who helped to bring about a change in the mind of the public: his book on the *Coutumes de Beauvaisis* (between 1280 and 1283), abounding with details which bring the period back to life, shows us how the diversity and chaos of the feudal world gradually gave place to order and unity. Philippe de Novare and Philippe de Beaumanoir were educated and even scholarly men; the author of *Récits d'un Ménestrel de Reims* (*c.* 1260) was apparently a *jongleur*, who related with considerable charm for the benefit of simple people the great events of the history of his time as reflected by popular tradition.

But all the books of knights, jurists, and *jongleurs* pale beside the incomparable *Histoire de Saint Louis* of JEAN DE JOINVILLE, seneschal of Champagne (*c.* 1224 to 1317). This is perhaps the masterpiece of French medieval literature. Joinville wrote, in extreme old age, at the request of Queen Jeanne. Louis IX had long been dead, but the aged seneschal, who had been his faithful companion-in-arms in the Holy Land, remembered as clearly as though they were yesterday the six wonderful years which he had lived in closest intimacy with a saint who was at the same time the King of France. The main theme of the book is the history of the Seventh Crusade, to which he added a certain number of incidents and anecdotes of the king belonging either to the time before or after the Crusade. If the plan of the book is not well arranged, its charm is such that we hardly notice it. In a series of episodes full of magnificent colour, two characters hold the stage almost throughout: Louis IX, a great Christian and an admirable king, the finest figure of the Middle Ages, and close at his side his companion and future historian, Joinville. Joinville was neither a saint nor a great man, but what a perfect gentleman! It is his subtle, resolute, smiling personality, let us not be afraid to say so, which makes the supreme attraction of his book. Simple, natural, religious within measure, brave without affectation, tempering the most solid good sense by a touch of humour, with something luminous and affable about him, Joinville was one of the most accomplished types of men produced by the 13th century. He would do honour to any society, but when he is replaced in the society in which he lived, how much better we understand it, with how much more sympathy do we regard it. He who wishes to know the spirit of feudal France in all its purity and in its finest flower has but to read this book of

Joinville's. When, however, it appeared in 1309, St Louis, its hero, had been dead nearly forty years and its author was 85 years old. Around him a new world had been born or was about to come into being.

## § II. FROM THE BEGINNING OF THE HUNDRED YEARS' WAR (1337) TO THE RENAISSANCE

The Hundred Years' War (1337–1453) arrested the normal development of the institutions and the public opinion of France. The 13th century led to the establishment of a centralising monarchy, guardian of the general welfare, allowing the nobles their share, but leaning above all on the middle classes.

In the 14th century, the necessity for defending the kingdom gave a new lease of life to the feudal régime. It was absolutely necessary to have recourse to the services of men whose trade was fighting. The military classes therefore took front rank once more. Having renounced the fight for Christendom in the Orient they could at least fight for France in France itself. It was a good opportunity for showing that they deserved their privileges, but they did not take advantage of it. They produced great captains like Du Guesclin, but, on the whole, their pride and their incapacity were their ruin.

Scorning all that was not noble, they were unable to organise the commons of France and were beaten by the commons of England. They allowed the kingdom to be invaded and the people of France to be crushed. Through their fault a period of atrocious massacres and misery was hopelessly prolonged. The feudal régime, which weighed heavily on the country, had no longer any justification. Hence the terrible revolt, so terribly repressed, of the Jacquerie, in the country districts, and violent popular movements in Paris. When salvation came at last, it was to a large extent the work of a daughter of the people, Jeanne d'Arc, who brought what was lacking more and more in the feudal nobility—an ardent love of her country and a profound faith in its destiny. In such dark times we can hardly expect to find flourishing a literature whose aim it was to give pleasure. Almost all the kinds of literature which were in vogue during the preceding period disappeared, and no new kinds were created. History alone, which did not lack matter, shows any brilliance.

Not that all attempt at poetry had been abandoned. The people of that age even thought they had great poets among them. We of to-day can easily perceive their mediocrity, and we know that genius itself would have been doubtless unable to triumph over such circumstances. The poets may be divided into three groups, which cover the time of this long period of the Hundred Years' War. To the first group belong Machaut, Deschamps, and Froissart. They continued, on the whole, the traditions of the courtly lyric, exaggerating still more its artificiality. What had been the pastime of an elegant society, animated, in imagination at least, by a refined ideal, became in their hands the occupation of qualified professionals. Not that the nobility had entirely ceased taking part in literary tourneys; witness the delightful book of the *Cent Ballades* (between 1386 and 1392) composed by several high-born authors of the period. But there was, we feel, no longer any harmony between this poetry and the spirit of the age. The nobles wrote and read love poems and protected the authors, chiefly because it was good manners to do so. Similarly they tried to introduce into the daily life of the time the colour of the prose romances of the Round Table, which at that time enjoyed a great vogue in high society. In both these ways an effort, doomed in advance, was made to maintain the ways of feeling, thinking, and acting which belonged to a past that was definitely done with.

In one thing, however, the poets of the 14th century were innovators: instead of insisting that every new lyric must have a form peculiar to itself, they fashioned forms which did not vary, but which repeated practically the same combinations of stanza, rhythm, and rhyme. Thus by the side of allegorical poems, whose persistent success gives evidence of the great influence of the *Roman de la Rose*, we find the *rondeau* and the *ballade*, which were to have a great future. Deceived by their superficial novelty, the age thought it was witnessing the birth of a new school of poetry in its midst.

Guillaume de Machaut (*c.* 1300–1377) was considered by all to be its brilliant founder. His *Voir Dit* (1363) is still readable to-day; it is a long romance in verse, in which he tells of the love and admiration with which he, in his old age, inspired a young maiden. Eustache Morel or Deschamps (*c.* 1345–*c.* 1405) was the most prolific of the disciples of Machaut. His immense work, consisting of ballads, rondeaux, and allegorical poems, has the interest of a chronicle, kept up from day to day by an honest, sensible, but rather surly observer who was also a clear-sighted patriot. Much may be learned of the feats and exploits of his contemporaries, of the customs and spirit of the times, but we must not look for poetry. FROISSART is superior to Machaut and Deschamps, or, at any rate, in several of his poems, e.g. *L'Épinette Amoureuse*, he has related episodes of his youth, be they fact or fiction, with more grace and freshness. As an example of this sort of autobiographical poem we might also mention his *Dit du Florin* (1389). But Froissart is above all a great historian, whom we shall meet again later.

Machaut, Deschamps, and Froissart belong almost entirely to the 14th century. The second group takes us into the 15th century. It includes Christine de Pisan and Alain Chartier.

CHRISTINE DE PISAN (*c.* 1363–*c.* 1430), the daughter of an Italian father, the doctor of Charles V, was a good Frenchwoman who did honour to the country of her adoption. She was very well educated and borrowed much from antiquity; her vocabulary and even her style were influenced by her intimate knowledge of the Latin authors. There is in her work already as it were a breath of the Renaissance spirit. But she was poor and lived by her pen; she wrote too much. There is more delicacy and sincerity in her love poetry than in that of Machaut and Deschamps, but in spite of her beautiful character and fine intelligence she was not a great writer.

ALAIN CHARTIER (*c.* 1385–*c.* 1430) had an immense reputation in the 15th century, which it is permissible to-day to consider exaggerated, but he certainly had to a greater degree than the others we have mentioned a sense of form. *La Belle Dame sans Merci*, in which a lover, rejected by his lady, dies of grief, is merely a playful trifle; but the poem, very commonplace as to its matter, is written with an elegant ease and wit unknown since the 13th century. It created a lively interest among the courtiers and ladies of the court of Charles VII—and this in 1424, one of the darkest moments of the Hundred Years' War. We see here in full the lack of harmony already mentioned between the poetry of the 14th and 15th centuries and the real life of the time.

Nevertheless Alain Chartier was a sincere patriot who thoroughly understood the gravity of the moment. In his *Quadrilogue Invectif* (1422) he points out the causes of the French misfortunes in vigorous strokes which hit the mark. The book is written in prose, and in language which attempts and often reaches eloquence. Here again there is a remarkable attention to form too rare in the work of his contemporaries.

The same interest in form is found in the poets of the third group: MARTIN LE FRANC (*circa* 1410–1461), whose *Champion des Dames* (1442) recalls the manner of Jean de Meun, and above all CHARLES D'ORLÉANS (1391–1465), whose collection of ballads and rondeaux is the masterpiece of courtly poetry of the 15th century. Charles, duke of Orléans, took part in all the great events and all the tragedies of the period. Taken prisoner at Agincourt (1415), he remained for 25 years in captivity in England, and it might have been expected that his poetry would have a deeper inspiration than that which animates his collection of short love verses. This is another example of the tyranny of fashion. But it must be admitted that this great noble has succeeded better in this kind of poetry than any of his predecessors. The matter is of small account, but great attention is paid to the form, which is often exquisite. Never prolix, never grandiloquent, never bombastic, the language is in keeping with the delicate sentiments expressed. This amiable poet never lacks grace; even when advanced in years, he wrote some charming verse on the disillusions and disappointments of old age. The last of the courtly poets of old France, he was also the most artistic.

Mediocre as the poetry of the 14th century is, it would be hard to find, apart from the historians, prose writers comparable to Machaut, Deschamps, and Froissart. We can mention only LE CHEVALIER DE LA TOUR-LANDRY and the author of *Le Ménager de Paris*. Le Chevalier de la Tour-Landry wrote in 1371–1372 a book which he intended to be a handbook of reading and French composition, and at the same time a handbook of practical morality, for the use of his daughters. His examples are taken from the Bible and from contemporary history. The tales from the latter are naturally more interesting to us; they are written in a very agreeable style, though it drags at times; they tell us much about the manners, customs, and even the fashions of the 14th century, and show us what conversation was like in the provincial high society of the period, even giving the subjects and the tone. Similarly *Le Ménager de Paris* introduces us into the *bourgeois* circles of the time.

But the literature of the 14th century owes its importance chiefly to its historical works. Two names stand out from all the rest: Jean le Bel and Froissart.

JEAN LE BEL (*c.* 1290–1369), canon of Liège between 1352 and 1361, wrote a *Chronique* of the events which took place in his own time in England and France from 1329 to 1361. His style is clear and rapid; the beginning of the book especially, where he relates the history of the Scottish campaign, is particularly interesting. Froissart, who recognised his merit, borrowed long passages from him, not without acknowledging it. But it has become difficult to appreciate justly Jean le Bel, because his work seems to such an extent to be incorporated with that of Froissart. There is however no doubt that he is inferior to Froissart.

JEAN FROISSART (1337–*c.* 1405) set himself the task of relating the whole history of the wars between France and England. Starting with the year 1325 he brought his account up to 1400, and there the fourth and last book stops abruptly; the conclusion is lacking. Froissart was twenty when he began the great work which was to be the occupation and the passion of his life, and at which he laboured until his last years. He kept to the established title of *Chroniques*, but he makes it definitely clear that his work is to be not that of a chronicler, but of a historian. In other words, he was not satisfied to set down in factitious chronological order a string of disconnected facts, which, in this artlessly simple arrangement, lose all relation to reality. He had a keen sense of reality, with all its colour and all its complexity, and it is this he wished to convey to us. He could only succeed in this by presenting the facts to us in all their multiplicity of detail. And this is just what he did his utmost to accomplish during a period of fifty years.

But these details, how were they obtained? By interrogating those who took part in the great events and who made history. And all his life, never shrinking from fatigue, never sparing expense, impelled by the most exacting curiosity, Froissart did in fact scour France, England, and Scotland, seeing kings, princes, knights, squires, and roving soldiers, saying little, listening much, asking questions and continually taking notes.

This method, inaugurated by Jean le Bel, was practised by Froissart on a much larger scale with uncommon energy and perseverance. We do not know if it has ever been adopted since. It was naturally bound to lead to some mistakes. The chronology of the *Chroniques* is not always accurate, far from it, and Froissart accepted more than one doubtful anecdote. But who else has ever succeeded in reviving with such intensity seventy-five years of the crowded and agitated life of two great nations? What author in any country has ever presented a picture of events so widely dispersed and so complex, a picture so vast, so powerful, so picturesque, and so true in colour? People have not always been just towards this great artist and historian, because they have been too severe on the man. They cannot forgive him for admiring, without qualification, the feudal nobility. Patronised by the great nobles of his time, and writing for them, he shared the greater part of their prejudices, and that is what he has been so bitterly reproached for. He has been criticised for not being ahead of his time. He belonged to a society which he thought would endure longer than it did. Such a mistake has often been made and will often be made again; it in no way detracts from the merit of Froissart. He exalts the knightly virtues and some of them well deserved it. If he had no sympathy for the popular movements of his time, he has at least described them minutely and in no way sought to diminish their importance. Froissart is the greatest name in the literature of the 14th century and one of the greatest in all French medieval literature.

During the first half of the 15th century the works that best deserve mention are once more the historical works. An unknown author—without doubt a clerk whose occupation it was to write for the nobles—has left us a *Livre des faits du bon Messire Jean le Maingre, dit Bouciquaut,* marshal of France and governor of Genoa (1409). This biography, based on documents furnished by members of the marshal's household, has weak spots and too much tedious erudition. But in general it is interesting and lively, the style clear, compact and agreeable. Bouciquaut was a fine type of knight of the last age of feudalism. At times he recalls St Louis, and the author of his biography has something of the charm of Joinville. No small praise, in either case.

*La Chronique du bon duc Loys de Bourbon* (1429) is a biography of the brother-in-law of Charles V, who died in 1410. The author was a "poor Picard pilgrim," JEAN CABARET, who drew his information from one of the Duke's companions-in-arms. He has evidently somewhat flattered and idealised the portrait of his hero; but this unpretentious history, written in popular and rather racy language, makes pleasant reading. It contains a number of interesting details of the life of a great feudal noble, and of his relations with his vassals and subjects.

*Le Journal d'un Bourgeois de Paris* is anonymous; it is an invaluable picture of Parisian life from 1405 to 1449, in particular during the Burgundian and English domination. It shows what were the impressions made by the events of the time on an intelligent man, a priest and member of the university, and a fiery partisan to boot. *Le Journal de* CLÉMENT DE FAUQUEMBERGUE, a registrar of the Parlement of Paris from 1417 to 1435, is far from offering the same attraction as regards the curious and the picturesque, but it would be hard to find another work of the time which gives us a more intimate picture of the life of the Parlement, that great body in which were gathered together more and more the élite of the *bourgeoisie* of the day.

Apart from the *Chroniques* there is hardly anything worth mention among the works of this time, except those that are related to the *Roman de la Rose*. This was in fact the moment when the tendencies which guided Jean de Meun began to be quite clear to all his readers, when the most enthusiastic advocates and the most fierce antagonists of his book appeared. The names of the antagonists are best remembered. Christine de Pisan, whom we know already, rose against Jean de Meun in defence of women, and JEAN GERSON, ecclesiastical chancellor of Paris, in defence of religion. The most important work stimulated by this quarrel was a prose treatise by Gerson, *Contre le Roman de la Rose* (1402) written in particularly firm and vigorous language. On the other hand, and quite apart from all these polemics, the influence of Jean de Meun is found in a number of works, both prose and poetry, which took up and developed some of his ideas or were inspired by his spirit. Here must be mentioned above all *Les XV Joies de Mariage* (*c.* 1420), in prose, one of the most finished works of the 15th century, in which the keenest observation is tinged with the subtlest irony. The title is an added touch of raillery, for all the time we have to do with the sorrows of marriage. The author has remained unknown, but we may conjecture that he was a secular, perhaps a country, priest; the scenes he describes are placed in provincial circles of the petty nobility. His book, written in a nervous close-packed style, in which every stroke is driven home, leaves an after-taste of bitterness. It is the work of a man who thinks, not without a certain proud satisfaction, that he sees to the bottom of the vanity of all things.

It will be noticed that the majority of the works hitherto mentioned were written for the nobility, or even when addressed to others were not intended to go outside a small circle of generally highly cultivated readers. Some of them were mere jottings which owed their publication to a fortuitous concourse of circumstances. There was nothing written with a view to please that large public which for centuries delighted in the *chansons de geste* and the *fabliaux*. Was this public therefore completely forgotten during the 14th and 15th centuries? No! for in the latter part of the Middle Ages dramatic performances took the place of the *jongleurs*, who had almost disappeared as early as the beginning of the Hundred Years' War.

The theatre did not of course begin all at once in the 14th century, but until then there is no proof that its popularity was very extensive. At all events what remains from the 12th and 13th centuries is of small account: *La Représentation d'Adam* (second half of the 12th century), *Le Miracle de Saint Nicolas* by JEAN BODEL of Arras (middle of 13th century), and *Le Miracle de Théophile* by Rutebeuf. We have already mentioned the few works which belong to the domain of comedy.

*La Représentation d'Adam* shows us Adam and Eve after the Fall, the death of Abel, and the procession of the Prophets announcing the coming of a Redeemer. The stage directions are given in Latin and we learn that the stage was close to the church, probably right up against the portal. These two circumstances are explained by the origin of the serious drama. It arose gradually out of religious ceremonies, which for many years were completed by dramatic representations within the church itself. It was Latin before it was French. In the 12th century it was definitely installed in the public square. *Adam* is written in several metres, but the octosyllable predominates, and this metre remained essentially the dramatic verse of the Middle Ages, just as it was the narrative metre *par excellence.*

The *Miracle* is a play dealing with a miraculous episode in the life of a saint, or a supernatural intervention on the part of the Virgin. This kind of play, known as early as the 13th century and perhaps earlier, was certainly very popular in the 14th century. One manuscript has preserved for us forty *Miracles de Notre Dame* which, judging from the way they resemble each other, must have been composed for the same audience. Long before this there had been formed in the towns associations of citizens called *puys*, with a view to holding poetic festivals in honour of the Virgin Mary.

The forty plays of the Cangé manuscript were apparently written by various authors at the end of the 14th century for one of these *puys.* The characters are often princes, but they were created by men who had only seen great nobles from a distance. They are at their best when they depict the life of the *bourgeois*, or even the lower classes, not so much by giving us picturesque details, though this side is not forgotten, as by rendering the ordinary feelings of everyday life. Hence the flavour of originality in these little dramas; no other work of the 14th or 15th century teaches us more of the heart of this nameless crowd which, beneath the nobility and clergy, constituted at that time the majority of the French people.

Other associations sprang up side by side with the *puys*, such as the *Confrérie de la Passion*, which, as early as the beginning of the 15th century, had an established theatre in Paris. This *Confrérie* gave plays of the same type as the ancient *Représentation d'Adam*, but, probably under the influence of the disciples of St Francis of Assisi, they abandoned theological subjects in order to devote themselves to the outstanding scenes from the life of Christ and especially the Passion. The *mystères*, as they were afterwards called, soon began to enjoy an extraordinary popularity. The performance of a mystery play lasted several days and was made the occasion of a magnificent city festival, which drew great crowds from every direction. They not only appealed to religious feeling, but also to the taste for pompous displays and rich costumes which was very strong at the time.

The action of the play was very varied and introduced the most surprising episodes The scenery was peculiar, in that all the different scenes of the entire action (Paradise, Hell, City, Sea, etc.) were set up side by side, and the personages never left the stage. This very extraordinary system spread all over Europe, introduced everywhere by the foreign students who crowded to the lectures of the University of Paris and saw the performances of the *Confrères*. The artists of every country were inspired by these grandiose spectacles, which instilled new life into the sculpture of the period.

It is a pity that the mysteries themselves have so little literary value; their execution is mediocre. We cannot even make an exception of the masterpiece of this kind, *La Passion* of ARNOUL GRÉBAN, written and acted about 1450. The play is at any rate full of life, especially in the scenes from the life of the people, in which appear shepherds, servants, sergeants, devils, etc.; these scenes teem with phrases and characteristic touches from common life. The religious discussions and arguments, on the other hand, abound in learned phraseology and pedantic latinisms. This is a very curious mixture, which corresponds to the differences of class in the audience. The spectators of the mysteries included all classes of society, but those plays were specially relished by the populace and belong to popular literature.

At the end of the Hundred Years' War, France took on a new aspect. Nobles still existed, but feudalism was dead. The royal army took the place of the feudal army. The authority of the king increased daily and tended towards absolutism with the consent of the nation itself, which accepted the means in view of the excellent end: the re-establishment of peace and order, better government and growing prosperity. At the death of Charles VII (1461) the nobles hoped to arrest the development of the monarchy. For long they struggled against Louis XI. The most persistent of them was Charles the Bold, the powerful Duke of Burgundy. But by sheer force of will and calculating cunning the new king was able to master all opposition, and to impose his rule on the entire kingdom. France was then a modern State and Charles VIII was about to lead it into Italy on its first adventure (1494). The period from 1453 to 1494 is therefore for the most part still a period of warfare, but not of violent and brutal warfare against a foreign invader who devastated the land. It was a bitter rivalry between Frenchmen, a struggle between the selfishness of the nobles who sought only their own interest and the selfishness of the king, who at any rate had the advantage of identifying his own interests with those of the country. It was a period in which underhand and cunning diplomacy were more important than fine feats of arms. The time for the practical man had come.

Nevertheless this utterly matter-of-fact generation can boast of a true poet, the greatest French poet of the Middle Ages, François Villon (1431 or 1432–after 1463). He led a wretched and even a criminal existence, but this existence was undoubtedly for him the source of the rarest poetry. A Bachelor of Arts and Master of Arts of the University of Paris, he killed his adversary in a quarrel and fled from Paris. He obtained pardon and returned, but he took part in a serious robbery at the Collège de Navarre and disappeared once more. Before leaving Paris he published a merry farewell to his friends in which he professes to bequeath to them imaginary legacies; this poem, *Les Lais* (1456), was the beginning of his career as a poet. Then suddenly we come upon Villon again, at the age of 30, in the prison of Meun-sur-Loire—for what misdeed we do not know. At the accession of Louis XI he was liberated, but he had suffered cold, hunger, and much cruelty from his gaolers. More than that, he had withdrawn into himself and was overwhelmed at the thought of his lost youth and at the closing of every honourable career to him. At the same time he became conscious of his genius. *Le Testament* (1461 or 1462) is a sort of diary in which Villon related, at times in veiled language, his sufferings and wretchedness at Meun and afterwards, and recorded precisely the feelings which stirred his impressionable mind. The framework of the poem, as indicated by the title, is similar to that of the *Lais*, but the theme is taken up again with a much wider view and with incomparably more spirit. The stanza is the eight lined stanza with three rhymes, made fashionable by Alain Chartier in *La Belle Dame sans Merci*. But that is all Villon owed to his predecessors. No poet in the Middle Ages, nor perhaps since, was ever more personal. Physical suffering, dark poverty, the anguish of sickness and premature old age, solitude of the soul, it is his very life which he has described; and he speaks of death as one who has often been confronted by its spectre, in tones and with an intensity of vision that are unforgettable. The style is in perfect harmony with the rest; in his picturesque verse, so full of colour, the images stand forth in striking relief. Into the body of the *Testament* Villon has interwoven several *ballades* of which the finest and the best known are the *Ballade des Dames du temps jadis*, the *Ballade pour sa Mère*, the prayer *pour l'âme du bon feu maistre Jehan Cotart*, and *Les Contredits de Franc Gontier*. The admirable *Ballade des Pendus*, written later (1463), at the moment when he barely escaped hanging, is perhaps his masterpiece. This poverty-stricken outcast, this gaol-bird, was the first modern lyric poet.

The year 1456, in which Villon began to write, was also the year in which ANTOINE DE LA SALE (1388–*circa* 1469), warrior, great traveller, and preceptor of princes, wrote *Le Petit Jehan de Saintré*, one of the works of the 15th century which show originality. La Dame des Belles Cousines, partly from idleness, partly from inclination, undertakes to make a young page of the Court, *le petit* Saintré, into a perfect knight. She succeeds, but when the name of Saintré is gloriously celebrated throughout all Europe, the lady takes offence without reason, abandons the knight and becomes enamoured of a loutish abbot, who treats her to sumptuous repasts. It begins as an idyll of chivalry and ends in the key of the *fabliaux*. The earlier chapters, except for a certain surprising pedantry (the lady cites from memory the Latin authors, text and translation), are full of a charming grace and delicacy.

But the last part of the book, where the monk comes between Saintré and his lady, is even better. The scene in which Damp Abbé wrestles with and throws the young Saintré while the lady looks on, jeering, is written and handled with consummate art. This perhaps gives us a glimpse of the idea of the author: the ecclesiastic gets the better of the knight; the former represents a prosaic age which prefers the good things of life to glory, and he triumphs where the knight of high ideals, the man of the past, fails. Saintré, the brave and loyal nobleman, the heir of all the fine feudal traditions, is brutally thrown to the ground by a burly plebeian who cares nothing for the feats of arms of a noble. It is the triumph of physical force over the more refined ideal of a select class which was on the point of disappearing. This marks one of the strongest trends of the century.

Antoine de la Sale showed so much talent in his subtle and witty romance that there has been a temptation to attribute to him a large part of the anonymous works of the century when they were rather out of the ordinary. In spite of what critics have said, he was not the author of *Les XV Joies de Mariage*, nor has he been proved to be the author of *Le Livre des faits de Jacques de Lalaing*, or *Les Cent nouvelles nouvelles*. In its final form *Le Livre des faits* was not earlier than 1468. It is another portrait of the model knight according to the old conception. But Saintré, although he bore the name of a 14th century nobleman, was only an imaginary person in the book of La Sale, while the exploits of Jacques de Lalaing, who died in 1453, were still fresh in everyone's memory. He reminds one of Boucicaut but he had not his manliness and broad human sympathies. He goes from joust to joust, giving and accepting complicated challenges, a regular knight of the Round Table as conceived at the time—a pale and conventional figure which was still the ideal of the aristocracy of Western Europe, France, Spain, Portugal, and England. But side by side with the belated champions of this factitious unity live, increasing in influence, the men who were building up the modern nations. The burgesses and villeins of Ghent, against whom Lalaing fights towards the end of the book, are very real individualists.

*Le Jouvencel* (between 1461 and 1468), by JEAN DE BUEIL, depicts the nobility in a less brilliant but more attractive light than the *Livre des faits*. It is a military novel. Within the framework of a story, the main incidents of which are borrowed from 15th century history, the author has presented the whole theory and practice of the military art of the period. He shows us the warlike aristocracy of the end of the Hundred Years' War actually at work, with all the detail of their daily life. We see especially how they grew fat on war, and what importance was attached to questions of the allotment of prisoners and the division of spoils. The idealistic side of the profession is also clearly indicated, and as we go along we meet with a great number of characteristic manners and customs. It is told in a brisk, lively fashion, and the style is very good. Altogether it is one of the most interesting books of the 15th century.

Beside the romancers who made history serve their purpose must be placed the historians proper. MATHIEU D'ESCOUCHY (*c*. 1420–*c*. 1482) brings his *Chronique* to a conclusion about 1465; it was a continuation of that of MONSTRELET (died 1453), who himself continued Froissart from 1400 to 1444. Mathieu d'Escouchy wrote in a clear, very readable, but colourless style. He had a sane, well-balanced judgment and, a rarer thing at this time, a strong feeling of humanity. GEORGES CHASTELLAIN (*c*. 1405–1475) undertook in 1455 a *Chronique des choses de ce temps*, a great part of which is lost to-day. It is hard to decide whether he deserved the very great reputation which he enjoyed among his contemporaries.

The author of *Les Cent nouvelles nouvelles*, wishing to write a collection of tales, turned to oral tradition, and he therefore often chose the same subjects as the *fabliaux* of the 13th century. His point of view, too, is not very different from that of the *jongleurs* of old. Not so coarse in style, quite as licentious at bottom, his chief aim is to make us laugh. He has no satirical trend, but constant good humour and often plenty of spirit. There is more art than in the *fabliaux*, and the details are more happily grouped with a view to giving the illusion of real life. But nevertheless it is always art of an inferior kind. Beneath the uniform method and manner the work lacks the impress of an individual style. The real originality of the book is that it is in prose. Here may be traced the influence of Boccaccio, from whom the author explicitly claims descent. But he was inferior to his model, nor can his work be compared with *Les XV Joies de Mariage* or *Le Petit Jehan de Saintré*. He introduced into France the prose tale briskly and merrily told—this was his chief merit. His book was presented to the Duke of Burgundy, Philip the Good, at Dijon, probably in 1462.

As for the theatre, the great vogue of the mysteries continued. The tendency was to make them ever longer and to write them in vast cycles, which in some cases took weeks to perform. We may mention especially the *Mystère du Vieux Testament*, which consists of nearly 50,000 lines.

But during this period the serious drama can offer nothing to equal the simple farce *Maître Pathelin* (1464), one of the masterpieces of the 15th century. It is an amusing story of a rogue of a lawyer who makes a dupe of Guillaume the draper, and is in his turn duped by a simple country shepherd. Pathelin, a consummate actor, pretends to be ill when Guillaume comes to demand the price of some cloth delivered that very morning, and Guillemette, the lawyer's wife, having been well rehearsed, plays her part admirably. Her husband has been in bed for weeks, so how could he have bought the cloth? And Pathelin talks deliriously in several languages. His cunning tricks and devilish arts succeed in convincing the stupid Guillaume that he has been dreaming. The same day the draper summons before the judge his shepherd Thibaut, who has robbed him of several sheep. The case is clear and Thibaut could never have been acquitted, if it had not been for his brilliant advocate Pathelin, who suggests that he should pretend to be an idiot and answer "Baa!" to every question. So Thibaut, on being examined, bleats away with all his might. But the draper, suddenly perceiving Pathelin resuscitated and perfectly well, is choked with indignation, forgets Thibaut, and begins talking about his cloth. The judge, at a loss to understand all this confusion, keeps shouting at him, *Revenons à nos moutons*. The case, of course, is dismissed. But the best of it all is that, when Pathelin claims his fee, Thibaut can say nothing but "Baa!" and bleats for all he is worth. Pathelin had found his match.

This farce was written by some one who had an instinctive sense of stage-craft. The two plots are very skilfully blended;

nothing can be more comic than the angry impatience of the judge, brought about in the most natural way from the entanglement of the two different plots. The characters are not complicated, but how picturesquely and clearly they stand out, and how alive they are! What vivacity in the quick repartee! How breezy and lively the language! The play well deserves its celebrity. It is a pity we do not know who the author was. We know no more of the author of *Le Franc-Archer de Bagnolet* (1468 or 1469), a dramatic monologue as perfect in its way as the farce of *Pathelin*. It is a subtle and amusing satire of the country militia instituted by Charles VII; the "Francs-Archers" had a reputation for cowardice and the warrior of Bagnolet is a boastful coward.

The twenty years which saw the appearance of *Le Testament*, *Le Petit Jehan de Saintré*, *Les Cent nouvelles nouvelles*, *Pathelin* and *Le Franc-Archer de Bagnolet* certainly constitute a brilliant period of medieval literature. However, apart from Villon, who belongs to his century only in the external form of his work, this literature lacks grandeur and imagination. It is somewhat hard, and at times depressing. *Lalaing* and *Le Jouvencel* are more elevating, but they look backwards. The tendency of the present was undoubtedly to extol Damp Abbé or Pathelin. The majority of these books are animated by the harsh realistic spirit of the time of Louis XI, which was not favourable to flights of imagination. So that it is not surprising to find that this literature came to an end abruptly. As early as 1470 the production seems to have ceased. There is only one more great name, Commines; the rest is mediocrity or vacuity. We may except, however, the charming story of *Jean de Paris*, written towards the very end of the century.

The mysteries continued to stir the enthusiasm of the crowd, but their artistic value was no greater, and in the 16th century they disappeared before the opposition of the religious feeling awakened by the Reformation. Farces continued to be written, some of them amusing, but we must wait until we come to Molière to find anything that can compare with *Pathelin*.

Poetry fell very low. GUILLAUME COQUILLART imitated the picturesque style of Villon, but without his finish, and his matter was very thin; his poetry (1477–1480) is that of a law student. He was, however, very superior to the *grands rhétoriqueurs*, who had neither art nor inspiration, and vainly sought after originality in ridiculous difficulties of technique.

Medieval literature at least ends worthily with a fine work, the *Mémoires* of PHILIPPE DE COMMINES (before 1447–1511), written in the last decade of the century. Commines was first in the service of Charles the Bold, then from 1472 in that of the king, Louis XI, whose cunning, calculating statecraft was more after his own heart. His book is intended to be a political manual for the use of princes and their counsellors. He therefore tries to get to the bottom of an intrigue, to discover the causes of a war, and the meaning of a treaty of peace. He compares the situations, contrasts the individuals, and tries to set forth the main lines of a policy. Hence the abstract and intellectual side of his *Mémoires*. They are rather deficient in life and colour; furthermore such a method as his needs a clear, concise style, and his style is too often diffuse and heavy. But his work is that of a highly intelligent man who sees clearly, reasons accurately, and penetrates beneath appearances. Men thus gifted rarely wrote in French during the Middle Ages; the example of Commines was a great novelty. Kings and princes interest him particularly, because their personal ambitions influence the course of events; above all he closely observes Louis XI and Charles the Bold; he is not deceived by them; he criticises them freely. Had he been allowed, he would willingly have suggested reforms. He is not indifferent to the lot of the people, and sees how every action of its chief affects the nation for good or evil. Moreover, he does not believe that the course of events depends entirely on the king's caprice and pleasure. He often calls attention to a sort of avenging justice, inflicting punishment for errors or crimes, in which he sees clearly the hand of God.

After Commines medieval literature produced nothing more. It might perhaps have been renewed by seeking inspiration in the great works of the 12th and 13th centuries, but these were unknown at the time. Buried in castle or convent libraries, the old French manuscripts were no longer read, the chief cause being perhaps that they were no longer understood. The language had undergone profound changes in the 14th century; from this time onwards the works of the early Middle Ages appeared to be written in a foreign tongue which was considered, quite wrongly, an inferior form of the language of the day.

Thus the 15th century had exhausted its rather scant inspiration and it was unable to find support in the centuries that had gone before. Salvation had therefore to come from other sources. This was to be the work of the Renaissance. But the inglorious end must not make us unjust to French medieval literature as a whole. Let us remember that in the 13th and 14th centuries it was admired and imitated throughout all Europe, and that it produced such works as *Roland*, *Érec* and *Perceval*, the *Renart* poems, *Aucassin et Nicolette*, *La Châtelaine de Vergi*, the prose *Lancelot*, *Le Jeu de la Feuillée*, *Le Roman de la Rose*, the book of Joinville, the *Chroniques* of Froissart, the poetry of Villon, the farce of *Pathelin*, and the *Mémoires* of Commines.

## BIBLIOGRAPHY.


Gaston Paris, *La littérature française au Moyen Age* (*xi*[e]–*xiv*[e] *siècles*), 5th ed., 1914; *Esquisse historique de la littérature au Moyen Age depuis les origines jusqu'à la fin du xv*[e] *siècle*, 2nd ed., 1913; *Légendes du Moyen Age*, 4th ed., 1912; *La Poésie du Moyen Age*, 2 vols., 1903–1906.

J. Bédier, *Les Légendes épiques*, 4 vols., 1912–1917. A. Jeanroy, *Les Origines de la Poésie Lyrique en France au Moyen Age*, 2nd ed., 1904. L. Foulet, *Le Roman de Renard*, 1914. F. Lot, *Études sur le Lancelot en prose*, 1918. J. Bédier, *Les Fabliaux*, 2nd ed., 1895. E. Faral, *Les Jongleurs en France au Moyen Age*, 1910. E. Langlois, *Origines et Sources du Roman de la Rose*, 1891. Ch.-V. Langlois, *La Société Française au xiii*[e] *siècle d'après dix romans d'aventure*, 3rd ed., 1911. *La vie en France au Moyen Age d'après quelques moralistes du temps*, 2nd ed., 1911.

J. Mortensen, *Le Théâtre français au Moyen Age*, 1903. L. Petit de Julleville, *Les Mystères*, 2 vols., 1880.

Gaston Paris, *François Villon*, 2nd ed., 1910. P. Champion, *François Villon, sa vie et son temps*, 2 vols., 1913.

Constans, *Chrestomathie de l'Ancien Français*, 3rd ed., 1906.

**La Vie de saint Alexis*, ed. G. Paris, 1917.

*La Chanson de Roland*, ed. Gautier (édition classique), Tours.

*Le Roman de Troie*, ed. Constans, 6 vols., 1904–1912.

Marie de France, *Lais*, ed. Warnke, 2nd ed., Halle, 1900.

Thomas, *Tristan*, ed. Bédier, 2 vols., 1902–1905.

*Béroul, *Tristan*, ed. Muret, 1913.

Chrétien de Troyes, ed. Foerster, Halle; *Érec*, 2nd ed., 1909; *Cligès*, 3rd ed., 1910; *Yvain*, 4th ed., 1912; *Lancelot*, 1899.

*Romances et Pastourelles*, ed. Bartsch, Leipzig, 1870.
*Floire et Blanchefleur*, ed. du Méril, 1856.
*Aucassin et Nicolette*, ed. Suchier, 8th ed., Paderborn, 1913.
**La Châtelaine de Vergi*, ed. Raynaud-Foulet, 2nd ed., 1912.
*Guillaume de Dôle*, ed. Servois, 1893.
Villehardouin, *Conquête de Constantinople*, ed. N. de Wailly, 3rd ed., 1882.
Jean de Meun et Guillaume de Lorris, *Le Roman de la Rose*, ed. F. Michel, 1864.
Rutebeuf, *Œuvres*, ed. Jubinal, 3 vols., 2nd ed., 1874.
*Adam de la Halle, *Le Jeu de la Feuillée*, ed. E. Langlois, 1911.
*Philippe de Novare, *Mémoires*, ed. Kohler, 1913.
*Récits d'un Ménestrel de Reims au xiii^e^ siècle*, ed. N. de Wailly, 1876.
Philippe de Remi, sire de Beaumanoir, *Coutumes de Beauvaisis*, ed. Salmon, 2 vols., 1899–1900.
Joinville, *Histoire de Saint Louis*, ed. N. de Wailly (édition classique), Paris.
Froissart, *Chroniques*, ed. Luce-Raynaud, 11 vols. (down to 1385), 1869–1899; ed. Buchon, 3 vols., 1837.
*Les XV Joies de Mariage*, ed. Jannet, 2nd ed., 1857.
*Villon, *Œuvres*, ed. Longnon-Foulet, 2nd ed., 1914.
Antoine de la Sale, *Le Petit Jehan de Saintré*, ed. Guichard, 1843.
*Les Cent nouvelles nouvelles*, ed. Wright, 2 vols., 1857–1858.
*Pathelin*, ed. Schneegans, Strasbourg, 1908.
Commines, *Mémoires*, ed. B. de Mandrot, 2 vols., 1901–1903.

The editions marked * are published in *Les Classiques français du Moyen Age*, ed. Mario Roques.

# CHAPTER IX

## ARCHITECTURE

### § I. FRENCH ROMANESQUE

Art dormant from 5th to 10th century. Charlemagne's attempted revival. Renaissance of the 10th century. Influence of Roman Art. Division of art into provincial schools. Provence. Toulouse. The French *chevet*. The vault. The flying buttress. Aquitaine and the domed church. Auvergne. Burgundy. Normandy. Review of the Romanesque period.

ARCHITECTURE, the master art which touches mankind most closely, for though we may live without painting and sculpture, we must have houses to shelter us and buildings in which to meet, is more subject than the other arts to local and social influences. These influences it is the proper part of the art to express; and when it is in a healthy state Architecture will reflect faithfully the country and society in which it exists. Nowhere did the art better satisfy this condition than in France during the Middle Ages.

In the earlier part of this period, France was divided into semi-independent principalities, governed by great feudatories, who faintly acknowledged the distant and shadowy sovereignty of the king; and this division is well illustrated by the distinct provincial styles into which Architecture fell in Burgundy, Toulouse, Aquitaine, Anjou, and Normandy. The distinction was most strongly marked during the Romanesque period; though it was never quite lost as the kingdom gradually became consolidated under Louis VI, Philip Augustus, and his successors. For though Gothic art, which was developed in the Ile-de-France, the Royal domain, to some extent made its way into the distant provinces, it was never fully accepted in the South and West. The Gothic cathedrals at Limoges and Clermont-Ferrand seem out of place where they are, intruders, and almost impertinences.

No province of the Roman Empire was more thoroughly latinised than Gaul. Roman learning flourished in the schools of Trêves, Lyons, Arles, Toulouse, and Bordeaux, and Italy herself can show no finer remains of Roman work than those at Nîmes, Arles, Vienne, Orange, and the Pont-du-Gard. The advent and settlement of Visigoths and Burgundians did not at first interfere with Roman culture, or disturb the life of the great Roman nobles and the pursuit of peaceful arts.

The picture which Sidonius Apollinaris, writing in the 5th century, gives us of his villa at Clermont recalls Pliny's description of his Tusculanum, and we read of great churches being built at Lyons, Tours, and Clermont with ranks of marble columns, windows with tinted glass, and gilded ceilings that vied with the sunshine. But Sidonius lived to see the end of the Western Empire and the subjection of his own Clermont to Gothic rule: and in the following generation Roman culture in Gaul was overwhelmed by the tide of barbarism. During the next five centuries the arts were dormant, and it was not till the 10th century that we find any trace of native architecture. Charlemagne at the end of the 8th century had attempted to revive Roman art, but his Capella Palatina at Aquisgranum or Aix-la-Chapelle, imitated from the Byzantine church of St Vitale at Ravenna, adorned with the spoils of Theodoric's palace, and built no doubt by Italian architects, was an exotic on the soil of Austrasia and founded no school in northern France.

When at last the arts awoke to fresh life, Architecture followed a different line in each part of the country. It was in the southern half of France that Latin culture had reached its highest development and lingered longest. The people there were less exposed than those in the North to the intrusion of Germanic tribes and the mixture of Teutonic blood; and they retained, as they probably do still, more of the old Gallic strain. It was there, especially in Provence, that the finest examples of Roman work remained, and that the influence of classic art was felt most strongly through a great part of the Middle Ages. In Aquitaine, farther west, a new element appears in the remarkable series of domed churches, resulting probably from the trade route of Byzantine commerce that passed through that part of France. Auvergne developed a style of its own, partly affected by classic example, but highly original. In Burgundy, the cradle of French monasticism, classic tradition had great influence, though the architecture is developed on a different line from that in Provence. Normandy owes less than any other part of

France to ancient example. It lay too far from the centre to have ever had the fine buildings of Provence, for Roman work was coarser and more barbarous in proportion to its distance from Italy; and what there may have been did not survive the havoc wrought by the Normans, the most ferocious of all the barbarians who desolated France. The Ile-de-France, which was afterwards the cradle of the Gothic style, has little to show of the Romanesque period. Its extent was small compared with that of the greater feudatories, and it had been harried and laid waste by the terrible Normans, who besieged Paris and sacked and destroyed both churches and monasteries. It was not till the latter part of the 12th century that the development of architecture, which brought to an end the reign of the Romanesque style, began in the Royal domain.

Such in a few words is a sketch of the Renaissance of French architecture from its temporary eclipse during what are called the dark ages; and in describing it in detail, province by province, it is natural to begin with that part of France where Roman tradition was strongest. For all art is progressive, founded on something that has been done before; and when artistic life began to stir in men's veins once more, their first care was to find a model from which to work. The only suggestions open to them were those of the ancient art of the Roman Empire, and the finest models of that art remaining on Gallic soil were in the South and especially in Provence.

**Provence.** When some sort of order had succeeded to the first chaos of barbarian settlement, we find Provence, the old Provincia of the Romans, forming part of the kingdom of Arles; and when that came to an end Provence survived as an independent kingdom, and was not united to France till 1481. It was natural therefore that its art should take a different course from that of the provinces feudally connected with the French crown. The country was full of remains of Roman art; and these, being nearer the source, were of a higher and more refined quality than the Roman work in more remote provinces. The Romanesque artist in Provence had no lack of good examples of architecture and sculpture to inspire him, and his work from first to last is based in a great measure on classic example.

The church of NOTRE-DAME DES DOMS at AVIGNON has a porch so classic in design that it has mis-led the unwary to believe it a Roman work, though it cannot, at the earliest, be older than the middle of the 9th century, and is probably rather later. In the same church is a central domed lantern, not unlike those of the later Byzantine churches[1], though we can hardly attribute it to a Byzantine inspiration. There is, however, a distinct trace of Byzantine influence in the curious building known as the Pantheon at Riez near Draguignan[2], which has a central octagonal dome carried on eight pillars within an aisle which is enclosed in a square; the square being brought into an octagon by exedrae or apses in the corners, as at the church of Ezra in Syria, or that of SS. Sergius and Bacchus at Constantinople. The baptistery at Fréjus is somewhat similar to this, and Mr McGibbon illustrates a church on the island of St Honorat which seems a purely Byzantine building[3]. But these are exceptions, and Provençal architecture is Latin rather than Byzantine. As a rule the churches are basilican; the dome plays no part in their construction, and it is only in some of the figure sculpture and ornament that Eastern influence can be traced.

The great churches in Provence are covered with barrel vaults of stone, pointed in section, in order to reduce the thrust, and forming one solid structure with the gabled roof, instead of being protected by a separate roof of timber (Plate II, fig. 1). The thrust of this great mass of stone had to be resisted by massive walls, and the nave was sometimes supported by quadrant vaults over the aisles. The church of ST TROPHIME at ARLES, which was consecrated in 1152, is a good example of this mode of construction; but the great glory of this building is the splendid portal (Plate I) which, with the still more elaborate one at the neighbouring church of ST GILLES, forms the highest achievement of Provençal art. Classic tradition shows itself in the colonnaded jambs carrying a horizontal entablature enriched with figure sculpture; in the statues that stand in the inter-columniations; the acanthus scrolls on the cornices; the guil-loche or Greek fret; the Corinthian capitals of the columns and

[1] Illustrated, Viollet-le-Duc, *Dict. rais.*

[2] Texier and Pullan, *Byzantine Architecture.*

[3] *Architecture of Provence and the Riviera.*

ARLES. St TROPHIME—WEST PORTAL

# PLATE III.

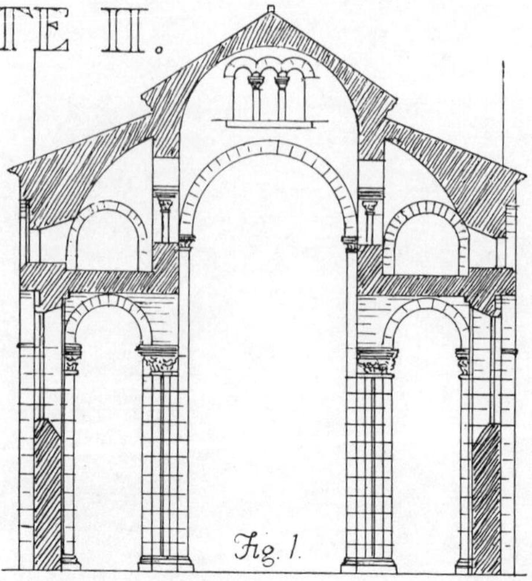

Fig. 1.

CLERMONT FERRAND—SECTION OF NAVE

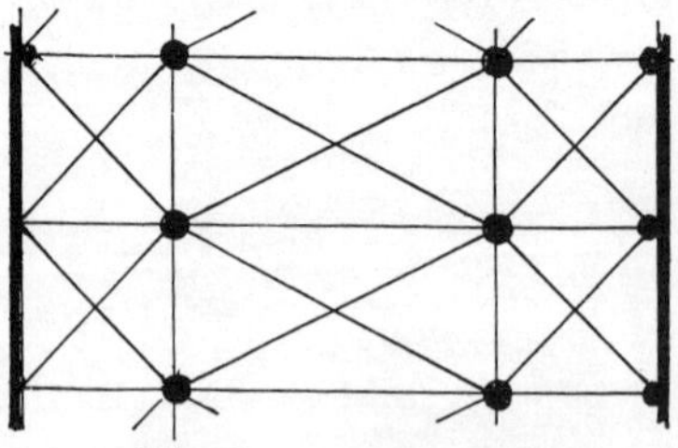

Fig. 2.

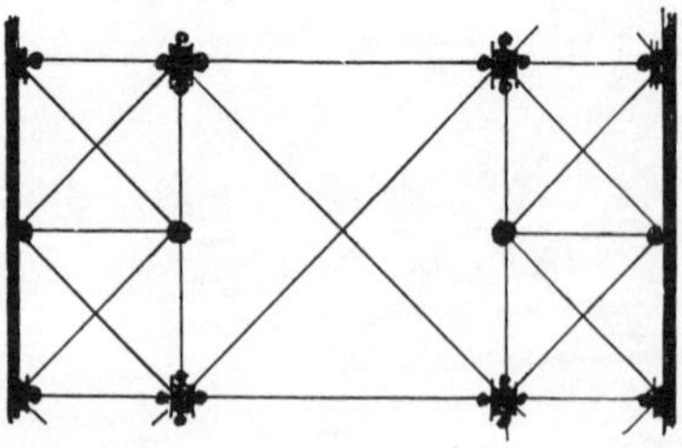

Fig. 3

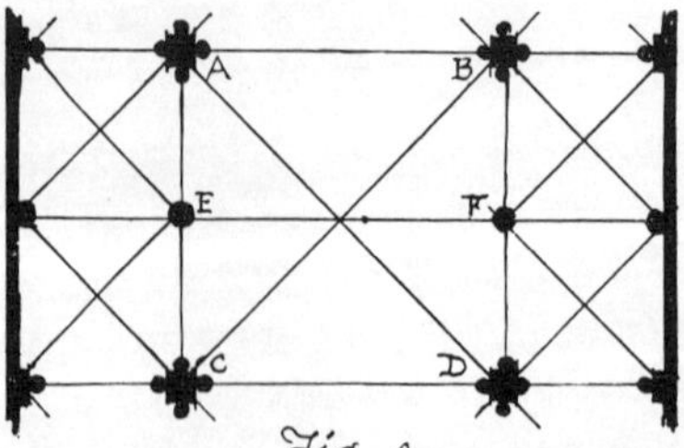


Fig. 4.

PLANS OF VAULTING

the fluted pilasters at the jambs of the doorway. The figures seem to show Byzantine influence, from which the architecture is free, and they were probably modelled after the ivories, woven stuffs, and illuminations, of which a great quantity found its way into Western Europe from the East. The beautiful cloister of St Trophime is not less remarkable than the portal. This too is full of classic detail: there are fluted pilasters, corinthianising capitals, mixed with others containing figures, and the buttresses are fluted piers surmounted by capitals of a Corinthian type. The covering is a semi-circular vault of stone. There are similar cloisters at Montmajour near Arles, at Elne, at Thoronet, and on the island of St Honorat.

The art of Provence was not progressive; it stood still, and Viollet-le-Duc, with whom Northern Gothic of the 13th century is the standard of excellence, depreciates it, and compares the portals of Arles and St Gilles unfavourably with those of Notre-Dame at Paris. This comparison, however, ignores the genius of the place. The severer Gothic style was unsympathetic to the Provençal: it was only admitted late; and was never really assimilated in the land of the Troubadours; and architecture in Provence passed from the Romanesque style to that of the classic Renaissance. One might, in a figure, regard it as infected with the languor to which the delicious climate was conducive; but with the languor it has also the delicacy and refinement of the South and of an ancient civilisation. Provençal Romanesque is Romanesque without its rudeness; and while the monks of Peterborough were building their sturdy nave, with huge round columns and plain cushion capitals, the men of Arles and St Gilles were busy fashioning their solemn statues, and carving their lovely scrolls and friezes, their reliefs and frets, with a dexterity of technique that leaves nothing to be desired. Like the enchanting land which they adorn, these buildings have a flavour of poetry and romance which we do not find in the more scientific and masterly styles of the north.

**Toulouse.** The neighbouring county of Toulouse, where the Visigoth kings had had their capital, was for a long time, like Provence, disconnected from the French crown, and was only annexed after the cruel persecution of the Albigenses in the 13th century. The ravages of these religious wars, which reduced the most civilised part of France to a desert, have left but few buildings there of an early date, and the unsettled state of the province is illustrated by the fortified churches that remain in several places. Here too, in a certain measure, may be traced the influence of Roman example. The south porch of St Sernin at Toulouse has a very classic-looking cornice on the south porch, carried on projecting modillions. But the classic strain is not so pronounced here as in Provence; the sculpture is less influenced by ancient example, and though there are figures to be found not unworthy of comparison with those at Arles and St Gilles, the generality has degenerated into extravagance and grotesqueness. The art was in the stage of infancy, though full of promise of a vigorous future life on a fresh model. This is the character of the sculpture in the fine portal of the abbey church at Moissac, where the figures though carved with some spirit, especially in the smaller friezes, are drawn out to attenuation, with bent knees, and draperies that seem glued to their limbs. The church to which this porch is attached is single-aisled and ends in an apse. The body of it was rebuilt in the 15th century, but the western tower, to which the porch was added, is Romanesque, and was turned into a fortress with crenellated parapet, very significant of the disturbed state of the province. The cloister of this church is one of the finest in France. An inscription gives the original date as 1100, but though the sculptured capitals and piers belong to that time, the superstructure was rebuilt afterwards with pointed arches.

A better style appears in the figure sculpture at St Bertrand de Comminges, and in the little church of St Just at the foot of the hill on which that abbey stands.

The country near Toulouse and on the foot-hills of the Pyrenees abounds in village churches of the 12th century, often very small and humble, but sometimes, as at St Aventin, near Luchon, of considerable size. They have barrel vaults divided into bays by transverse ribs, apses with semi-domes, towers with mid-wall shafts and arcaded cornices. The doors often have sculpture, sometimes of marble, and fairly well executed.

The church of St Sernin at Toulouse is an immense edifice, cruciform, with a later central tower over the crossing, double aisles to the nave, aisles on both sides of the transept and an apse with an ambulatory and five projecting chapels. It has, therefore, every feature of French ecclesiology. The apse with its ambulatory aisle and crown of chapels is an early example of the *chevet,* which became a persistent feature in all the succeeding styles of architecture in France. A Romanesque church of the primitive type ended eastward in a simple apse, like the basilican churches of Italy, Salonica, and the East; and where there were side aisles, the aisles also ended each in an apse. The cathedral of AUTUN is a good example of a basilica of this kind ending in three apses. The next step was to continue the aisles round the central apse instead of finishing them with apses of their own; and the wall of the great apse was pierced with an arcade of columns and arches opening into this ambulatory, which at first was covered with a waggon-vault forming a ring round the drum of the middle apse. From the outside of this ambulatory aisle chapels were projected, one or more, the number increasing as occasion arose. This composition of a lofty central apse, and a lower aisle round it with chapels attached, is the French *chevet,* and with rare exceptions all French churches during the Middle Ages ended eastward in this fashion (Plate V). The Normans brought it to England with them; all the great cathedrals with which they replaced the older churches of the Saxon style were originally apsidal, and all but a few had the circumambient aisle and coronal of chapels. But with us the fashion did not take; Peterborough and Norwich still retain their Norman apses, and they survive in the crypts of Gloucester, Winchester, and Worcester, but most of the great churches before long pulled down their apses and reverted to the square east end of the Saxon type, and the still earlier Celtic buildings. At Westminster the Abbey has a *chevet* on the French plan though with English detail, but it is the only perfect example in England, and it was built under French influence. Tewkesbury and Pershore have apses with ambulatory and chapels, but they are very irregular and have no resemblance to the French type. In Germany the *chevet* came in with the Gothic style which was adopted ready-made from France. In Italy, except where Northern influence appears, as at Milan, and in some of the churches in the Norman kingdom of Naples, the *chevet* does not occur, though the churches are apsidal.

The earlier churches in France of the 10th and 11th centuries had wooden roofs over both nave and aisles, and the skill of the builders was exhausted in constructing a semi-dome of stone over the apse, and perhaps vaulting the lower stage of the towers. But these churches were constantly destroyed by fire, and the builders from the first aspired to the safety and dignity of a stone roof. Their first achievement was to vault the aisles. Each bay or compartment of an aisle measured from pillar to pillar was practically square, and the space was but moderate, so that they soon learned to cover it with the Roman cross vault, formed by the intersection of two equal cylinders. It took some time for them to venture to vault the wider span of the nave, and they began with waggon- or barrel-vaults semi-circular in section. They soon found that the thrust of these vaults, especially when loaded above as has been described with a gable of solid masonry, pushed the walls out, and in order to reduce the thrust they gave the roof a higher pitch and made the section a pointed arch instead of a round one. The thrust of these vaults was of course continuous along the whole range of the wall, while buttresses could only be placed at intervals. At St Sernin, and many other churches, as for instance those of Auvergne, support was given by covering the triforium with a quadrant barrel-vault, half a semi-circle (Plate II, fig. 1), and this, so long as the outer wall was substantial enough, was effective. But it had the disadvantage of making the nave very dark, for it made the clerestory which lighted the nave of a basilican church impossible. Obviously the remedy was to cross-vault the nave like the aisles, so that the transverse vault should allow windows to be opened in the side walls above the aisle roofs. This seems to have been successfully accomplished first in Burgundy, perhaps at Vézelay. The effect was to relieve the side wall between the pillars from any thrust, and to concentrate the whole of it on isolated points over the pillars. The danger of this concentration was not at first perceived, and the builders found their walls giving way at these points, to which, on account of the aisles, no buttress could be directly applied. This suggested the flying buttress which carried the thrust of the high vault overhead across the aisle to a solid pier beyond; thereby completing the theoretical system of Gothic construction. It cannot be claimed that it was entirely original, for cross-vaulting was a Roman invention, and the concentration of thrust on isolated points of support with the need of support at those points was thoroughly understood by the Ancients. But this system of construction was certainly developed further by the mediaeval men, who succeeded in making almost a new method of it, for the idea of bridging the aisle by a flying buttress to bring the thrust upon a pier beyond was as novel as it was audacious. Construction of this kind, where thrust was opposed to thrust, and the building stood by equilibrium of forces, began in the latter part of the Romanesque period and was thoroughly developed in the 13th century. It will be more fully explained when we come to that period.

**Aquitaine.** The western and south-western parts of France formed the vast territory of the Dukes of Aquitaine, which included Poitou, most of Guienne, the Limousin, and Augoumois. The Romanesque architecture of this district is very distinct and stands apart from that of the other provinces in many particulars. The line of commerce with the East, and especially with the Byzantine Empire and Venice, ran through this part of France, from Aigues-Mortes on the Gulf of Lyons through Limoges to Rochelle, whence commercial intercourse was continued by sea to Britain and the north of Europe. At Limoges was settled a colony of Venetians, of which traces survived till the 17th century, in the names of streets, and ruins of houses. The Byzantine connection was reflected in the local architecture, and resulted in a remarkable series of churches in which, as in the East, the dome forms the principal motive of the design.

The most famous, though not the earliest, example of this group of buildings is the church of St Front at Périgueux. It is in plan almost an exact reproduction of the church of St Mark at Venice, which itself was copied from Justinian's church of the Holy Apostles at Constantinople, affording a conclusive proof of a Byzantine and Levantine derivation. The 10th century church of St Front was burned in 1120. Retaining part of the nave and transepts which had escaped the fire, a vast church was added eastward in the form of a Greek cross with five domes, one over each arm, and another over the central crossing. Unlike St Mark's as it now exists, the same domes show internally and externally, so that, like St Sophia at Constantinople, there is not an atom of combustible matter in the whole construction. The appearance of the outside, with its cluster of domes, and an enormous western tower, is surprising in Western Europe. The construction of the domes, especially of the pendentives, differs in some degree from the Byzantine method, showing that though the domical idea was derived from the East it was carried out by native architects in a way of their own, in which indeed they had been working for many years before the date of St Front[1].

The cathedral of CAHORS which dates from 1119 has two great domes which show outside, but they are covered with timber and slate. At SOLIGNAC the nave is ceiled with a succession of domes which are hidden under a continuous roof. At ANGOULÊME there is a series of three domes over the nave, and at FONTEVRAULT, where the domes are destroyed, there was the same arrangement, in both cases covered by a long continuous roof; but at Angoulême a fourth dome over the crossing is carried up into a central tower and there is a similar feature at NOTRE-DAME, POITIERS. There are many other instances in this province of churches with domical construction either over the whole or part of them, but except in those instances which have been mentioned, the domes are treated as ordinary vaults, not exposed outwardly but hidden under roofs. Those hitherto described are formed with pendentives on the true principle of dome construction, but at St Hilaire in Poitiers and in the cathedral of Le Puy, which may be counted as belonging either to the style of Aquitaine or that of Auvergne, there are octagonal domes resting on squinches in the angles of the square bay, and these of course are not domes in the true sense of the word, though inspired by the domical idea. The same may be said of the strange church of St Ours in the castle of LOCHES, which consists of something like four steeples in a row.

LE PUY, one of the most romantic and picturesque places in the world, has a wonderful cathedral built on a steep declivity,

[1] For St Front see R. Phéné Spiers, *Architecture, East and West*; and for domed churches generally F. de Verneilh, *L'Architecture Byzantine en France*. For illustrations see T. G. Jackson, *Byzantine and Romanesque Architecture*, vol. II.

so that you enter at the west end by a storey below the church floor, to which you ascend by flights of stairs. An old monkish chronicler has it that "you enter the church by the nostril and leave it by the ears," that is the transepts. It is built of basalt, the product of that volcanic region, mixed with yellow freestone and brick, which especially in the cloister forms a polychromatic decoration, in rough mosaic patterns, bands, chequers, and alternate voussoirs of arches. On a needle of rock two hundred feet high is the little chapel of St Michel de l'Aiguille, with a fascinating doorway where all these coloured materials are used in combination with marble. The tower of the cathedral is a fine example of a form of campanile, typical of the district. It rises with a succession of stages diminishing so much that the upper part is carried on an inner wall from the ground upward, within the outer wall of the lower stages. The whole of this cathedral and its appurtenances is so singular, and so strongly stamped with originality as almost to place it in a class by itself. Some of the capitals of the south porch in particular are hardly like European work in their strange fantastic richness.

Aquitaine is not so rich in sculpture as Provence or Burgundy, but the façades of Angoulême and Notre-Dame at Poitiers are covered with tiers of niches containing figures. The latter of the two is a delightful piece of Romanesque; the ovoid pinnacles or spires on the angle turrets and the central cupola are covered with scaling, and so is the cupola at Saintes, like the domes at Périgueux, to which all these examples bear a certain affinity. The west front at Civray is especially interesting, and the churches at St Junien, St Leonard, St Savin, and Chauvigny should not be missed by those who would understand the Romanesque of western France.

**Auvergne.** The county of Auvergne, with its capital at Clermont-Ferrand, was subject sometimes to Aquitaine and sometimes to Toulouse, and its architecture is influenced from both directions. But the Auvergnat style has also a strong individuality, distinguishing it from that of the other provinces of France. The typical examples, at Clermont, Issoire, and St Nectaire, all date from the beginning of the 12th century; Brioude is a little later, and the churches of Chamalières and

St Saturnin also belong to the same group. Their plan is cruciform, with ambulatory *chevet* and central tower. The transepts are of two heights, only the part ranging with the aisles being carried up to the full height of the nave, and the extreme bays being kept lower. This gives a fine broad shouldered base for the central tower. All four arms of the cross have barrel-vaults, counter-thrust by quadrant vaults over the triforium (Plate II, fig. 1), so that there is no clerestory, and the nave is somewhat dark. The aisles are generally cross-vaulted, but occasionally have barrel-vaults. The gabled roof is of solid masonry united to the vault. Like the work at Le Puy, which is related to that of Auvergne, the exterior is decorated with polychrome masonry, the local basalt being inlaid with white freestone in coarse mosaic patterns with excellent effect. Bands of this decoration surround the drum of the apse, surmounted by a cornice with modillions in the classic fashion, and at Clermont other patterns fill the spandrels of the window arches and the gables on the ambulatory. Polychrome masonry is rarer in France than in England and of course in Italy, and the fashion was perhaps suggested in Auvergne by some Venetian traveller, struck by the capabilities of the local material for use in this way. Of these churches those at Issoire and Brioude are the grandest, that of Notre-Dame du Port at Clermont is the richest in decoration and in sculpture, and that at St Nectaire is the most picturesque, situated in the fine sub-mountainous country south of the Puy de Dome. They are all very much of the same date, and their characteristic style, when once thoroughly developed, stood still and led to nothing further—it is indeed so complete in every respect that there seems no opening for anything to come from it. The churches of Auvergne and Le Puy fill a chapter in art by themselves, and there are no buildings in France more fascinating and delightful.

**Burgundy.** With Burgundy we open a new chapter of French Romanesque. All the schools already described, those of Provence, Toulouse, Aquitaine, and Auvergne, bear traces, more or less distinct, of a Roman or Byzantine derivation, and these traces they never lost. In Burgundy, though Roman tradition played a large part in the decorative detail, fresh influences were at work, and the style began to move onward to novel developments which resulted in the style we know as Gothic. Burgundy was the cradle of French monasticism. From the great mother-house of Cluny and her daughters at Cîteaux and Clairvaux sprang hundreds of Benedictine foundations throughout Western Christendom. In the 11th century three hundred and fourteen monasteries and churches obeyed the Abbot of Cluny, who struck money in his own mint like the King of France himself, and within twenty-five years from its foundation the Cistercian Order had spread over Europe and numbered 60,000 brethren. Wherever they went they carried with them their own type of habitation: the convent was in a manner standardised, conformed to an accepted plan in general arrangement, and even to some extent to certain dimensions. In tracing the remains of one of these institutions one knows pretty nearly where, in relation to the great church, we shall find chapter-house, cloister, refectory, dormitory, and domestic offices. Thus with the spread of the monastic Orders a great school of architecture arose, and while the passion for monasticism was at its height, the conventual buildings for several centuries eclipsed the cathedrals and churches of the secular clergy. The great minster of Cluny which was rebuilt between 1089 and 1131, the narthex, a great church by itself, not being finished till 1220, was the largest church west of the Alps, and St Etienne the original cathedral at Périgueux is a very humble affair compared with the abbey church of St Front.

The rule of St Benedict prescribed manual labour in the fields or the workshop, besides literary labour in the scriptorium; and as in France there were few laymen skilled in craftsmanship, the monks had to be their own masons, carpenters, glaziers, and builders. For the cloister, in those days of social disorder, was the only place where the peaceful arts could be cultivated. The monks were not necessarily clerics; most of them were laymen, and in early times they were discouraged from taking orders. A great number of them were artisans, and by the rule of St Benedict they were to continue working at their crafts, though they were forbidden to take any pride in them, a hard counsel of perfection. In every convent were workshops; the specification sent from Cluny for the buildings at Farfa provides a building 125 feet by 25 for the work of the glaziers, jewellers, and goldsmiths; other workshops would be in proportion. In these hives of industry traditions of art would insensibly grow up, schools of design would naturally be formed, and uniformity of style would result through ut the country over which the brotherhood spread its branches.

The abbey of CLUNY was founded in 909 by William, Duke of Aquitaine, in order to reduce to stricter discipline the prevalent lax observance of the Benedictine rule. But Cluny itself, as it grew in power and wealth, became luxurious, and a fresh reforming party seceded to Cîteaux in 1098. By the Cistercian rule everything was reduced to extreme simplicity. The architecture became austere, there was to be no painting or sculpture, the windows were to be of white glass, and the tower to be low and unpretending. St Bernard who entered the convent of Cîteaux at the age of 22, and became abbot of the daughter-house of Clairvaux two years later, inveighs against the architectural display, the sculpture, the ornaments, and the enormous size of the buildings of the Cluniacs: but the Cistercians themselves in time deserted this Puritan standard.

Of the great church at CLUNY very little remains, and the abbey church of VÉZELAY, which was begun in 1089, is now the finest example of the richer kind of Burgundian Romanesque. It is remarkable also as the place where probably the first successful attempt was made to cover a nave with cross-vaulting, and so to recover the clerestory which illuminated the wooden roofed basilica, but had been impossible with the barrel-vault. The choir and transepts were rebuilt in a later style between 1198 and 1200, but the Romanesque nave of 1102 remains, and the narthex of 1132. In the latter, which, like that at Cluny, is a church by itself, with nave and aisles three bays long, the pointed arch appears: all the nave arches are round. The great west door, leading from the narthex into the nave, is the finest piece of Burgundian Romanesque carving (Plate III). It is round-arched with a central pillar supporting a horizontal lintel, above which the tympanum is sculptured with a figure of Christ in a vesica dispensing the holy Spirit to his disciples, epresented by rays emanating from his fingers, and directed on them severally. Small subjects in the arch represent the

VÉZELAY—NARTHEX AND WEST PORTAL

signs of the Zodiac, and various arts and trades. The sculpture has not the grace of Arles or St Gilles, and is more like the semi-grotesque of Moissac in attenuation of the figures and extravagance of gesture. But the work has nevertheless that air of life and sincerity that is of the essence of true art, inevitably leading on to perfection. There is a similar portal to the cathedral of AUTUN, under a fine open porch, which being a secular building is not enclosed as a narthex like that at Vézelay. Both these buildings show classic tradition in their details. The sculpture in the chapter-house at Vézelay is thoroughly Corinthian in character, and the vaults at Autun are supported on fluted pilasters with Attic bases. Similar details occur in the church of St Jean at Autun and the cathedral of VALENCE, where the buttresses of the east end are square piers with Corinthian capitals. Classic tradition is strong also at VIENNE, where a Roman temple remains, besides other ancient buildings. At LYONS, though the Gallo-Roman church celebrated in an ode by Sidonius Apollinaris no longer remains, the gigantic columns in the church of AINAY may be some of his *Fulmenta Aquitanica superba*, and the capitals of the pillars are based on Corinthian examples.

The same classic feeling is observable in the capitals of the interesting church of AVALLON, and in its splendid portals, which are among the triumphs of Burgundian Romanesque.

At the east end of the abbey of ST BÉNIGNE at DIJON remains the lower part of a curious circular chapel, built to contain the tomb of the titular saint, which was dedicated in 1018 and was still standing in 1739. It was built by Abbot William of Volpiano in Lombardy, a notable figure in the story of French architecture. Two concentric and vaulted aisles surrounded a central space, which was originally open to the sky, and there were two storeys of them above the crypt which still exists. The work is rude in the extreme, but when complete the rotunda in spite of its barbarous detail must have been very striking. It is curious that excavation has lately discovered the foundations of a similar rotunda on a smaller scale at the east end of St Augustine's abbey church at Canterbury, in a position exactly corresponding with that at Dijon. It was built by Abbot Wulfric in 1049, after his return from France, where he may have seen that at Dijon[1]. Abbot William was a great builder, and imported artisans of various trades from his native Italy.

The abbey church of PONTIGNY, where Becket spent some of the time of his exile, is a fine example of Cistercian work, built according to St Bernard's Puritan ideas. But with all its severity it is a beautiful building, and shows by its chaste simplicity that architecture may do without ornament, and yet delight us. Though sculpture was forbidden, opportunities for the artist remained in nicety of proportion, judicious outline, delicacy of detail in moulding, in profile of base and capital, and the austere Cistercian rule has given us some of the most lovely buildings in Gothic architecture, such as Rivaulx, Fountains, and Tintern abbeys in our own land. Puritan asceticism may suppress all ornament, but the true artist will show that he can, if he is obliged, do without it. And yet the severity of this restriction, in the 12th century, had the effect of retarding the progress of Romanesque architecture so long as it remained in monastic hands.

Architecture found a fruitful soil in Burgundy in which to flourish. There, and in the neighbouring county of Champagne, were quarries of splendid stone, and the people had a natural bent towards the manual crafts. A Byzantine historian records that "there is a barbarian people beyond the Rhine called Burgundians, who had an easy life, for nearly all of them are craftsmen, and make a good living thereby."

**Normandy.** Normandy, as has been said already, owes less than the other parts of France to classic example. Of all the barbarian invaders and settlers in Gaul the Northmen were the most ferocious and destructive, and if any remains of ancient art existed in that remote part of the Roman empire, they must have been swept away by the new-comers. When, therefore, they settled down, and from being the most disorderly became the most orderly of all the provincials, and from ravagers of convents and murderers of priests the most devout children of the Church, the Normans had none of those monuments of ancient art before their eyes which inspired the men of Provence and the South, nor had they brought with them any traditions

[1] This discovery at Canterbury was made in 1915. See report and plans in *Archaeologia*, vol. LXVI.

of native art from their old rude homes in Denmark and Norway. No sooner, however, did they settle down in their new territory than they adopted the art of the conquered race as they did the religion and the language; and with that adaptability which was a Norman characteristic they soon became Frenchmen, as in England they became English, and in Italy Italians. They also became at once great builders, and within a century and a half they covered their new country with vast structures, both secular and ecclesiastical. Their work has little or no sculptured decoration; their pillars bore plain cushion capitals, in which it was long before any simple foliage began to appear, and their rare attempts at figures were childish and barbarous. The typical enrichments of Norman work are conventional—billets, nail-heads, zigzags, bosses, and channellings—such as an ordinary mason would easily chop out, and with these simple means they managed to produce an effect of surprising richness.

At the end of the 10th century the dukes sought for aid in the more cultured parts of France, and Duke Richard II (996–1027) persuaded William of Volpiano to come from Dijon to reform the ecclesiastic disorders of the province. William, as we have seen, was a great builder, and the influence of the Lombard school was thus introduced into France, whence with the Norman conquest it passed into England. This connexion was strengthened by the appointment of another Lombard to the abbey of Bec, who also was a great builder, Lanfranc of Pavia, afterwards the Conqueror's Archbishop of Canterbury. From Lombardy came those solemn and massive naves, with sturdy piers and cushion capitals that impress us with their majestic simplicity and somewhat barbaric grandeur at JUMIÈGES and CAEN, at Winchester and Peterborough, and in Germany at Worms and Mainz. In Germany too, at Cologne and elsewhere appear arcaded exterior galleries round the apses borrowed from Lombardy, like those at Milan and Como, Parma and Modena, Borgo St Donnino, and Pavia, perhaps derived at second-hand from Pisa and Lucca. This, however, was a feature that did not find acceptance in France or England.

Abbot William's practical help in founding a school of architecture in Normandy was invaluable. He is recorded as "giving no slight assistance by his advice in laying foundations."

Architecture at that time was only beginning to revive in France, and Normandy would be the most backward of the provinces in the arts. There was a dearth there of skilled workmen, and the abbey of Fécamp implored the monks of Dijon to send craftsmen to finish their buildings for them. The Normans were apt pupils, and more than that they were not without originality, for when they began to find themselves in the new art, their work took a distinct line of its own, differing considerably from that of the rest of France. In the great churches of MONT ST MICHEL and CERISY-LE-FORÊT we may perhaps see the hand of Abbot William. The fine church of ST GEORGE DE BOSCHERVILLE is later, dating in its present form probably from 1116, though it had been founded between 50 and 60 years before. In this church and at Cerisy-le-Forêt there occurs the gallery across the ends of the transepts of which we have an example in Bishop Walkelyn's cathedral of Winchester. Canterbury had the same, till it was removed because the pillar supporting it in the middle of the north transept was in the way of the pilgrims to the "martyrdom."

St Etienne—the ABBAYE AUX HOMMES—at CAEN was founded by the Conqueror and consecrated in 1077, Lanfranc of Pavia being the first abbot. Like all early Norman churches the aisles only were vaulted and the nave was originally roofed with wood like Peterborough. It was vaulted later. The design is marked by a stern severity, but shows the Norman style already advanced to a greater degree of refinement, and there is even some rude attempt made at imitating the Corinthian capital. The proportion allotted to the triforium is remarkable, for it is nearly equal to the arcade below, and this is a characteristic feature of the great Norman churches both in Normandy and in England, as for instance at Ely, Norwich, Peterborough, Southwell, and the early part of Winchester. There is somewhat the same proportion between the two storeys at S. Ambrogio in Milan, with which Lanfranc would have been familiar in his native Lombardy.

La Trinité—the ABBAYE AUX DAMES—at CAEN, the other great foundation of the Conqueror and his wife, has been more altered, and is now mainly a 12th century building. The choir is aisleless, and is finished with a semi-dome over the apse, quite a southern feature. The capitals are rudely Corinthian, and there is considerable ornamentation by frets, billets, and other conventional devices.

Caen abounds in examples of the Norman style, early and late, and there are fine churches in all the villages round about. The later round-arched work is splendid with zigzags, billets, and the other ornaments of the style, but there are few attempts till later at any more advanced or more natural forms in sculpture.

The Norman style, however, may be studied as well, or perhaps better, in England than in its native Normandy. For the conquerors were no sooner settled here than they set to work to cover the land with stupendous buildings, that not only threw into the shade the Saxon buildings, which for the most part were destroyed to make way for them, but excelled in scale and magnificence the buildings the new-comers had left behind in Normandy.

**Ile-de-France.** The Ile-de-France, the Royal domain, has comparatively little to show of Romanesque architecture. It was ravaged by the savage Northmen, who besieged Paris, and destroyed churches and monasteries in the country round about. But besides the havoc made by the barbarians, the number of the earlier buildings was reduced by the great outburst of building in a more advanced style that followed the gradual consolidation of the monarchy in the later part of the 12th and in the 13th century by which the Romanesque style was brought to a conclusion in Northern and Central France

The BASSE ŒUVRE at BEAUVAIS is the nave of the original cathedral, which has been attributed to various dates. Viollet-le-Duc dates it in the 8th or 9th century. On the other hand, Bishop Hervé is said to have laid the foundation in 990. It has been so extensively restored in modern days that very little trace of antiquity remains, but in a dark corner a small piece of the ancient exterior work can still be seen, and this certainly seems to be of the later date. It is basilican in plan, with nave and aisles divided in the simplest way by plain and square piers of masonry carrying round arches cut square through the wall without even a chamfer on the edge. The roofs are of wood, and the windows are wide and round-arched, the stone voussoirs alternating with tile. The front seems to have been altered from the original design. Only three bays of this church remain, beyond which begins the colossal mass of the Gothic cathedral.

The nave of LE MANS, built in the 11th century, is a fine Romanesque work enriched with reticulated masonry in front, and with well-developed Corinthianising capitals. Though not strictly at that time in the Royal domain it seems to belong to it in point of style. The desecrated church of the abbey of ST EVREMOND, on an island in the river at CREIL, has some beautiful Romanesque detail, showing classic influence in the flat buttresses surmounted by capitals. With the abbey of ST DENIS, founded in 1122, we reach the end of the purely Romanesque period, and touch that of the transitional style, through which the early work passed into the Gothic of the 13th century.

From the preceding brief account of French Romanesque, necessarily superficial for want of space, it will have been gathered that it covers a wide field of design, and possesses infinite variety. It is herein that it differs from the Romanesque of other countries; for while in them the steady progress of the art can readily be followed as a simple subject, in France in each province it followed a different course, and fell into different schools. The churches of Arles and St Gilles do not differ from the Auvergnat buildings at Clermont and Issoire more than these do from Vézelay and Autun, or the domed churches of Perigord and Poitou from any of these, or those of Normandy from all the rest. It is this that gives French Romanesque its special value as a thoroughly representative art, expressive in each case of the district and people to whom it belongs. But it is not only on the ground of historical and social propriety that it is to be enjoyed: if Romanesque was nowhere else so varied, it was also nowhere more beautiful. The gracious portals of St Trophime and its neighbour, the vigorous and masculine churches of Burgundy, the cavernous domes of Périgueux and the mysterious hollow pyramids of Loches, the arcaded and storied façades of Poitiers, Civray, and Angoulême and the neighbouring buildings that have been mentioned, are full of young struggling life, and a strange romantic loveliness; they are more interesting for their very imperfections, showing the passionate ardour with which the artists were struggling ever upwards in the scale of art. When at last perfection, within certain limits, was reached in the 13th century, this element of striving and human effort drops out of the art; to some extent its interest is lessened, and one often looks back with regret from the placid content of achievement to the youthful vigour and earnest endeavour of the earlier schools.

## § II. EARLY FRENCH GOTHIC

Consolidation of the kingdom. The new Cathedrals. The Communes. The lay architect. The pointed arch. Rib and panel vaulting. Noyon. The transitional style from Romanesque to Gothic. Paris, Laon, and the beginning of Gothic. Bourges. Chartres. Reims. Gothic fully developed. Amiens. Beauvais.

The consolidation of the French monarchy was accompanied and illustrated by a corresponding change in French architecture. It passed, in fact, by gradual steps, from Romanesque to Gothic. The firmer establishment of royalty began with Louis VI—*Le Gros*. His grandson Philip Augustus took Artois and Vermandois from one great feudatory the Count of Flanders; and Normandy, Maine, and Anjou from another, John of England. The cruel persecution of the Albigenses gave Toulouse to the Crown; the English were finally expelled in 1451; Louis XI acquired Dauphiné, Burgundy, and Provence; and his son Charles VIII acquired Brittany by marriage.

The growth of the central power was marked at first by an astonishing outburst of building. During the reign of Philip Augustus, 1180 to 1223, new cathedrals were begun at Paris, Chartres, Bourges, Laon, Soissons, Reims, Meaux, Noyon, Amiens, Rouen, Cambrai, Arras, Tours, Séez, Coutances, and Bayeux, and nearly all were completed before the end of the 13th century. It was like the passion for building in England that followed the Norman Conquest; and except the construction of railways in our own day there can hardly have been such another marvellous building epoch in the world's history.

This was not only the age of the growth of royalty, but also that of the growth of civic liberty and the decline of monasticism. Most of the French cities like those of Italy and England acquired charters during the 12th century and that following, and with municipal independence they increased in wealth and power, at the expense of their old lords, whether spiritual or temporal. The regular clergy had become great feudal potentates as well as the bishops, and fared no better than they; for if the Bishop of Laon was murdered by his townsmen, the abbey of Vézelay was sacked by the people in alliance with the Count of Nevers, and the Abbot of St Vif at Sens was slain in an insurrection of the townsmen whose charter had been revoked. Everywhere they revolted against bishop, abbot, and chapter. "It is by the emancipated bourgeoisie," says Luchaire, "that the laic spirit arrived at modifying from top to bottom the character not only of public powers and social relations, but also of the literature and intellectual life of the country[1]."

As in Italy, so in France, the communes signalized their triumph by the adornment of their native cities. Everywhere the old cathedrals were pulled down and rebuilt on a grander scale, especially in the northern and central parts of France. If during the preceding period the cathedrals had been eclipsed by the great monastic churches, they in their turn were now thrown into the shade by the size and splendour of the great cathedrals with which each newly enfranchised city strove to outdo its neighbours. In this movement the bishops and the communes were united, for the bishops had long been jealous of the regular establishments which were exempt from episcopal control, and had always been a sore in their sides.

Architecture therefore emerged at this time from the cloister, and awoke to new life like the society of the day. The architects were no longer clerics but laymen, as they had long been already in Italy. All the names of architects of this time that have been preserved are those of laymen[2], and this change of artists resulted in new developments of the art, which had been retarded by the conservatism of the regular Orders. And yet it was in a great abbey at St Denis and in the work of a monk, the Abbot Suger, that the first sign of the new movement is to be found. Viollet-le-Duc suggests that Suger, conscious of the decline of monas-

[1] Lavisse, *Histoire de France*, vol. II. pt ii. p. 356.

[2] M. de Lasteyrie gives a long list of their names from the end of the 11th century onwards. *Arch. relig. en France*, p. 237.

ticism, was anxious to show the world an abbey in the van of progress, instead of restraining the art within the narrow limits of Cistercian austerity.

The old church of St Denis, founded by Dagobert in 625, had been rebuilt more than once when Suger was elected abbot in 1122. From his modest cell, where he led the simple life of a monk, he directed the policy of the kingdom, and ruled as Regent while Louis VII was absent on his ill-managed and disastrous crusade. The church which he found at his election was so small and inconvenient, that "the women," he says, let us hope only figuratively, "ran over the men's heads to the altar, as on a pavement." He began at once to rebuild it on a grand scale: the western part was finished in a little over three years and dedicated in 1140, and the body of the church followed, with the eastern end.

Suger has left us in his writings a lively picture of his interest in the work; of his journeys to the quarries at Pontoise, which he suggests were revealed to him providentially, and to the forest of Yveline to find suitable timber; of his care in directing the sculptured and other ornament, and in giving their subjects to the carver, the glass-painters, the goldsmiths, and in supplying the inscriptions. The bronze doors were modelled with scriptural subjects, and in the arch of the left-hand portal he placed a mosaic picture, "though," he says, "contrary to the new fashion." He longed to rival the basilicas of the East with their wealth of gold, mosaic, and jewels, and he tells us, "I used to confer with men from Jerusalem, and I took pleasure in learning from those to whom the treasures of Constantinople and the ornaments of St Sophia had been displayed, whether in comparison with them anything here could be said to have any value[1]." Some of the mosaics from St Denis may now be seen in the Musée de Cluny: but the art of the mosaicist did not establish itself in France.

The greater part of Suger's building has been replaced by the 13th century work of Pierre de Montereau, but we still have his western part and the lower storeys of the east end, and in Suger's design we see the beginning of a new phase of mediaeval art. St Denis is remarkable as the building where the pointed arch

[1] *Gesta Sugerii Abbatis*, cap. XXXII.

and the scheme of Gothic construction were first shown on a grand scale. In the façade round and pointed arches appear together, but the pointed arch rules in the construction, and henceforth it won its way to the final extinction of Romanesque tradition of the classic form. Though there are still traces of Romanesque ornament at St Denis, the construction may fairly be called Gothic. The chapels are fitted between radiating buttresses, and have each two pointed windows though those of the crypt below are round-arched.

The construction of the early vaults of the Romanesque period has been briefly described already (see Plate II and p. 338): but so long as the arches remained semi-circular it admitted of very little development, for it is obvious that round arches of different span could not rise to the same level, and consequently it was difficult, and sometimes impossible, to manage well the intersection of the wide longitudinal vault of a nave with the narrow cross-vaults containing the clerestory in the side walls. This difficulty disappeared when the pointed arch superseded the inelastic round one, for arches of different spans could now be brought to the same level at the crown. Equal cylinders were no longer needed and irregular spaces could now be covered with a vault as easily as a regular one.

In order, however, to get a good intersection of these unequal vaults, a fresh improvement was now introduced by the adoption of a system of ribs to mark the intersection of the arched constructions as they crossed one another. Although by giving the cross-vault a pointed section, admitting of variation in each case, vaults of different span could be brought to the same level at the crown, yet the groins or lines of intersection could not be brought to lie in one plane, but had a tendency to twist, and the surfaces between to wind like the fluke of a screw propeller. The result was not only unsightly but insecure, and the geometrical problems suggested were troublesome. It occurred to the architects therefore, as the groins would not come straight of themselves, that they should be made to do so by disregarding their proper geometrical intersection and building an arched rib on the diagonal line with a true and regular curve, like the transverse rib which divided the bays at each column. This gave them a nervature of good and true arches on the four sides and the

PLATE IV

AMIENS—SECTION OF NAVE

two diagonals of the bay, and between them they filled in the panels with smaller stones arched from rib to rib, which could be allowed to take a winding surface without danger to the construction, or without spoiling the appearance, for the ribs gave a true arched form to the vault in every direction. This was a great innovation and revolutionised the design of Gothic vaulting, both in France and in England. From the first simple rib and panel vaults of the early 13th century came all the later developments, when intermediate ribs were introduced; sheaves of ribs sprang from one capital as at Exeter or Winchester, traceries branched from rib to rib as at Gloucester, and at last rib and panel were fused together into one solid construction of masonry as at King's College, Cambridge, and the royal chapels at Westminster and Windsor. It was in England, however, that Gothic vaulting developed into these intricate and splendid ceilings: in France it remained simpler to the end of the Gothic period.

This double revolution of the adoption of the pointed arch and the system of ribs and panels completed the scheme of the Gothic vault. It only remained to utilise the new mode of construction to the utmost, by suppressing all unnecessary material, and economising supports. By the system of cross-vaulting the thrust of the whole vault was concentrated on isolated points at each pier or pillar, and if these were fortified by exterior buttresses either directly applied, or flying across the aisle to buttresses beyond, the structure was rendered safe. Consequently the curtain walls between the piers were relieved of any lateral pressure, and had only to carry themselves, and to stay the piers by arches into the aisles, at the triforium, and over the clerestory windows, these last being loaded with the upper wall on which the great roof rested. The clerestory windows were made larger as this came to be better understood, and occupied the whole width from pier to pier with a wall of glass set in tracery. Of this final development of French Gothic, Amiens cathedral (Plate IV) affords the most perfect example: the supports are reduced to the slenderest proportions consistent with stability, and the proportion of the voids to the solids is exaggerated to the verge of insecurity. The church has indeed been tied together longitudinally with iron.

This perfect development of the construction just described did not take place at once; there was a period of transition from Romanesque to Gothic, to which we owe some of the most important and beautiful architecture in France.

The fine church of Notre-Dame at SENLIS, the choir of which is dated between 1150 and 1165, has the same mixture as at St Denis of round and pointed arches; and here, as elsewhere in churches of this period, it may be noticed that while for constructional reasons the pointed arch is used in the vaulting, in the interior arcades and in other structural parts, the round arch survives in windows and ornamental features, where questions of construction do not arise; as if the artist parted with reluctance from a form sanctioned by centuries of use. This church has one of the most splendid steeples in French Gothic art, full of lovely detail, though the outline leaves something to be desired[1].

The cathedral of SENS, built between 1143 and 1168, except the west end which is later, has the system of Gothic construction fully developed. The arches of the great arcade are pointed, and are carried by clustered piers alternating with cylindrical columns, coupled one behind the other, like those at Canterbury cathedral, where William, an architect from Sens, was employed on the new choir from 1174 till his accident in 1179, when he left his work to be continued by William the Englishman. This alternation of stouter and slighter supports is connected with the system of sexpartite vaulting, which requires to be explained.

In the quadripartite vault (Plate II, fig. 2) the wide vault of the nave ranges with the narrow vault of the aisle bay by bay. It was not possible to do this well or at all, so long as the round arch was used, which demands that the crossing cylinders shall be equal, or else there will be trouble. In some early vaults, as at St Ambrogio in Milan, this was got over by making each bay of the nave equal to two of the aisle, and like them square (Plate II, fig. 3). The cross cylinders being equal, the intersection was on a true line in one plane. But at Sens and some other early churches a variation was introduced. The vaults were planned as at St Ambrogio with one nave bay to two aisle bays, but the lateral triangular spaces were bisected by a rib,

[1] This church is reported to be seriously damaged by the Germans.

PLATE V

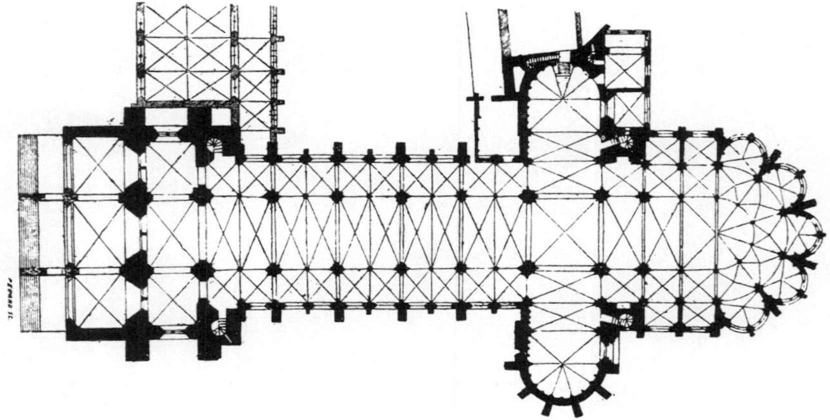

NOYON CATHEDRAL, from V.-le-Duc

dividing the vault into six. In the Abbaye aux Dames at Caen, the rib is a simple arch carrying a thin wall across the nave vault, but in the Abbaye aux Hommes and at Sens a vault is turned over each of the two subdivisions from the main diagonals to the new rib introduced between them (Plate II, fig. 4). This is the sexpartite vault, which gives occasion to an alternation of the supporting members, larger clustered piers *A, B, C, D*, having most to carry, being placed at the angles of the square double bay, and slender piers or simple columns under the intermediate ribs at *E, F*.

The cathedral of NOYON (Plate V) was begun in 1150 after a disastrous fire and was finished about 1190 or 1200, the choir being the earlier part of the building. Here, too, we have round and pointed arches used together. It is, or was, for I fear it has been partly ruined during the late war, one of the most interesting buildings in France: none showed better the transition from Romanesque to Gothic. In the choir we find round arches, and there are columnar buttresses outside the chapels of the apse which belong to the Romanesque style, though the apse windows and arches are pointed. The transepts are apsidal. In the nave there is an alternation of clustered pier and plain column, as if for a sexpartite vault, but the present vaults are quadripartite. The proportion of the triforium is lofty, and it is vaulted, which occasions a second triforium arcade above, corresponding to the aisle roof outside. This makes the elevation of the bay four-storied instead of being as usual only of three stages. The west front, which is later, is singularly fine, and the projecting porch or narthex and the cloister and chapter-house, which belong to the next century, are rich with exquisitely natural carving of fruit and flowers.

The transitional style may also be studied at ST GERMAIN-DES-PRÉS in Paris, and in the churches of Châlons-sur-Marne, and the fine church of ST REMI at Reims, if by chance it has escaped destruction during the late war.

In the churches of St Denis, Noyon, and Senlis, Viollet-le-Duc says we may see the cradle of pointed architecture. Romanesque traditions were not forgotten, round and pointed arches still seemed to struggle for mastery, primitive sculpture is to be found side by side with attempts at better interpretation of nature, and now with the cathedral of NOTRE-DAME at PARIS we seem to take another step forward. We still have the lofty proportion of the triforium, and originally there were four stages, though the alteration of the clerestory at an early date reduced them to three, and the nave-vaulting is sexpartite. But the round arch has finally given way to the pointed, which now at last rules everywhere.

The present building was begun by Bishop Maurice de Sully in 1163, and at his death in 1196 the choir and transepts were finished. Before the death of Philip Augustus in 1223, the nave and west front were completed, except the upper part of the towers which were finished between 1235 and 1240. There were at first no chapels between the side buttresses; they were added at the end of the 13th century and finished in 1315. There are two aisles on each side of the nave and choir, and they are continued round the apse. The transepts were lengthened one bay in 1258. The vaulting round the apse of the triple semicircle is very ingenious and interesting, the problem being a difficult one, and the contrivance is very clever and should be studied.

All the columns are cylindrical and carry pointed arches. The capitals show a great advance in design and technique; the Romanesque type has quite disappeared and the foliage, though preserving traces of the Corinthian arrangement, is based on nature.

The space corresponding to the upper triforium at Noyon was occupied at Notre-Dame originally by circular openings with a sort of wheel tracery. These roses have been re-set by Viollet-le-Duc in two bays: in the rest they have made way for lengthening the clerestory downwards; the triforium roof being at the same time flattened as was necessary.

The west front of Notre-Dame is on the whole the finest in France (Plate VI). It is simpler than those of Amiens, Reims and Bourges; the treatment is bold and masterly, and the proportions of the stages to one another is admirably contrived. The design of the upper stage of the towers is magnificent, and it is doubtful whether they would have had the same impressive effect if they had been finished with the spires that

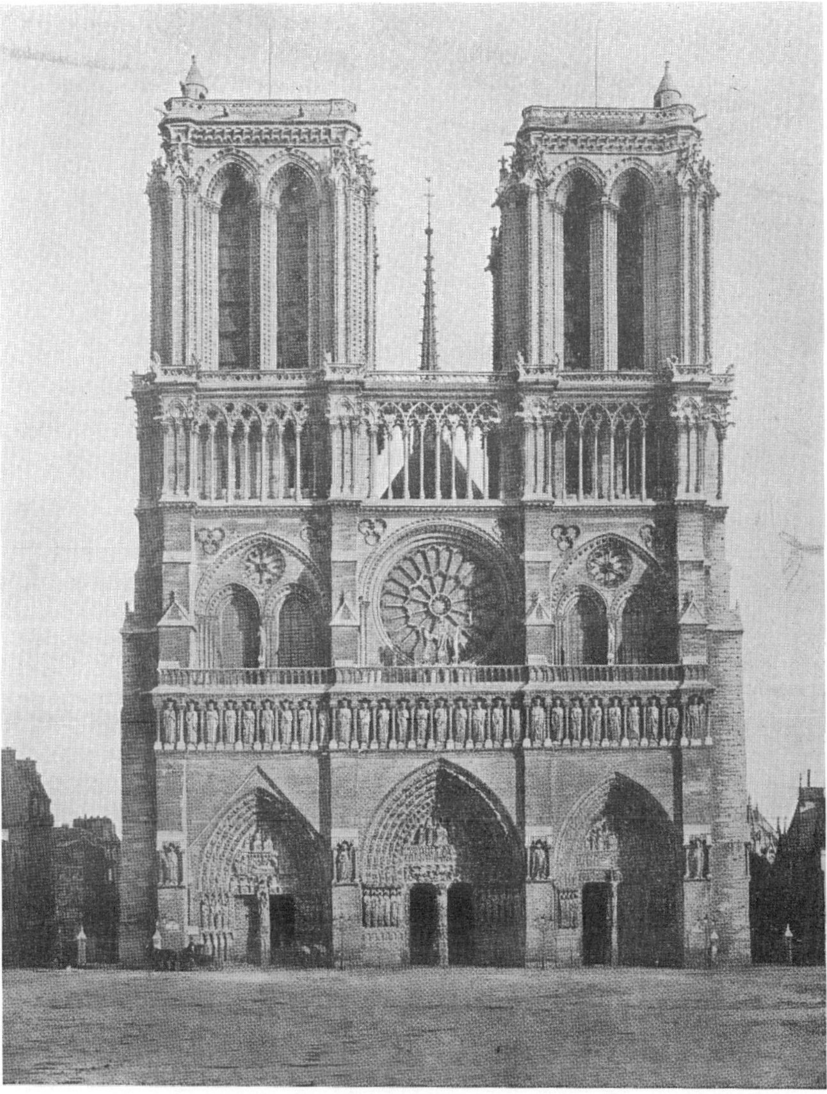

PARIS. NOTRE-DAME—WEST FRONT

were originally intended. The horizontal lines are strongly marked, more so than the vertical, and this perhaps is a survival of Romanesque and ancient Roman tradition. The broad spaces containing niches, windows, and traceried gallery, sweeping from side to side, give an air of solidity and dignity to this façade that is wanting in the more elaborate fronts that succeeded to it.

The novelty of the art shown at Notre-Dame will be appreciated if we compare it with what was going on in other parts of France at the time when it was being built. The domes of Périgueux were just finished; the fronts of Arles and St Gilles were in progress, and Auvergne and Burgundy still clung to their native Romanesque. In Notre-Dame we see the new Gothic art fairly launched on its course.

The splendid cathedral of LAON resembles Paris in some respects, but is rather coarser in detail. Crowning its lofty hill with its five steeples the mighty mass of choir, nave and transepts is a magnificent object in the landscape, and the situation may almost be compared to that of Durham. The five towers were intended to have been seven, two at the west front, two at each transept and another over the crossing, but one is missing from the transept on either side. Here again, the tradition of a lofty and vaulted triforium is observed, causing a second or pseudo-triforium stage above like that at Noyon. All the arches are pointed and are carried on mono-cylindrical columns with foliaged capitals. The church was begun as usual at the east end in 1160, and ended with an apse and an ambulatory. The nave and west front and transept were finished about 1205. The choir was then altered from an apse to a square end seven bays farther eastward, and the upper part of one tower at each transept was completed before the middle of the 13th century. The second intended transeptal tower never rose above the roof. A three-storied apsidal chapel on the east side of each transept is a singular and picturesque feature. Christchurch Priory, Hants, has a two-storied chapel of the same kind.

The central tower forms a lantern over the crossing, and this, though almost universal in the great English churches, is very unusual in France except in Normandy, where the architecture has several points of resemblance to that north of the channel.

The square east end, also, of which there is another instance in Laon at the fine church of St Martin, is not common in France though almost universal with us.

The towers at Laon are very original in design. Rising square up to the last stage they there become octagonal, and on each oblique face they have a tourelle consisting chiefly of columns and arches, up one of which the stair is contrived; and from between the shafts of the western towers peep out figures of oxen commemorating the legend of a miraculous ox which helped to draw stones to the fabric while it was building. These towers excited the admiration of Wilars de Honecort, an architect of the 13th century, who saw them in process of being built and sketched them in his album, writing against his drawing that he had been in many lands but had nowhere seen such a tower as that at Laon[1]. Originally the towers were surmounted by crocketed spires, which have now disappeared. That on the south transept tower was removed at the time of the Revolution, being dangerously distorted. The construction indeed seems too frail to carry them. There are cloisters attached to the cathedral of some interest, though not very accessible, being turned into cottages, and Laon has several other monuments deserving careful study, especially the great church of St Martin, the Episcopal Palace, and the Templars' Church.

The new art is carried further in the apsidal transept of the cathedral at SOISSONS[2], where we have again the four-storied bays, though the nave has only the usual three stages of arcade, triforium and clerestory. The same four-storied design occurs in the choir of ST REMI at Reims, which was rebuilt in the new style early in the 13th century. The nave of this fine church is remarkable for the strange way in which details of the 13th century are grafted upon very early and primitive work of nearly two centuries before.

The magnificent cathedral of BOURGES has side portals of beautiful Romanesque work which have been refixed in the newer building, and the northern of the two has a scroll of exquisite design on the lintel. They are covered by porches of unusual beauty, with a central shaft carrying a pair of trefoil

[1] *Sketch-book of Wilars de Honecort*, ed. Willis, Plates LXVII, LXVIII.

[2] This church is reported to be very seriously damaged by the Germans.

arches, round which are carved in one case a series of little owls, and in another little apes. These porches are placed where transepts would be expected, but there are no transepts at Bourges, the plan consisting of an unbroken nave with two aisles on each side, which are carried round the apse. Except for the omission of the transepts the plan resembles the original design of Notre-Dame at Paris; but the section and elevation are very different. The inner of the two side aisles is carried up half-way from the low outer aisle towards the lofty nave, and it has its own triple staging of arcade triforium and clerestory, the latter looking out over the outer aisle. The effect of this is to make the nave arcade enormously high, at the expense of the triforium and clerestory, which seem crowded up against the vault, and this is unsatisfactory. The general effect, however, at first sight of the interior is surprisingly fine; the long vault from end to end, unbroken by a transept, is magnificent. There is something like it in the interior of the cathedral at Exeter, where in the same way a fine unbroken vault runs from end to end of the church.

The cathedral of LE MANS has at the end of its Romanesque nave a 13th century choir, which like that at Bourges has the inner of two aisles carried up, with its own triforium and clerestory, like the central choir.

The cathedral at CHARTRES was rebuilt by Bishop Fulbert in 1028. The present north-west tower was added between 1135 and 1145, and the south-west one between 1145 and 1175. The magnificent Royal portals, which now align with the west front of the towers, stood originally in a line with their eastern side, leaving the towers exposed on three faces. They must have been brought forward to where they now are before 1194, when Fulbert's church behind them was destroyed by fire. The north-west tower had a spire of wood, which, after being twice burned, was replaced by the fine stone steeple of Jean Texier between 1507 and 1513. The famous south-west steeple was finished at once in stone, and in its stern majestic features forms one of the most splendid works of the transition from Romanesque to Gothic. The Royal portals with their sculptured tympana, and their jambs adorned with solemn mystic figures, drawn out to columnar proportions, form an important link in the history of French decorative sculpture. The heads are very characteristic, and that of Christ may be compared with the figures of our Lord at Reims and Amiens.

The rebuilding of the body of the church was carried on with such extraordinary vigour that it was practically finished before 1212. The conception was magnificent; the design contemplated no less than nine towers, two in the west front, two at each transept, two at the chord of the apse, and a central one over the crossing; but only the two first were built, the central one was never attempted and the other six only reached the eaves. The simplicity of the design still attaches it slightly to the transitional style, but it is decidedly in advance of Paris and Bourges. The vaults are quadripartite, the lofty triforium has been reduced to smaller proportions, allowing a lofty arcade, and there is a magnificent clerestory with a circle containing plate tracery in the head. The columns have attached colonnettes and foliaged capitals with early examples of the leaves *à crochet,* soon to be developed into the typical French capital of the later Gothic. The proportions of the interior are singularly happy; it has not the depression of Paris nor the extravagant altitude in relation to span of Amiens. The gradual advance of importance given to the arcade in proportion to the other stages will be seen by the following table, in which the elevation is in all cases divided approximately into 32 parts:

| | Paris | Chartres | Reims | Amiens |
|---|---|---|---|---|
| Arcade ... | 11 | 14 | 15⅓ | 16 |
| Triforium ... | 9 | 4 | 4⅔ | 4¾ |
| Clerestory ... | 12 | 14 | 12 | 11¼ |
| | 32 | 32 | 32 | 32 |

The two splendid lateral porches of Chartres are the finest product of French Gothic, especially the northern one (Plate VII), which was begun in 1250. The amount of sculpture in statues, arches, capitals, and bases is hardly to be believed: it is said there are 700 figures in the north portal alone. Some of them have a little trace of archaic stiffness, but others have a freedom and grace that puts them on a level with classic work. These portals afford matter for careful study of French Gothic at its best. The whole of this wonderful cathedral is full of interest and instruction,

CHARTRES CATHEDRAL—NORTH PORCH

PLATE VIII

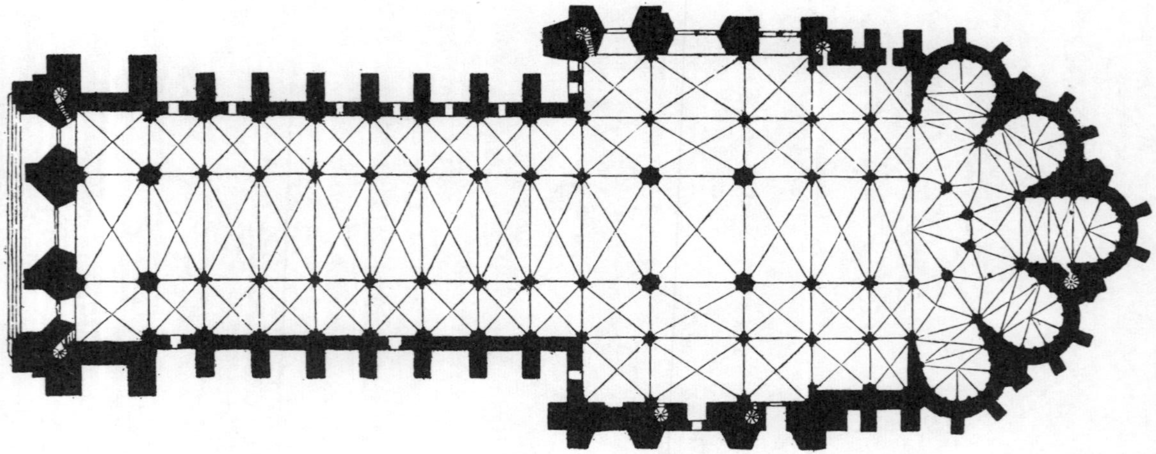

RÉIMS CATHEDRAL, from V.-le-Duc

and now that Reims has fallen, there is none other in France on the whole its equal[1].

Of REIMS one can only write retrospectively, as if it were still as it was in the summer of 1914. It was in my judgment incomparably the finest of French cathedrals, in the majesty and simplicity of its proportions, the purity and delicacy of its details, and the glorious perfection of its sculpture. How much of this is left, or can be recovered, I know not. It has been for four years the mark for German cannon, directed, we are told, by a passion for its destruction, irrespective of military purposes, and with its grievous defacement and partial ruin one chapter in the history of French art is wiped out.

The cathedral built by Archbishop Hincmar in 841 was burned in 1210, and on the first anniversary of the fire the new church was begun. The architect was Jean d'Orbais, to whom the exquisite east end with its ring of chapels is due. Jean de Loup was architect sixteen years and made the great west portals. After him came Gaucher, and then Bernard of Soissons was architect for 25 years, and built the five western bays and "*ouvra à l'O.*", the great western rose window. The church was not finished till late in the 14th century, nor the towers till 1427.

Like Laon, Reims excited the admiration of Wilars de Honecort, who saw the east end rising, and sketched the apsidal chapels, writing against his sketch "this is how the chapels at Cambrai will have to be if one does them rightly[2]."

The plan of the church (Plate VIII) is simple and shows a great advance on its predecessors. Only the eastern part has the double aisles of Paris and Chartres, the nave having only one aisle on each side, which is an improvement, the space seeming to expand as you advance eastward. There are fortunately no chapels between the nave buttresses, and the effect of the flank of the nave, with these great projections, is extremely noble. The chapels round the apse, which Wilars so much admired and proposed to copy, are unrivalled, and show the final perfect development of the French *chevet* (Plate IX).

[1] See M. and E. Marriage, *The Sculptures of Chartres Cathedral*, Cambridge, 1909.

[2] *Sketch-book of Wilars de Honecort*, Plates LIX and LX. "Dautretel maniere doivent estre celes de Cambrai son lor fait droit."

In them we see the first beginnings of bar tracery, the windows being of two lights carrying a circle with sexfoil cusping. The same design with certain alterations runs through the windows of the whole church. The elevation of the bay is severely simple, the vaulting quadripartite, and showing no sign of the tentative efforts of preceding buildings. The capitals are richly sculptured, sometimes mixed with figures as in the famous "vintage" capital, but towards the west end, which is later, they fall off in style and become confused and inexpressive. In the same way the refined Attic base of the eastern part is exchanged in the western bays for a simple section without the scotia or hollow moulding.

The upper part of the western towers is octagonal, and, as at Laon, has a slender tourelle at each oblique face, consisting mainly of colonnettes. A spire was intended between four spirelets, and was prepared for, but the structure looks too frail for such a load.

The front has three great portals, and their tympana have tracery, and are glazed, instead of the usual sculpture, but the jambs were filled with statues of extraordinary merit. They were by several hands, and those in the jamb of the right-hand door were archaic, and duplicates of some at Chartres, probably having been carved in advance and kept till the building was ready for them. The other figures were the highest achievement of French mediaeval art. Especially noteworthy was the group of the Annunciation with the smiling angel, and above all the group, by a different hand, of the visitation of Mary and Elizabeth which might be compared to the finest Greek sculpture. How many of these lovely figures have survived?

In a side doorway is a figure of Christ of great beauty and dignity.

The foundation of the great church at Reims, where French kings used to be crowned, was followed in a few years by that of AMIENS, which it is usual to regard as the perfect flower of the French Gothic style. It was begun by Bishop Evrard de Fouilly in 1220, the same year in which the foundation of Salisbury cathedral was laid. The nave and the west front up to the gallery were finished by 1236. The apse and its chapels seem to have been finished in 1247, after which the work was closed

REIMS CATHEDRAL—APSIDAL CHAPEL, from V.-le-Duc

PLATE X

AMIENS CATHEDRAL—WEST FRONT

for want of funds, and the choir was not completed till 1269. The west front, which had stopped at the gallery level, was continued in 1366, but the north tower was not finished till the next century. The chapels between the nave buttresses were added in the 14th century.

A labyrinth or House of Daedalus in the floor, now represented by a copy, gave the date 1212, the names of the bishop Evrard, King Louis VIII, and three architects successively employed, the first, to whom the main conception of the building must be attributed, being Robert de Luzarches. The inscription was placed by the last architect, Master Regnault, in 1288.

The plan, before the chapels were added between the nave buttresses, was very like that of Reims. The columns are round with attached colonnettes and simple capitals *à crochet*, the front colonnette being run up to carry the vaulting ribs. The bases are good examples of the Gothic version of the Attic base. The vault is quadripartite, the side bays much stilted, to allow space for an immense clerestory; the triforium consists of two three-light openings with a trefoil in the head, and below it runs a string beautifully carved.

The choir, which is later, is by another and an inferior hand: probably Thomas de Cormont had then succeeded to Robert de Luzarches. An attempt is made at greater splendour: the back wall of the triforium is pierced with windows and glazed, and the inner face is surmounted by an unmeaning and ungraceful pediment. The spacing of the columns in the apse is less successful than at Reims or Chartres: they seem too much crowded together, and the arches disproportionately tall and narrow, especially when contrasted with the immense expansion given to the clerestory windows in the side walls. But the agreeable spacing of the columns of the apse was a difficult problem, on account of the radiation of the bays in the surrounding ambulatory, and was not often successfully achieved.

The west front (Plate X) by de Luzarches is a splendid work, perhaps a little too full of ornament, but still a masterpiece and certainly superior to that of Reims. The sculpture here, and in the side portals, is by several hands and of unequal merit: that of the west front is the best, and the statue of Christ on the pier dividing the middle portal—*Le beau Dieu d'Amiens*—is deservedly famous.

The great portals are typical of the form that henceforth became nearly universal in France. They are brought forward to the front of the great buttresses and covered with a gabled roof. This, as the door is set back in the main wall, gives the porch a great depth, affording a splendid gradation of shadow. The sides are splayed and flanked with columns and statues, and the arch is recessed order by order conformably with the jamb. Each order in the arch is carved with figures in niches. These, as they come overhead, seem to hang from the arch, and indeed in some of the later examples the figures are actually suspended by hooks. There is an element of absurdity in these niches toppling overhead, when they should be upright, and the Romanesque portal, such as that at Arles, is more logical. Indeed, this method, by constant repetition in French portals, becomes in the end tiresome.

At Amiens we have the whole system of French Gothic construction thoroughly developed (Plate IV, *sup*. p. 355): the thrusts of the high vaults are concentrated on isolated points over the piers, where they are met by the counter-thrust of the flying buttresses, which in their turn depend for their stability on the exterior buttress piers beyond the aisles: the solids are reduced and the voids enlarged to their utmost extent: the columns are no larger than the load requires; the walls from pier to pier are relieved of all lateral thrust and are pierced with openings in each stage reaching from pier to pier, leaving only the arches of the great arcade with their spandrils to steady the columns, the traceries of the triforium, and the clerestory, in the latter of which the window takes the full width of the bay, and with the window-arch carries the solid wall above up to the plate level on which the roof rests. The whole construction is well balanced and scientific; theory is pushed to the very verge of insecurity, and in point of fact the bays have been tied together by iron carried in the triforium stage lengthways of the building. The whole structure is on an enormous scale, the height from the floor to the apex of the vault being no less than 141 feet, or nearly one-third more than the corresponding height in Westminster Abbey, which has the highest vault of any Gothic church in England.

PLATE XI

BEAUVAIS CATHEDRAL—INTERIOR

And yet in its very perfection one misses something of the charm of earlier work where theory was less supreme. The construction seems a triumph of engineering rather than of art, and is only partly redeemed from being merely a mechanical success by the splendour and beauty of the sculpture which is attached to it. One misses the effort and the vigorous striving upwards of the Romanesque work and the succeeding transition, which has subsided into the placid content of achievement; a phase more congenial to the temper of antiquity than that of the restless, ever progressive mind of modern Europe. However much one may enjoy the west front of Amiens, the interior strikes one with a certain coldness: the proportions seem too fine drawn, that of the arcade excessive, the height of the nave too great for its width, the detail of triforium thin and poor in the nave, and in the choir positively ugly. Of the crowding together of the apse columns and the contrast between those bays and the wide bays next them, I have spoken above. In all these respects Amiens is inferior to Reims, where, in my opinion, French Gothic reached its climax.

The men of BEAUVAIS resolved to rebuild their cathedral in 1247, after the old church of Bishop Hervé had been injured by fire. They watched with envy the magnificence of the great church which was rising at Amiens, and resolved that they would do something finer still. The vaulting of their choir was made 13 feet higher than that at Amiens, but it promptly fell. It was rebuilt in 1272 and fell again 12 years later. In rebuilding it a second time they strengthened the construction by introducing an additional column in each bay of the side walls, thus doubling the number of arches. No accident could have been more fortunate. It brought the side arches nearer to the span of those in the apse, and thus remedied the unhappy contrast which there is at Amiens between the narrow apse bays and the spreading bays next them. The result is to produce an interior of strange and haunting beauty. In all respects the effect is far superior to that of its neighbouring rival; if Amiens is coldly correct, Beauvais is entrancingly lovely (Plate XI). The excessive height of the arcade at Amiens is here reduced, and the clerestory is correspondingly lengthened with a magnificent effect. The back of the triforium is pierced with windows and glazed, thus making the whole choir a lantern of slender masonry set with glass.

In 1231 the monks of ST DENIS set about rebuilding the body of their church, though Suger's building had barely stood for a century. Pierre de Montereau was the architect, and with the exception of the west front and adjoining bays and the lower storey of the apse with its chapels the whole of the existing church is his work. It is in the fully developed Gothic style, remarkable for its lightness and the amount of glass-space. To the same architect is attributed the SAINTE CHAPELLE in the old palace of Louis IX at Paris, where the whole space between buttress and buttress is filled with windows in which bar tracery is fully developed. It was built between 1245 and 1248.

## § III. THE PROVINCIAL STYLES

The provincial styles. Normandy. Burgundy. The Plantagenet style. Limoges and Toulouse.

It is time to turn from the Ile-de-France, where the final triumphs of the pure Gothic style were achieved, to see what was being done in other parts of the country.

In NORMANDY, during the latter part of the Romanesque period, under the settled rule of its powerful Dukes, architecture progressed rapidly and outstripped the other schools of France. The Ile-de-France was weak and disorganised and architecture there had not yet come to its own. The conquest of England, which transferred the seat of power to the other side of the channel and drained the province of men and means, threw Normandy backward, and only one great cathedral, that of Bayeux, was raised there during the 12th century. When Normandy passed to the French crown in the next century the influence of the central Gothic school made itself felt: but though the great churches of that period at Caen, Rouen, Séez, Coutances and elsewhere are mainly in the new Gothic style, they are carried out in a manner of their own, with many differences, some of them as might be expected showing affinity to the Gothic of England. We find for instance round abaci instead of the universal French square or polygonal one, and labels over the arches inside the building, which are general in England, but not used in other French work. Corbel tables are common both in Normandy and England, and interlacing arcades are peculiar to Norman work not only in Normandy and with us, as at Canterbury, Christchurch Priory, St Cross, Castle Acre, and Iffley, but in Sicily and South Italy, whither the Normans carried this favourite device with them. The western rose window of most great French churches is rare in Normandy, but on the other hand the central tower, which is unusual in the rest of France, but almost universal in the great English churches, is found in Normandy at both the great abbeys at Caen, at Rouen in the cathedral and at St Ouen and St Maclou, at Bayeux, Lisieux, Coutances, Norrey, Bretteville, and numerous other churches both small and great, and is often open as a lantern to the church below. Apart from these and such like peculiarities, Norman Gothic conforms to that of the central school.

The fine cathedral of St Pierre at LISIEUX is thoroughly French in style, not unlike Notre-Dame in its vigorous simplicity. It was begun in the latter part of the 12th century and finished in 1218. The nave arcade has pointed arches on cylindrical columns and the vaulting is quadripartite and a good deal domed up. The interior of this church is as fine as anything in early French Gothic.

The cathedral of BAYEUX, built by the fighting bishop Odo, was burned by our Henry I in 1106, who afterwards rebuilt it. Earthquake and fire caused a fresh rebuilding in 1159, but the consecration did not take place till 1231. Its chequered history is reflected by the medley of styles in the nave, where late Norman arches and wall diapers of the 12th century are carried by massive clustered piers with 13th century capitals. The choir is of regular 13th century work, with features showing English influence, such as the passage in the clerestory wall inside the window, and the peculiar leaf of Early English capitals common to the style from York to Winchester, and Westminster to St Davids, but, so far as I know, found nowhere else in France.

The vaults are quadripartite, there is no western or transeptal rose window, and sculpture is sparingly used. The typical Norman ornamentation, as has already been mentioned, was conventional, and figure sculpture was developed slowly in that province, where there was a lack of the antique examples enjoyed by Provence and the South.

Another characteristic of English Gothic which is observable in Normandy is the greater use of mouldings in the arches. In the early Gothic of the centre of France the mouldings seldom amount to more than a simple roll on the edge of a square order, but in Normandy we find the deep hollows and rolls with which we are familiar in our early English and early Decorated work. The arcades of the cathedral at ROUEN afford an example of this.

The 12th century is represented there by the north-west tower—the "Tour St Romain"—and the two side portals of the west front. The nave was rebuilt after a fire and finished probably before 1240; the two side portals before the end of the century; the Lady chapel in the 14th century; the beautiful "Tour du Beurre" in 1487; and the gorgeous west front (Plate XIV) between 1509 and 1530. The nave has aisles so lofty as to cover the main arcade, and another above it, a sort of pseudo-triforium, which simply opens to the aisle as at Lucca, Genoa, and Rochester, though no doubt intended originally to have had a vaulted floor and a triforium storey in the usual way. The choir is in the more regular French style and finely proportioned. The choir of the ABBAYE AUX HOMMES at CAEN, which was rebuilt in the 13th century, has the vaulted triforium of Noyon and the early French Gothic, combined with the English characteristic clerestory passage with triple-arched inner tracery.

In the fine cathedral of SÉEZ the Normans, working more on the French model, pushed lightness of construction beyond the verge of security, and the fabric has had to be extensively repaired.

Normandy, like England, is famous for its stone spires, a beautiful feature of Gothic architecture which is much less common in France. Every village round about Caen has a steeple; some of them saddle-backed, others with fine belfry stages and stone spires. Those of ST PIERRE (Plate XII) and St Sauveur at CAEN, which seem to be by the same architect, are especially beautiful. That of St Jean in the same town was to have been similar, but is incomplete, the foundations having given way and stopped the work.

PLATE XII

CAEN. St PIERRE—TOWER AND SPIRE AND EAST END

PLATE XIII

COUTANCES CATHEDRAL—EXTERIOR

The two early western towers of the Abbaye aux Hommes at Caen are crowned with magnificent spires of the 13th century, and the churches at Norrey, Ifs, and Bernières follow the type of those at St Pierre (Plate XII) and St Sauveur at Caen. They have each a lofty graceful belfry stage, with a pair of two-light windows between a pair of narrow blank arches. The spire is octagonal, with a lofty spire-light on each direct face, and a pinnacle, hollow and shafted, at each angle of the square tower. The Normans had a keen eye for outline, and there are no other towers and spires in France to compare with them in this respect.

The magnificent cathedral at COUTANCES (Plate XIII) shows most of the peculiarities of Norman Gothic. The nave dates from 1208 and the choir from 1238 to 1248. The great glory of the church is its group of towers—a lantern over the crossing, and two splendid steeples at the west end. The latter are remarkable for a distinct staircase turret with spires of its own attached to the outer corner of each tower. The interior of this church is less successful than the outside, though it has many points of interest, but the exterior, from whatever point it is seen, makes it one of the most important and satisfactory in France.

In almost every province of France the architecture shows local differences, though they are not so pronounced as in the Romanesque period. In BURGUNDY the narthex, which forms so important a feature at Vézelay, Autun, Pontigny, and formerly at Cluny, occurs also in the Gothic churches of that province. There is one, though partly imperfect, in the church of ST PÈRE SOUS VÉZELAY, where there is also a fine arcaded front, something like that of the neighbouring abbey, and an extremely beautiful tower with a wooden spire, the belfry stage of which slightly recalls that in the towers at Laon. Behind this splendid façade is hidden a humble church, which was never rebuilt or brought up to the same standard of magnificence. The picturesque and romantic town of SEMUR-EN-AUXOIS has a remarkable church with a western narthex or triple-arched porch.

The church of ST URBAIN at TROYES is built of the splendid stone of Champagne which encouraged the architects of that province to attempt deeds of daring in construction impossible with inferior material. The church is a mere lantern of gorgeous stained glass framed in slender spars of stone: the mullions are slender like bars of iron, and the piers mere shafts. Clerestory and triforium form one window with two planes of tracery, between which is a wall passage, the outer plane being glazed in the triforium and the inner in the clerestory. The traceries are cut in single slabs of stone slid into grooves between the buttresses. The whole scheme of decoration by painted glass remains and is consistent and harmonious: a band of figure-work forms a zone of splendid colour round the building on a ground of grisaille which shimmers like a tissue of silver.

In POITOU and ANJOU Gothic architecture took a very special form, very unlike that of the Ile-de-France and the central provinces, with many traces of the Romanesque and the dome architecture of Aquitaine. The cathedral of ANGERS is an immense transeptal church without aisles, ending in a simple apse, ceiled with vast square quadripartite vaults, which rise so enormously, dome-fashion, in each bay, that, though not constructed domically, they seem reminiscent of the real cupolas of Angoulême and Solignac. Of this Angevin or "Plantagenet" style, as M. de Verneilh calls it, Angers has several examples. The HÔTEL-DIEU, or hospital, founded by our Henry II in 1153, is a vast three-aisled hall, 200 feet by 75, with a beautiful chapel of 1180 in the same style at one end, a cloister, and a fine granary in two storeys divided by pillars and arches into nave and aisles. The pillars in all these buildings are slender, and in the chapel and hospital carry pointed arches, and vaults which are highly domical. The ribs are merely rolls embedded in the vault, and do not stand out, being really only a moulding on the arris of the groin. The windows are plain with round-arched openings. The chapel, which is square, consisting of two bays each way, is vaulted and shafted in the same way.

The fine abbey church of ST SERGE, also at ANGERS, is perhaps a still more beautiful example of this singular style of architecture. Here too the windows are round-arched, though the arches of vault and arcade are pointed. In all these buildings, the vaults of the side aisles and of the middle space are of equal height.

The cathedral of POITIERS, which was founded about 1160,

is in the same style. Like St Serge it has three aisles of equal width, and almost equal height, though here the middle vault is lifted a few feet higher than the others. In other respects the same description applies to this building. It has a square east end with three shallow coves sunk in the solid wall to represent apses. The walls are panelled with a lofty blank arcade of round arches on slender shafts, carrying a wall passage that passes below the windows and behind the projecting wall-piers. This is a Romanesque feature, and occurs at Cahors and Solignac. The fine hall of the palace of the Counts of Poitou, now the Palais de Justice at Poitiers, has similar wall arcading.

The Angevin style is one of great beauty, and really forms a separate school of Gothic art, quite distinct from that which sprang to life in the Royal domain.

Farther south in the Limousin and county of Toulouse the Gothic of Paris and Amiens made still less impression on local architecture. It is a surprise to find it in the 13th century cathedrals at Limoges and Clermont, in the midst of very different work, and in Provence, as has already been said, the style was never accepted. At TOULOUSE, situate in a great plain with no local quarries, great use is made of brickwork, with excellent effect. The tower of the Jacobin convent has no stone in it except in the capitals of the little window shafts and some of the string courses. Moulded bricks are used for angle rolls, but the window-heads are made with ordinary bricks, not shaped, but placed in straight-sided arches, over two-light openings. The result is piquant and delightful. Another tower in the same town, of similar design, has been partly ruined.

There is an interesting group of towers at LIMOGES, of which the upper part is octagonal, but set obliquely, with an angle and not a face to the cardinal points, the corners of the square below being filled with a pinnacle or buttress partly detached.

Other local peculiarities will be noticed by the observant student in the different provinces of France; which, though they may lack the severe logical and scientific exactitude of the style which finds its perfect development at Amiens, will not for that reason be less grateful to the artist's eye.

## § IV. LATER FRENCH GOTHIC

Fourteenth century Gothic. Its dullness and monotony. Revival in the fifteenth century. The Flamboyant style. Its origin and development. End of French Gothic architecture.

In the foregoing sections the development of geometrical Gothic has been traced from its beginning at St Denis, where the pointed arch began to influence the construction, through the transitional work of Senlis, Noyon, and Sens, where Romanesque tradition had almost disappeared, to Paris and Chartres, where it was finally lost, and to Reims where the new art was fully developed and thoroughly carried out without any loss of the old constructional solidity. Another step taken at Amiens brought it to the verge of weakness, and at Beauvais this limit was overstepped and ruin followed, needing supplementary supports to be added.

In these last buildings every problem had been solved and brought to its logical conclusion. There was nothing more to be done: the style was complete so far as constructive science went, and at first the French architects saw no opening for any fresh artistic departure. In England it was different. Our geometrical Gothic, which may be considered to have reached its full development at the Chapter House at Westminster in 1250 and the "Angel Choir" at Lincoln in 1255, continued but for a short half century more before it began to pass into a new phase. In the Chapter House at Wells, built between 1293 and 1302, may just be detected the faintest tendency of the strict geometrical figures in the tracery to melt into flowing lines. In the choir at Bristol, built in 1306, and the steeple of St Mary's at Oxford of about the same date, the change is well-advanced, and by the middle of the century, in the Lady Chapel at Ely and the Octagon, the curvilinear Decorated style is perfected, and geometrical tracery forgotten. But in France, no corresponding change took place, and this chapter of Gothic architecture is wanting.

French Gothic during the 14th century therefore followed the lead of the 13th without its originality, reproducing the construction and architectural details of the masterpieces of that period, but without its vitality. Fine churches were erected, especially during the early part of the period, but the architecture gradually declined in quality and became mechanical and commonplace. The tendency was to exaggerate the lightness of the fabric, to increase the voids at the expense of the solids, and the result was an attenuation and feebleness of design that made the work uninteresting.

The vast church—an ex-cathedral—of ST QUENTIN, dating from the end of the 13th century, with a vault 127 feet high from the floor, is a favourable example of later French geometrical Gothic. It has two transepts, the only example, so far as I know, remaining in France; but they are not treated like those at Lincoln, Salisbury, or York, the second or eastern transept being rather unimportant. The nave, which is later than the choir, though still geometrical, is very striking, with a lofty clerestory of traceried windows, united by descending shafts with the triforium, a device which generally obtained during the later Gothic period. The sculpture of the nave capitals is very poor, consisting of detached sprigs of foliage planted round the bell, without any sense of spring or support. That in the choir, which is earlier, is better. There is a good deal of fine painted glass in various parts of the church, and at the east end remains part of an older Romanesque building. This fine church has suffered severely during the war, and is, I understand, partly in ruin.

The eastern part of the magnificent church of ST PIERRE at CHARTRES seems to date from this period, grafted on to a structure of various dates from the early Romanesque period onward. The whole clerestory is filled with beautiful painted glass, partly figure-work, partly grisaille, all of the highest interest, an almost unrivalled display and worthy of careful study.

The cathedral of CHÂLONS-SUR-MARNE is a good example of late 13th century Gothic. The apse is well contrived, and the whole effect pleasing; but the foliage of the capitals is poor and shows the decline of the style.

The great church of ST OUEN at ROUEN was begun in 1318 on the site of a Romanesque predecessor, of which a small part remains on the north side. The west front and its two towers are modern; the nave dates from the 15th century; and only the eastern part with the apse and *chevet* belongs to the 14th. The plan shows a return to simplicity; there are no lateral chapels; the transepts are short, which also is good; and the apse is designed with only three canted bays, which has a very good effect. But though the plan is excellent the detail is very disappointing. The main arcade is poor and thin, with meagre shafts and miserable little capitals. The aisle windows are enormous, and the solids are reduced to a minimum. The general effect of the interior from the west end is good, the proportion fine, and the plan simple, but beyond this there is nothing to interest, the details being poor and monotonous. The north transept of the cathedral at ROUEN with the *Portail des Libraires* is a typical example of the later French geometrical style. It is said to date from 1280, but looks later. It shows the decline of the art in the attenuation of all the details, in its thin and wiry mouldings, and in the shallow recessing of the planes.

The 14th century was not a happy time for France. She was harassed by English invasion during the hundred years' war, and devastated by the Black death in 1348 and afterwards, which swept away half the population. Comparatively few great buildings were erected during that period, and they show little of the spirit of the century before. Viollet-le-Duc writes of the great cathedral at Bordeaux that it is bare and cold, the work "plutôt d'un savant que d'un artiste." He says, further, that "at the end of the 14th century we no longer find the individual stamp which marks each building at the beginning of it. The general arrangement, the construction, and the ornament take already a monotonous aspect which favours mediocrity at the cost of genius. Science carries the day over art, and absorbs it. Solids are reduced to the least possible, windows enlarged to the greatest extent, spires rise on supports that seem unfit to carry them, mouldings are divided into an infinity of members, and piers are composed of bundles of colonnettes as numerous as the arch mouldings they support. Sculpture is starved by the geometrical combinations of the architecture. In spite of the excessive skill and logic which presides over the design it leaves you cold; and in its efforts you find more calculation than inspiration[1]."

[1] Viollet-le-Duc, *Dict. rais.* I. 154.

From this mechanical style, when art seemed sunk into commonplace and half dead, French architecture did not revive till the 15th century, when a fresh inspiration seized it; it sprang at once to a new life, and suddenly blazed out into the Flamboyant style, the last phase of French Gothic, in which it expired at the advent of the classic Renaissance. The suddenness of its appearance suggests that it was adopted from some foreign source, and M. Enlart and others trace its origin in the curvilinear Decorated style of England, which began a hundred years before, and which we had already abandoned for the rigid Perpendicular style with which English Gothic closed its career.

The history of architecture in the two countries at this time presents a curious contrast. Our curvilinear or flowing Decorated style, which began in the first years of the 14th century and continued till its last quarter, had been invaded as early as 1337 at Gloucester by novel methods of design, the first symptoms of coming change. The beautiful Percy tomb at Beverley, of exquisite curvilinear design, dated 1365, is contemporary with the east end of the choir at Gloucester in an early phase of Perpendicular architecture, and the eastern part of the cloister, which has a vault of fan tracery. Our architecture began to assume a severer form, and the luxurious sweeping lines of Selby and Carlisle stiffened themselves into rigid straight lines at Canterbury and Winchester, where new naves in fully-developed Perpendicular were begun in 1378 and 1394. In France, on the contrary, the stiff geometrical style persisted all through the period when in England architecture had yielded to the seduction of the softer flowing lines of the later Decorated; and it was not till some time after we had abandoned that style for one of more severity that the French broke through the rigid formality of geometrical architecture and flamed out into the brilliant and luxuriant style appropriately named Flamboyant.

It is difficult to see from what quarter but England the inspiration could have come. There was nothing like our flowing style elsewhere; the connexion between the two countries, even in spite of hostility, was close and constant and a great part of France had been under English rule. But though the suggestion of flowing lines may have been borrowed from an

English source, the new style in France went its own way and has little likeness to our more restrained 14th century work. Having once broken down their rigid geometrical forms the French could not twist and bend them enough, and the curvilinear of France often ran into extravagance. The Flamboyant style has been condemned as decadent, debased, and meretricious by purists who revere the 13th century as the period of true architecture; one can understand that it makes no appeal to pedantry. Flamboyant architecture has not the stern simplicity of Paris or Chartres, the majesty of Reims, the strict logical perfection of Amiens: that is incontestable. It is playful, piquant, full of clever surprises, joyous and amusing, sometimes frivolous, seldom serious and restrained: but there is room for it in the temple of art, just as in that of literature there is a seat for Ariosto as well as for Dante.

Whatever were its shortcomings, it was beyond question alive, and contrasted strongly and favourably with the worn-out art which it superseded and which had nothing to offer to the world but stale repetitions.

Normandy was still in English possession when the Flamboyant church of Caudebec was begun in 1426; and St Maclou at Rouen in 1432; and the gorgeous church of Notre-Dame de l'Épine near Châlons was built in 1419 only four years after the battle of Agincourt. After the expulsion of the English in 1456 the new style spread rapidly all over France. Even in the south, which had resisted all attempts of the sterner school of 13th century Gothic to gain a footing, Flamboyant architecture found acceptance, and appealed with success to the softer temperament of the people. In every part of the country new buildings were erected, and old ones remodelled in the new style, which pervaded the whole kingdom as completely as the Perpendicular style did that of England. The suddenness of its development is remarkable. In the last year of the 14th century the nave of St Quentin was built in regular geometrical Gothic, and yet as early as 1412 we find the Flamboyant style fully matured and generally adopted. The window traceries are drawn in flowing curves, like those of England seventy years earlier, though it must be confessed with less restraint and less beauty, often running into wild extravagance, and sometimes, as in certain cases at St Étienne, Beauvais, into positive ugliness. Elsewhere we find them shaped into fleur-de-lys and forms unsuitable to masonry. The mouldings also underwent great changes. In the early schools they had been very simple, often a mere roll on the angle of an order. Now they were elaborated far more than they had ever been even in England, where, at this time indeed, they were being simplified from the deep under-cutting of the earlier styles. In Flamboyant work they are hollowed and under-cut marvellously, the object being to get brilliant sharp edges and deep shadows, and the contrast is often managed in a masterly manner. The bases of columns, on the other hand, became simpler: the scotia or hollow of the Attic base disappears, the members are stretched out upwards, and lifted high above the floor. Another novelty is the frequent omission of the capital, and the continuation of the arch-moulding down the pier to the base in many cases, while in others the arch-mouldings are made to spring out of a circular column, in which they are imagined to exist in embryo, each moulding emerging logically at the proper geometrical point. This gave the mason many nice problems in setting out, so as to make the several members die into the cylindrical core, given by the column, without any awkwardness or mistake. These geometrical puzzles had a growing fascination for the masons, and the stonework of the Flamboyant period is full of intricate devices, where difficult intersections seem purposely provoked in order to show the cleverness of the workman in overcoming the difficulty. Nothing is more ingenious than the way in which mouldings are made to interpenetrate one another, a small feature being intercepted by a larger, but coming again into view beyond it at the true geometrical point, as if it had run through the member in which it was submerged, and emerged again without being any the worse for the interruption. These interpenetrating mouldings and the perverse ingenuity which delighted in them provoked the ire of Ruskin, who has many hard things to say of Flamboyant architecture.

The style in its earlier form is well shown in the church of St Maclou at Rouen. It was designed and begun in 1432, though not finished till the next century. The lace-work spire is modern. The clerestory and triforium form one composition in the interior, an arrangement now become general; the windows have flowing tracery of good design; the mouldings are sharp and keenly edged, divided by wide and deep hollows, and those of the arch run down the pier to the floor with no interruption from a capital. The whole design is light and elegant, and as yet there is no want of substantial effect. There is a splendid porch in the same style at the west end, of which it forms the principal feature. It is canted in five bays to suit the street, and all the resources of the style are lavished upon its pierced traceried gables, pinnacles, and lace-work parapets. The statuary which completed its adornment is unhappily lost.

The west front of the cathedral at ROUEN (Plate XIV), which inspired one of Turner's beautiful drawings for the engravings in *The Rivers of France*, is a marvel of delicate traceries, pinnacles, pierced work in gables and parapets, from amid which modestly peep out two rude Romanesque portals. To the north it is flanked by the Romanesque "Tour St Romain"; to the south by the splendid "Tour du Beurre," which is perhaps unrivalled in its own style. Through several stages enriched with panelled buttresses, pinnacles and traceried windows, it rises squarely to the top stage, where it is converted into an octagon, set between four tourelles at the angles, pierced, and connected by little flying buttresses to the central octagonal lantern. The central tower of ST OUEN in the same city is like it in some respects, but the octagonal lantern stage is larger and higher in proportion, and the angle tourelles are more important. It is difficult to say which of these two splendid towers is the better; but that at the cathedral has the advantage of being seen from the ground to the top, while that at St Ouen is placed over the crossing, and is only seen from the roof upwards. From some points of view it has the disadvantage of appearing rather small for the great church which it surmounts so finely.

Of all the Flamboyant buildings in France there is none superior to the unfinished church of St Wulfran at ABBEVILLE. The façade is, I think, unrivalled in the style: though abundantly ornamented it is not overloaded with detail, and there is enough plain wall to give relief (Plate XV). The whole composition is admirable, well-proportioned, and agreeably broken up by the buttresses, which are judiciously profiled to give a good outline.

PLATE XIV

ROUEN CATHEDRAL—WEST FRONT

ABBEVILLE. St WULFRAN—WEST FRONT

I know nothing more beautiful in the style than this front. The nave vault is quadripartite, and quite like a late English one, with intermediate and ridge ribs and bones at the intersections. The triforium, however, is quite French with bold Flamboyant tracery and a pierced parapet.

These parapets to the triforium are a special feature of the Norman churches, and are found in buildings of earlier date as well as later.

A few miles from Abbeville brings one to the gorgeous Flamboyant abbey church of St Riquier, which was begun in 1457, restored after a fire in 1487, and finished in 1517. The interior is in a simpler and earlier style than that of Abbeville, and at the west end is a tower and below it a portal which is decorated with all the extravagant profusion of Flamboyant architecture in its most lavish mood. The whole is inferior to its beautiful neighbour at Abbeville.

The church at Caudebec on the Seine between Rouen and Havre has an interior of unusual beauty. The columns are cylindrical, and the arch-mouldings interpenetrate curiously as they spring, but there are good capitals, octagonal, with nice carving of foliage, instead of the mere intersection of mouldings and column described above. The effect of this interior is excellent.

At the south side of the church stands the tower with a gorgeous spire of pierced stone work, girdled with coronets in relief throwing shadows on the octagonal pyramid, of which each face is sunk from the edge to the middle. I understand it is a rebuilding, but after the original design. It is a work of great beauty.

The Romanesque north-west tower of the cathedral of Chartres is crowned with a fine steeple, designed and built by Jean Texier of La Beauce, and finished in 1512. It consists of several stages, square and octagonal, superimposed, and placed obliquely and directly alternately, with pinnacles and pediments successfully disposed so as to fill out the design to a good outline..

The citizens of Beauvais, not content with a choir 13 feet higher than that of their near neighbour Amiens, were provoked to further emulation by what was told them of the new church of St Peter at Rome. The report of its extraordinary height reached them just as they had built the first bay of the nave, which was equal in elevation to the choir. A new fit of megalomania seized them: they would not be outdone by Rome, and over the crossing they ran up an enormous tower nearly 500 feet high, which stood for a little more than 20 years, and then, in 1573, the overladen piers gave way and the whole came down in ruin, bringing with it parts of the adjoining choir and transept. The reconstruction included three of the legs of the central tower, only the south-eastern one having survived. Beauvais has now no tower. The adjoining south transept, which was begun in 1500 and finished in 1548, does not seem to have suffered by the catastrophe of 1573. It is very heavily buttressed, and has an air of ponderous solidity, which contrasts unfavourably with the light construction of the 13th century choir. It is gorgeously decorated with panelling, traceries, pinnacles, and gables, with all the profusion of the style, and the delicate intricacy of the detail emphasizes, by contrast, the heaviness of the masses over which it is spread. The tympanum of the south door is filled with niches instead of the usual sculpture, and that of the north transept has a Jesse-tree, which has lost its statuary.

The church at SENLIS has a very similar transept of Flamboyant work.

The fine church of ST JACQUES at LISIEUX is an interesting example of the Flamboyant style. It is ten bays long, with side aisles, but no division between nave and choir, though there may have been, or at all events was intended to be, a *jubé* or rood screen, for which a stair is provided in one of the columns. It has an apse of three cants, and the aisles end square at the chord of it. The window tracery in the clerestory is devoid of cusping. The great arcade has deeply moulded arches dying into cylindrical columns without capitals in the manner already described.

The church at SAINT-LO in Normandy has a 14th century nave with two western towers and spires. To this a Flamboyant choir with double aisles was added in the 15th century; both aisles are carried round the choir, and very shallow chapels open from the outer one. The vaults are quadripartite with acutely pointed ribs, and the mouldings die into the circular columns

ALBI CATHEDRAL—SOUTH SIDE AND PORCH

ALBI CATHEDRAL—THE CHOIR

as at St Pierre, Lisieux. The irregularity of the plan, which is accommodated to the street, causes some nice problems in groining, which should be studied, as well as much picturesque variety in the interior effect.

The well-known church of BROU-EN-BRESSE is extraordinarily rich in Flamboyant work; but nowhere can the detail be studied better than in the cathedral of ALBI. This great church was begun in the 14th century, and is a vast pile of brown brick with round bastions for buttresses, more like a castle than an ecclesiastical building. On the south side is attached to it a Flamboyant porch (Plate XVI) of extraordinary magnificence, and the interior is rich with painting, screens, and statuary almost beyond belief. It consists of one vast nave undivided, with uninterrupted quadripartite vaulting from end to end, and on either side chapels in two storeys, the partitions between which are the great buttresses that support the vault. The choir is not defined in the main building, but is formed by screens parallel to the outside walls, but set inwards, so as to leave a passage all round outside them. The span of the main building is so vast that there is room for a very spacious choir within (Plate XVII). The screens are of stone, traceried, panelled, and full of niches with excellent statuary on the outside towards the passage, and the inside is lined with superb tabernacle work, canopies and pinnacles of stone, decorated with colour, over the stalls. The intricacy of the sculptured foliage is amazing: the long serrated leaves of the artichoke are twisted, interlaced, passing under and over one another, turned forward and backward with extraordinary ingenuity. Every one of the great crockets and finials of the entrance pediment is a study in itself, and the artifice with which it is managed cannot be fully realized till it is examined closely from the gallery on the top of the screen.

This plan of an enclosed choir within and clear of the church walls with a passage all round it on the outside occurs elsewhere in the south of France at St Bertrand de Comminges, and in the abbey of Moissac. It is a sort of glorified version of the enclosed *schola cantorum* in the churches of St Clemente and St Maria in Cosmedin at Rome: but the screens here are lofty enough to receive the tabernacle work and the aspiring canopies of the choir stalls inside them.

It was during the Flamboyant period for the first time that civil and domestic architecture began to play an important part in the art. The day of the baronial castle was over: in the 15th century public order had begun to make private warfare obsolete. In the old castles loopholes were enlarged into spacious windows letting in light and air, and new buildings were designed without regard to military conditions. Earlier than this great civil buildings had arisen within the safe bulwarks of the wealthy trading cities of Italy and the Low Countries, the most beautiful and one of the earliest of the latter being the great Cloth Hall at Ypres, now a melancholy heap of ruin. In France and England municipal buildings of the middle ages are rare, but ROUEN, in the PALAIS DE JUSTICE, has a splendid example of Flamboyant architecture applied to a civil building. The lower storeys have fine wide open arches and windows; above these is an arcaded parapet, with pinnacles and statues, which breaks up at intervals into dormer windows, which are smothered in pediments, buttresses, pinnacles, and other devices of the style so much that the window itself can hardly be seen for the luxuriance of its surroundings. The general effect is gorgeous, but confused, and wanting in simplicity. Dormer windows are treated handsomely, but with greater sobriety and with delightful effect in the part of the château of BLOIS which was built by Louis XII and finished about 1515.

BOURGES is remarkably rich in domestic work of this period. The present Hôtel de Ville was the MAISON DE JACQUES CŒUR built by that unfortunate minister of Charles VII inside the old Gallo-Roman wall, on which the back of the building rests. The site was bought by him in 1443. A gateway, over which is the chapel, with paintings by Italian artists, admits to a courtyard, on the opposite side of which is the palace of the great financier, who housed himself with not less magnificence than the great nobles and prelates of the Church, his contemporaries. The Hôtel at Paris of the Abbot of CLUNY, now a museum, is not more important than this house of a mere commoner.

The HÔTEL CUJAS at Bourges, now a museum, is another interesting domestic building there: and in another part of the town is the so-called HOUSE OF CHARLES VII, now the Lycée. It has a handsome staircase tower with pedimented doors and windows, and little figures of guards or warders peeping out from behind imaginary shutters.

SAINT QUENTIN has a charming little HÔTEL DE VILLE, more in the manner of those in the Low Countries, and significant of the neighbourhood of the frontier. It is a very beautiful building, and has points of interest within, notably a grand fireplace with a projecting hood.

The influence of the Italian Renaissance of Roman Art was felt towards the end of the 15th century. Even earlier than that classic details begin to steal into compositions which are Gothic both in England and France. In the Flamboyant front of Rouen, built by the brothers Le Roux between 1507 and 1530, are twisted shafts with Renaissance details serving as pedestals for statues. At St Riquier there are similar semi-classic features supporting Gothic niches. In the same way Italian arabesques are introduced into the Gothic chantry of Lady Salisbury in Christchurch Priory, Hampshire. In both countries a mixed style arose where details borrowed from classic art were used in the Gothic manner and in combination with Gothic forms. For a long time these buildings may still be classed as Gothic buildings in spite of their columns, Doric, Ionic, or Corinthian, and their architraves, friezes, and cornices. Chenonceaux, Chambord, Chaumont, Fontainebleau, and Blois, are still in the main Gothic buildings free from Palladian formulae, like Kirby, Longleat, Burleigh, and Audley End in our country. The east end of ST PIERRE at CAEN (Plate XII) has no decorative feature that can be classed with any school of Gothic art: every one is supposed to be in the new fashionable style, and yet it is in all respects a Gothic construction: the windows are filled with tracery of a kind: the arches are round, but they are moulded very differently from classic work: we have the regular French *chevet*, with ambulatory and chapels like Senlis or Reims; the full Gothic construction of vaults sustained by flying buttresses springing from piers loaded with pinnacles to resist the thrusts just as at Amiens or Beauvais, and while every feature in the detail pretends to be classic, which it certainly is not, the whole system of construction, in which, and not in its decorative features, the real essence of the design consists, is as much good sound Gothic work as Amiens itself. The church of ST EUSTACHE at PARIS affords another example, and a more important one, of the same curious mixture of styles, for though there is not a single decorative feature like those of the Middle Ages, the construction itself is as absolutely Gothic as that of Notre-Dame.

Time had come, however, for the old art of the Middle Ages to die and make way for a successor. It died hard, both in England and France, as we have seen; and in a manner it never really quite died out, for its influence affected the new style in both countries, though less in France than with us. The final phase of French Gothic, though it has suffered from many detractors, is surely not the least interesting in its history. Through trial and difficulty the early men of the 10th and 11th centuries plodded on, with many a failure and set-back, till in the 12th they began to see their way to making their work sound and durable. Working ever onward, they diligently improved, and perfected finally a complete and scientific principle of construction, which they embellished with the choicest treasures of their new-found art. To this the men of the 15th century succeeded. The constructive labours of their hardy predecessors had made everything easy for them. All problems of construction had been solved for them, and all methods lay ready to their hand. When Leo X assumed the tiara he said "Poichè Dio ci ha dato il Papato, godiamolo": and so we may imagine the men of the last age of Gothic saying "Our forefathers have saved us all trouble in making our buildings, let us enjoy them." The result was the Flamboyant style in which the Gothic art of France expired in a blaze of glory.

## BIBLIOGRAPHY

It is impossible within this compass to go deeply into technical details of construction, or to illustrate as many of the monuments as would be desirable in order to make the description intelligible. I have therefore referred in the notes to works where illustrations of certain buildings may be found, and I may perhaps add that drawings of nearly every building mentioned in the text will be found in my larger works on the same subject.

T. G. J.

E.-E. Viollet-le-Duc. *Dictionnaire raisonné de l'Architecture française du XI^e au XVI^e siècles.* 10 vols. 1854–1868.
F. de Verneilh. *L'Architecture Byzantine en France.* 1851.
*The Sketch-book of Wilars de Honecort,* ed. R. Willis. 1859.
R. Phéné Spiers. *Architecture, East and West.* 1905.
Sir T. G. Jackson. *Reason in Architecture.* 1906.
—— *Byzantine and Romanesque Architecture.* 2 vols. Cambridge. 1913.
—— *Gothic Architecture in France, England and Italy.* 2 vols. Cambridge. 1915.
R. de Lasteyrie. *Architecture religieuse en France.* 1912.
C. Enlart. *Origines francaises de l'Architecture gothique.*
J. F. Colfs. *Les Écoles gothique.*

# CHAPTER X

## SCULPTURE, GLASS, PAINTING

In the development of those arts which we are to survey, there are certain moments of special importance, such as are called epoch-making, and these it will be well to name at the outset.

The first and least enduring is the Carolingian Renaissance at the end of the 8th century, which extended over the greater part of the 9th.

Then, in 1142–4, Abbot Suger gathered all the best artificers of France to cooperate in the rebuilding of his church of St Denis. Their achievement in architecture, sculpture, metal-work, and glass-painting exercised a very great influence on the generation that followed.

The reign of St Louis, 1223–64, coincides with the great epoch of church-building, and is the golden age of Gothic sculpture, painting, and glass.

Charles V, Charles VI, and Jean, Duke of Berry, whose activities extended from 1364 to 1422, were three great patrons of art and learning. Under them painting especially flourished: and, coincidently, great sculptural works were undertaken for the Dukes of Burgundy.

Of these epochs, the second, which roughly covers the years 1220 to 1280, is incomparably the most important. In it France attained an uncontested supremacy over all other races in the domain of art.

Another short general statement may be permitted before we begin our review.

In studying Greek art, it is agreed that sculpture forms the backbone of the subject. In mediaeval art it must be subordinated to architecture, to which it was in the main ancillary.

Painting in our period was feeling its way. In two departments it attained a height never since reached, namely, the illustration of books, and the making of coloured windows. This last is a very special form of art tightly restricted by limitations of material, ancillary, again, to architecture, yet partaking of the nature of painting. Its immense importance in the country and time with which we are concerned justify it in claiming a separate treatment.

There are certain other special forms of art which I have been compelled to leave entirely out of sight. The chief of these are enamelling and tapestry.

## § I. SCULPTURE

As in literature and learning we can justly speak of a Renaissance in the days of Charlemagne, so can we in the domain of the fine arts. The Carolingian period saw the production of remarkable works in painting, building, calligraphy, and, to a less extent, in what may be called sculpture.

We have, I believe, no single stone image which can be assigned to this period. There is an equestrian statuette in bronze of Charlemagne (probably), which was once a treasure of the Cathedral of Metz and is now in the Musée Carnavalet at Paris; and this, it is contended, is really a work of the 9th century. The fact that equestrian statues of Roman date were brought from Italy to Aix-la-Chapelle shows that an artist there could have found models on which to base his work. Whether this statuette was actually made in the 9th century I will not undertake to determine; but the attempt which has been made to lower its date to the 16th is pretty clearly a failure.

By far the greater part of the extant carved work of Carolingian times is in the form of ivories, mostly plaques intended to be placed on the covers of liturgical books. Of very few of these can it be confidently said that they were made in the region we call France: the great abbeys of Germany and Switzerland must be regarded as the place of origin of most of them. The traditions of both east and west have been drawn upon by the artists of these reliefs. On some we see the true Byzantine angel bearing his long cross-tipped staff, on another (the Psalter of Charles the Bald at Paris) one side transcribes into carving such a drawing as we find in the Utrecht Psalter, illustrating the text of a whole Psalm (in this case the 56th) in a single composition, while the other side shows the story of Nathan and David as it might have been pictured in the 4th century illustrated copy of the Books of Kings which we know as the Quedlinburg fragments. Both the Utrecht Psalter and the other MS. are of Italian descent. Still more strongly are we reminded of the Quedlinburg book by an ivory in the Louvre which represents the interview of Joab and Abner and the young heroes of Helkath-hazzurim (2 Sam. ii.), a subject untouched, we may say, by later art, and of no symbolical significance.

In short, the ivory-carvers were influenced very largely by the pictures in the books of their time, just as they were five centuries later. In a review of the general development of sculpture there is neither space nor necessity to say more about them.

Sculpture cannot be said to have made a real beginning before the 11th century. We do hear of images on the portals of churches in the 9th and 10th centuries, and of others (like that of St Faith at Conques) which were objects of devotion. The image of St Faith (of wood covered with metal) still exists to show how very infantine were the efforts of the first sculptors. Equally childish is the carving of a lintel dated 1020–1 at the church of St Genys-des-Fontaines (Pyrénées-Orientales), on which Christ in majesty with two angels and six apostles are represented. There is no room to dwell upon this stage of the history.

It should be realised that, until Suger's work at St Denis gave an impulse and furnished a model, that part of France which afterwards attained supremacy in this art had really nothing to show. All the best Romanesque sculpture is to be found well to the south of Paris, in Languedoc, Auvergne, Poitou, Burgundy, and Provence. It is possible for the student of style to discriminate the schools of these various regions: but upon this side of the matter I shall say little, and rather attempt to point out the great works and their broad characteristics.

When we come to deal with the 13th century we shall find that the sculptural decoration of a great church follows a prescribed plan carefully thought out. In the Romanesque period this is not the case. There is indeed a fairly constant fashion of adorning the space in the head of the arch of the principal door with a representation of Christ in majesty or the Last Judgment. And in certain districts we find a preference for a well-defined set of subjects. But unity of conception is confined at most to the western façade of the church.

Among the most famous of Romanesque sculptured façades are two in Provence, those of St Gilles, and of St Trophime at Arles (see above, p. 334, Pl. I). It has been contended that these are largely based on a study of surviving Roman sculpture and are to be regarded as the sources of the great works of the 13th century. Such is the view of the German critic Vöge: it is traversed by M. Michel, who sees in the work at St Gilles an eclectic composition, in which the single statues are adaptations from the rising school of the north and the reliefs owe their inspiration in part to the ancient Christian sarcophagi, plentiful in the district, and in part to the sculptures of Lombardy; while the Arles façade is an inferior product of the same character. In other words, the school of Provence is a decadent one. If the French view is the right one (and it seems solidly based) it is well to place these monuments on one side at the outset. They still remain (especially at St Gilles) wonders of beauty and richness: the frieze illustrating the life of Christ which surmounts the portals at St Gilles is full of interest at every point: it finds a parallel in the north on the west front of Chartres.

We turn to works of less doubtful character.

Toulouse was never a more important centre of art than during this period. The great Romanesque basilica of St Sernin (Saturninus) has in the wall of the choir-aisle at the east end certain low reliefs in marble representing Christ, angels, and apostles (one on each slab) which may be assigned to the end of the 11th century, and a tympanum of about 1125. But the great glory of Toulouse in this department was in the destroyed cloisters of some others of its churches. In these were a multitude of capitals, either historiated, that is, carved with scenes, or decorative; and a large number of them have been preserved and are now in the city museum. In their richness, intricacy, and delicacy of execution they represent the best work of the school: in subject they exemplify the curious want of system which characterises the period. The most diverse subjects from Old and New Testament and from lives of saints occur upon them. It is true that in this case we have only the capitals themselves and no clue to their original arrangement: but another case, that of the cloister of Moissac, which is intact, demonstrates the truth of the statement. Here are some of the subjects: Beheading of John Baptist, Nebuchadnezzar eating grass, martyrdom of Stephen, David and his musicians, Jerusalem, the devil chained, miracles of the Syrophenician and the Centurion; or again: Raising of Lazarus, the Beatitudes, Cain and Abel, Alexander flying in the air, David and Goliath. The capitals in the church at Vézelay or in Autun Cathedral yield similar lists. Perhaps those which remain from the destroyed church of Cluny are the most singular: a series of these, it has been shown, represents the several "tones" of Gregorian music; others show the Seasons, the Virtues, the Ages of the world.

Besides these capitals Toulouse affords certain statues of apostles from the cloister-door of St Étienne which are of extraordinary interest.

Within the sphere of influence of Toulouse, perhaps, are three works of great importance: at Moissac, Beaulieu (Corrèze) and Souillac (Lot). Besides its cloister, Moissac has a portal which was at least begun before 1115. The tympanum has Christ with the four evangelistic beasts, two angels, and the 24 Elders: and a lintel covered with wonderful decorative work. There are figures of Isaiah and St Peter on the sides of the door and the central shaft is composed of a mass of animal forms. This feature recurs in yet more curious guise at Souillac. Then, within the porch on left and right are high reliefs under arcades. Dives and Lazarus, the Annunciation, etc. are the subjects. This feature connects Moissac with Beaulieu, where the corresponding sculptures are of Daniel in the den visited by Habakkuk, and the Temptation of Christ. Beaulieu's tympanum represents the Last Judgment, and the lintel below it has magnificent monsters and decorative work. It is later than that of Moissac. Lastly, Souillac has (inside the west end of the church) its pillars composed of beasts and of the sacrifice of Isaac, and, above, a relief, flanked by two seated statues, of the famous story of the Virgin delivering Theophilus from his contract with the devil. In their vigour and raciness these Souillac carvings are as striking (though not beautiful) as any works of the time.

Other churches possess famous tympanum-sculptures. The abbey of St Faith at Conques (Aveyron) has a great Last

Judgment, notable for its many inscriptions, and for the introduction of the patron of the place, St Faith, with her church, and the fetters from which she delivered prisoners, hung up in it. There is no fineness of execution about this work. Far superior in this respect is the tympanum at Cahors (Lot), in which again the patron, St Stephen, is introduced with his story, and mingled with a composition of the Ascension.

At Vézelay (see above, p. 344, Pl. III), the most northerly of the churches with which we have to deal, the narthex has a triple portal. The date is 1132. The central door shows Pentecost: Christ in the centre is shedding from His hands rays upon the Apostles. The lintel below has reliefs which have never been satisfactorily interpreted. The statues of St John Baptist on the central shaft and of Apostles at the sides are very notable.

There is also a triple portal on the outer west wall; but in this case the sculptures have been severely restored.

Autun Cathedral is the last to be noticed. It was once rich in sculpture of the Romanesque period, of which only the tympanum with the Last Judgment, and fragments of a side-portal (a remarkable figure of Eve hiding herself in the Garden was found and is figured by M. Michel) and of a mausoleum-shrine of St Lazarus, now remain, together with a number of historiated capitals inside the church. At Autun, if anywhere, one might have expected that classical influences would show themselves in figure-sculpture, as they surely do in the architecture of the interior of the cathedral. But it is not so: Autun, says M. Michel, is here the offspring of Vézelay; and a comparison of the two tympana justifies his statement.

One work of a different class must be mentioned before we turn to another district, namely, the wooden doors of the cathedral of Le Puy, carved with scenes of New Testament story in low relief, which are accompanied by verses of which the lettering is strangely worked into monograms. It is the only monument of its kind known to me in France, but recalls the doors of S. Maria im Capitol at Cologne.

The western region remains. It is here that we note some special local features; the habit, for instance, of making the whole façade of the church exhibit a single composition. At Angoulême this is variously described as the Last Judgment and the Ascension: the latter seems to be right. Ste Croix, Bordeaux, has Christ in majesty, Prophets and Apostles: at Notre-Dame la Grande, Poitiers, lessons from the Christmas office (from a sermon ascribed to St Augustine) have been taken as the basis of a composition showing the Incarnation and its prefigurements. Here too we have recurring subjects: the triumph of Virtues over Vices, the Ten Virgins, the months and signs, and sometimes these are carved in the voussures of the arches, in a fashion of which our own Norman portals illustrate the beginnings, and which in the next century becomes extremely important. Characteristic of the churches of Poitou is also the placing in a shallow arched recess beside the portal, or higher up, an equestrian figure, sometimes called Charlemagne, but apparently in truth intended to represent Constantine. Some or all of these peculiarities are illustrated in the churches of Parthenay le Vieux, Melle, Civray, Ruffec, St Jouin-lès-Marnes, Aulnay, Argenton-Château, and not a few others.

Nothing in the development of art, any more than in any other department of human activity, comes out of the blue without preparation or harbinger; and of course the sculptural decoration of the great 13th century French churches is no more than the climax of a process which had got a long way in the 12th.

Probably if Suger's great church of St Denis had kept its western façade intact we should have seen in it the germ and more than the germ of the façade of Chartres. Its date was *c.* 1142. I speak thus abruptly of façades, for in façades and portals the flower of French sculpture is concentrated, not, as in classical times, in great single statues—cultus-images—or in groups. Lines of single statues, meant to be seen in combination, and high and low reliefs are the staple of our material.

The triple western portal comes to be the standard form: but single ones, especially in the earlier years, have also to be considered.

Taking the single portal as our unit first, we see that the following parts of it receive decoration.

On the *trumeau* or central shaft between the doors there is a statue, and on either side of this, in the splay of the doorway, are more statues on the same level. Below the feet of these are sometimes pedestals carved with relevant figures and bas-reliefs. On the jambs of the doors and sides of the *trumeau* are small figures. The head of the arch is filled in with stone, and this area, the *tympanum*, is filled with high reliefs in several horizontal bands. The recessings or voussures of the arch are filled with zones of small figures or groups.

Such is the canvas upon which the web is woven. Of the web itself much has been written. It has been rightly said that a great French church of the 13th century is a "Sum of Theology" in stone. In other words, it is evident that a definite programme underlies the scheme of sculptural decoration, and one drawn up by men who were masters of the learning of their day. Without elaborating this thesis, which is generally accepted, we will see how the different portions of a western façade with triple portals were allocated when the scheme was fully developed. But let it be noted that no single one of the statements which I am about to make is true of all the examples.

The central portal is that of Christ. He stands on the *trumeau* with the Apostles on either side.

In the tympanum is the Last Judgment: in the voussures angels and saints who witness or take part in it.

The jambs of the door have the Ten Virgins.

Of the other portals, that on the spectator's left (I name it so for convenience: it is chosen really as being on Christ's *right*) is the Virgin's. If there be a *trumeau*, she occupies it. The side statues may be those of typical figures of the Old Testament (as Abraham, Melchizedek, Solomon and the Queen of Sheba) or pairs or trios of figures representing the Annunciation, Visitation, Presentation. The tympanum shows the Death, Burial, and Coronation of the Virgin: the voussures, types of her, or incidents in her life.

The right-hand portal is that of the patron saint of the place: his effigy and those of other local saints occupy the *trumeau* and sides: his life is in the tympanum and very likely in the voussures as well.

The pedestals of the statues and lower parts of the wall may have sculptures relevant to the statues above them: or cycles such as the Story of the Creation, the Virtues and Vices, the zodiacal signs and occupations of the Months, the Seven Liberal Arts.

Above the portals is a line of statues of kings, representing the royal ancestors of the Virgin, known as a *Galérie des rois*, and formerly thought to represent kings of France. It was, by the way, a favourite fashion to identify many of the statues on churches as portraits of founders, benefactors, and contemporary worthies: in hardly any case can these interpretations be held valid.

The side portals, of the transepts or aisles, are often in importance comparable to those on the west front: but the subjects treated on them were not prescribed to the same extent. In a majority of cases, perhaps, a legend of local interest is selected for treatment. However, the evidence of Chartres, Rouen, and perhaps Troyes and Sens might suggest that it was the proper place for the Old Testament.

In the interior of the church there was always, I suppose, a rood-screen or *pulpitum* of stone (called, in France, a *jubé*) and often a stone screen separating choir from aisles (choir-enclosure). Practically all *jubés* and most choir-enclosures are gone—swept away by the Chapters of the 18th century, who preferred wrought-iron gates and grilles. Surviving fragments show that in the 13th century the Life of Christ was nobly illustrated in relief on *jubé* and choir-enclosure.

The germs of all this treatment can be seen in the 12th century. *Tympana*, single figures, on the *trumeau* or at the sides, bands of figures in the ornament of the arch; but they are sporadic and undeveloped. One element, which we have seen to be highly important in the Romanesque period, disappears into the background (though it is not wholly extinguished) in the 13th century, and that is the historiated capital.

A brief statement of the order in time of the great portals will best introduce our more detailed examination.

St Denis, 1142; gone.

Chartres (west), 1150–75; triple.

North and south transepts 13th cent., the north the earlier.

Le Mans (lateral: single), *c.* 1170; sometimes dated 1137: if correctly, a very important member of the succession.

Senlis (single), *c.* 1190.

Laon (west: triple), *c.* 1200.

Paris, Notre-Dame, *c.* 1220; most influential; one portal preserved from the earlier church and of the same workmanship as one (R.) at Chartres.

Amiens, *c.* 1230.

Reims (west), 1280; N. a little earlier.

Bourges, 1250–60 (and 16th cent.).

Slightly, but only slightly, less important are:

(Troyes, N. portal (single) of which all the imagery has gone, and only the inscriptions remain.)

Sens.

Auxerre.

Less important again, but following the form laid down:

Poitiers.

Meaux.

Bazas.

The lateral portals of Rouen, and the façade of Lyons, both deprived of their statues, but both conspicuous for their wealth of small bas-reliefs, perhaps trespass into the 14th century.

The list, I need not say, is not exhaustive: it is, however, representative.

We will now go through some of these examples, and, without entering into minute detail, set out the schemes of them.

**Chartres.** Here the retention of the earlier western portals drove the artists of the 13th century to concentrate on the northern and southern porches—for these are real porches with detached columns.

*West front:*

C. Statues: probably ancestors of the Virgin. This applies to all the three western doors.

Tympanum: Christ in glory.

Voussures: the 24 Elders, etc.

L. Statues: see above.

Tympanum: the Ascension.

Voussures: Months and Signs.

R. Statues: see above.

Tympanum: The Virgin and Child; The Annunciation, etc.

Voussures: Arts and Sciences.

Capitals, extending all across the front: Life of Christ and of the

Virgin. This is a feature we shall not meet again. The frieze at St Gilles recalls it, and there may have been borrowing of design.

Above: Gallery of Kings.

*North Porch* (see above, p. 362, Pl. VII). Entrance to central bay:

Statues relating to Samuel and David: reliefs of their lives below.

In the arch above: Creation.

C. Statues: Anne on the *trumeau*. Joachim, Patriarchs, Prophets.

Tympanum: Death, etc. and Coronation of the Virgin.

Voussures: Jesse-tree, etc.

Entrance to L. bay.

Statues: Church, Synagogue, etc.; some gone.

Reliefs: Virtues and Vices.

In the arch: Active and Contemplative Life: Heavenly Beatitudes.

L. Statues: Annunciation, Visitation, Prophets.

Tympanum: Nativity, Adoration of Magi.

Voussures: Ten Virgins, Psychomachia (Battle of Virtues and Vices), Fruits of the Spirit.

Entrance to R. bay.

Statues uncertain: local saints on R.

Reliefs: Arts and Sciences.

In the arch: Months and Signs.

R. Statues: Old Testament worthies.

Tympanum: Stories of Solomon and Job.

Voussures: Stories of Samson, Esther, Judith, Gideon, Tobit.

*South Porch:*

Detached pillars of the porch each sculptured with 24 reliefs.

From L. 1. Martyrdoms. 2, 3. Twenty-four Elders, and Virtues and Vices. 4. Confessors (scenes from their lives).

In the arches above: L. The Ten Virgins; C. Prophets and Virgins; R. Angels and Apostles.

*Portals:*

C. Statues: Christ and the Apostles.

Tympanum: Last Judgment.

Voussures: nine orders of angels.

L. Statues: Martyrs (six).

Tympanum: Story of St Stephen, continued in the voussures.

R. Statues: Confessors.

Tympanum: Stories of SS. Martin and Nicholas.

Voussures: Story of St Giles, and saints.

Statues above: Kings of Judah.

The late choir-enclosure (begun in 1514) has the Lives of the Virgin and of Christ. The *jubé* was destroyed in 1763.

**Le Mans** (lateral, single portal).

Statues: eight, ancestors of Christ.

Reliefs: Peter and Paul.

Tympanum: Christ in glory and Apostles.

Voussures: Angels, Life of Christ.

**Senlis.** The single western portal is a very remarkable work. There is a growing freedom in the statues and an emotion in the reliefs which heralds a new age.

Statues: Abraham, Moses, Simeon, St John Baptist.
Tympanum: Death, Burial, Coronation of the Virgin (said to be as early as any example of this subject).

**Laon.** All the statues are new.

C. The Virgin's door here.
Tympanum: Last scenes and Coronation.
Voussures: Jesse-tree, etc.
L. Again the Virgin.
Tympanum: Early scenes of Christ's life.
Voussures: types of the Incarnation, with inscriptions.
R. Christ.
Tympanum: The Last Judgment.
Voussures: Ten Virgins, etc.
Above, in the Towers: the Creation, and Arts and Sciences.

**Paris, Notre-Dame** (see above, p. 358, Pl. VI). The statues are largely restorations.

C. Statues: Christ and the Apostles.
Reliefs: Virtues and Vices; Months and Signs.
Jambs: Arts and Sciences.
Tympanum: Last Judgment.
Voussures: Ten Virgins; Riders of the Apocalypse, etc.
L. Statues: The Virgin, St Denis, etc.
Tympanum: Death, Burial, Coronation; Prophets.
Voussures: Jesse-tree with prophets and ? sibyls.
R. "Porte Ste Anne," *c.* 1185.
Statues: St Marcellus and local saints.
Tympanum: Virgin and Child; Early Life of the Virgin.
In the wall between C. and side-portals: Church and Synagogue.
Above: Gallery of Kings.
N. Transept: Early Life of Christ.
S. Transept: St Stephen (commemorating a demolished Church of St Stephen on this site).
Choir-enclosure: Life of Christ.

**Amiens** (see above, p. 365, Pl. X). On the whole, perhaps the best preserved of all, and the stateliest.

C. Statues: Christ, Apostles, Prophets.
Reliefs: Virtues and Vices; illustrations of the Prophets' writings.
Jambs: Ten Virgins.
Tympanum: The Last Judgment.
Voussures: Angels, Saints, etc.
L. Statues: St Firmin (patron) and local saints.
Reliefs: Months and Signs.
Tympanum: Story of St Firmin.

R. Statues: The Virgins and typical figures (Solomon, etc.).
Reliefs: illustrations of the statues; types of the Virgin.
Tympanum: Death, Assumption, Coronation.
Voussures: Angels and Elders.
Above: Gallery of Kings.
S. Transept: Statues: Virgin, St Honoratus and local saints.
Tympanum: Story of St Honoratus.
Voussures: Prophets, etc.

**Reims.** The culmination of the art in some ways: the beauty of the single statues has provoked the inquiry whether antique models were not copied here.

The tympana of the western portals are here unfortunately replaced by tracery and glazing. The reliefs are pushed down to the lintels above the doors (these are partly destroyed) and up into the gables. Supplementary sculptures occupy the angles of the towers. The principal sculpture of the Last Judgment is on the N. side of the church[1].

C. Statues: The Virgin, The Annunciation, Visitation, Presentation, Adoration of the Magi.
Jambs: Months and Elements.
Gable: Coronation.
Voussures: Saints.
L. Statues: Local saints.
Jambs: Arts and Sciences.
Gable: The Crucifixion.
Voussures: Life of Christ.
Side-buttresses: W. Face: Invention of the Cross. N. Face: St John Baptist.
R. Statues: Patriarchs and typical figures; local saints.
Jambs: Virtues and Vices.
Gable: Last Judgment.
Voussures: The Apocalypse.
Side-buttresses: W. Face: The Apocalypse.
S. Face: Life of St John Evangelist.
Above, in the Rose: Life of David, Gallery of Kings, Baptism of Christ.

There are two portals on the N.

1. Statues: St Sixtus and local saints.
Tympanum: Acts of SS. Nicasius and Remigius.
2. (Blocked) Statues: Christ and the Apostles.
Tympanum: Last Judgment.
Voussures: Ten Virgins, and Saints.
Above, in the Rose: Story of Genesis.

**Bourges** has five western portals. The statues are gone.

C. (xiii). Tympanum: The Last Judgment.
Voussures: Saints.
The Ten Virgins in the Rose above.

[1] Reims is, I think, unique in having the *inside* of the West wall (and of the S. transept wall) covered with statues in niches.

Reliefs (in spandrels of lower arcade: extending across R[1] and R[2]): Story of Genesis.

L[1] (xiii). The Virgin.
Tympanum (partly xvi): Death, Assumption, and Coronation.
Voussures (xvi): Saints.
Reliefs (xvi: extending over L[2]): Life of the Virgin and of Christ.

R[1] (xiii). St Stephen (the patron).
Tympanum: Story of St Stephen.
Voussures: Saints.

L[2] (xvi). St William of Bourges.
Tympanum: Story of St William.
Voussures: Saints.

R[2] (xiii). St Ursin.
Tympanum: Story of St Ursin.
Voussures: Saints.

The N. and S. portals are of cent. xii, preserved from an earlier church.

N. Statues: two only, female (? Queen of Sheba and Sibyl).
Tympanum: Virgin and Child, Adoration of Magi, etc.

S. Statues: Christ and six? Old Testament figures.
Tympanum: Christ in glory and Apostles.

Three more examples, of great interest, demand notice.

**Troyes.** The single portal on the N. transept has preserved its inscriptions, but its imagery disappeared at the Revolution. It was known as *le beau portail.*

Statues: probably Christ and the Apostles.
Reliefs below: said to have been from Genesis.
Tympanum: the Crucifixion[1] (not, as usually stated, the Last Judgment).
Voussures (7):

1. The Twenty-four Elders (without inscription).
2. The Church and Synagogue: the Deaths of the Apostles.
3. Sixteen prophets (incl. St John Baptist).
4. Life of Christ?
5. Ages of Man. Seven deadly sins.
6. Seven Liberal Arts. Seven Sacraments?
7. Months and Signs.

**Sens.** Statues gone.

C. Tympanum: Christ in glory and Story of St Stephen the patron.
Jambs: Ten Virgins.
Reliefs: Arts and Sciences, Months, Marvels of Creation.

L. Tympanum and Voussures: Life of St John Baptist.
Reliefs: Liberality and Avarice.

R. Tympanum and Voussures: The Virgin, Life and Death.
Reliefs: 14th cent. single figures.

Higher up in a niche on R. a broken equestrian figure.

N. Transept (xv). Voussures: The Twelve Patriarchs, Prophets, Sibyls (?).

[1] I judge by the inscription "Behold and see if there be any sorrow like my sorrow" and the rest. The prophecies also bear on the Passion.

**Auxerre.** Statues gone.

C. Tympanum: Last Judgment.
Voussures (late): Lives of the Apostles.
Below the statue-niches: Prophets?
L. Tympanum: The Virgin: Coronation.
Voussures: Life of the Virgin, Infancy of Christ.
R. Tympanum: Story of St John Baptist.
Voussures: scenes from life of Christ and of St John Baptist.

Below the statue-niches: groups of the story of David and Bathsheba; Arts in the spandrels.

Reliefs, extending across the northern half of the front: Story of Genesis, ending with Joseph.

On the southern half:
Story of Job (?) and of the Prodigal Son.
Life of David.

In a niche above on R. a large group of the Judgment of Solomon.

*North Transept:*
Tympanum and Voussures (late): Life of St Germanus of Auxerre.

*South Transept:*
Tympanum: Story of St Stephen (patron).
Voussures: Angels.

Three examples of less importance are:

**Poitiers.** Statues gone.

C. Last Judgment.
L. The Virgin.
R. St Thomas the Apostle: his acts in India.

**Meaux.** Statues gone: some, an inscription says, were sainted bishops of the place.

C. Last Judgment.
R. The Virgin.
L. St John Baptist (xv).
S. Transept: St Stephen.

**Bazas.** Statues gone.

C. Last Judgment.
Voussures: Life of St John Baptist (patron).
L. Life of St Peter.
Voussures: Genesis.
R. The Virgin.
Voussures: Jesse-tree, Months and Signs.

Of all these multitudes of statues and reliefs there are a few which have attained almost a popular renown. The two Christs of Amiens and Reims (the "Beaux Dieux"), the Virgin, Joseph, Elizabeth, and Gabriel of the central door of Reims are among these. In the latter group the memory of the great classical art is at once evoked by the Virgin and Elizabeth, while the Joseph has a really astonishing vivacity. Of the former, the Reims statue has suffered from re-touching: that of Amiens remains, perhaps, the noblest presentation of its great subject that can be seen. The St Theodore of the south porch of Chartres I should rank as the finest warrior saint before Donatello's St George.

The reliefs at Amiens tell their stories with amazing skill: that of the Vision of Isaiah is surpassing in simplicity and nobility. Some of the later Genesis series at Auxerre, particularly in the story of Joseph, recall the antique as vividly as the Reims statues. Direct borrowing of *motifs* is possible in both cases, in view of the number of Roman monuments that must still have remained fairly intact in the country: but personally I do not feel driven to suppose it.

These "appreciations," however, might be multiplied *ad infinitum*. The study of detail, intensely interesting as it is, must be subordinated here to the general scheme and conception which was paramount in the minds of the directors and planners of these great works.

The other great vehicle of expression for the sculpture of the 13th century was the tomb. And here the material is, in comparison with that which we have been reviewing, woefully scanty. The deliberate destruction wrought at the Revolution has deprived us of all but a very small fraction of the effigies in enamelled metal and in stone which were once multitudinous in the monastic and secular churches of France. The metal tombs which survive may be counted on the fingers of one hand. The children of St Louis at St Denis and the two episcopal effigies at Amiens are, I believe, the only ones of first-class importance that remain. And the rarity of stone effigies in general in French churches will surprise anyone familiar with those of England.

The custom of placing a representation of the deceased person upon the lid of his tomb was begun in the 12th century, but only tentatively. The curious marble mosaic figure of Fredegond at St Denis dates from about 1180.

It was the work of the 13th century to develop the conception of the tomb-effigy. The type chosen was not that of a corpse, but of a living person with open eyes, recumbent, gazing upon the light of the other world. An animal (commonly a dragon) couched beneath the feet, typified originally, it seems clear, the conquest of Death, of Sin, or of the lower passions. As time went on this conception became blurred, and a hound or lap-dog or beast of chase was thought equally fitting. In this effigy there was no attempt at portraiture: M. Mâle (whose whole treatment of the subject is admirable) is no doubt right in saying that the rule was to depict the dead as he would be when he rose again: all men, it was said both in East and West, would rise with bodies of the age of 33 years, as did their Lord. We do not, in France, meet with the cross-legged Crusader with his hand on his sword-hilt, so familiar to us here. Calm and beauty are the key-notes.

Besides the recumbent effigy there were bas-reliefs and statuettes upon the great tombs, illustrative, it may be, of the funeral cortége or of events in the life of the dead. Tombs at Limoges of the end of our period show the Judgment, or again patron saints. That of Dagobert at St Denis gives the legend of a vision of his rescue from the devil seen after his death. But of all the monuments that can be called sepulchral the tomb-shrine of St Stephen of Aubazine at Aubazine in Corrèze is the most perfect and beautiful work known to me. The effigy lies beneath a ridged canopy with sloping sides, upon each of which, under an arcade, is sculptured in high relief a procession of Cistercians adoring the Virgin and Child: upon one side they are on earth, on the other they are risen or rising from the dead. The triangular spaces at the ends are filled with lovely compositions of foliage and birds.

In the last quarter of the century the practice of making death-masks began, and portraiture was the direct and natural consequence.

The sculpture of the 14th century, like its architecture, is less important in France than that which preceded and that which followed it. It created no great type. Delicacy and charm it had in abundance: witness the multitudes of small reliefs of Biblical subjects, lives of saints and grotesques, which cover the pedestals of the lost statues on the N. and S. portals of Rouen and Lyons cathedrals: those of Rouen belong to the last years of the 13th century: some canopies at Lyons decorated with small figure-sculpture can hardly be surpassed for grace and richness. The beautiful reliefs on the outside of the apse at Notre-Dame of Paris are also 14th century work.

The niche-statue and the single figures of saints and Madonnas are important factors in the total output of this century. A St James the Great in the museum at Beauvais is a very striking example of the single figure.

Among the broad and general characteristics which now affected all branches of pictorial art we note the insistence on the pathetic, specially noticeable in the crucifixes. Here the suffering of the Lord is emphasised, the posture of the body is contorted, the feet are pierced by a single nail, the crown of thorns sometimes appears on the head. The very multiplication of crucifixes is an indication of this attitude of mind. It is not confined, however, to the expression of painful emotions: we see it in the added tenderness and homeliness of such subjects as the Virgin and Child. The Pietàs and Entombments, which insist still more strongly on pathos, belong to the 15th century. Of course the devotional literature of the time plays a very great part in this development, and so does the dramatic, in the form of the Passion or miracle-play: but upon this aspect of the subject it is not for me to dwell.

The names of artists—comparatively rare in earlier days—begin to be heard of in some numbers. André Beauneveu, Jean de Liège, and Jean de St Romain are among these, but it seems that we cannot safely attribute to either of these the famous figures of Charles V and his wife Jeanne de Bourbon, which, once on the portal of the Celestines at Paris, are now in the Louvre. Other portrait-statues of great excellence are to be seen on the northern tower of Amiens (*c.* 1375), in the great hall of the palace at Poitiers, and of course at St Denis, upon the tombs of Du Guesclin and Louis de Sancerre.

The portrait-statue, as we have seen, was an outcome of the tomb-sculptor's art, and this art was very prominent in the 14th century. Two innovations, destined to have a great vogue, were, according to M. Mâle, made in this period: the kneeling effigy of the dead, and the representation of him as a corpse—the *cadaver*, in which once more we see the "pathetic" tendency emerging. But apart from these there are many stately tombs—those of the Avignon popes at Avignon itself and Villeneuve-lès-Avignon, at La Chaise Dieu, at Uzeste (Landes), of prelates at Narbonne, Limoges, Comminges, Carcassonne; and there was a very large industry, centred at Paris, for the manufacture of incised tomb-slabs (corresponding to the sepulchral brass of Flanders and England, which is hardly to be found in France) which sent its wares to every part of the country.

The last years of the 14th century saw a remarkable group of works initiated at Dijon, of which considerable remains exist. It was in 1385 that Philip the Bold of Burgundy founded the Carthusian monastery of Champmol, just outside Dijon. The church of it was dedicated in 1388. In the following year we first hear of Claus Sluter, a Hollander (possibly his father was of Mainz). He is mentioned in the first instance as a carpenter, but soon he succeeds Jean de Marville as chief sculptor. Of Jean de Marville we may have a work in the statue of the Virgin on the portal of the church of Champmol: those of St John the Baptist as the Duke, St Katherine as the Duchess, may all be by Sluter.

In 1395 Claus Sluter began his best work, the great Calvary outside the church, of which the base, known as the Puits de Moïse, remains in the garden of the lunatic asylum that occupies the site of the Chartreuse. What we now see is a hexagonal base standing in the centre of a well, and bearing on its faces statues of Moses, David, Isaiah, Jeremiah, Zechariah and Daniel. They bear scrolls inscribed with prophecies of the Passion, and above their heads is a row of weeping angels. This base (which no one who has seen it will ever forget) was formerly surmounted by a great crucifix. All six statues were made by Sluter: Moses, David, and Jeremiah were set up in 1401: before his death in 1404 he had finished the others, and had designed the angels, which were carved by his nephew Claus de Werve.

This second Claus completed in 1411 another work which became a type and model—the tomb of Philip the Bold († 1404) which, with the later and less fine tomb of Jean-sans-Peur, was saved and hidden at the Revolution and—not wholly intact—is to be seen in the Dijon Museum. The particular fashion which it made popular was the placing in niches round the altar-base of the tomb of a series of figures representing the funeral cortège, and mourners—commonly called "pleureurs." These are exquisite statuettes of men (not monks or clerks) draped in funeral cloaks with deep hoods almost concealing their faces—"inky cloaks" such as survived, in a modified form, into our own day.

To complete the story of this Burgundian school let it be said that the tomb of Jean-sans-Peur, on the same lines as that of Philip, was ordered of Juan de la Huerta in 1443, and lingered on many years in the making. Antoine le Moiturier took it in hand in 1463, and it was set up in 1470.

Instances of "pleureurs" have been cited dating back well into the 14th century: but, as has been said, the tomb of Philip gave them their vogue. Throughout the 15th century they are to be found on most great tombs. They grow in importance as an element in the composition: in one splendid instance, but an isolated one, the tomb of Philippe Pot (*c.* 1480) now in the Louvre, they are life-size figures carrying the tomb-slab on which the dead man lies.

The industry of the English alabaster-carvers of Nottingham, which began some time in the 14th century and attained its zenith in the early years of the 15th, made its mark, I think, in France. Not only were the alabaster tables imported into the country in great numbers, but at least one important series, at St Seurin at Bordeaux, seems to me to owe a good deal to English influence. It illustrates the lives of St Severinus and St Martial among other subjects.

It was, finally, a sculptor trained in the 14th century, and probably at Paris, who executed the bas-relief of the Coronation of the Virgin which M. André Michel justly ranks as a masterpiece, and which stands over the portal of the Château of La Ferté-Milon (Aisne), built by Louis d'Orléans about 1400.

Something has been said of the ivories of an earlier epoch: it will be right to notice, however briefly, those of the Gothic period. It is noticeable that the great age of stone sculpture yields practically no ivories. In the late 13th century they became commoner, and in the 14th they are exceedingly numerous. We have single statuettes or even groups in the round—

Madonnas, Saints, a wonderful Deposition from the Cross (in the Louvre)—and we also have the tablets carved with reliefs and hinged together which form by far the most numerous class of the religious ivories. The subjects found on these tablets are most commonly the Virgin and Child with angels, surrounded by scenes from the early life of Christ: then came in the Passion and the Death and Coronation of the Virgin. These diptychs or triptychs were carried about in the pouches of travellers and used as objects of devotion in their chambers. They are uniformly of most skilful workmanship, but of few of them can more be said. In subject and in treatment alike there is undeniable monotony, and a visible dependence upon the works of the book-illustrators. With all their defects, however, it must be confessed that mediaeval art has not left us many more immediately pleasing productions than the better class of ivories, be they statuettes, tablets, or crosier-heads.

Ivory carving was also extensively employed for secular uses: caskets, mirror-boxes, combs, were decorated with reliefs, in which, as in the tablets, a very strictly limited cycle of subjects was represented. There were love-scenes, hunting-scenes, and scenes from romances (these last being often not easy to interpret) and the changes were rung on these *ad infinitum.*

The centre of production of the Gothic ivories of the types which have been indicated (for I leave Italy out of the question) is agreed to have been Paris. Ivories were doubtless produced elsewhere, in Germany and in England, but only a few of them can be clearly marked off as native to those countries. Imitation of the French—the Parisian—style was the well-nigh universal rule. The production went on during the 15th century, but the art was decadent, and there is no need to dwell upon it. I believe it cannot be said that at any time, early or late, the ivory-carvers exercised any appreciable influence upon sculpture in stone.

The mastery over material which had been growing throughout the 14th century increases still further in the 15th. The feats accomplished in undercutting and in the making of stone-work into filigree are surprising. Realism is also insisted upon, and enters into the treatment of sacred subjects, largely under the influence of the miracle-plays. The multiplication of guilds all over the country is an accidental factor which bears upon art, for a demand arises for images of the special saints at whose altars and in whose chapels the members made their offerings and said their devotions.

Such are a few of the marks of 15th century sculpture. In greatness of conception it cannot hold a candle to that of the 13th, but, in skill and virtuosity, it naturally surpasses it.

Little was said—there was little to say—of the architectural sculpture of the 14th century. We now see a large amount of this produced; many of the great unfinished churches receive completion of a sort or embellishment: not a few large churches are wholly the work of this age. St Wulfran at Abbeville and St Riquier near by afford good specimens of Flamboyant façades which have retained their statues, and here we see tokens of the concentration of popular interest upon a selection of saints: Adrian, Eustace, Nicholas, the three Maries. Both churches have conspicuous images of the Trinity, a feature wholly alien to the art of the 13th century. The voussure-sculptures, here and in many other places, take the form of groups under canopies, terribly difficult to decipher.

The Lives of the Apostles on the west front of Auxerre, and that of St Germain on the north, and, again, at Vienne the types (drawn from the *Biblia Pauperum* and *Speculum salvationis*) which are placed above the western portals, are notable examples. Nantes Cathedral is another church which was at one time very rich in sculpture of this pictorial type. Its statues are gone and its reliefs sadly mutilated, but the long series from Genesis which overflows the west part and, penetrating into the interior, is yet unfinished, is worth mentioning as showing a vivid interest in Bible story. Richest, best preserved, and most interesting in selection of subject is perhaps the portal of the collegiate church of St Theobald at Thann in Alsace. We sink from this by slow degrees to the horrors of the west front of Orleans.

Three great churches have preserved examples of interior sculptural decoration which cannot be omitted from any survey such as this. The choir-enclosure at Chartres tells the story of the Virgin and of Christ in a long series of groups of amazing delicacy of execution. The latest of these are of the 17th century.

Amiens has four sections of screens (there were formerly many more of the same kind) consisting of canopied reliefs. They illustrate the stories of St John Baptist, St Firmin (these two are coloured), St James the Great, and the Jewish Temple. The St Firmin screen with the beautiful effigy of the donor Adrien de Hénencourt below it is deservedly one of the most popular objects in the church. The choir-stalls at Amiens are almost unique in France in presenting hundreds of scriptural groups. They were finished in 1504. Historiated wood-carving is noticeably rarer all over the country than in Germany or even England.

The third instance is Albi: here the choir-enclosure (1473–1502) is equipped with a very complete series of patriarchs, prophets and sibyls—single figures, coloured—on the outside, and apostles inside. In these a good deal of Flemish influence is perceptible.

With these sculptures it may be allowable to class the life-size groups representing the Entombment of Christ (the most famous of which is at Solesmes). One of the earliest of these is that at Tonnerre, which is not later than 1454 and was made by Jean Michel and Georges de la Sonnette. They have all a certain interest as exercises in the expression of a particular emotion, but, as in the case of the crucifixion-scenes, only a great artist can import freshness into the scheme, once fixed.

The names of sculptors become yet more common throughout the 15th century: documents are more plentiful, and the work done for royal and secular patrons is larger in amount. But in very few cases can we couple the name of an artist with an extant work. An exception is Jacques Morel of Lyons, who died in 1459, after a very troublous life. His great work seems to have been the monument of Cardinal de Saluces at Lyons (destroyed in 1562): we still have another, the mutilated but beautiful tomb of Charles de Bourbon and Agnes de Bourgogne in the abbey church of Souvigny (Allier) which was finished in 1453. M. Michel thinks that a fine coloured sculpture of the Agony in the Garden in Rodez Cathedral may also be his.

Our concern in this review is with the development of *Gothic* sculpture: and therefore it is out of place to touch upon the beginnings of the revival of classical forms. Considered from this point of view it is to be feared that the 15th century must rank as a time of decadence, in spite of the marvellous skill of the stone-carvers, and the greater freedom attained in the portrayal of emotion and in the production of portraits. The presence of a learned guiding mind behind the design ceases to be felt: we are dealing with skilled craftsmen, not with theologians and poets. Perhaps the point finely observed by M. Mâle in the tomb-effigies of the 15th century may be taken as significant and characteristic. Their eyes are no longer open to the next world, but only closed on this.

## § II. GLASS

The statement that had long passed current among writers upon stained glass, that we possess portions of windows as old as the 11th century is now challenged, and so good a critic as M. Mâle declares that it is unsafe to regard any glass in France as older than the remains of Suger's windows at St Denis (*cir.* 1144).

Previous writers had allowed—chiefly perhaps on the authority of Richer—that a fragment of an Ascension at Le Mans might plausibly be attributed to the days of Bishop Hoel (1097) who is recorded to have given glass to his church. It was also customary to cite a figure of St Timothy in the church of Neuweiler in Alsace as possibly anterior to the 12th century—to say nothing of a few examples outside France.

It will be best perhaps not to insist upon these scanty relics. If it were possible to date them with certainty, they would be exceedingly interesting, of course: but in the absence of agreement we can afford to neglect them. We know from Richer's chronicle that there were storied windows late in the 10th century, and we may be content to acquiesce in the view that none now exist much earlier than the middle of the 12th.

Even for the 12th century the number of examples is small enough. We have a few of Suger's medallions at St Denis and records of others poorly drawn for Montfaucon's *Monumens de la Monarchie Françoise* in the 18th century. We have the western windows at Chartres, especially the Jesse-tree and the Madonna of "la belle Verrière" (N. choir aisle): fragments, including the lower part of the Ascension, at Le Mans, a Virgin and Child at Vendôme, the crucifixion-window (the eastern one) at Poitiers in which Henry II and his queen appear, and something at Angers.

In these the technique does not differ in any essential particular from that of the next century, nor does the choice of subject. We have enough remains to show that the two great types—large figures destined for the upper windows, and medallions to fill the lower windows—were both in use.

There were also grisaille windows in which colour was sparingly, if at all, employed, and which contained no figures but only decorative designs. These were used, perhaps invented, by the Cistercians, whose objection to pictures is well known. The earliest extant examples are at Aubazine (Corrèze).

Very probably, after St Denis, Notre-Dame de Paris received great accessions of stained glass. Its clerestory was filled with figures of bishops by 1182: Le Vieil, who wrote on the making of stained glass in 1768, tells us what happened to it:

> On comptoit encore à Paris, il y a 40 ans au plus, au rang des monuments de la Peinture sur verre du 12e siècle quelques anciens vitreaux dans le haut du chœur de l'Église de Paris, dont j'ai démoli en 1741 les deux derniers, pour les remplir de vitres blanches.

A little before this he speaks of a window given to the church of Paris by Suger:

> Dont quelques parties qui avoient été conservées dans un des vitreaux de la galerie du chœur, représentoient, très-grossièrement à la vérité, une espèce de triomphe de la Ste Vierge, mais qui ont été démolies depuis peu.

When we add to the deliberate removals of glass by the legitimate authorities the wholesale demolition of buildings at the Revolution, we need not be surprised if the relics of 12th century glass, never, I suppose, very plentiful, are now so very rare.

In the churches which weathered the storm there was no such systematic breaking of windows as took place in England in the Civil Wars, and so we find a large number of buildings which have kept their original equipment of glass practically intact.

Such, in fact, is the abundance of old glass in France, and so great, moreover, are the difficulties which beset the comparative study of it, that much still remains to be found out about its pedigree and relationships. Especially is this true of the 13th century. We have few dated windows, few names of artists: comparison of windows in different churches is hard, because reproduction of the originals in photography is hard, and faithful tracings or engravings are few.

A good photograph can be made of a 16th century window or of one of any period which has large figures; but many of the medallion windows of the 13th century are so placed, or are in such a condition, as to defy the camera.

Yet a certain amount of comparison has been done: and the fact seems to emerge clearly that Chartres in the early years of the 13th century was the *foyer* of the manufacture and designing. And Chartres is linked up with St Denis, for, as M. Mâle points out, in the Chartres window which tells the story of Charlemagne and Roland several medallions are identical in design with some formerly at St Denis, which are engraved by Montfaucon. Further, he finds identity of decorative design in the borders of windows at Chartres, Sens, and Canterbury, and of subjects and treatment at Chartres, Bourges, Tours, Le Mans, while a window at Rouen is actually signed by Clemens Vitrarius Carnotensis. Chartres, then, was for a time the diffuser of this art over northern France and England (at least, Canterbury). We have seen how carefully thought out was the plan of the Chartres sculptures. We find the same quality in some of the windows which Chartres supplied to other churches: they illustrate the correspondence of the Old Testament with the New (here following a St Denis model) or they interpret the Parable of the Good Samaritan or portray that of the Prodigal Son. The scheme of some of the Biblical windows at Canterbury (mostly now destroyed) testifies to like learning: but I hesitate to attribute all this to Chartres influence, for I see reason to believe that it was a specially English habit to elaborate types and antitypes.

The Chartres influence was not confined to medallion (or narrative) windows: the large figures of the clerestories appear also to have been made there. To the subjects of these we will return when we come to consider the schemes of the decoration.

M. Mâle distinguishes one school of glass as independent of Chartres in this first half of the 13th century, and that is at Lyons.

The cathedral windows there show similar technique and colouring, no doubt, but a different iconographical tradition, with eastern connexions. For example, St John the Evangelist is bearded, and the Virgin at the Annunciation is spinning. These are Byzantine traits.

In the middle third of the 13th century Chartres ceases to hold its dominant position. The glaziers of Paris are at work on the Sainte-Chapelle (finished by 1248) and on many churches in the city and neighbourhood, even possibly as far off as Clermont-Ferrand. It becomes increasingly difficult to mark out relationships and spheres of influence.

The rapidity of production had effects not wholly favourable upon the product. The decorative borders became less interesting, and, M. Mâle adds, an excessive use of violet is noticeable. Still, the effect is one of great splendour.

Experiments in the use of grisaille glass combined with colour are not unfrequent in the latter part of the 13th century. Medallions, single figures, and even groups of figures are set on a background of opaque white glass.

The 14th century, while giving us some few really exquisite works, is of less interest than the 13th and the 15th. It discards narrative windows and substitutes for them rows of single figures under canopies. This feature, of the canopy, now attains great, and, I think, excessive importance. The whole fashion was more or less dictated by the rich stone tracery which now filled the windows.

The invention of a new colour, the yellow stain, and the growth of a liking for white glass are two factors which characterise the glass of the 14th century.

The painters relied for their best effects upon delicacy of drawing, and moderation in the use of strong colour. Their work may be seen at its best perhaps in the clerestory of Évreux Cathedral, where one window, dated 1400, appears to me to be one of the loveliest in the whole range of the art. Its composition is of the simplest—adorers presented by patron saints to the Virgin and Child—and it is almost wholly silver-white with small admixture of blue and ruby.

The 15th century retains the single figure and canopy, of

course, but as time goes on it reverts to the narrative window, sometimes disregarding wholly the limitations of the stone mullion and tracery, and spreading a single picture over several lights: sometimes filling each light with small square panels illustrating successive scenes, and inscribing the explanation under each. This particular form of narrative window attains its perfection in the first quarter of the 16th century, and at that point—before the introduction of enamel-glass—we will leave the survey of the art.

As in other departments, so here, we witness the emergence of individual artists whose names we can couple with existing works: such are Enguerrand Leprince (Jesse-tree, etc. at St Étienne, Beauvais), Jean Cousin (Sens, Fleurigny, etc.), the Pinaigriers (St Étienne-du-Mont at Paris, etc.). The names of many more *peintre-verriers* are known, especially at Troyes, and much of their work remains there: Paris can also give us many names, but little to show for them.

A little may now be said of the subjects of windows and of their placing in the churches. Let us suppose a church consisting of nave, aisles, transept, and apse with radiating chapels, and retaining its glass of the 13th century. Its clerestory will be filled with single figures, as has been said. In the choir there are likely to be the Apostles with clauses of the creed and the Prophets with corresponding prophecies. The apse has the Virgin, Christ, the patrons. The bishops of the place and its own saints may extend into the nave. The great windows of the transept may be roses; so may that at the west end. If so, they contain such compositions as the Last Judgment, Christ and the angelic hierarchy, the Arts and Sciences, the Months and Signs, Winds, Seasons, Elements, the Ten Commandments. So far for the upper windows. For the triforium, if it be glazed, as it is in some few churches, no rule can be laid down. The lowest range of windows, usually single lights, will be narrative windows filled with figured medallions, lozenges, quatrefoils, in various combinations, to which the iron work that frames the glass will be made to correspond. In the choir the easternmost chapel is the Virgin's, and her life and the Jesse-tree and the early life of Christ will be there.

The other apsidal chapels have their several patron saints

whose legends we expect to find in the windows. The portions of the choir aisle walls which are not interrupted by chapels will have glass of more general significance—types of Christ, the Prodigal Son, the Good Samaritan, Dives and Lazarus, the story of Joseph, in no settled order. Those in the nave aisles have single stories which, again, are not subject to any principle of arrangement: an Old Testament history and the story of an obscure local saint may be next door to one another. Many of these narrative windows were the offerings of guilds or crafts, and it was customary for the donors to mark their gift by representing, at the bottom of the window, persons exercising the particular craft or trade—tanning, carpentering, forging of metal, or weaving of cloth. The individual donor will also appear, of course: in the large upper windows we often see him holding a model of his gift in his hands, and his armorial bearings will be features of immense importance from the decorative point of view. In the later centuries (to digress for a moment from the proper theme of this paragraph), the element of the donor and his arms tends to usurp a larger and larger share of the window space (commonly in the form of his presentation to the Virgin by his patron saint), while the purely religious subject will be relegated to the small tracery lights.

Of the churches which have preserved their 13th century glass Chartres is the first in order: both upper and lower windows are filled with it. Bourges comes next. Le Mans (choir), Auxerre (choir), Châlons-sur-Marne cannot be omitted from the list. The Sainte-Chapelle at Paris is an instance of smaller compass: it has suffered greatly from restoration and other disasters.

For the 14th century Évreux affords the most beautiful examples.

For the 15th there is a good deal at St Ouen (Rouen), at Le Mans, at Évreux (Lady Chapel); Ambierle and Eymoutiers are two examples of churches almost wholly filled with glass of this time. For the very last years of the century I know nothing finer than the great storied windows of the nave clerestory at Troyes. Perhaps the most beautiful of all 15th century windows is one in the chapel of Jacques Cœur on the north side of Bourges.

The first quarter of the 16th century offers a multitude of fine examples: the minor churches of Troyes, the cathedrals of Sens and Moulins (Allier), the church of St Florentin (Yonne), that of Montmorency near Paris, and the chapel of Champigny-sur-Veude (Indre et Loire) would be universally acknowledged as of first-class interest in this regard. And to these I would add the splendid range of windows in the choir of Auch (Gers), finished and signed by Arnaut de Moles in 1513.

Of the subjects of some sets of windows in each of these periods I must take such account as was done in the case of sculpture.

At Chartres the three western windows (12th cent.) have respectively the Jesse-tree, the early, and the later life of Christ. Above them (13th) is a Rose of the Last Judgment. The north transept Rose is of the Virgin. The great lights below it have St Anne and four typical Old Testament figures with contrasts, e.g. David and Saul, Melchizedek and Nebuchadnezzar. The south Rose is of the Christ of the Apocalypse with the Beasts and Elders: below it are the four major prophets carrying the four evangelists. The clerestory has in the main single figures of Old and New Testament worthies, and of saints, interrupted occasionally by subject windows with a few pictures in them.

The lower range of windows are practically all narrative-windows. Without giving the whole list a few samples may be taken to show the apparent want of system. In the north side of the nave, beginning from the west, we find in successive windows: the story of Noah, of St Lubin, of St Eustace, of Joseph, of St Nicholas; then a type window of Old and New Testament, the Prodigal Son, St Laurence (the Ten Virgins—destroyed), an unidentified legend, St Nicholas again—there is yet a third history of him farther on—St Thomas the Apostle, St Julian the Hospitaller, etc. etc. The whole number of existing windows of this type is 39.

Taking a similar glance at Bourges, and omitting notice of glass later than the 13th century, we find in the upper windows of the choir (of which there are here two rows—Bourges has double aisles and no transepts) Apostles and Prophets, the Virgin, St John Baptist, St Stephen: the Virgin, Christ as Judge, SS. Stephen and Laurence, sainted bishops of Bourges. The windows of the nave are in grisaille with small roses at the top containing usually pairs of figures of saints.

In the lower row, in the ambulatory and chapels of the choir, beginning from the N.W.: The Parables of the Rich Fool and Dives and Lazarus: chapel with SS. Mary of Egypt, Nicholas, Mary Magdalene: Invention of St Stephen, the Good Samaritan: chapel with SS. Denis, Peter and Paul, and Martin: The Prodigal Son, type-window: Lady Chapel with late glass: The Last Judgment, the Passion: chapel with SS. Laurence, Stephen, and Vincent: the Apocalypse, St Thomas the Apostle: chapel with SS. James the Great, John Baptist, John Evangelist: Joseph. Here we see that the windows in the chapels tell the stories of particular saints, and the intermediate ones (with exceptions) are devoted to Biblical subjects.

It is easy to exceed in this drawing up of lists: but one more favourite must be allowed a place: that is, Auxerre. Here the windows suffered a good deal in 1567 from the Huguenots, who knocked out the lower parts of a good many of them. There has also been displacement of medallions; whole windows have been redistributed piecemeal. Here again we take account only of the choir with its 13th century glass.

Upper range: the windows are surmounted by roses, one of which has the Virtues and Vices and another the Arts. The main figures are of our Lord, Apostles, Prophets, patron and local saints.

Lower range: narrative windows. Creation (part): mixed, SS. Peter, Martin, Germanus (these medallions fill two windows); Life of David; St Mammes; Creation; Noah, Abraham, Lot; Joseph; St Margaret; St Andrew; Samson (called *Sensum Fortin!*) + Invention of St Stephen; St Laurence; Theophilus; St Eustace + parts of Adam and Eve, Moses, St James; St Nicholas; Prodigal Son; St James + the Apocalypse and St Eligius; St Nicholas continued + Apocalypse, St Eligius, St John; St Mary of Egypt + St Vincent; St Mary Magdalene + St Vincent; St Peter, St Vincent, and miscellaneous panels; St Katherine.

An interesting feature here is the large amount of Old Testament history which was represented. The same is the case in the very difficult windows of Poitiers cathedral, and also in the Sainte-Chapelle. The sculptures of Auxerre, we have seen, were also very full of Old Testament subjects.

We must pass to the 14th century, and here we find ourselves among votive windows and single figures of saints. The interest shifts from the subject-matter to the drawing, and to the personalities of the donors, and their heraldry. And the same is true in great measure of the windows of the early part of the 15th century. To catalogue these in any given church would be rather tedious. Perhaps St Ouen at Rouen may be allowed to form an exception, for here the clerestory contains, in glass of the 14th and 15th centuries, a continuous line, running all round the church from N.W. to S.W., of Old Testament, New Testament and Christian characters, a scheme which shows that directing care which we associate with the earlier times.

In our last period (*c.* 1480–1530) we return to the narrative window and occasionally find an iconographical scheme governing a series of windows, as in the Lady Chapel at Évreux and in the choir of Auch. We will glance at two or three examples.

At Troyes the nave of the cathedral has very large clerestory windows and a glazed triforium filled with magnificent pictures of the last years of the 15th and first of the 16th century by men whose names are recorded, and some of whom glazed the south transept at Sens. The subjects of the histories are as follows: on the south side of the nave beginning from the east, twelve saints by Verrat and Godon: a Jesse-tree on a glorious ruby ground by Lyénin: next, the Prodigal Son; Joseph; Daniel: on the north St Peter; Tobit and Tobias; Job; St Sebastian; the Story of the Cross, and the Wandering Jew by Verrat.

Next I will take the transepts of Sens. South transept, east side, Jesse-tree with prophets, Sibyls and types of the Incarnation; St Nicholas. South Rose, the Last Judgment; below it, St Stephen. West side: Invention and Translation of St Stephen. These are by Troyes glaziers. North transept, east side: Story of Jacob and Joseph; Archbishops of Sens. North Rose, Christ in glory; below it, appearances of Gabriel to Daniel, Zacharias, the Virgin; Michael overthrowing anti-Christ. West side, Story of Abraham; local saints.

Third, the church of St Florentin (Yonne): in the choir ambulatory and apse are these histories, beginning from N.W.: St Julian the Hospitaller, the Apocalypse, St John Baptist (two windows), St Nicholas, St Florentinus, St Martin (east), the Creation, Emblems of the Virgin. The clerestory windows, which are later, have the Passion, one scene in each window. The narrative windows, which are of *c.* 1525–32, are some of the brightest and most pleasing in France.

Lastly the choir ambulatory and chapels of Auch. These were done by Arnaut de Moles between 1507 and 1513. In these eighteen windows there is a series of patriarchs beginning with Adam, prophets, Sibyls, and Apostles. Most of the windows have small scenes at the bottom, illustrating something in the life of the figure above. Thus the sixth window has Moses, the Libyan Sibyl, and Enoch; and below are the Burning Bush, the Sibyl and Octavian, and the Translation of Enoch: the ninth has Caleb, St Bartholomew, Obadiah: below is the flaying of St Bartholomew: in the tracery are SS. Mary Magdalene, Katherine, Barbara, Apollonia, and Lucy. The prominence given to the Sibyls, who also figure in the carved work of the stalls, is a notable feature here. It is only in late works that we find the whole set of twelve: a single Sibyl may be seen here and there in the 13th century, as at Laon. The Renaissance, when Lactantius began to be popular again, brought them forward: his works are full of quotations from them.

Some of the best known windows of the early part of the 16th century are those which depict allegorical subjects: the Triumph of Christ, the Ship of the Church, and so on. These are in spirit as well as in actual date products of the Renaissance, and do not fall within my scope.

## § III. PAINTING

The remains of mediaeval painting in France, as elsewhere, fall into two main categories: those intended to adorn buildings, namely mural paintings and easel pictures, and those which illustrate books. At some periods we find that the same artists employed themselves on both branches of the art.

The book-paintings form an infinitely larger and completer series than the other. It is mainly upon them that we depend for our knowledge before the 16th century. All manner of accidents have befallen the mural paintings in churches, palaces, and castles. The buildings have been dismantled or their walls scraped or whitewashed. The easel pictures, altar-pieces, and so on, never so numerous as in Italy, have perished in wars of religion and in revolutions. Of this class of objects some few, no doubt, await discovery; but they can be only few. Of mural paintings many must still lie hid under the whitewash in small provincial churches; but it is not likely that any of these will prove to be absolutely novel in character or of first-class value as works of art.

I shall deal first with the mural and easel pictures.

**Mural and easel pictures.** We have nothing remaining from the age of Charlemagne in this department. Among the works of the Carolingian poets there are many *tituli*, inscriptions in verse intended to be inscribed upon wall-paintings: but the paintings are gone. Those of St George's church at Oberzell on Reichenau are of the end of the 10th century, and are not by any stretch of language to be called French; but they are practically the oldest we have, and it is likely that the decorations which we read of in French churches were very similar to them. These paintings represent scenes of the Gospel history, and do not, naturally, differ in any essential from the illustrations in the books of the time. They represent the brief renaissance, as it is not unjustly called, which took place under the Ottos.

The first monument which France proper has to show is the cycle of paintings, dating from some time not early in the 11th century, which decorates the great abbey church of St Savin-sur-Gartempe (Vienne), east of Poitiers. The greater part of this is fairly well preserved, and is all reproduced in a folio by Prosper Mérimée. In the western porch, below, are scenes from the Apocalypse: above is the Passion, now very faint. The nave roof has the most interesting series, the Old Testament history from the creation to Moses, unhappily with considerable gaps. The choir and chapels contain mostly single figures, of Christ, Apostles, and saints; in the crypt is the story and passion of the Saints Savinus and Cyprianus, who are patrons. For this last cycle at least the artist had no ancient model to follow: for the Bible pictures he might have had, and those of the Apocalypse in particular show resemblances with the tradition that was current later on and can be traced back to a quite early date. The technique of the paintings is simple: few colours are the staple; yellow, brown-red, white, and green: blue is very rare.

The system, says M. Mâle, is closely allied to that of the Byzantine painters as handed on to the West by "Theophilus" in his treatise on the arts; but there is no reason to look upon the designs of the pictures as Greek. We do find definite borrowings from Byzantine art in other parts of France, but not here.

The west and centre of France possess a good many other relics of painting of the 12th century. It was a very widespread fashion to represent Christ in majesty, with the Apostles, on the roof of the apse; fragments of some such composition are probably the commonest in these regions as in others. More peculiar are the remains of the Psychomachia or Battle of Virtues with Vices; most curious among those cited by M. Mâle is the mystic marriage of St Katherine with Christ, a subject we associate with late mediaeval and Renaissance times. It occurs —for the first time—in the apse of the church at Montmorillon (Vienne). Biblical cycles seem uncommon, but there are remains of one from Exodus in the desecrated church of St Julian at Tours.

The mural paintings of Le Puy and its district have received minute attention at the hands of M. Léon Giron. It is here that we find the blue backgrounds characteristic of Byzantine art, and also certain Byzantine schemes, notably that of the Transfiguration. There is a fresco of this in Le Puy Cathedral which shows the Greek scheme exactly, our Lord in a mandorla with five rays proceeding from Him, and a crouching Apostle in front: the two others at the sides, Peter speaking. The same tradition, by the way, is followed in a western window at Chartres (12th century).

If the great church of Cluny, so needlessly and cruelly destroyed in the early years of the 19th century, had been allowed to stand, we should have seen in it and in the refectory of the abbey a series of paintings of great importance. Nothing is left there, but M. Mâle refers to the church of Berzé la Ville, within Cluny's sphere of influence, as possessing paintings (the legend of St Blasius) which may serve as samples of the Cluny style. These I have not seen.

It remains to be said that neither in the South nor in the North are there sufficient specimens of wall-painting to merit description here. But it will be allowed that the Bayeux tapestry affords an idea of the kind of design which would be followed in the wall-decorations of a great castle hall in Normandy.

In sum, there is enough painting of the Romanesque period to show that it was a normal part of church decoration and that it had attained a considerable degree of excellence.

In the 13th century, when book-decoration was at its very best, there is a singular dearth of mural painting. The fact is that the artists who might have produced it had all their energies absorbed in the designing of stained glass. Interest is shifted from the wall to the window. It is true that colour decoration was employed, sometimes very extensively, in the interior of churches, for roofs, walls, columns, and imagery. The Sainte-Chapelle is a famous example. Figure-subjects were introduced into this decoration: but they were subsidiary to the general effect. It is therefore the fact that no mural painting of transcendent excellence belonging to the golden age of art in France can be cited. Some interesting samples of secular pictures have survived. They illustrate romances and sports. Such are the paintings at the Château de Saint-Floret (Puy-de-Dôme).

We have to pass to the middle of the 14th century before we meet much that is germane to our purpose. The oldest easel picture in France is probably the portrait of King John of France now in the Bibliothèque Nationale. It may be the work of the king's favourite painter, Girard d'Orléans, who accompanied him in his English captivity. For we now begin to hear of names of artists. Girard d'Orléans (*fl.* 1361) did important works, including a history of Julius Caesar, at the Château Vaudreuil, work which was finished by Jean Coste. For Charles V histories of Charlemagne and of Theseus were painted at Paris, as well as other wall-decorations representing *verdures* or landscapes of a sort. When we see the paintings, uncovered not long ago in a room of the papal palace at Avignon, of people gathering fruit, fishing, etc., we are reminded of these, and we suspect Italian influence, for all the paintings at Avignon, sacred and secular, are by Italian hands.

The patronage of Charles V and his circle attracted painters from many quarters. Some of the best, e.g. André Beauneveu and Jean or Hennequin de Bruges, came from Flanders. This latter was the man who in 1375 designed with the help of an illustrated manuscript the existing tapestries of the Apocalypse in the cathedral of Angers. Of Beauneveu we have no work remaining except in manuscripts. The most beautiful thing of the period (it is dated between 1364 and 1377) is the altar-frontal of silk with drawings of the passion and portraits of Charles V and queen Jeanne de Bourbon (at the Louvre) which is known as the *Parement de Narbonne,* and which M. le Comte P. Durrieu would like to attribute to Jean d'Orléans.

Charles VI and Jean Duke of Berry were as active patrons of painting as of sculpture and building, and so were the great nobles about them. Inventories tell us of many easel pictures and altar-pieces, and the names of the men who painted them. The Dukes of Burgundy who employed Claus Sluter and the rest on the sculptures of the Chartreuse of Champmol, employed Jean de Beaumetz, Melchior Broederlam, Jean Malouel, Henri Bellechose to paint pictures for the cells of the monks. Portions of an altar-piece by Broederlam are at Dijon: a picture of the houseling and martyrdom of St Denis attributed to Malouel and to Bellechose is in the Louvre. But the relics, it must be said once more, are very scanty. A work which has been assigned to a French artist of this time (before 1399) is the famous Wilton diptych representing Richard II of England and his patron saints before the Virgin: but English criticism contests this. Certainly French, however, is a lovely drawing on vellum of the death, assumption, and coronation of the Virgin (in the Louvre), which seems likely to be a design for a large wall painting.

Mural paintings in churches become commoner in the 15th century in France, just as they do in England; and, as in England, they are usually rather rough productions. A good typical example are those in the Old Cathedral at Digne (Basses-Alpes) where the N. wall of the nave has a large Last Judgment, combined with a set of Virtues and Vices in an arcading, the Vices being in the lower row, with a chain connecting their necks. Of greater merit is the Dance of Death at La Chaise Dieu (Hte Loire), parts of which are figured by Mâle. A painting at Chauvigny (Vienne) of Christ helped by all sorts and conditions of men to bear His cross is interesting from its subject. Better known is the painting of the Liberal Arts in the Chapter-house at Le Puy, and those of the Sibyls (1506) at Amiens, but these carry us into the domain of the Renaissance.

The painters of separate pictures, on the other hand, assume very great importance as the 15th century goes on. It is only of late years that the discrimination of French from Flemish pictures of that age has been seriously taken in hand; for the influence of the van Eycks and their followers was very strong, and earlier critics were not unnaturally content to label as Flemish anything that was not obviously Italian. But justice is now done to the French primitives, and the works of Enguerrand Charonton, Jean Fouquet, and the Maître de Moulins—to name but three out of a considerable number—are recognised and honoured. And besides pictures which can be definitely assigned to this or that master, there are in the galleries of Europe a good many works undoubtedly of the French school of 1450–1500 which at present remain anonymous. To traverse rapidly the ground so admirably covered in the chapter on painting in the *Dawn of the French Renaissance* seems wrong: it may just be recorded here that, of the artists I have mentioned, the principal work of Charonton is a picture at Villeneuve-lès-Avignon, variously christened at different times the Trinity, or the Coronation or Triumph of the Virgin. It was painted in 1453–4 and we have the contract for it, in which very minute details are prescribed to the painter; and he has followed out his orders carefully. The picture has a superficial resemblance to Dürer's Trinity at Vienna. Fouquet we shall meet again as a miniaturist: all the best work of his that we have was done in books, but there are also a very few pictures—all portraits—attributed to him, and he is known to have designed mural paintings of great merit at Tours, his home, as well as tapestries (of the story of Troy, etc.), a few of which exist. The Maître de Moulins takes his designation from a triptych at Moulins Cathedral, which is his best work: three or four other pictures are assigned on the evidence of style to his hand.

**Pictures in Books.** Probably the two earliest manuscripts containing pictures which have been assigned by anyone to French artists are the Pentateuch of Tours and the Gospels of St Augustine's of Canterbury.

The former is an uncial MS. of the 7th century with a number of curious full-page illustrations; but the last pronouncements on its provenance make it either Italian or Spanish. The latter (Corp. Chr. Coll., Cambridge, 286), of near the same date, has two full-page paintings; it, again, is more likely to be of Italian than of French origin.

The few 7th and 8th century books which are undoubtedly of French origin and contain ornament (e.g. an Orosius at Laon, and the Sacramentary of Gellone at Paris, *cir.* 750) are infantine in execution; and they have no real pictures, but symbolic forms, and initials composed of fish and birds. We have to pass to the 9th century and the age of Charlemagne before we can speak of paintings in books to any purpose. Then we do find Bibles, Gospel-books, and Sacramentaries with large frontispieces and elaborate initials. Some of the earliest of these were produced at Tours in the abbacy of Alcuin; but it is not possible to say that his English nationality influenced the style of the pictures in them. Rather we detect an attempt to revive and adapt classical models in the figures, and to use Celtic (and sometimes Byzantine) patterns for the initials. Ireland, so marvellously skilful in purely decorative work, could furnish no help in the other department.

Three great Bibles of the beginning of the 9th century are reckoned as Tours productions: those of the British Museum, (*add.* 10546), of Zürich, and of Bamberg: two more of *c.* 850–60, the Bible of Charles the Bald at Paris, and that of St Paul's at Rome, the latter written and perhaps painted by one Ingobert, represent the later work of the school, as also do the Autun Sacramentary (at Autun) and the Golden Gospels of Soissons, (Bib. Nat. lat. 8892) to which some award the palm among all Carolingian books. But it is ill enumerating the score or more of sumptuous manuscripts which remain to attest the vigour and skill of the artists of that age both from Tours, from Metz and its district, and from the great German abbeys, which, after all, furnish the greatest number and some of the very finest examples.

One group of books however must be dwelt upon. The Utrecht Psalter is written in uncials and contains outline drawings illustrating the text of each Psalm. These drawings closely resemble the Anglo-Saxon pictures of the 10th century in their peculiar rapid lightness of style.

This Psalter was for a long time in England, probably at Canterbury, and copies or imitations of it, undoubtedly English, exist; one is the Harley MS. 603 of the second half of the 10th century, another the Eadwine Psalter at Trinity College, Cambridge, written certainly at Christ Church, Canterbury, early in the 12th century. It has been shown independently by Durrieu and Goldschmidt that the Utrecht Psalter is closely connected with a group of books done in the diocese of Reims in the 9th century (816–845), and most likely at the abbey of Hautvillers. The principal representative of this group is the Gospels of Archbishop Ebbo of Reims, now at Épernay. Its system of illustrating the Psalms is paralleled in more than one French Psalter (one at Troyes, one at Oxford, Douce 59), as well as on an ivory on the Psalter of Charles the Bald already mentioned. It derives from an older tradition, but it is not a direct copy of a single ancient archetype.

There has been an inclination to regard this Utrecht Psalter as the parent of the characteristic Anglo-Saxon school of drawing: but this is a doubtful proposition. The best part of a century separates the Psalter from its earliest copy (Harley 603), and so far no continuous chain of connexion between the two periods or schools has been brought to light.

However this school of Reims of the 9th century must be regarded as one of the most remarkable of its time, both in itself and in the influence which it did undoubtedly exercise in at least one English centre.

The object of this review is to emphasise the great periods in the development of the art; and with this in view we are justified in passing over the 10th, 11th, and most part of the 12th centuries with hardly a word of comment. Broadly speaking it seems that France has very little of first-rate interest to show in these centuries, even in the early part of the 12th, in comparison with England; and that English influence is perceptible in the works produced in the great northern abbeys such as St Bertin (at St Omer). A Psalter at Boulogne with beautiful small pictures in the initials, done at the very beginning of the 11th century, deserves to be singled out, and so does the great

Bible of Souvigny (at Moulins) of the 12th century, which contains frontispieces to several of the books that are comparable to those in the Winchester and Lambeth Bibles. The most famous picture-book of this period, the *Hortus Deliciarum* of Herrade of Landsperg (burnt at Strasburg in 1870) must be reckoned to Germany rather than France. In it the borrowings from Byzantine books are most noteworthy.

In the same way the chief product of the South must be reckoned to Spain: this was a series of elaborately illustrated copies of the commentaries of Beatus on the Apocalypse and of Jerome on Daniel, which reproduce with slavish faithfulness the pictures of an archetype that was doubtless Spanish.

But towards the end of the 12th century a new era opens. One of the greatest of all pictured books must be assigned to the years about 1200. This is the Psalter of Queen Ingeburge, now at Chantilly with the rest of the collection which the Duc d'Aumâle bequeathed to the Institute of France. It bears such marked traces of English influence that some have claimed it as an English work: but they are not likely to be right. It is a Psalter of the English type, no doubt, with pictures of Bible history prefixed to it; but that its scribes and painters were French need not seriously be questioned. On the other hand, a somewhat earlier Psalter which afterwards belonged to St Louis and is now at Leyden may be safely regarded as English.

It is in the Psalters of the first half of the 13th century that we can most easily trace the rise of the art to its highest point. The Psalter being the one book of devotion which the laity might be expected to own at this period, the best available artists were employed in the adorning of it, as, in the later 14th century and all through the 15th, they were employed upon the books of Hours of the Virgin. It was the custom, a custom of English origin, as I believe, to prefix to the Psalter a series, longer or shorter, of illustrations of Bible history. In the Old Testament, Genesis and the life of David were most copiously illustrated; in the New, the early life of Christ, the Passion, the Death of the Virgin, and the Last Judgment; less commonly, the ministry of our Lord. Effigies of saints were added to these cycles, varying with the particular surroundings and devotions of the person for whom the book was made. It is in these pictures that we find our chief material.

M. Haseloff has pointed out, rightly, as I think, that in the Psalters from 1220 onwards the influence of the prolific craft of the glass-painters is perceptible, and that in the same way about 1250 the influence of architecture and sculpture replaces that of glass. The pictures are arranged in a series of medallions on the page, as in a window, or they are set under architectural canopies. The former is the case in a Psalter in the Rylands Library (Lat. 22), the latter in the Psalter of St Louis (Bib. Nat. lat. 10525) and in its sister-book that belonged to Isabel of France (?) and has recently, and most fortunately, been secured for the Fitzwilliam Museum, Cambridge: two books which represent the best achievement of their time.

There is another series of pictures, long in the Phillipps collection at Cheltenham, and now in that of Mr Pierpont Morgan, which cannot be omitted in any survey, however compressed, of French miniature art. In its present form it is a fragment of rather more than 40 leaves, consisting wholly of Bible pictures (Creation to near the end of David's life) with short Latin rubrics written in an Italian hand. The pictures are undoubtedly French, probably by more than one painter. He who illustrated the Books of Samuel is an artist of very great power and imagination. Most of his compositions must be quite original, for he portrays many incidents in the story which are quite outside any traditional cycle. His observation and his *verve*, coupled with his feeling for colour and his wonderful touch, give him a place by himself in the line. These pictures were very probably intended to form part of a stately Psalter. A reproduction of one leaf (at Paris) may be found in Vitzthum's book *Die Pariser Miniatur-malerei*.

All these great books are Parisian. Paris becomes the centre of this, as of other arts, in the first quarter of the 13th century, and retains its supremacy until well into the 15th.

The number of books which its many *ateliers* turned out is astonishing: particularly active were they in the production of small Bibles, few of which contain really important ornaments, though the best excel in beauty of script and in such decoration as they do possess. These small Bibles were unknown to the 12th century. They usually contain a type of text which was authorised by the University of Paris, and perhaps represents a revision made by the Dominicans there, a revision of which Roger Bacon says very hard things.

One great work of imagery which had a short life about this time, and of which the development is due to the Paris school, is that of the *Bibles moralisées*. The system of these is that on every page a set of medallions illustrates consecutive incidents in the Bible, and a parallel set gives a spiritual interpretation of each. Every one of the canonical books was so treated: a frankly impossible task, and one which resulted in great monotony in the series of interpretations. Only three copies of the best period are known, and these are dispersed and fragmentary: one is divided between Paris, Oxford, and London, another is at Vienna, the third, a fragment of eight leaves, belongs to Mr Pierpont Morgan. The latter is the finest: it contains the end of the Apocalypse, and has portraits, probably, of St Louis and his queen.

In the fifty years from 1270 to 1320 we approach the time when individual artists begin to be known by name. One such, Honoré, ruled perhaps the best Parisian *atelier* at this period, and it must be noted that certainly in these years, and probably a good deal earlier, the production of fine books had passed away from the religious houses (of the capital, at least) and was in the hands of lay professionals. We have not many works by Honoré: the finest undoubted one is the Breviary of Philippe le Bel of the year 1296 (B.N. lat. 1023): a leaf from a *Somme le Roi* in the Fitzwilliam Museum is also generally accepted as his.

English (or is it Flemish?) influence is strong in the east and north-east in the early years of the 14th century, and shows itself in the multiplication of grotesques: a Breviary, of which one volume is at Verdun and another in private hands, and the Brooke Pontifical given by Mr Yates Thompson to the Fitzwilliam Museum are striking examples of this tendency, which cannot be said to have been potent at Paris.

Jean Pucelle is the next great name, and he represents the years 1320 to 1350. With him we connect a group of beautiful books: the Belleville Breviary (B.N. lat. 10483–4), finished by 1342, and distinguished for its singularly elaborate treatment of the Kalendar (here fragmentary) in which the fall of the Jewish church and the rise of the Christian is depicted in conjunction with the Apostles' Creed, the utterances of the Prophets, and the preaching of St Paul, according to a very carefully thought-out scheme which is expounded in a prose preface. This same Kalendar reappears in more than one Book of Hours in a complete form; notably in that of Jeanne II, Queen of Navarre, executed between 1336 and 1349, and lately in the Yates Thompson collection.

Another masterly production of this *atelier* is a book of the Miracles of the Virgin in French verse which was, until the war, at the Seminary at Soissons: its present whereabouts is a mystery.

Nor should the great French Bible projected by King John be unnoticed. It was to be translated by Jean de Sy and to be accompanied with comments, and maps, and pictures. The king's defeat and captivity in 1356 interrupted the work, and it was never finished: 46 quires (368 leaves) survive and only a few of them have been illustrated; but what has been done is of the very finest kind; Delisle would attribute it to Jean le Noir.

We come next to the period of the influence of Charles V, Charles VI, and Jean Duke of Berry. The inventories of the libraries formed by these three were edited and most thoroughly investigated by Léopold Delisle: he succeeded in identifying as extant rather more than a hundred of the 1239 books entered in those of the two kings. Not all Charles V's books were written for him; some were heir-looms, others were bought; but a great many were not only transcribed, but composed or translated at his order. Augustine's *City of God*, Aristotle's *Politics*, Bartholomew's *Properties of Things* are but a few of the books that now appeared in French, and beautiful copies of them were placed in the king's library. Pictures of the presentation of the book to the king, tricolor borders to the pages, and the royal arms supported by lions are characteristic marks of these: and so is the use of grisaille in the miniatures. We have many names of artists for Charles V's time, but very few can be coupled with existing works.

A symptom of the prolific output, and of the rather mechanical methods to which it led, is the frequent occurrence at this time of rough pencil sketches on the margins of books, made by the director of the *atelier* to indicate the composition of the intended illustration, and also of written notes in the vernacular telling the artist what he is to draw. Moreover we find not a few instances of the repetition of the same composition in different books, and this not only in the case of familiar sacred subjects, but in histories and romances where some originality might have been looked for.

Perhaps of the single artists André Beauneveu may have been the most distinguished; he has been mentioned already in connexion with other painting-work and with building. The one piece of book-illustration which can be safely attributed to him is a splendid series of Apostles and Prophets in a Psalter (B.N. fr. 13091).

Under Charles VI and Jean Duke of Berry magnificent work continued to be done. We see closer observation of nature in the rendering of landscape, increasing skill in portraiture; and the influence not only of Flanders but of Italy becomes obvious.

The *Très Riches Heures*[1] of the Duke of Berry (at Chantilly) with its unrivalled series of pictures of the occupations of the twelve months may be taken as representing the highest point of the art. Unfinished at the death of the duke in 1416, the decoration of it was completed by inferior hands later in the century: but the three brothers de Limbourg—Pol, Jehannequin, and Herman—had executed some 71 pictures in it, large and small. Until 1904 there was another production of the same artists which could be set beside it, in the Hours of Turin, done for William IV, Count of Holland: but in January of the year named it was burnt, and only one of its miniatures had been even photographed. These brothers de Limbourg were perhaps nephews of Jean Malouel, who has been named above as a painter.

One more bibliophile of the next years must be mentioned in the person of John Duke of Bedford (*d.* 1435), who in 1425 purchased the whole library of the Louvre. For him two very famous illuminated books were produced by some Paris *atelier* unknown—the Bedford Breviary (unfinished) at Paris, and the

[1] This is the designation in the inventory. There are also the *Grandes Heures* (B.N. lat. 919) and the *Très Belles Heures* (Brussels 11060), which are assigned to Jacquemart de Hesdin.

Bedford Hours at the British Museum. From the same very skilful hands came the Sobieski Hours at Windsor Castle.

Practically it is with the death of Charles VI that Paris ceases to be the centre of art. And, generally speaking, the middle part of the 15th century is poor in work of really fine quality. The markets were deluged with illustrated Books of Hours, nobles went on ordering and getting sumptuous Chronicles and Romances, prelates had handsome missals and Pontificals: but I believe that these two adjectives are, on the whole, the right ones to use. Yet one great name, that of Jean Fouquet, marks that generation. Born at Tours, he did some of his best work between 1450 and 1460 and died at Tours between 1477 and 1481. An expedition which he made to Italy before 1450 left its impress on him, and so, naturally, did the potent Flemish school of his time. It has been said above that he was a painter of easel and mural pictures; but what we can now judge him by is the not inconsiderable number of miniatures which survive. Foremost among these is the series cut from the lost Hours of Étienne Chevalier (treasurer of France), which form a beautiful little gallery of their own at Chantilly. These were done between 1455 and 1460. I find it difficult to characterise them otherwise than by saying that they are at once recognised as the work of a really great painter.

Like many others in these years, Fouquet was called upon to illustrate the French version of Boccaccio's *Cas des nobles hommes et femmes*. This book is at Munich (fr. 6): a third commonly assigned to him is a copy of the *Grandes Chroniques de France* (B.N. fr. 6465).

His pupil Jean Bourdichon is the last who will be named here. He also was of Tours, and he survived well into the 16th century. His fame rests chiefly upon the *Grandes Heures* of Anne of Brittany (*c.* 1497), which was deemed worthy of a complete reproduction in colour in the middle of the last century. Full-page pictures with large half-length figures are characteristic of Bourdichon (and his school), and also careful studies of flowers, which he paints in his borders, adding their names. All this work is very skilful, and its early popularity is not to be wondered at; but it is not inspired, and it is not even very well suited to its purpose, that of making beautiful pages in a book.

It must be said once again that this review of French miniature art, or painting in books, is, in comparison with the wealth of existing material, absurdly compressed; scores of highly important examples have been passed unmentioned. My object has been to lay stress on the great moments in the development. Periods of transition and the achievements of most of the provincial schools have been advisedly neglected.

## BIBLIOGRAPHY

*Histoire de l'Art depuis les premiers temps Chrétiens jusqu'à nos jours*, ed. André Michel, esp. vols. II (1905) and III (1907). E.-E. Viollet-le-Duc, *Dictionnaire raisonné de l'architecture française du xi^e au xvi^me siècles*, 10 vols. 1854–1868. W. R. Lethaby, *Medieval Art*, 1904. M. and E. Marriage, *The Sculptures of Chartres Cathedral*, Cambridge, 1909. E. Mâle, *L'Art religieux du xiii^e siècle en France*, 1898; *L'Art religieux de la fin du moyen âge en France*, 1908. H. Martin, *Les Miniaturistes français*, 1906. G. Graf Vitzthum, *Die Pariser Miniatur-malerei*, Leipsic, 1907.

## NOTE

The sculptures of Reims cathedral suffered grievously in the Great War. Many of the figures were more or less injured, some were decapitated, some totally destroyed. Most of the damage was done in 1914, but the Beau Dieu (see above, p. 402) was decapitated in 1918. The Virgin of the Annunciation (see *ib.*) is among those injured.

# INDEX

The letters ff. after an entry implies that there are references to the same subject on at least two immediately succeeding pages. Princes are indexed under their Christian names, persons of noble birth and those usually known by their surname under their surnames.